Relevance and Precision

Relevance and Precision

From Quantitative Analysis to Economic Policy

Essays in Honour of
PIETER DE WOLFF

Editors
J. S. CRAMER, A. HEERTJE, P. VENEKAMP

1976

SAMSOM PUBLISHERS, ALPHEN AAN DEN RIJN

NORTH-HOLLAND PUBLISHING COMPANY
AMSTERDAM - NEW YORK - OXFORD

Publishers
Samsom Publishers, Alphen aan den Rijn
North-Holland Publishing Company, Amsterdam - New York - Oxford

Distributors for the U.S.A. and Canada
Elsevier/North-Holland Inc.
52 Vanderbilt Avenue
New York, N.Y. 10017

Library of Congress Card Number 76 47610

ISBN Samsom 90 14 02473 8
ISBN North-Holland 0 7204 0534 3

Preface

At the age of sixty-five, Pieter de Wolff is taking his leave from the University of Amsterdam. This book is a tribute to him by his pupils and friends. Their individual contributions have no common subject, yet they have by and large a common theme: the application of precise reasoning, mathematics or quantitative methods to questions that are relevant to economic and social issues of the day. This reflects the dominant preoccupation with economic policy of Pieter de Wolff, who was originally trained in the sciences.

Of the fourteen papers, which have been ordered according to the seniority of their authors, four deal with questions that are directly or indirectly related to personal income distribution. Three articles treat economic theory – welfare economics, growth theory, and the capital controversy – and there are two each on the practice of macro-economic policy and on consumer behaviour. The remaining three papers are concerned with an input-output model, index numbers and the teaching of economics respectively. The main appeal of this collection lies in the economic implications rather than in the methods that are used.

It is over two years since we began preparation of this volume, and we wish to thank the contributors and the publisher for their cooperation.

The Editors

Contents

Pieter de Wolff

Pieter de Wolff, who was born in Amsterdam on 25 May 1911, passed his final schoolexamination in 1927. In the short space of five years he then completed his academic studies in mathematics and physics. From September 16, 1931 he worked as a demonstrator at the Physics Laboratory of the Municipal University of Amsterdam, at which he was studying. On 16 October 1933 he had to give up this function. During the period of crisis in the thirties De Wolff was unable to pursue his career with the same rapidity as he had completed his studies. On the contrary, it took him almost three years to start well and truly on a career which was nevertheless to prove spectacular.

However, De Wolff did lay the foundations for his career during that period. His interest in science coupled with that in social problems lead him to attend lectures by Tinbergen. This decision had far-reaching consequences for the course of his career. In the meantime De Wolff was able to make both ends meet by giving private lessons.

On 17 April 1935 Tinbergen made him take part in the activities that aimed at a reorganisation of the Statistics of Wholesale prices. Due to ill-health of a civil servant, the Central Bureau of Statistics in The Hague had a temporary vacancy. Here De Wolff made his first acquaintance with the field of statistics. Little could the C.B.S. have imagined that, at that moment, they were appointing a future chairman of the Central Committee of Statistics! His first position with the C.B.S. was, however, to be a brief one and lasted only until 22 August 1935. Fortunately, he was able to resume work on 27 April of the following year, this time to assist in the writing of the introduction to the publications in which the C.B.S. was to account for the results of its census of industry of 1930.

Though De Wolff was still employed on a very temporary basis, his relationship with the C.B.S. began to take more definite shape. On 1 August 1936 he became a clerk in temporary service. On 1 August 1940 he got a permanent appointment which lasted until 15 January 1942 when he left the Bureau in order to accept a position in industry.

So the year 1936 provided De Wolff with some social security, due to the fact that Tinbergen managed to get him a position in a new department of his creation, which was to deal with the research of business cycles. With this an important phase had started, a phase in which De Wolff developed into a statistician and an econometrist. It has been of great importance to him that he was allowed to interrupt his 'C.B.S.-period' from 1 October 1938 till 4 September 1939 so as to be able to work with Lundberg and Svennilson at the Konjunktur Institutet in Stockholm, and another month with Frisch in Oslo, thanks to a stipendium provided by the Rockefeller Foundation. When in 1942 De Wolff became a staff-member of the Department of Central Precalculation and Planning of Philips Ltd. in Eindhoven – where he became head of the department Marketing Analysis later on – his name was already held in high repute in the world of science.

As was to be expected, as soon as the war was over De Wolff was approached by the Faculty of Economics of the Municipal University of Amsterdam. They needed a lecturer in statistics. Having fulfilled a teaching assignment in descriptive statistics and in mathematical analysis in statistics from 16 October 1946 until 1 June 1947, De Wolff then accepted an appointment as reader in statistics at the Faculty. From that moment a new phase in the teaching of those subjects came into being.

The function that De Wolff was to accept in 1947 had previously been taken care of by the Bureau of Statistics in Amsterdam. This tradition was continued and, consequently, De Wolff left Eindhoven to perform the functions of both director of the Bureau in Amsterdam and reader at the Municipal University there. In contrast to his predecessors De Wolff was also assigned to lecture on the applications of statistics and mathematics in economics. His inaugural lecture was entitled 'The Meaning of the Sample for economic-statistical Research'. The fruits of his teaching were soon embodied in a book entitled 'Business Statistics', which was published in 1950. By 1969 this textbook and guide to the solution of many practical problems had seen its tenth revised and enlarged edition.

De Wolff also had a considerable contribution to make as director of the Bureau of Statistics. He clearly left his mark upon the publications of this Bureau and he procured a prominent position for it as a pioneering institute in the field of statistical research both in the Netherlands and abroad. For the municipality too, the

Bureau became an increasingly important source of information and it developed into a considerable advisory authority. The coordination of its research activities with those of other municipal institutions has been much improved by De Wolff. During the period in which he worked as an Amsterdam municipal official his appointment as a part-time professor was confirmed. After a four months' period, in which he worked as an expert in Egypt, he prepared to take up his professorship. The public ceremony took place on 30 November 1953 with an inaugural lecture on 'Mathematical Economics and Econometrics, their Task and Method'.
In every respect De Wolff made the most of the possibilities that his new position offered him. His influence in the fields of education and research increased rapidly. Many students and those engaged upon research have profited by his work. In this context we should mention some ten candidates for a Ph.D.-degree whose work he supervised and who have attained important positions. It should be stressed that De Wolff has meant a great deal for the shaping of their personalities. Particularly a sense of objectivity, a critical attitude and attentiveness to exact formulations are qualities that have been much stimulated by him.
As a lecturer De Wolff not only inspired many people in Amsterdam, but elsewhere in the Netherlands and also abroad many people are indebted to him. For instance, for some four months in 1953 he gave a series of lectures in Egypt. From 1 July 1964 until 21 June 1965 he was a research professor of economics at Harvard University, in Cambridge, Mass., where he held the Frank W. Taussig-Chair. He also gave a number of lectures upon 'Economic Planning in the Netherlands' for the Roager Fund in Berkeley, in May 1965. From January until August 1973 he was a visiting professor there. Following the period of the Taussig professorship he gave a course of lectures in Argentina. In 1966 De Wolff gave a series of 6 lectures in Curia, Portugal, during a summer course organised by the Gulbenkian Foundation and the Scientific Committee of N.A.T.O. on 'Forecasting on a Scientific Basis, Aspirations and Realisations'. Finally, mention should be made of the lectures he gave in May 1966 for 'Studium Generale' as part of the course of the Documentation Bureau for East-European Law at Leyden.
On 1 March 1957 De Wolff changed his status of municipal official for that of government official: he was appointed director of the Central Planning Bureau. This meant an important shift of accents in the 'block' of his activities: now economics and econometrics were given more emphasis than statistics. From that date on De Wolff became a most prominent adviser of the Dutch government, both as a researcher and as a planning economist. Though he gave up the function of director of the C.P.B. at the end of 1966 on the occasion of his appointment as a full professor, he is still called in to advise the government, witness his active

participation in the recommendations of the 'Oosterschelde-Commissie'.
During the period when De Wolff was at the head of the Bureau of Statistics of the municipality of Amsterdam he established several important contacts, both in the Netherlands and abroad, which were intensified and extended after 1966.
He has been chairman of many committees operating in the Netherlands, and also of a large number of international committees. In this context the 'Working Party 4' of the O.E.C.D. of which he was chairman during the period 1960–1974 is especially worth mentioning. He attended many meetings organised abroad and also for other reasons did he carry on his profession beyond the Dutch borders.
In 1960 he was in the U.S.A. from 27 March until 27 May in connection with a Leaders Grant he received under the terms of the 'United States Information and Educational Exchange Act'. The following must also be mentioned: his visit to Washington in January 1965 as a participant in a Seminar, organised by the I.M.F.; his participation in a conference at Harvard University on 'Pakistan's third 5 Years Plan', under the auspices of the Development Advisory Service of the above mentioned university in May 1965, and, in August 1967, his participation in a conference in Ulricehamn in Sweden, on Incomes Policy, organised by 'Studieferbundet for Naringlar och Samhülle' (the Industrial Council for Social and Economic Studies).
Moreover, De Wolff took part in the activities within the framework of the Seminar on Methodology of current economic development and Short-term Planning, under the auspices of the O.E.C.D. in Opatija in Yugoslavia, and, in December of that year, also in the Seminar on technological Forecasting in Warsaw, organised under the auspices of the Economic Commission for Europe. He was a discussant during the Flemish scientific Congress in April 1971 at Brussels.

It must not be forgotten that, for many years, De Wolff has been a member of a group of economists from both Western and East-European countries, who, thanks to the Ford Foundation, are able to meet yearly under the auspices of the International Economic Association, to exchange ideas about Labour Productivity.
Finally we should mention his activities in connection with the Pierce Memorial Lectures in Ithaca (New York Cornell University) in April 1972, and his consulting work as an O.E.C.D.-expert during the conference 'Higher Oil Prices and World Economy: an Appraisal of Adjustment Policies' (Brookings Institute, Washington) in November 1974.

De Wolff has been active on behalf of many institutions and societies. Since 1957 he has been a member of the Social Economic Council of the Netherlands. From 1960 till 1974 he acted as chairman of Working Party 4 (on Incomes Policies) of the O.E.C.D. During the period 1956–1958 he was chairman of the Netherlands Society for Statistics, Biometrics, Econometrics and Operational Research; in the years 1961 and 1962 he was also chairman of the Society for Political Economy. Since 1 January 1974 he has been chairman of the Central Committee of Statistics. Furthermore, he is a member of the Royal Netherlands Academy of Arts and Sciences and of the Dutch Society of Sciences.

From 1967 until 1 January 1974 he was chairman of the Committee for Medium-Term planning of the E.E.C. He has also been chairman of many other committees, such as the Committee Computing and Date Processing Equipment (C.R.I.V.A.), the Committee 2000, a Committee concerned with wages, the Committee of the Handicraft Trade Organisation, the Trade Organisation for Retail Trade, and the Council for Small and Medium Business, the Committee Building Planning, the Board of Examiners for Statistics for the State Certificate for modern business administration (S.P.D.). He is still a member of the Econometric Society (as a Fellow), of the International Statistical Institute, of the American Statistical Association, and of the Union Internationale pour l'Etude Scientifique de la Population. On 1 January 1975 he became vice-chairman of the Advisory Council for Science Policy. One of his latest activities which must not be omitted here concerns his discourse upon 'Economic-Technological Consequences of Scarcity', on 7 February 1975, in connection with the 700th anniversary of the city of Amsterdam for the Palace Meetings 'Tussentijds Bestek'.

All these aspects of De Wolff's professional life have been honoured in three special ways. In 1969 the University of Groningen appointed him Doctor Honoris Causa, Prof. Dr. H. Rijken van Olst acted as his promoter. It must be left undecided whether this appointment is of more significance than that of 'Ridder in de Orde van de Nederlandse Leeuw', an important Dutch Royal Honour, on 30 April 1960. Anyway, both events clearly indicate that De Wolff's work is held in great esteem both among the general public and in academic circles.

Finally this esteem has also been demonstrated at the end of a career that had led to the function of full professor in mathematical economics at the interfaculty of actuarial sciences and econometrics, which he had helped to found and of which he has always been the driving force. The function of vice-chairman of the Advisory Council for Science Policy, which demanded a great deal of his attention, and that of full professor which was especially intensified by increasing demands of management, were difficult to combine. Then De Wolff was enabled to resign from this latter function and yet remain at the Interfaculty for, to round off his career, he was appointed a personal professor; indeed a richly varied career during a period that has been marked by the rise of econometrics and the flourishing of the Interfaculty of actuarial sciences and econometrics.

P. E. Venekamp

Bibliography of Pieter de Wolff

1. De vraag naar vervoer per tram (Demand for tramway transport), *De Nederlandsche Conjunctuur*, 1938.
2. The Demand for Passenger Cars in the United States, *Econometrica*, 1938.
3. A Simplified Model of the Causation of Technological Unemployment (with J. Tinbergen), *Econometrica*, 1939.
4. Indexnumbers Illustrating the Development of Swedish Foreign Trade since 1920, *Meddelanden fran Konjunkturinstitutet*, Ser. B, 1, Stockholm 1939.
5. Eenige gegevens in verband met de distributie van suiker en peulvruchten (Some remarks on the rationing of sugar and pulse), *De Nederlandsche Conjunctuur*, 1940.
6. Income Elasticity of Demand, a Micro-Economic and a Macro-Economic Interpretation, *The Economic Journal*, 1941.
7. Enkele nadere gegevens betreffende de leeftijdsopbouw van de bevolking (New data concerning the age-distribution of the population), *Maandschrift van het Centraal Bureau voor de Statistiek*, 1941.
8. Onnauwkeurige getallen (Inaccurate numbers). In: O. Bakker, *Statistiek*, Deel I, Purmerend 1941.
9. Resultaten van een inventarisonderzoek in de gemeente Rotterdam, ingesteld door de Schade-Enquête Commissie aldaar, in 1941 (Results of an investigation into the property of durables made by the Schade-Enquête Commission, in 1941), *Maandschrift van het Centraal Bureau voor de Statistiek*, 1943.
10. *Handboek der bedrijfseconomische Statistiek* (Business Statistics; with J. G. Stridiron, J. Tinbergen en B. G. F. Buys), Second ed., Utrecht 1943.
11. *De betekenis van de steekproef voor het economisch-statistisch onderzoek* (The importance of sampling for economic and statistical research), inaugural speech as lecturer of statistics, Alphen a.d. Rijn 1947.
12. Statistische kwaliteitscontrôle (Statistical quality control), *Tijdschrift voor Efficiëntie en Documentatie*, 1948.
13. Het prijsindexcijfer van het gezinsverbruik (The cost of living indexnumber), *Kwartaalbericht van het Gemeentelijk Bureau van Statistiek*, 1949.
14. De prijsvorming van aardbeien, een theoretische aanvulling (Determination of the price of strawberries), *Statistische en Econometrische Onderzoekingen*, 1950.

15. Het ontstaan van een frequentieverdeling (Origin of a frequency distribution), *Statistica*, 1950.
16. *Oefeningen in Statistiek* (Exercises in statistics); Deel I, opgaven (Exercises; with O. Bakker), Groningen 1950.
17. Toepassing van de bezettingstheorie op een coderingsvraagstuk (An application of the occupancy theory on a coding problem), *Statistica*, 1951.
18. De bioscopen in Amsterdam (Cinemas in Amsterdam), *Kwartaalbericht van het Gemeentelijk Bureau van Statistiek*, 1951.
19. De ontwikkeling der reële inkomens (The development of real incomes), *Kwartaalbericht van het Gemeentelijk Bureau van Statistiek*, 1951.
20. *Oefeningen in Statistiek* (Exercises in statistics); Deel II, uitwerkingen (Solutions; with O. Bakker), Groningen 1952.
21. La mortalité à Amsterdam selon les quartiers (with J. Meerdink), *Population*, 1952.
22. *Wiskundige economie en econometrie; hun taak en werkwijze* (Mathematical economics and econometrics; their task and methods); inaugural speech as professor of statistics and econometrics at the University of Amsterdam, Alphen a.d. Rijn 1953.
23. On the Samuelson' Theorem from the Theory of Production, *Econometrica*, 1953.
24. Infant Mortality by Social Groups in Amsterdam (with J. Meerdink). Paper for the 28th session of the International Statistical Institute in Rome, 1953. Reprinted as: La mortalité infantile à Amsterdam selon les groupes sociaux (with J. Meerdink), *Population*, 1954.
25. De intelligentie te Amsterdam in verband met demografische en sociologische kenmerken van de bevolking (Intelligence in Amsterdam in connection with demographic and sociological characteristics of the population; with J. Meerdink), *Statistica Neerlandica*, 1955.
26. *On a System of Regional Social Accounts for the City of Amsterdam* (with P. E. Venekamp). Paper for the 29th congress of the International Statistical Institute in Rio de Janeiro, 1955.
27. De nieuwe prijsindexcijfers van het levensonderhoud (The new cost of living indexnumbers), *Kwartaalbericht van het Gemeentelijk Bureau van Statistiek*, 1955.
28. Steekproeven bij administratieve contrôle (The application of sampling in auditing), *Statistica Neerlandica*, 1956.
29. *Operations Research*, 's-Gravenhage 1956.
30. De invloed van de keuze der gewichten op de hoogte van een gewogen indexcijfer (The influence of the choice of the weights on the value of an indexnumber), *Statistica Neerlandica*, 1957.
31. *Openbare vermakelijkheden en publiek te Amsterdam* (Public Entertainment and the Public in Amsterdam; with A. C. Hissink), Amsterdam 1957.
32. La fécondité des mariages à Amsterdam selon l'appartenance sociale et réligieuse (with J. Meerdink), *Population*, 1957.
33. De statistische basis voor financiële en monetaire analyses (The statistical base for financial and monetary analyses; with Ph. J. Idenburg), *Economisch-Statistische Berichten*, 1957.
34. Stellung der Arbeitnehmer in der modernen Wirtschaftspolitik; Landerbericht Niederlande. In: *Internationale Tagung der Sozialakademie Dortmund*, edited by Hans Bayer, Berlin 1958.
35. *Public Entertainment and the Public in Amsterdam* (with A. C. Hissink). Paper for the 30th congress of the International Statistical Institute in Stockholm, 1958.
36. On the Application of Stratified Sampling to an Auditing Problem, *Contribution to the Volume in Honour of Prof. Dr. Corrado Gini*, Rome 1959.
37. Produktiviteitsverhoging bij accountantscontrole door toepassing van gelaagde steekproeven (Higher productivity in auditing after application of stratified sampling), *Statistica Neerlandica*, 1959.
38. De methodiek van het Centraal Economisch Plan (Methodology of the Central Economic Plan), *Economisch-Statistische Berichten*, 1959.

39. *Recent Experiences in the Application of Econometric Models in the Netherlands.* Paper for the 21st European Meeting of The Econometric Society in Amsterdam, 1959.
40. Intellectual Resources and the Growth of Higher Education. In: *Forecasting Manpower Needs for the Age of Science*, Paris 1960.
41. Wirtschaftsprognose als Grundlage der Volkswirtschaft unter besonderer Berücksichtigung der niederländischen Verhältnisse. In: *Wirtschaftsprognose und Wirtschaftsgestaltung*, Internationale Tagung der Sozialakademie Dortmund, edited by Hans Bayer, Berlin 1960.
42. Het Nederlands Centraal Planbureau (Le Bureau Central du Plan néerlandais), *Etudes Economiques*, 1960.
43. *Economisch-Statistische Vraagstukken* (Economic-statistical exercises; with answers); Deel I (opgaven) en Deel II (Uitwerkingen), (with P. E. Venekamp), Groningen 1960.
44. De ontwikkeling der lange-termijnplannen in Nederland en hun betekenis voor de economische politiek (The development of long-term planning in the Netherlands and its importance for economic policy), *Tijdschrift voor Economie*, 1961.
45. *The Problem of Rising Prices*; report to the OECD of a group of experts consisting of: William Fellner, Milton Gilbert, Bent Hansen, Richard Kahn, Friedrich Lutz and Pieter de Wolff, 1961.
46. The Estimation of Reserves of Ability (with K. Härnqvist). In: *Ability and Educational Opportunity*, Report for the Conference organized by the Office for Scientific and Technical Personnel, in collaboration with the Swedish Ministery of Education in Kungälv, 1961.
47. State Budget and Planning (with Th. A. Stevers). In: *Les Prévisions Budgétaires dans le Cadre des Prévisions Economiques et leurs Adaptations*, 1961.
48. *Planning op Langere Termijn bij Overheid en Bedrijfsleven* (Long time planning; with J. E. Andriessen). Den Haag 1961.
49. Door meten tot weten in de sociale wetenschappen (Knowledge by measurement in the social sciences), *Statistica Neerlandica*, 1962.
50. Hulpmiddelen van de economische politiek (Instruments of economic policy). In: *Theorie van de Economische Politiek*, edited by J. E. Andriessen and M. A. G. van Meerhaeghe, Leiden 1962.
51. *De economische groei in de westerse wereld* (The economic growth in the western world); discussion paper for the 1962 meeting of the Vereniging voor Staathuishoudkunde (The Dutch Society for Economics), 's-Gravenhage 1962.
52. Les techniques de la planification néerlandaise. In: *Les Problèmes de la Planification*, Editions de l'Institut de Sociologie, Université Libre de Bruxelles, 1962.
53. The Scope, Methods and Tools of Planning. In: *Planning*; papers read at the Business economists' Conference at New College, London 1962.
54. *Employment Forecasting Techniques in the Netherlands.* International seminar on forecasting techniques organized by the OECD, Brussels 1962.
55. *Oefeningen in elementaire statistiek*, Deel I: opgaven, 8th ed. (Exercises in elementary statistics; with O. Bakker and P. E. Venekamp), Groningen 1963.
56. Mogelijkheden tot vaststelling van begaafdheidsreserves (Possibilities to establish the reserves of talents), *Weekblad van het Genootschap van leraren aan Nederlandse gymnasia en lycea en de R.L.V.*, 1963.
57. Instrumenten van economische politiek (Instruments of economic policy), *De Economist*, 1963.
58. *Ten Years of Forecasts and Realisations*: an inquiry into the quality of the predictions by the Netherlands' Central Planning Bureau, 1953—1962 (with C. A. v.d. Beld). Invited paper. 34th Session I.S.I., Canada, 1963.

59. *Economische aspecten van het aardgas* (Economic aspects of natural gas). Report for a meeting organized by the Royal Dutch Academy of Sciences, Groningen 1964.
60. *Wages and Labour mobility*. Report to the OECD of a group of experts consisting of M. R. Deroo, M. A. Liorzou, Mrs. S. Münke, C. E. Odhner, H. Phelps Brown, G. Saunders, L. Ulman, C. Vannutelli and P. de Wolff (chairman).
61. Probleme der Einkommenspolitik (Problems of incomes policy). Discussion paper for a Round table conference, University of Kiel, 1965.
(Reprinted in *Review of Social Economy*, 1966, as: The OECD contributions to the development of incomes policy as an economic policy instrument of central governments).
62. *Oefeningen in elementaire statistiek* (Exercises in elementary statistics), Deel II: uitwerkingen (answers), 7th ed, (with O. Bakker and P. E. Venekamp), Groningen 1966.
63. The Depreciation Multiplier, *The Review of Economics and Statistics*, 1966.
64. The Use of Mathematical Models in Planning. In: *Governmental Planning and Political Economy*, Institute of Business and Economic Research Institute of Governmental Studies, University of Berkeley, 1967.
65. *De economie van het onderwijs* (The economics of education; with R. Ruiter), Discussion paper for the 1968-meeting of the Vereniging voor Staathuishoudkunde (Dutch Society for Economics), 's-Gravenhage 1968.
66. *Eenvoudige economisch-statistische vraagstukken*, Deel I: opgaven en Deel II: uitwerkingen, (Simple economic-statistical exercises with answers; with P. E. Venekamp), Groningen 1968—1969.
67. De financiën van de Nederlandse overheid in de periode 1850—1914 (Governmental finance in the Netherlands during 1850—1914; with J. W. B. van Overhagen), *Economisch Historisch Jaarboek*, 1969.
68. Sectorstructuurpolitiek (Structural policy for industrial branches). In: *25 jaar Centraal Planbureau*, The Hague 1970.
69. De financiën van de Nederlandse Provinciën en gemeenten in de periode 1850—1914 (Finance of the Dutch provinces and municipalities in the years 1850—1914; with W. Meyer and J. W. B. van Overhagen), *Economisch Historisch Jaarboek*, 1970.
70. Bijdragen voor *Encyclopedie van de bedrijfseconomie*, Deel VI: Mathematische analyse, Statistiek. (Mathematical analysis, Statistics; Encyclopaedical contributions), Bussum 1971.
71. Technical Progress Functions and Kaldor's Models of Economic Growth. In: *Schaarste en welvaart*, volume dedicated to Porfessor Dr. P. Hennipman, Leiden 1971.
72. *Incomes Policy in the Netherlands and Germany with Comments on the Present U.S. Policy*. Paper for a conference on incomes policy at Cornell University, 1972.
73. *Bedrijfsstatistiek* (Handbook of industrial statistics), 11th ed., Alphen a.d. Rijn 1972.
74. The Relation between Income, Education and Social Background (with A.R.D. van Slijpe), *European Economic Review*, 1973.
75. De economie van het onderwijs (The economics of education; with A. R. D. van Slijpe). In: *Economie in Overleg*, opstellen aangeboden aan Professor Dr. C. Goedhart, Leiden 1974.
76. Price Formation and the Inflationary Process in a Small Open Economy (the Netherlands), (with W. Driehuis and A. van Heeringen), *De Economist*, 1975.
77. A Sectoral Wage Price Model for the Netherlands Economy (with W. Driehuis). In: *Inflation in Small Countries* (ed. H. Frisch), Vienna 1976.
78. Note on Incomes Policies. In: *Inflation Theory and Anti-inflation Policy* (ed. E. Lundberg and E. A. G. Robinson), to be published in 1976.
79. Het prijsindexcijfer van de gezinsconsumptie (The cost of living indexnumber; with J. D. Lock), *Jaarboek van de Nederlandse Vereniging voor Marktonderzoekers*, to be published in 1976.

The Role of Occupational Status in Income Formation

Jan Tinbergen

Introductory

During the last decade numerous attempts have been made to estimate the impact of various 'explanatory variables' on individual income. There is a tendency away from the purely stochastic approach, whose latest representative probably is Christopher Jencks [4]. Among those interested in this search into the income formation process Professor Pieter de Wolff, to whom this volume is dedicated, has supplied us with an interesting study on the impact of years of schooling, differentiating between years with a smaller and years with a larger impact [8], and using Torsten Husén's material [3]. In the present essay another part of the income formation process will be tackled.

Among the variables included by a number of authors on the subject the one called occupational status (O) appears [4] [1]. One of the advantages of using this variable is its relative reliability, in the sense that people differing in social position and consulted at different points of time do not show very diverging opinions on it. What is less clear in some of the empirical analyses performed is the precise role O, according to the authors, plays in the income formation process. One can imagine three, rather different roles. Two of them assume that O has an immediate impact on incomes; and this impact may be of different nature. One way in which O influences income may be that O is a measure of *psychical income*, adding to the job holder's satisfaction alongside money income. The other is that O is a measure of an *effort* to be made to perform the job. In the former case money income I will have to depend negatively on O; in the latter case it will have to depend positively, since the effort needs a compensation.

The relationship we are now discussing is known under the name of 'earnings function'; it expresses income (here assumed to be identical with earnings) as a function of a number of degrees to which the individual income recipient possesses certain qualities relevant to do the job satisfactorily.

Elsewhere [7] I went into the question about the nature of the earnings function. In terms of economic analysis this function is a 'price equation', that is, expressing a price in terms of supply and demand factors. The variables appearing on the right-hand side of the function usually are only supply factors, however. This does not mean that the earnings function is a supply equation; for then also the numbers employed should appear in it. The reason why often demand factors are not explicitly shown is that the group for which the function has been estimated faces one and the same market. Demand factors are constant, therefore, and their impact is hidden in the intercept and the coefficients of the earnings function. The best known supply factors considered are years of (various types of) schooling and years of experience on the job (see, e.g., [5]). One theme of this essay is, then, whether in addition, occupational status is one of the supply factors and which of the two alternative interpretations of it seems more likely (cf. Section 3).

An additional theme we are going to deal with only makes sense if O constitutes a measure of effort. Assuming that effort compensation leads to 'justifiable' income differences, in contradistinction to differences due to scarcity rents, we may obtain a very crude impression of the relative importance of justifiable income differences (cf. Section 4).

The third role of O we propose to deal with is to attribute to O an altogether different role, namely that of a factor co-determining the choice of the length of the *education process*. This implies that the impact of O on income is an indirect one. To test this alternative we make an attempt to 'explain' years of schooling S with the aid of occupational status O, adding one or more other independent variables (cf. Section 5). This implies that a *different path* of causation is introduced, where occupational status is planned before or during the educational process, and the latter, apart from depending on other generally accepted phenomena, also depends on occupational status sought.

Material Used

Our study is meant as an illustration of how to go along and its results are highly tentative. This is so because the material available to this author at the moment of writing is the best he had available, but lacks information on a number of supply factors of a non-cognitive character which may well be relevant. For this reason —and possibly for other reasons as well—the multiple correlation obtained for the earnings function is 0.595 only; that is, the variance explained only 0.355. This is very close to the results obtained by De Wolff and Van Slijpe for Husén's total sample, amounting to $R^2 = 0.332$. The material used is that of Duncan, Featherman and Duncan as shown by Bowles and Nelson [2] [1]. It has the advantage of covering, for the four age groups considered together, about 10,000 persons. Bowles and Nelson supply a correlation matrix for the age groups 25—34, 35—44, 45—54 and 55—64 years, respectively, and our estimations have been entirely based on their Table A 1. Readers interested in the considerable number of details added as footnotes to that table are referred to that source.

'Explanation' of Income with the Aid of Four and Two Independent Variables

As a first test an attempt was made to construct an earnings function (or 'explanation' of income), with four independent variables, namely, occupational status O, years of schooling S, childhood IQ (Q) and socio-economic background (B). In standardized variables the multiple linear regression equation for the age-group of 45—54 years runs:

$$I = 0.43\ O + 0.00\ S + 0.03\ Q + 0.22\ B;\ R^2 = 0.355 \tag{1}$$

Our choice of independent variables is based on the direct relationship Bowles assumes to exist in his path analysis (containing S, Q and B), adding O as another independent variable, representing either effort or psychical income, as announced. In comparison to Bowles's result, R^2 increases from 0.255 to 0.355, but the positive algebraic sign of O excludes its interpretation as psychic income. Only on the assumption that O constitutes an effort can we accept (1). The virtual absence of an influence exerted by years of schooling remains an unsatisfactory feature of (1), however.

By dropping Q and B as directly affecting variables we obtain an alternative result:

$$I = 0.48\ O + 0.12\ S;\quad R^2 = 0.323 \tag{2}$$

which is only slightly less in explanatory power, but again shows an (even increased) impact of O in its role of an effort index.

Excluding O as an explanatory variable, and taking as the only independent variable S, we obtain:

$$I = 0.44\ S, \quad R^2 = 0.197 \tag{3}$$

which implies a considerable fall in explanatory power.
The evidence so far shown gives more support to O as an effort indicator than as a representative of psychological income.
As a check on the preceding result equ. (2) has also been estimated for the other age groups considered by Bowles and Nelson. For the four groups we obtain Table 1.

Table 1

Regression Coefficients and R^2 for O and S: Four Age Groups

	Regression Coefficients		
Age Group	for O	for S	R^2
25—34	0.41	0.03	0.184
35—44	0.50	0.10	0.324
45—54	0.48	0.12	0.323
55—64	0.41	0.11	0.242

The material used of course limits the possibilities of experimenting. Various alternative ways of explaining income variance are conceivable, if one had access to measured independent variables whose appearance in the earnings function would make sense. From a Dutch sample of a few hundred higher employees a wealth of other variables has become available .Whereas a full analysis of this new material is to appear elsewhere, one feature may already be mentioned. In contradistinction to actual years of schooling, years of schooling required for the jobs held appear to explain about 85 per cent of income variance. Keeping this in mind, one may wonder whether there is not a high correlation between occupational status and schooling required. Introduction into equations (1) or (2) of that variable might therefore change the algebraic sign of O and hence leave room for the physical income assumption. We will not pursue this issue in the present essay, however.

'Justified' Income Differences: Those Compensating for Effort

Elsewhere [7] I have introduced a theory of justice with regard to income differences and proposed to consider as justified income differences those constituting a compensation for effort. Other components of income, especially scarcity rents of inherited capabilities or inherited wealth, are not considered, in my theory, elements of an equitable incomes-and-jobs distribution. On the assumption (i) that our variable O constitutes a proper measure of effort connected with each type of job, we may use our results in order to estimate which portion of income variance is justified in the above sense. Using standardized variables x_i (exogenous) and y (endogenous) and assuming (ii) that the variance 1 of the latter can be completely explained by a number I of variables x_i we have:

$$1 = \Sigma b_i r_i \quad 1 \leq i \leq I \tag{4}$$

where b_i are the regression coefficients in

$$y = \Sigma b_i x_i \tag{5}$$

and r_i is the simple correlation between x_i and y. To any one of the x_i we can then attribute a contribution $b_i r_i$ to the unit variance of y. Further assuming (iii) that the b_O we found in our incomplete ($I = 2$) regressions are the same as the ones needed in the complete regression (5) we find for the contribution of O, as a percentage of total variance, 18, 28, 27 and 20 respectively for the four age groups mentioned in Table I.

The reader will be aware of the heroic cumulation of assumptions used, however.

Occupational Status as a Codeterminant of Education Chosen

We will now tackle the third subject announced in Section 1. This means the attribution to O of a different role in the path analysis presented by other authors, namely the role of *co-determining the length of the schooling process.* This exercise will be carried out in a number of alternatives. First, O will be used as the only exogenous variable determining the number S of years of schooling. Secondly, various second exogenous variables will be added, in turn: to begin with income I, considered as 'income aimed at'; next, parents' income P, socio-economic background B and father's education E. Thirdly, three exogenous variables will be used, namely O, P and E. The material used did not permit the estimation of other three-variable regressions, or a four-variable one. The results obtained are shown in Table 2.

Table 2

Schooling 'explained' by (a) occupational status (O) only, (b) by O and income I, (c) by O and parents' income P, (d) by O and father's education E, (e) by O and socio-economic background B, (f) by O, P and E, (g) by P and E, for four age groups. Regression coefficients are shown in column headed by exogenous variables used. Variance explained is indicated by R^2 (Regression coefficients and R^2 in per cent).

	a		b			c			d			e			f				g		
Age	O	R^2	O	I	R^2	O	P	R^2	O	E	R^2	O	B	R^2	O	P	E	R^2	P	E	R^2
25—34	74	55	73	1.5	55	60	28	61	63	23	59	56	33	62	56	23	16	63	42	33	42
35—44	73	54	70	6.5	54	60	23	57	62	23	58	54	30	59	54	17	19	60	42	34	42
45—54	63	46	62	9.4	46	52	30	53	58	28	53	47	39	57	49	22	21	56	45	28	39
55—64	63	40	59	8.8	41	47	35	49	54	24	45	44	36	49	43	30	15	51	46	25	38

The following conclusions can be drawn.

1. In nearly all cases somewhat more than half of the variance in S can be explained.
2. The regression coefficient for O is in almost all cases 0.5 or more.
3. The multiple correlation coefficients obtained are highest for the youngest group and in all cases falling with rising age.
4. The impact of parents' income and of father's education is practically equal; that of socio-economic background clearly somewhat higher.
5. Occupational status O contributes significantly to the explanation of schooling S: additional variance explained can be read from cases (f) and (g) and amounts to 21, 18, 17 and 13 per cent respectively, for the four age groups considered. Practically the same results are found by comparing results under (e) with the single correlations between S and B, not mentioned in the table.

As a further check on conclusion (5) a few more estimates were made for the age group 25–34 only. An 'explanation' of S was attempted using O, childhood IQ (Q) and socio-economic background (B) and another one without including O among these exogenous variables. Variance explained by the inclusion of O amounts to 0.64 as compared with 0.46 without O. The regression coefficient for O was 0.52. Thus, as the main conclusion of this section we may retain conclusion (5).

Conclusions

Our exploration of the role to be attributed to occupational status O using the material of Duncan, Featherman and Duncan suggests that:

1. if O is assumed to co-determine income it is a measure for effort needed in performing one's occupation rather than a measure for psychical income;
2. the latter possibility can only be opted for if income is determined to a high degree by schooling required as distinct from actual schooling and if a high correlation exists between occupational status and schooling required;
3. assuming, on the basis of (1), that O represents the effort needed to perform the occupation chosen, we can estimate what portion of income variance is 'justified' in the sense of Section 4; and this portion would then be in the order of 20 to 30 per cent;
4. if O is assumed to be a co-determinant of the years of schooling rather than of income, its role appears to be significant: its addition to other determinants such as income, parents' income, father's education, socio-economic background or childhood IQ raises the portion of variance explained by some 18 per cent in the various cases studied.

References

[1] Bowles, S. and V. I. Nelson: The Inheritance of 'IQ' and the Intergenerational Reproduction of Economic Inequality, *The Review of Economics and Statistics*, 1974.

[2] Duncan, O. D., D. L. Featherman and B. Duncan: *Socio-Economic Background and Occupational Achievement: Extensions of a Basic Model*, Washington 1968.

[3] Husén, T.: *Talent, Opportunity and Career*, Stockholm 1969.

[4] Jencks, C.: *Inequality*, New York 1972.

[5] Mincer, J.: *Schooling, Experience and Earnings*, New York 1974.

[6] Tinbergen, J.: Substitution of Academically Trained by other Manpower, *Weltwirtschaftsliches Archiv*, 1975.

[7] Tinbergen, J.: *Income Differences: Recent Research*, Amsterdam 1976.

[8] Wolff, P. de and A. R. D. van Slijpe: The Relation between Income, Education and Social Background, *European Economic Review*, 1973.

Developments of Goals of Economic Policy in Sweden

Erik Lundberg

The goals of general economic policy as pursued by the central Government have become more and more ambitious and complicated during the post-war period. This is true in all Western countries. The case of Sweden may be interesting from several points of view. The social-democratic Government in Sweden made pioneering efforts already in the early 1930's in order to find ways of balancing the total economy. These goals were broadened and became successively more ambitious during the thirty years after the war. The specific political and social processes behind the policy developments in Sweden are of course of great interest – not least in a country with the same social-democratic party in power during the whole epoch. However, in this essay I concentrate the attention on the factual development of the policy aims with emphasis on the problems of goal conflicts that arise when the setup of targets becomes manifold and complicated. It should be noted that I limit the discussion to the *general* policy goals adopted by the Government such as stability of the price level and full employment, excluding such more specific targets as for instance refer to housing and agricultural policy.

Aims and Means

There was a time when the general economic policy in Sweden had but a single purpose – to maintain the parity of the Swedish Krona with gold. It was that way for more than 40 years prior to 1914, and it was that way again for a short time (1924 – 1931) after the reinstatement of the gold standard. Since then the fundamental aims of Swedish economic policy have gradually become more numerous and more ambiguous, with ever larger areas of conflict, all of which has led to increasingly difficult problems of weighing and evaluation, with respect to the tools of economic policy available. It is interesting to consider the conglomeration of issues involved in the economic policy of today against the background of a process which has advanced from the very simplest and least ambitious of aims to a multiplicity of goals of a more and more pretentious nature. It may be useful to try clarify the relationship involved in the distinction between aims and means concepts of the Government's economic policy. One can very easily conceive of such aims as price stability, full employment, a high rate of growth, as well as a more equal distribution of income, as ultimate goals – with ample reservation for difficulties in definition and problems of quantification. But, seen from another point of view, aims such as these become rather a means of achieving other and more fundamental goals; goals which lie to a great extent beyond the economist's capability of definition, such as for instance 'quality of life'. This relative nature of economic targets is something we should be aware of. Thus, it is evident that rapid growth and a high GNP per capita can never be considered as ends in themselves, but only as means, within the framework of given resources, of attaining various welfare goals.

Neither can a stable price level only be regarded as an ultimate aim. It can be regarded as a type of *ethical requirement*, e.g. as a way of minimizing systematic treachery or as a means of attaining a balanced economy (see below). In the same way a more equal income and wealth distribution may be understood as a moral claim based on egalitarian prinicples. It is of interest to note that distribution goals differ from such aims as a stable price level or full employment in the sense that there is actually no limit to distribution aims. Each new stage in a process of evening out inequalities will give rise to dissatisfaction with the results attained and new efforts to reach more ambitious aims will be provoked. But again it is not only a question of ethical norms. A more even distribution of wealth, including less concentration of shareholding, may be taken as means to attain a lower degree of confrontation between capital and labor and thereby more of 'social harmony' and economic democracy. Profit- and wealth-sharing schemes are in Sweden sometimes regarded as ways of reaching an improved social climate within the firms, perhaps contributing to more responsibility and higher productivity in work.

My intention in mentioning these points has been to show that apparently simple presentations of policy aims may refer to a complicated background of deeper intentions. It should also be mentioned that some of the usual means of economic policy may sometimes acquire or be given the character of aims. The interest rate is generally considered to be an instrument of economic policy, but under certain circumstances a low interest rate has assumed the character of a secondary aim (e.g., for the purpose of holding down the level of rents). By the same token, fixed rates of exchange can be given the character of an essential secondary aim, just as the maintenance of substantial reserves of foreign exchange acquires a high priority of its own. In this article, the purpose of which is not to delve deeply into these concepts, I consider these latter types of aims as means and restrictions, respectively, to be utilized for the purpose of attaining primary goals of the type exemplified above.

Stability of the Price Level

One might express it paradoxically and say that the typical feature of the *gold standard* was that the government's general economic policy did not strive toward any specific aims. The gold standard represented a technique of countering minor disturbances in the flow of payments between countries, using small means, chiefly changes in the discount rate. The system functioned reasonably well as long as the disturbances were of a minor nature, but not under such heavy strains as the first World War or the Great Depression of 1929–1931. During the years of the gold-standard, one might say, the general level of prices in Sweden, as well as the fluctuations in the business cycle, were determined mainly by international developments. But the economic policy conducted had scarcely such aims in mind. In the years following 1920, on the other hand, the government consciously maintained a deflationary policy with a view to restoring the old parity of the krona with gold, and thereby returning to the gold standard (which took place in 1924). The downward pressure on price and wage levels in Sweden after 1920, and the severe unemployment situation at that time, served as *instruments* in attaining the goal of regaining the old parity of the krona.

Upon the abandonment of the gold standard and the introduction in September 1931 of a free currency system with flexible rates of exchange, Swedish economic policy assumed a more independent status, pursuing more autonomous goals. In the fall of 1931 the Riksbank declared that the sole guiding aim of monetary policy was to bring about 'a stabilization of the purchasing power of the Swedish krona in the hand of the consumer'. In the beginning, oddly enough, this price stabilization objective had an anti-inflationary intention; a general increase in the level of prices was feared as a consequence of the sharp depreciation of the krona. Soon, however, the principal question in the years 1932–1933 became one of preventing the spread of strong international deflationary tendencies. Radically new was the fact that for the Swedish Government—and thus not only for the economists—*price stability* became a primary, independent aim of economic policy, while at the same time exchange rates were regarded as secondary targets and on occasion only as an instrument of the stabilization policy.

The authorities actually took this price stabilization objective seriously during the 1930's; indeed, right up to 1946. Certain important modifications were successfully introduced when external conditions changed and were expressed in specific terms. Price increases resulting from a deterioration in the terms of trade, increased taxes, agricultural regulation, and the like, should be tolerated and not offset by price reductions in other areas. Reduced productivity (as during the war years) should also be permitted to find expression in the form of increased prices, and the reverse. Such considerations had belonged to an old tradition in the Swedish professional debate, opened up by Knut Wicksell and David Davidson already 40 years earlier.

In the monetary policy programs at the end of World War II it was declared by the Government that the price level could be expected to decline after the war, when productivity began to rise and cheaper raw materials and fuels again became available. Once again it was a question of a serious intention of the Government to focus upon these objectives, underscored by a substantial appreciation of the krona in July, 1946. Actually this program failed completely because of world inflation and bad stabilization policies at home. As in other countries strong political pressures, trade union behavior in full employment conditions plus expansive monetary and fiscal policies were accompanied by a continuously rising price leval. The policy goal of the Government with regard to the price level adjusted itself to political and economic reality and to the policy possibilities when full employment was given a dominating priority. The prize stabilization goals was watered down to formulations such as 'highest possible stability', actually implying an acceptance of the actual long term rate of increase of the consumers' price index by around 4 per cent per year during the period up to the end of the 1960's.

Economic Stability and Full Employment—Variations in Goal Ambitions

It is worth noting that the maintenance of a stable price level in the old days was not only considered as an essential aim in itself, but was also looked upon as an expression, or indication, of economic balance in the economy as a whole, signifying that the demand for goods and services was, taken as a whole, neither too great nor too small. The goal of a stable price level was thus interwoven during the 1930's with the objective of *economic stability.* A policy of economic stabilization should thus serve the dual purpose of restraining sharp price increases during boom periods, and preventing deflation in times of declining business activity. In this debate of the early 1930's the Swedish economists – such as Erik Lindahl, Gunnar Myrdal and Bertil Ohlin – were following up and extending the analysis of the conditions of economic balance pioneered by Wicksell and Davidson. The remarkable fact in Sweden was that the Government during the 1930's accepted the main ideas of the economists and actually tried to apply them. The attempts in the direction of an expansive monetary and financial policy during the 1930's were thus motivated by these aims of economic policy, i.e., for the purpose of stimulating an upswing, whereby stability in the areas of price and foreign exchange could be looked upon as restrictions.

The necessity of reducing unemployment was naturally a part of the goal of economic stability, although the *full employment* objective was not specifically formulated until the closing years of the war. William Beveridge once coined the phrase 'full employment: more jobs than men', which he even defined quantitatively as 3 % unemployment.

In Sweden the expression came into use primarily through the so-called 'Postwar Program of the Labor Movement' of 1944. There was not, however, any effort to define the goal in quantitative terms: the only attempt in this direction was a very vague and general statement: 'It is our wish that the average level of unemployment in the long term be lower than that which was characteristic of the so-called good years of the latter half of the 1930's'. Neither does one find the goal clearly defined in 'The Trade Union Movement and Full Employment', published by the Confederation of Trade Unions in 1951. It is interesting to note, however, that a full employment condition was considered to prevail on the Swedish labor market during the years 1948 – 1950, when unemployment was, in fact, just below 3 %.

During the postwar period, the goals of price stabilization and full employment have both undergone modification with respect to their degrees of ambition. The aim of a stable level of prices has been retained in its verbal formulation in the official declarations, but its meaning has become modified in favor of an increasingly greater tolerance of inflationary tendencies. During the 1950's and the 1960's, the actual average 4 % rate of inflation came – as said above – to be looked upon as both natural and endurable. There have been certain reactions in the economic policy to the acceleration (to 6 – 7 %) which began in 1969, but it appears that this rate of inflation may also come to be looked upon as tolerable in view of the 10 – 12 % rate of increase experienced in 1974 and 1975. In this respect there seems to have occurred a successive adaptation of the goals to actual experiences, a creation of inflation tolerance that comes with expectations and adjustments to live with inflation. There are no quantitative Government pronouncements of price stability goals any more, only *forecasts* in the national budgets of continued inflation at high rates that may be taken as '*revealed preferences*'.

With regard to the goal of *full employment*, developments have mainly gone in the opposite direction – toward an increasingly higher level of ambition. The relatively low total unemployment conditions which existed during the periods of high economic activity have been labelled full employment. During the 1960–61 period, as well as in 1965 and 1970, we experienced an unemployment rate of 1 to 1,5 %, according to manpower surveys carried out by the Central Bureau of Statistics. Unemployment at the low point of the recession periods, on the other hand (2,5–3,5 percent), have been considered too high. Support for this interpretation may be found in various declarations, but principally in the reactions of economic policy. Restrictive measures adopted during periods of high business activity may however sometimes be difficult to interpret. It might be contended, for example, that the employment rate was considered to be too high in consideration of the pressures created on the labor market and on the balance of payments, thereby motivating restrictive measures. Another interpretation is that the level of employment might be considered sufficiently high (a goal of satisfaction) to permit the adaption of anti-inflationary measures without serious inconvenience. In this case it would be a matter of weighing the effects of measures which influence the level of employment and the rate of inflation, since these goals are in a trade-off position to each other.

Since the end of the 1960's, however, the discussion of these problems has begun to center on the concept of *incomplete employment*. Even with full employment (at 1–1,5 % total unemployment), the unemployment rate in certain areas may be unacceptably high. In counties having large forest areas, the level of unemployment has consistently been 2 to 3 times higher than that of the larger cities. The risks of unemployment vary greatly among the various branches of industry, being significantly higher in the construction industry and in textiles than in manufacturing and especially engineering. Unemployment varies considerably among occupations, as well as according to education, age, and sex. Unemployment hits woman to a greater extent than men, as well as poorly-trained and elder workers. There are increasing numbers of persons who have found themselves out of work because of plant shutdowns, etc., and who are difficult to place. In addition to these inperfections in the labor market, there are also the large, indefinable groups of *latent* unemployed; people who would accept employment if there were vacancies suitable from the point of view of geographic location, and such factors as education, wages, etc. A gradual increase in the rate of employment (particularly for married women) is part of the long term goals of an increasingly ambitious labor market policy.

The irregular distribution of job opportunities has always been a problem. There is no doubt, however, that this inequality has been taken more and more seriously, and is regarded as a functional defect of the labor market; the tasks of labor market policy, including the tasks of the labor exchange, have been successively expanded. The wider ambitions of policy, with respect to employment goals, are thus being focused upon this desire for a more equitable distribution of unemployment hazards among the various regions, industries, occupations, age groups, etc.

Growth Targets – and Conflicts with Other Goals of Policy

In the beginning of the 1950's, *growth goals* came into the picture in earnest. During the 1930's, just as during the early part of the postwar period, the goal of economic stability was dominant; no independent growth goal existed. With the inception from the end of the 1940's of the series of Government long term plans, a high growth rate of the GNP over a five-year period became an important objective.

It was mainly a matter of bringing about a rapid increase in the total availability of resources in order to meet all of the increasing needs expressed in these five-year studies: public and private consumption, investments, and exports. A number of *secondary aims* were thus called for as well: a high and increased proportion of investments and savings, respectively, a rapid improvement in efficiency or productivity, and continued structural transformation. The goal of keeping up full employment was of course included; at a given rate of productivity growth with regard taken of the shortening of working time, a sufficiently high rate of GNP growth gives a condition on the demand side for full employment.

For a long period of time, from the end of the 1940's to the end of the 1960's, the economic policy was dominated by the goals discussed above; stability of business conditions, full employment, and high growth rates. The levels of ambition and the relative importance of the various goals changed from time to time, but discussions concerning economic policy concentrated upon these matters, while conflicts involving the objectives themselves seemed limited. After the end of the 1960's, however, this comparatively harmonious constellation of goals became disrupted. There were three principal reasons for this: 1. the satisfactory measure of achievement with regard to the aims of growth and full employment had created a certain saturation; the results attained began to be taken for granted; 2. success, in itself, brought about new problems in the form of disturbances in the development process; 3. other and partly new goals began to come to the forefront of attention: goals concerning the environment and the distribution of income and wealth, goals related to industrial policy, involving the structure of the economy (including the share of the public sector), new goals dealing with job satisfaction and job security, and economic democracy.

Obviously, these different goals did not just appear suddenly: questions involving aspects of industrial policy, a more equitable distribution of income, and the levelling-out of wage differentials had already been discussed intensively in the middle of the 1940's (for example, in the Postwar Program of the Labor Movement; the 27 points). But complications and conflicts of aims first became prominent when the objectives began to have a direct bearing upon the framing of actual economic policy.

Let me illustrate the new possibilities of complication by examining the conflicts which have arisen in recent years among the goals of growth, employment, and income distribution. Mobility of labor may be considered an important condition for a high rate of growth. And the continuous rapid increase in wages and salaries, that during the 1960's was constantly threatening profit margins, might be regarded as one of the prime movers in the process. There is both theoretical and empirical evidence to indicate that a large share of the increase in productivity was traceable to a structural transformation, with rapid transfers of manpower and capital resources from low productivity or stagnant firms and industries that could not pay the heavy labor costs to high productivity and expanding ones. This was the melody of the optimistic 1950's, and it also became the theme of the policies of the 60's. Consequently, one of the tasks of the labor market policy was to create a condition of high mobility, both geographically and by occupation. This type of policy, oriented as it was to the market, was undoubtedly highly successful from the point of view of growth and efficiency.

But there were serious drawbacks and conflicting aims. The stern rationalization and structural conversion process in industry and trade that was strongly induced by the rapid rise in wage costs dealt harshly in many instances with certain categories of manpower, primarily older people and unskilled workers. Pockets of unemployment appeared in stagnating areas. The labor mobility policy proved to have limited possibilities of solving these problems. It became more and more apparent that the high productivity increase of the 1960's was purchased at the cost of heavy sacrifices in human welfare concentrated among the groups mentioned.

They were subjected to unemployment, early retirement, and low incomes—even the objective of income equalization was therefore in danger. At the same time relatively high profits with a high degree of self-financing in rapidly expanding corporations gave rise to uneven wealth distribution.

It may be noted that Swedish labor market policy from the end of the 1960's has tended to shift more and more from activities designed to increase mobility toward those intended to preserve and stimulate employment at the local level, in the individual business and within the region. The high priorities given to growth goals from the 1950's are on the way to be abandoned. New laws governing job protection and the measures taken to promote employment seem to have precisely this in mind. Under an extensive policy of this kind, often colliding with the requirements of an efficient market, a conflict of purpose arises between full employment and a high rate of growth. Of course, the benefits to be gained through increased job security, less relocation, more pleasant surroundings in which to live and work etc., might very well be worth a certain amount of sacrifice in productivity growth.

A new phase of employment policy—containing conflicts between productivity and employment goals—has appeared during the recession of 1975 in Sweden. Open unemployment as registered in the manpower surveys has so far (up to September 1975) been kept low at around 1.5 % (close to the full employment target) although the development of real GNP has stagnated and the volume of industrial production has declined since 1974. A certain lag of employment behind production is the rule but this time the preservation of employment *within* the firms has become a new goal. Employers are subsidized for keeping people in training programs and for making investments and repairs. Special subsidies are being paid out for supporting increases in inventories under the condition of not reducing employment. New laws and rules make it very difficult and expensive to dismiss workers. The result will be the benefits of more security in employment at the cost of lower efficiency in the plants and worsened allocation of labor. To these effects might be added a regrettable deterioration of the unemployment statistics (a larger concealed unemployment) and as a consequence still more unreliable Phillips curves!

There are also important conflicts between *income distribution goals* on the one hand and growth and stability aims on the other. The strong pushing up of the low wage groups in relation to higher wage and salary groups has been quite a successful part of the egalitarian wage policy of Swedish trade unions from the second half of the 60's. These efforts have in the main implied a confrontation with the market forces implying negative side effects on inflation and unemployment.

The progressive direct income taxes – as means of income equalization – have tended to aggravate wage inflation. The relation between marginal and average direct taxes for a common worker is often such that a 10 per cent rise in nominal gross wages will on the average result in only 6 % net increase in disposable income (after tax). This progressive tax system therefore works as an enlargement mechanism as to claims for wage increases, aggravating the inflation tendencies and may also have negative effects on incentives.

There are also serious conflicts between growth targets and the functional distribution of income. As in other countries a continuous squeeze of profit margins has been going on since the end of the 1950's. It can be said that this development has been an accepted policy goal not only with regard to a more even income and wealth distribution but also for satisfying growth and stabilization aims. The pressure from rising wage costs (incl. rapidly increasing charges for covering pension and other social reforms) has (as mentioned above) apparently been accompanied by a very rapid rise in industrial productivity (by 7 – 8 % per year in the 1960's). On the other hand falling profitability and declining possibilities of self-financing of investments out of profits have tended to keep down investment activity. This tendency has, however, been successfully counteracted – especially in the 70's – by a selective investment policy by Government agencies, using investment fund techniques, tax rebates, local subsidies, special credit injections as means of an expansive policy. In fact the increased dependence of Swedish industry on Government funds and support has become a kind of neo-mercantilist policy with ambitious aims of steering the structural development of the economy.

Changes in Priorities – Some Concluding Remarks

It should be observed that the goals of economic policy undergo changes and become subject to reappraisal also as a consequence of the *instruments* of policy which are used and made available. If, for various reasons, an active rate of exchange policy – implying appreciations of the Swedish krona to neutralize international inflation – is not under consideration, a tolerance can be created toward a high rate of inflation through expanded protection against its harmful effects, e.g., by index regulation of loans, wages, taxes, and of social welfare contributions. In this way, people can learn to live with a high rate of inflation and adapt themselves to it, but the risk of an acceleration is built into such a system.

In Sweden the preservation of free collective bargaining and the independent status

of the trade unions in this respect has been a fundamental goal in itself. Therefore Government control or freezing of wage rates as a means of stabilization has been politically impossible—in contrast to Dutch and British experiences. In this respect there is until now no change in Swedish attitudes.
Among the changes taking place in goals priorities, the objective of *growth* tends to be declining from its position of prominence. This point has been discussed above. Such objectives as job security, regional balance, a more even distribution of income, pleasant working conditions, and various environmental aims, are given priority at the expense of GNP-growth. In addition, new restrictions are being imposed upon the growth process with respect to the uncertainties regarding future access to energy and raw material resources. These restrictions (which can assume various forms of expression within the framework of the economic policy being pursued), emanate from a mixture of environmental considerations (in the broadest sense of the term), and an indefinable heedfulness to the needs and interests of future generations. It is not reasonable to set up something called zero-growth as a goal in order to achieve a happier state of society within the limits of available resources. It is sooner the case that all the other goals discussed here (including consideration of future shortages of raw materials and energy), involve such restrictions upon possible growth that with a certain amount of guidance in the form of economic policy, the growth rate may be forced to decline to a level substantially below that of the 1960's (say for Sweden an annual GNP growth of 2–3 % instead of 4–5 %). Such a change in priority can very well be combined with a general *goal of efficiency*; that is, to produce and utilize resources in the most efficient way possible, within the bounds of given objectives and restrictions.

One consequence of a retarded rate of production increase would be that the satisfaction of demands for a *more equitable distribution of income* would lead to increased tensions. There would be a greater number of income groups than before who would be obliged to adjust to a reduced standard of living (real income after direct taxes), in order to provide the desired room for low income groups. The problem is rendered more difficult as a somewhat reduced share of the GNP increase becomes available for internal needs, since a deterioration in the terms of trade (oil prices) and increasing aid to developing countries are to be balanced in the long run by increasing export surpluses. The degree of pressure upon various wage earner categories would naturally also depend upon how rapidly the share allocated for public services would be allowed to rise. A continued high rate of inflation (which could partly be a result of an intensified conflict between these goals) might possibly conceal or moderate the tensions.

This complex of problems involves the question of *distribution of wealth* as well. Here we find the most recent and important development in the Swedish debate of policy goals. A high rate of inflation tends to yield large profits on quick transactions of various kinds, thereby increasing the disparity in the distribution of wealth. There are conflicts of aims between desires for a more equitable distribution of wealth and for reasonable productivity increases in industry. In the Swedish debate the problem lies primarily in the relatively large profits for the most productive and expansive corporations in each industry. One result of a egalitarian wage policy as carried out by the central trade union organizations means that wage costs are largely determined independently of profits and wage-payment capacities of individual firms. The most profitable units or branches, having the largest rise of productivity and often expanding more rapidly than the average, tend to receive extra high profits, as a consequence of being protected by the marginal firms with no or low profits which are hardly able to pay the increased wage costs. The intramarginal profits (the quasi rents in Marshall's terminology) are used for financing investment and expansion of the firms in question. This type of capital formation will imply increased wealth going to a small minority group of share-holders. The Swedish trade union economists maintain that this wealth increase rightly belongs to labor as it has abstained from exploiting the surplus profits by means of differential increases of wages and salaries. The proposals of profit-sharing now presented in Sweden aim not only at a more equal distribution of industrial wealth formation but ultimately also at a radical transformation of the economy and the general power structure. The wage funds to be created in order to take over the new issues of shares corresponding to the profit-sharing, will according to the proposals in 15 – 20 years imply employee-majority of shareholders in the main industrial companies.

There are many alternative possibilities of mitigating the conflict between the goals of tolerating comparatively large profits for an efficient and expansive private sector of the economy, and at the same time accomplishing a reasonable distribution of the resultant accumulation of capital. Future political debates concerning different systems of achieving more of economic democracy are likely to be very lively in Sweden. However, there will be lots of research, Government committee work, some practical experimentation, and a long political process before a revolutionary change of this kind will be put in force. The present, very active debate on these issues of profit sharing, socialization of savings, and economic democracy, demonstrates clearly how much more complicated and politically inflamed the issues of policy goals have become since the simple worlds of the 1930's and the 1950's.

Pareto Optimality: Value Judgment or Analytical Tool?

P. Hennipman

Welfare Economics . . . remains to some extent a mystery.

J. R. Hicks, The Scope and Status of Welfare Economics, *Oxford Economic Papers*, November 1975, p. 307.

L'économiste . . . est mieux armé que quiconque pour éviter toute confusion entre jugement de fait et jugement de valeur.

A. Wolfelsperger, *Les biens collectifs*, Paris 1969, p. 12.

. . . each economist, however, tainted the pure science of his economic analysis with moral weightings so subtle as to be unperceived by himself or even his colleagues and critics.

Norman Mailer, *St. George and the Godfather*, New York 1972, p. 143.

I

In modern welfare economics Pareto optimality, together with its *alter ego*, the Pareto criterion, occupies the centre of the stage. In hundreds if not thousands of books and articles it has served as Ariadne's thread to the solution of an ever widening range of problems. This leading role was not augured by its inconspicuous birth in a few crabbed paragraphs tucked away in the treatises of its spiritual father. Till it was rescued from oblivion or reinvented in the thirties, it dwelled in obscurity, only very occasionally coming to the fore, as in Barone's classic article [16].

Despite its present eminence, the position of the Pareto principle is in several respects ambiguous. Foremost specialists declare it to be 'universally accepted' (Arrow [14], p. 96; see also Sen [105], p. 1407). Yet it is regularly subjected to criticisms, and a distinguished economist like Morgenstern figures among its detractors [76]. In recent years its dominance has twice been fiercely attacked at book-length (Nath [81]; Rowley and Peacock [95]). Particularly important is the fact that its methodological status is surrounded by uncertainty, although this problem has been debated relatively little. The idea of Pareto optimality started its life as a purely economic concept. It continues to be used in this sense, but nowadays this interpretation is not the most usual one. In the course of its successful career during the past decades it has been transformed into something totally different, an ethical judgment or 'value proposition' (Bergson [25], p. 23). Probably the majority of welfare economists assign this meaning to it at present.

The Pareto principle experienced yet another metamorphosis in the theory of social or collective choice, which stands in an ill-defined relationship to welfare economics. Here it is generally listed as one of the conditions of an acceptable choice rule or 'constitution'. This requirement is plainly a value judgment. In the shape of a general constitutional rule the principle far transcends the boundary of economics.[1] The wider connotation will be ignored in this paper, which is restricted to welfare economics in the more traditional sense.[2]

Because of the transformations the concept of Pareto optimality has undergone, it has come to mean different things to different people, and even different things to the same person at different times. This circumstance, together with the fact that the various meanings are not always kept as clearly distinct as should be done, accounts for much of the confusion befogging its status. It also explains how it can be considered non-controversial in one context, the theory of social choice, and highly debatable on its homeground of welfare economics.

II

The two contrasting interpretations of Pareto optimality mentioned above reflect a fundamental disagreement about the character and purpose of welfare economics in general and the Paretian theory in particular. On the one hand the subject is considered to be a branch of positive economic theory, as neutral and objective as any other part. According to Archibald the theorems of welfare economics are 'theorems in positive economics' ([12], p. 320), and Van Den Haag argued that welfare economics 'is no more normative than mathematics or physics' ([111], p. 182). Recently Hicks also observed that 'there is nothing especially normative about allocation theory' ([49], p. 316).

Diametrically opposed to this opinion is the currently dominant one that welfare economics is essentially different from positive economics because it is based upon ethical value judgments and yields normative propositions.[3] To quote Hicks once more: 'Welfare Economics is commonly thought of as a normative (or shall we say quasi-ethical?) subject' ([48], p. 6). As Samuelson put it: 'the very discussion of welfare economics implies certain ethical assumptions' ([98], p. 775). Little even characterised it as 'essentially an ethical study' ([63], p. 86) and others have called it 'unashamedly normative' (Dasgupta and Pearce [35], p. 15).

According to this interpretation of the nature of welfare economics the Pareto theory of efficient allocation is part of a wider normative scheme, which also includes income distribution. It is a matter of dispute among the adherents of the ethical conception whether or not the grand design of Bergson and Samuelson, the social welfare function, is a useful device in this connection. It is held in low esteem by some of them, like Little and Mishan, who dubbed it 'a pleasing and nebulous abstraction' ([73], p. 747). But in any case the followers of the ethical persuasion also concentrate their efforts mainly on the problems of efficient allocation and tackle them with Paretian tools. The essential point is that they usually conceive of the Paretian allocation theory as being normative in itself, incorporating 'Paretian value judgments'. Some authors, however, adopt an intermediate position by regarding it as a positive part of welfare economics as a normative discipline (e.g. Millward, [69], p. 96). So the contrast between the two schools, if we may call them that, amounts in practice to little more than a difference in interpretation of substantially the same body of thought. Hence the term welfare economics will be regularly employed in this paper to indicate the Paretian theory, although the argument may have, at least partly, a wider application.

III

Welfare economics has not always been bedevilled by the contradiction sketched in the preceding section. For many generations, of course, there have been numerous advocates of a close link between economics and ethics, assigning to economics the duty of shedding light on or even offering solutions for the moral problems of economic life. Excursions into this borderland have sometimes been seen as a special type of welfare economics, e.g. by Myint in his historical survey ([78], ch. XI). The views of the authors discussed by him differ, however, in essential respects from the ethical version of modern welfare theory. They did not envisage the theory of efficient allocation as an ethical study and hence as an answer to their pleas.

Without any doubt welfare economics was, in its beginnings, taken to be a purely economic subject, wholly innocent of ethical pretensions. To Pareto, to go no further back into the past (for instance to Dupuit), the theory of collective ophelimity was an essential part of pure economics, which he saw as completely independent of ethics ([85], p. 19). He introduced the principle that was destined to become famous as nothing more than a definition of maximum collective ophelimity. As is well known, Pigou likewise regarded the theory of economic welfare as a positive science. When, in the thirties, welfare economics came of age as a separate subdiscipline, it continued to be dealt with in purely economic and positive terms; value judgments were mentioned sporadically, if at all. Illustrative is Hicks's renowned article of 1938 with its affirmation that welfare economics, which he equated with the theory of efficiency, is an integral part of economic theory ([44], p. 307). This trend of thought remained prominent well into the forties. Lerner's great treatise of 1944 [61] may be seen as its culmination.

Meanwhile Bergson, with his seminal paper of 1938, had planted the time-bomb which was to destroy the harmony. A striking feature of his essay is that he did not present his 'reformulation' of welfare economics, which he described as concerned with 'ethical counseling' ([20], p. 43), as fundamentally a new departure, but as a self-evident and general truth. In the very first sentence he applied it retroactively to all his precursors, including Pareto and Pigou. His conception made little impact till Samuelson took it up in the *Foundations*. After that the idea that welfare economics is unavoidably linked to value judgments rapidly gathered momentum and gained the ascendancy remarkably soon. The revolution was accomplished with little overt resistance, although the victory was not complete and in the course of time there occurred some counter-attacks, to be mentioned later. A peculiar fact is that the schism has never elicited a thorough exchange of views between the two camps. They live, on the whole, next to one another in a state of peaceful coexistence, each part rarely bothering to argue its own opinion against the competing one.

The inner division of welfare economics is all the more regrettable since it is in a much healthier state than the strong misgivings about its future abounding in the fifties would have led one to expect. It has shown far more vigour and fruitfulness than it was given credit for by many critics at the time. During the last decades it has grown in breadth and depth, steadily exploring new territory. It is true that the tendency to disparage welfare economics and all its works persists in some quarters; Boulding, for instance, has condemned it as a 'monumentally unsuccessful exercise' ([28], p. 12), although elsewhere he calls the Pareto optimum 'a very important concept' ([29], p. 90). But now the prevailing mood is one of optimism, as is borne out by Baumol's observation 'that there is a great vitality in the field of welfare economics' ([17], p. 45) and by the statement of Arrow and Scitovsky that welfare economics has recently increased greatly in importance ([15], p. 1). The incertitude about the central concept of Pareto optimality casts a shadow, however, on its gratifying progress.

This situation is an anomaly welfare economics cannot be proud of. It may be a consoling thought that it has not noticeably hampered the advance of research, yet it is not altogether innocuous. It raises a barrier to mutual understanding, the costs of which have not been negligible, and these may very well increase perceptibly in the near future. In recent literature there are signs that the confusion it entails is spreading and that the dissension threatens to become detrimental to the further performance of welfare economics. Already, for example, it is confounding its most important practical application, cost-benefit analysis. It is a piquant but disconcerting symptom of its schizoid condition to find Mishan, a tireless champion of the normative cause, arguing forcefully in favour of basing this technique on the principle of potential Pareto improvements as a purely economic criterion, and against the introduction of political value judgments ([74], pp. 90 f.), to be promptly confronted with the retort that value judgments cannot be avoided (Nash *et al* [80], pp. 122). If this unhappy state of affairs persists, the divided counsel on the character of its propositions could impair the not too robust confidence gained with difficulty by welfare theory from those it is deemed to inform. Its practitioners would be well advised to rid themselves of their philosophical self-doubt before long.

IV

The problem has a rather elusive quality because substantive differences of opinion are intermingled with verbal ones.[4] It may be noted, though perhaps superfluously, that it is not commensurate with the general one of the necessity, possibility or desirability of value-free economics. The issue at stake with respect to welfare economics is solely whether it is methodologically different from the rest of economics because of its subject-matter or purpose. A positive answer to this question does not imply a denial of the possibility of value-free economics, nor does a negative answer exclude the influence of ideology and interests. The problem has nothing to do with the hoary question of whether economists have the right to make judgments, which of course they have. Yet the general problem of *Wertfreiheit* is relevant to the dispute under consideration in that the normative conception of welfare economics may seem to fly in the face of the central tenet of the Weberian doctrine, namely that it is beyond the competence of science to furnish ethical appraisals and prescriptions.

A promising starting-point for an attempt to elucidate the problem appears to be the thesis, common to all adherents of the ethical school, that neutral welfare economics is inconceivable. (To start with the opposite assertion that ethical welfare economics cannot exist would be less apposite, as such a denial hardly ever occurs in so outspoken a form in the literature.) This assertion sharply highlights the division of minds and has, moreover, the appearance of a refutable proposition. This property may be deceptive; at least occasionally the statement looks suspiciously like a tautology, being merely the reverse of a definition of welfare economics as a normative subject. If intended as such it would stultify a fruitful debate at the outset. It will not do to settle the issue aprioristically by laying down definitions of the nature of welfare economics. A definition of one kind can easily be met with a contrary one. Even if questions of definitions cannot be avoided entirely, the proposition that neutral welfare economics is impossible conduces to an unbiased examination only if it is understood as one that can be critically assessed and that might be refuted on logical and empirical grounds.[5]

At first sight falsification of the impossibility thesis may seem to be extremely simple, as it suffices to appeal to the palpable fact that the neutral version of the welfare theory does exist. But it is not all that easy; the rebuttal will at once and somewhat contemptuously be met with the counter-argument that the so-called neutrality is imaginary and that at the present time only the exceptionally naive and unenlightened cling to the belief that it can be real. The unavowed value judgments are declared to be implicit in the theory, hidden in its premises and conclusions, if not in its vocabulary. The only correct procedure is to bring them squarely into the open. To do otherwise would be tantamount to self-deception and to leading other ignorants astray, unwittingly if not wilfully, by presenting results emanating from value judgments as purely scientific and objective. The inescapable consequence of this argument is that the founders of the subject themselves, Pareto and Pigou, not to mention many lesser mortals, were victims of self-delusion.

This reasoning clearly rests on the supposition that it is not possible to expunge the tacit or the explicit value judgments. They are considered to be inherent in the subject, not to be eliminated without doing violence to its intrinsic meaning. It is with this theorem that the present author ventures to disagree. The second main contention of this paper is that the neutral conception is demonstrably the most adequate one.

There have been some earlier revindications of positive welfare economics, apart from a number of scattered casual comments in its favour.[6] In 1946 Radomysler stated the case pointedly in a few pages ([91], pp. 89 f.). Some years later Myint, in his above named historical work, cogently pointed out the ethically neutral character of 'the Paretian theory of the Optimum' and stated as one of his conclusions that 'it is still possible to have a workably objective welfare analysis' ([78], pp. 118, 219). In 1959 Archibald castigated, in a more extensive treatment of the problem, the 'muddle' and the 'unnecessary difficulty and confusion' caused by dragging in value judgments ([12], p. 316). The positive character of the theory of allocation has also been persuasively argued by Buchanan ([30], pp. 4 f.), while in a recent note Ng ([83], pp. 1016 f.) again succinctly defended the objective interpretation, with special reference to Pareto optimality. Hartog, too, denies in his textbook the special character of welfare economics as compared to price theory ([42], pp. 2 f., 25]. Van Den Haag's spirited critique of the normative conception has already been referred to. Other examples might be mentioned to show that the positive interpretation is still very much alive and even appears to be gaining ground again.

It is to be deplored that these protestations have evoked hardly any response from the supporters of the opposite view. Archibald's powerful argumentation, for instance, was dismissed by Mishan on very weak grounds in a single, though complimentary, footnote ([70], pp. 7 – 8)[7]. This attitude may be seen as evincing how deeply rooted the conception of welfare economics as an inherently normative subject is. A further elaboration of the problem in order to test the impossibility thesis may therefore not be amiss.

V

The special character of welfare economics is regularly derived from what is considered its quintessential purpose, the making of policy recommendations. It is submitted that the view that it is merely the servant of economic policy and thus an 'applied science'[8] is far too narrow, particularly with regard to the Paretian theory of allocation. First and foremost it is a theoretical subject in its own right, quite independent of any preoccupation with policy problems. An illuminating example is the theory of comparative advantage, one of the earliest seedlings and one of the best cultivated trees in its garden. Whatever its relevance to economic policy may be, it is in the first instance a piece of theoretical analysis with a life of its own. There is reason to surmise that the tendency of the ethical school to subordinate the whole subject from the outset to its practical aim is to a considerable extent responsible for the fact that the two parties in the debate tend to argue at cross-purposes. Many defenders of positive welfare economics envisage primarily the substantial body of pure theory it contains.

These contrasting views are closely connected with different interpretations of the subject matter of the Paretian theory. It is generally agreed that it is concerned with the utility or economic welfare the individual members of society derive from the use of economic resources. But behind this consensus lies a subtle, yet crucial, disagreement. In its original neutral form the theory takes the individuals' utility functions directly as the starting-point for the study of collective utility maximisation. It was the distinguishing mark of the old tradition in welfare economics, in the Pigovian as well as in the Paretian variant, that its problems were analysed purely in terms of utility.[9] The ethical version of the theory, on the other hand, usually deals with utility at one remove by defining welfare economics as 'being concerned with the extent to which the objectives of society as a whole are fulfilled rather than the private objectives of its members.' (Winch [113], p. 13). It introduces the 'Paretian value judgment' that utility maximisation is consonant with 'social welfare', or, in a somewhat different formulation, it assumes that this judgment is held by society. Approbated in this way, utility maximisation is taken as the policy objective to which the recommendations of welfare economics are directed. This approach has been described epigrammatically by Mishan: 'welfare economics is founded on ethics, not utility'. ([72], p. 976).

With this dictum Mishan summarily banishes Pareto from the field in which he was a pioneer. This absurdity alone proves that the detour via 'the objectives of society' or the concept of social welfare is redundant. It is, moreover, objectionable because it obscures the elementary fact that economic theory is primarily interested in utility for its own sake. Even if all historical credentials are disregarded, economic theory cannot evade the duty of occupying itself with collective utility. It is an economic variable of great importance and its analysis the natural extension of the theory of individual utility maximisation. Buchanan is therefore surely right when he calls the study of efficient allocation 'the central part of economic theory' ([30], p. 4). One may even, as Pareto himself and his immediate followers were inclined to do, consider the problem of optimal collective utility as the supreme challenge to economic theory and its solution as the cap-stone of its edifice.

Evidently this basic problem owes its abiding interest, like many theoretical topics, not merely to its relevance to economic policy. It is an autonomous theoretical subject requiring attention quite apart from ethical or 'social' considerations. The problem is not primarily a teleological one: it is not necessary to assume that efficient allocation is deliberately willed by anyone.

As utility pure and simple is the authentic stuff from which the intricate web of deductions in welfare theory is spun, the countless contemporary Paretian models may most sensibly be viewed as building, also in this respect, on the foundation laid by the master. As a matter of fact they often relate overtly to unalloyed utility, and if they are clothed in the language of 'Paretian value judgments' the lifting of this veil brings out more clearly what they really are about. Lately Hicks has expressed the same opinion concerning the purport of modern allocation theory ([49], p. 316).

In the same essay he wonders why we should study 'welfare' if it is not a 'good thing'. ([49], p. 311) This question occupies the representatives of the ethical school a good deal. At least some of them believe that welfare economics should direct itself to a worthier object than so vulgar a thing as mere utility. According to Bergson its concern is 'the welfare of Social Man' ([20], p. 49) and Mishan considers it to be a 'weird exercise' if it is not based on a concept of welfare with 'broad ethical appeal.' ([70], p. 8 footnote). But surely the ethical quality of utility is irrelevant to economic theory. We do not investigate profit maximising behaviour and the trade cycle because they are 'good things'. For better or worse it is the lot of economists to study individual and collective utility and it has always fascinated them. Over the centuries they have acquired a certain expertise and all the attempts to deflect the efforts of welfare economics from this homely topic to the higher sphere of 'Social Man' have borne hardly any fruit. The ethical school has in fact offered no viable alternative; to replace utility with an unspecified ethical concept of welfare turns the 'weird exercise' into a vacuous one.

One of the advantages of retaining the original Paretian conception is that it is the most natural and straightforward one, unencumbered by circumlocutions about 'social welfare'. It is therefore, contrary to Mishan's claim in favour of the ethical approach ([72], p. 976), a considerable simplification. The grand theme of collective utility gives rise to manifold complex analytical problems which can only be adequately handled in the spirit of pure theoretical inquiry, without the intrusion of alien elements. The actual practice of welfare theory reflects the compelling force of this feature. Pure welfare theory is a self-contained world of economic concepts and conclusions, where the moral philosopher would be completely at sea.

As a part of pure theory welfare economics is obviously positive and not normative. The arguments advanced by Archibald, Buchanan, Ng and other authors mentioned above to demonstrate this carry full conviction. Propositions like those that, under certain assumptions, perfect competition is a sufficient condition of Pareto optimality, and that monopoly, tariffs and externalities cause a welfare loss are positive statements, which are true or false, independently of ethical or ideological beliefs.

If it is agreed that welfare economics is primarily a chapter of pure theory, it cannot be maintained that the concept of Pareto optimality is inherently an ethical one, 'normative to the core' (Alexander [4], p. 108). On the contrary, it is basically a theoretical notion, as it was in the mind of its originator. As such it is a neutral analytical tool performing a descriptive and not a prescriptive function. In this context it is not true that 'there is of course an implicit assumption here that if we are not at a Paretian optimum moving toward it is a good thing'. (Boulding [29], p. 91). That the Pareto criterion allows only a partial ranking is a direct consequence of its objective character, once empirical interpersonal comparisons of utility are thought to be unfeasible. So it is an error to think, as some do (e.g. Rowley and Peacock [95], p. 144), that this restriction ensues from a value judgment.

It would make no sense to waft away this neutral theory as being 'impossible'. One may, if one wants to, decline to dignify it with the name of welfare economics,[10] but then one should not deal with allocation theory under this label as if it were necessarily linked with value judgments.

VI

To accentuate the theoretical foundation of welfare economics is not to underrate the fact that it owes much of its interest to the discussion of policy measures which may enhance allocative efficiency. The next question to be examined is whether the treatment of allocation policy renders it necessary to introduce the value judgment that Pareto optimality is a 'good thing' and hence a desirable end.

It is immediately obvious, from elementary considerations, that the answer must be negative. The one step needed is to assume that efficient allocation may be a desired end. The objective is taken as 'given' in the sense that the theory does not evaluate its ethical worth, having no reason to do so. The analysis yields instrumental or teleological propositions indicating suitable means of attaining the presumed end, for instance the equation of price and marginal cost. It is a commonplace that such statements are positive, not normative (Machlup [65], p. 116; cf. Pareto [85], pp. 29–30). One may quite easily detect the complete analogy existing between the conditions for optimal allocation and those for profit maximisation in the theory of the firm (Hartog [42], pp. 2 f., 25).[11] Hence the policy recommendations concerning the achievement of the Pareto optimum are not categorical rules; they pretend to no more than hypothetical validity, also because the policy measures directed towards that end are not costless and may not be ethically and politically neutral. Merely in this conditional sense may it be said, as is often done, that the Pareto criterion 'commands' or 'justifies' certain actions, but it would be preferable to avoid the rather common expression 'Pareto rule' on account of its mandatory tone.

In the theory of allocation policy it need not be assumed that efficient allocation is the unique, unreservedly desired goal. Its being a policy objective does not preclude that policy makers and members of the public will want to weigh it against competing aims. So there is no reason to identify Pareto optimality with 'social welfare' as the supreme objective of society, nor to postulate it as a necessary condition for optimal 'social welfare'.

The Paretian optimum cannot even be considered as the only proper goal 'from the economic point of view'. The relative character of the Pareto criterion as a standard of judgment is sometimes expressed by stressing its purely economic character (e.g. Wolfelsperger [114], p. 40–41). This is correct in itself, but may nevertheless lead to a misunderstanding. Boulding, for example, once described it as a standard which judges events and politics 'as "economically" desirable, even though on other grounds (political, national, ethical) they might be judged undesirable' ([27], p. 3). As the inverted commas show, the term 'economic' is not unambiguous. His formulation seems to imply that a distinction can be made between economic and non-economic ends, and moreover that Pareto optimality is the only right economic end of policy. This view runs counter to Robbins's persuasive argument that 'there are no economic ends' ([92], p. 145).If one accepts his definition the satisfaction of consumers' wants is no more an economic phenomenon than, for example, the achievement of policy makers' objectives which are more or less independent of individual preferences. According to this reasoning Pareto optimality is not 'economically desirable' in an absolute sense. Even if this point is waived as a semantic one, it is still not correct to see Pareto optimality as the uniquely right economic end, for on account of its static character it rests on a restrictive definition of economic welfare. The wants of future generations are disregarded and static efficiency may on Schumpeterian or other grounds conflict with innovative activities.

One of the main reasons for attributing no more than relative practical validity to policy recommendations concerning allocative efficiency is of course its interconnectedness with income distribution. If efficiency and equity are deemed to clash, and as lump sum transfers can seldom be employed in practice to remedy the conflict, the former may be renounced for the sake of the latter. Among representatives of the ethical school it is the prevailing view that, irrespective of income distribution, Pareto efficiency is not a worthwhile objective. Samuelson, for in-

stance, remarks with regard to the conditions for optimal efficiency that their 'whole *raison d'être* disappears if the additional ethical conditions are not adjoined' ([98], p. 1096) and Sen observes that, if distribution is left out of account, a Pareto-optimal economy can be 'perfectly disgusting' ([103], p. 22). [12]
Suchlike value judgments are out of place in the neutrally formulated theory of allocation policy, which does not aspire to enounce 'full welfare judgments'. The theory does, of course, provide knowledge about the distributional effects of allocation policy, as well as the fundamental insight that Pareto optimality is not a unique position but, as Buchanan argued forcefully, it has completed its task by formulating the conditions for optimal efficiency, leaving the problems of distribution unsolved ([30], p. 195). As a rule the ethical school does the same since it usually introduces income distribution only in a formal way.[13]
This abstention also extends to the question of whether those whose welfare decreases as a consequence of measures to improve efficiency ought to be compensated. This is not a matter of allocation policy and is, moreover, a problem outside the bounds of positive theory. It is true that, if there are any unindemnified losers, the attainment of Pareto optimality is only a 'potential' improvement, but this need not prevent it from being pursued as a policy objective. The theory may also, of course, take actual Pareto improvements as a given end. A great deal of attention has in fact been paid to the problems involved in compensation or bribing possible losers; neither this objective nor potential improvements should, however, be regarded as prescribed by the Paretian theory.

VII

The conclusion that a positive welfare theory is perfectly possible would be vitiated if, behind the façade of impeccable neutrality, value judgments are tacitly lurking. To render full justice to the impossibility theorem of the ethical school we have to scrutinise the places where they are supposed to be inevitably ensconced, and to examine whether they are phantoms or real beings.
Value judgments that allegedly prevent a strict objectivity are detected by some economists in the 'emotive' and 'persuasive' terminology welfare economy employs. In the first place 'welfare' and 'welfare economics', as well as terms like efficiency, optimum and Pareto improvement, are said to carry ineradicable normative overtones. Little, in particular, ascribed the ethical nature of welfare economics almost entirely to those linguistic peculiarities ([63], ch. V, also Nath [81], p. 1). As Archibald effectively criticised this view in his above mentioned essay it need not detain

us long.[14] Admittedly it contains a core of truth, but we are not bound to capitulate so readily to the wiles of language as Little and likeminded economists do. We are not will-less slaves to our vocabulary; we are free to exorcise its disturbing normative associations or to substitute colourless terms for value-loaded ones.[15] Robertson's 'ecfare' may serve as an example ([93], p. 30). It also requires no uncommon sophistication for economists to keep in mind that words like efficiency and optimal are technical terms.[16]

It is remarkable that Little spurns the neutralising therapy. If the analysis were clothed in a neutral language it would, according to him, no longer be welfare economics ([63], p. 80). Here the reasoning becomes circular: after the subject is characterised as being necessarily ethical because of its emotive terminology this language is praised as being just the one that suits the subject-matter. So Little joins Mishan in expelling Pareto, with his 'theory of collective ophelimity', from welfare theory. The linguistic argument also ignores the fact that in some other languages like German and Dutch the equivalents of 'economic welfare' and 'welfare economics' are not ethically coloured to the same degree as in English. This underlines the spuriousness of the notion that the contents and character of a branch of science are determined by its name and terminology. The impossibility of a neutral welfare theory cannot be sustained on suchlike semantic grounds. The name welfare economics may not be quite fortunate, too grandiose and, as Hicks says, presumptuous ([49], p. 316). Allocation theory or theory of social efficiency, the title of Bohm's textbook [25], would be more appropriate. But surely the label attached to the theory is of the least importance. Weighty discussions about this question would have earned the disdain of Pareto, who took pride in his extreme nominalism and whose favourite maxim was: 'One should never quarrel about words' ([86], § 16, p. 10).

While the semantic argument has a subordinate place in the justification of normative welfare economics, the so-called Paretian value judgments are of great moment in this respect. The expression refers to the two standard postulates of the Paretian theory as well as to the concept of Pareto optimality. The first of these holds that the individual's preferences are the only yardstick of the utility or economic welfare he enjoys, the second that the economic welfare of a society or collective utility comprises the welfare of every member of the community.

These postulates are regularly presented as being value judgments in and by themselves. If this were true they alone would suffice to stamp the theory as indelibly normative, from the base upward as it were. As they largely determine the content of the Paretian optimum, it would owe its normative character at least in part to the underlying value judgments. This explanation is, however, usually combined with a contradictory one which, so to speak, lets the value judgments come in at the top. According to this view Pareto optimality as a policy norm takes pride of place and the postulates are subsequently elevated to an ethical status as a condition of its normative quality. On that account it is often called the 'basic Paretian value judgment.'

The most plausible solution of this contradiction is to consider the second motivation as decisive. Once Pareto optimality is assigned a normative function, it may seem natural to introduce the postulates from the outset as value judgments. That they are in themselves ethical presuppositions without being linked beforehand to the 'basic Paretian norm' is highly questionable, and very scant efforts have been made to prove it. At any rate the idea that they are inherently 'Paretian value judgments' is easily refuted.

The first postulate is nothing but the convention, regularly adhered to since the beginning of the nineteenth century, of defining utility in a theoretical sense, as distinct from the everyday use of the term (see for instance Say [99], I, pp. 81–2 and Dupuit [38], p. 104). This ancient definition is thus in no way especially 'Paretian', although Pareto coined the neologism 'ophelimity' to exclude all ethical associations. It is ironic that, of all concepts, the one which is the most venerable example of successful neutralisation should be looked upon as sheltering a value judgment. 'As every student knows', taking the individual's preferences as 'given' by no means implies condoning them. Scores of authors have pointed out that utility may be trivial, morally reprehensible or harmful to the individual's well-being and hence is not intrinsically a 'good thing'.

So one cannot but agree with Mishan that 'all that is utility is not welfare' (in the ethical sense) ([71], p. 35). No less true is Archibald's observation that to inquire into the efficiency of arrangements for the satisfying of given wants no judgment of these wants is called for ([12], p. 317). Consequently the notion of the Pareto optimum does not imply approval and it is therefore mistaken to assert that it embodies what Alexander christened the 'pig principle', the value judgment that 'more is better' ([5], p. 24; [4], p. 107). The Paretian theory merely assumes, like economic theory in general, that people prefer more economic welfare to less, but an ethical appraisal of this presumed trait of human nature lies outside its brief.

It is equally unjustified to read into the convention of starting from given wants an advocacy of consumers' sovereignty. As a matter of fact this expression, which is often employed in a normative sense (e.g. by Musgrave [77], p. 14 and Lerner [62], p. 258) had better be avoided as a designation of that practice. It is also otiose to turn Pareto's simple factual statement that the individual is the 'only judge of what pleases or displeases him' ([85], p. 62) into the 'Paretian value judgment' that everyone is the best (or the best and sole) judge of his own welfare, as is commonly done in the ethical interpretation of the theory. This embellishment cannot even claim the merit of satisfying the hankering after a concept of welfare with 'broad ethical appeal', as wants are still accepted as 'given'.

It is reasonable to stipulate as a condition of utility maximisation that consumers have enough information about the properties of commodities not to be disappointed in those they choose, but this assumption is not an ethical value judgment. The doubts frequently raised concerning the welfare significance of the satisfaction of given wants, as in recent lively discussions on merit wants, the moulding of preferences by advertising and the consumer society, as well as in the more esoteric disquisitions on the conundrums of preference and choice, carry less weight as objections to welfare theory if the latter has no normative pretensions than if ethical worth is attached to utility by means of a 'Paretian value judgment'. These problems are situated on another plane, the practical relevance of the Paretian theory.

The neutral concept of utility or economic welfare dispels the worries that have plagued many as to whether or not economic welfare is a separable part of total welfare. If this problem really had any importance it would also be a stumbling-block in the theory of consumers' behaviour, where nobody pays attention to it.

In its recent development the Paretian theory has displayed considerable flexibility concerning the variables included in the utility function. By broadening its scope in this respect it has been greatly enriched, although on the other hand the tendency to employ ever more comprehensive utility functions is not entirely propitious, as the concept of Pareto optimality becomes correspondingly less tangible and operational.[17] Be this as it may, the fact that a certain latitude exists in deciding which preferences are to be taken into account does not detract from the neutral character of the utility concept. The decision about its specification rests on a methodological or theoretical, not on an ethical value judgment.[18] One may, of course, delineate the concept with the intention of making it useful for normative purposes, but this consideration lies outside the concern of pure welfare theory, and the ethical school has seldom had recourse to this method.[19]

With regard to the second postulate the question is still simpler. It is quite gratuitous to dress it up as a 'Paretian value judgment'. It is an arithmetic truism that 'every individual counts' when the economic welfare of the members of society is the subject of inquiry, just as every apple counts if the weight of a basketful of apples is to be determined. Regrettably, the Paretian theory excludes the yet unborn from the scene, but this limitation is due to the analytical difficulties their presence would entail and not to the value judgment that their welfare is of no consequence.

On account of the two postulates it is widely held that welfare economics reflects an 'individualistic' view of society. According to Klappholz's formulation welfare economics denies the existence of 'such a thing as an independent community interest apart from the interest, or the welfare, of the individuals comprising the community' ([57], p. 106; cf. Samuelson [97], p. 243). But surely the fact that welfare theory confines itself to a particular problem, the satisfaction of the wants of the individual members of society, does not in the least imply that other problems are assumed not to exist. This mistaken view was disproved in advance by the creator of the 'individualist' theory of collective ophelimity himself, who, after all, developed as its complement an elaborate theory of 'social utility'. This he relegated to sociology, for he was anxious to preserve intact the separate identity of economics while stressing the necessity of sociology as its supplement.

VIII

The hunt for the elusive implicit value judgments, hitherto unavailing, cannot be called off yet, for there is another possible hiding-place demanding inspection, the theory of allocation policy. It has been shown that, in spite of all denials, it is perfectly possible to formulate it entirely in positive terms. But it is only truly objective if the conditional nature of its advice on policy is clearly recognised and expressed. This condition has by no means been always fulfilled. Welfare economists have often tended to claim absolute normative validity for their policy recommendations, presenting them as definite, scientifically founded prescriptions for a sound policy which the government ought to follow. This practice conforms to the age-old belief of economists that their science enables them to establish binding rules for policy and that they are even in duty bound to act as its master-guide. This ambition gained a particularly strong hold on welfare economics and has not yet been abandoned completely. Its practitioners occasionally still address governments in the imperative mood.

Without trying to explain fully the inclination to adopt this attitude, a few of the main reasons may be mentioned. If it has been found that tariffs and monopoly bring about welfare losses, it is tempting to think of this deprivation as inherently bad and rectifying measures as naturally desirable, the more so because these consequences may be ascribed to ignorance, arbitrary meddling or abuse of power. Strictly speaking, this mode of thinking is inconsistent with the principle of abstaining from passing judgment on wants and their satisfaction. But when policy problems relating to economic problems crop up, this axiom is easily lost sight of, and more economic welfare is appraised as being naturally better than less. So it comes about readily that Pareto improvements, as they do not harm anybody's economic welfare, are taken to be self-evidently meritorious.[20]

Historically a major factor has been the idea, largely of utilitarian origin, but perhaps more often held intuitively than explicitly, that promoting the economic welfare of the community is the one rational purpose of government policy. So the economist can take this preordained end as an objective norm, and offer definite prescriptions to attain it. This vision is akin to Hick's 'Economic Welfarism' which finds 'the *ends* of economic life *within* economics' ([46], p. IX; p. 96). In theory it is rarely accepted without restrictions, as Smith's adage about defence exemplifies, but the qualifications tend to be ignored when it comes to devising policy recommendations. This approach is, moreover, often combined with the notion that the state is, in fact, entirely animated by the desire to further that immanent goal, waiting only to be enlightened by economists about the means of achieving it.

Small wonder that welfare economists have fallen under the spell of this philosophy, which conforms to their deepest professional longings. It entitles them to assume, with a clear conscience as to their scientific objectivity, the role of benevolent lawgivers disposing of revealed knowledge about the supreme end of society, counting on their lessons being respectfully received. This welfare theorist's paradise is, of course, a mirage. The view that the desirability of maximum economic welfare is a scientifically ascertained objective fact has long been discredited. Myrdal's scathing denouncement of this 'methaphysical conception' might be said to have delivered the finishing stroke to its credibility ([79]; cf. also Albert [3]; Bohnen [26] and Weber [112]). Yet its attraction to welfare economists is so strong that it still lingers on in their minds and tends to colour their thinking. Wrestling itself free from this pervasive influence has been for welfare economics a long and painful process which has not yet been concluded.

Especially in the older literature, the desirability of welfare maximisation has been, for whatever reason, all too often taken for granted or put forward as an objective truth under the cloak of factual statements. Sometimes austere theoretical analysis slips imperceptibly into a normative posture as, for example, when Kahn suddenly calls a certain rearrangement of production 'socially desirable' ([55], p. 21) and Hicks in similar fashion praises a change that satisfies the compensation test as 'an unequivocal improvement' ([45], p. 329; cf. Little's comments on this passage [63], pp. 92 f.).

The ardently sought-for concealed value judgments are at last detected here in the policy norms which are seemingly derived from economics and postulated as if they had objective validity, although in this twilight sphere the distinction between implicit judgments and quasi-objective explicit ones is not always crystal-clear. The more or less surreptitiously introduced notions about welfare maximisation as the true end of policy have in the past haunted economic thinking to the detriment of its scientific integrity. They have got welfare economics a bad name as an ideologically biased pseudo-science. So it is gratifying that critical reflection has driven them out of hiding. The members of the ethical school, though by no means the first and only economists to spot the methodological sin, have rendered a useful service by making welfare theorists more conscious of its dangerous lure. It is partly due to them that this faulty kind of reasoning, although not quite extinct, has definitely become outmoded.

At times the designation of optimal economic welfare as the proper end from the economic point of view, or as economically desirable, has been branded as the most common and a particularly deceptive disguise of a value judgment.[21] It is true that such a characterisation shades rather easily into the idea that policy ought to grant this goal absolute priority. As economists have undeniably shown themselves prone to be caught in this trap, the indictment is justified to a certain extent. Yet it is incorrect to see the offence as necessarily associated with expressions like 'economically desirable'. As has been argued above, they are, though not unexceptionable, in many cases employed with the intention of stressing the relative significance of welfare judgments, for instance by no one less than Pareto ([86], § 2129, p. 1339).

IX

Apparently the ethical school, contending that welfare economics, set forth in neutral terms, harbours implicit value judgments, has a case. This discovery does not, however, supply a shred of evidence for its impossibility theorem. To drive out the illicit intruders is a most simple operation. Now and then human fallibility may allow them to slip back, but it is hardly an unattainable virtue to be on one's guard against this frailty.

Nor is it true that the contributions of all those who deal with welfare economics as a positive subject are crypto-normative. The most impressive example to the contrary is Pareto himself. He was, as Tarascio has explained, 'fully aware of the restrictive nature of the Pareto optimum criterion of economic welfare' ([108], p. 8). To ascribe normative significance to it would contradict his strongest scientific convictions. The ethical neutrality of science even became, as the same Pareto scholar remarked, an obsession with him ([109], p. 113).[22] His thinking was also devoid of the utilitarian and cognate notions that have been responsible for surreptitious value judgments in much of British welfare theory.[23] The distinction he drew between collective ophelimity and social utility shows that he was far from identifying the former with some ultimate good for society. Accordingly, he never tired of repeating that pure economics by itself could solve no practical problem and disavowed any intention to convey recipes for the achievement of happiness, utility or welfare ([85], p. 3). In his observations on a socialist economy he considered maximum ophelimity a possible and not a predetermined natural goal ([85], pp. 360, 362). So the neutral interpretation of the Paretian theory, untainted by implicit value judgments, is clearly the authentic one.[24] Surely he would have abhorred the now fashionable idea that the theory bearing his name is based on 'Paretian value judgments'.

It is a testimony to the strength of the normative propensity of economists that some of his most distinguished disciples have been less circumspect. Barone, in his famous paper on the collectivist state, posed the problem of how production 'ought to be directed' ([16], p. 245). Allais went still further by stating that a rational economy could pursue no other goal than the maximisation of economic welfare ([6], p. 34).[25] One should hasten to add, however, that suchlike propositions do not occur in other works on the Paretian theory by this profound student of Pareto (e.g. [7, 9, 11]).[26]

The position of Pigou is somewhat less clear-cut than Pareto's because of his presumption that an increase in welfare will in most cases enhance total welfare as well. The present author nevertheless questions the prevailing opinion that Pigou was mistaken in regarding his monumental work as 'positive science'. But, although not everyone will consider Pigou to be a convincing witness, there are other authors following the positive tradition who cannot possibly be reproached seriously with implicit normative proclivities. Presumably no one will feel slighted if Koopmans's magisterial study [59] is singled out as an example.

The most convincing proof that the subject is not naturally fettered to ethics is provided by the fact that many adherents of the ethical persuasion, and among them the most eminent ones, have greatly contributed to the positive type of analysis in this field. Striking instances are several studies by Bergson on central topics of welfare economics, like allocation under socialism ([19], especially ch. 14, [21]; marginal cost pricing [22] and monopoly welfare losses [23]), which are completely exempt from allusions to value judgments. Various publications of Samuelson and Mishan might also be mentioned.

X

The falsification of the impossibility theorem does not by itself disprove that, at least with regard to the theory of allocation policy, the ethical conception is justifiable. The possibility remains that installing value judgments here in a seat of honour is preferable to expelling them. As a matter of fact, there is little, if anything, to be said in favour of this program and much to be said against it.

The difference between the neutral theory and the ethical conception may appear slight in that those who subscribe to the normative interpretation do not hold that economics by itself is the source of the value judgments in welfare economics (cf., e.g., Samuelson [98], p. 1103). They are regarded as belonging to what Samuelson calls its 'ascientific area' ([98], p. 1129; cf. Bergson [20], p. 62, on the 'extra-scientific' part of the subject). They enter as data into economics, the scientific part, whose function is to 'neutrally interpret' them (Samuelson [98], p. 1129) as an 'unpretentious deductive mill' (Samuelson [98], p. 1103; cf. Bergson [20], p. 35, on 'the application of the logic of choice').

According to this dichotomy the concept of Paretian welfare economics is wider than the Paretian welfare theory as a branch of economics. It is doubtful whether it is felicitous to subsume the ascientific hinterland under welfare *economics*, but this is a relatively minor point. Far more important is that the set-up, although entirely compatible with the Weberian thesis of the neutrality of science, differs in a crucial aspect from the positive version of the Paretian theory of allocation policy. It does not take the end as given in the sense that it may be *desired* but it introduces, by way of 'a simple assumption' (Samuelson, [97], p. 236, cf. also [98], p. 1103), the judgment that Pareto improvements are good or *desirable*. In this minute variation lies the core of the controversy.

In many minds the image of the Paretian theory as a normative doctrine has replaced its original meaning. By a strange twist in the history of ideas the apocryphal interpretation is imputed to Pareto himself (see e.g. Samuelson's remark on '*his* best state of the world' [98], pp. 1099 – 1100) and is now called the orthodox one (e.g. Rowley and Peacock [95], p. 2). What the advantage of this transformation of the theory is supposed to be has never been satisfactorily explained. The desirability assumption is at best redundant. It does not enhance the practical relevance of the Paretian theory, which depends on the degree of efficiency actually desired. Yet, if it were merely pointless, it might, at a pinch, be tolerated as an irritant. But it brings in its train vexatious complications and even imperils the status of the theory. So it is a ready candidate for Occam's razor.

The description of welfare economics as postulating a desirable policy end makes good sense as a picture of the erstwhile too common practice of passing off purely economic criteria as objectively valid norms. By so doing, welfare economics was unwittingly engaged in recommending an end as desirable. That this characterisation is retained as being applicable to modern welfare theory appears to stem from an urge to continue the ingrained habit of laying down 'definite' policy rules [cf. Samuelson [97], p. 236), although now in a more respectable manner by basing them on explicit value judgments. This attempt is an empty gesture. It can merely succeed in masking the relative purport of welfare judgments with a spurious aura of absolute validity. By tending to keep alive the fallacy that welfare economics is entitled to provide objectively and generally valid prescriptions, this conception is only slightly less misleading than the former, condemned practice.

The ethical school appears, in fact, to be wavering between the idea that welfare economics provides a firm base for policy prescriptions which 'economists are entitled to make' and the recognition that this ambition is a will-o'-the-wisp. It has even, with some truth, been indicated as the main point of welfare economics that it only warns against ascribing any welfare significance to decision rules (Millward, [69], p. 89). But if this caveat is expressed by stressing the ethical or normative character of the rules, it is very likely to be misconstrued, especially by the uninitiated, as endowing them with ethical worth and obligatory moral force. The praiseworthy aim will be better served by presenting them as one-sided economic maxims which need to be supplemented or may be qualified by ethical and political judgments. The desirability assumption is, however, frequently not intended as just a warning signal, but employed as a warrant for the prescriptive function ascribed to welfare economics, as, for instance, when Pareto optimality is considered to be a necessary condition of optimal social welfare.

XI

A first drawback of the normative interpretation of the Paretian theory is that it has engendered protracted and inconclusive disputes about its true message. Most often the Pareto criterion, translated into the judgment that 'it is a good thing to make one man better off if nobody else is made worse off' (Graaff, [41], p. 10) is regarded as the fundamental norm. In this way it is pressed into a role for which it is ill-suited on account of its incompleteness as a welfare criterion. This becomes manifest in the familiar situation that policy measures aiming at a Pareto optimum make some people worse off. In view of this problem it is asserted, on the one hand, that the 'Pareto optimal approach' only postulates the desirability of increasing potential economic welfare, or, in other words, of Pareto efficiency (this view is clearly stated by Cordon [33], p. 104). On the other hand it is argued that in 'the Paretian framework one cannot legitimately *recommend* courses of action identified as potential improvements' (Culyer [34], p. 116). A similar opinion is that 'the Pareto criterion, strictly interpreted, requires compensation' (Hochman [50], p. 326). According to another, rather popular variant, the criterion implies the injunction that 'no one should be made worse off' (Boulding [29], p. 92). This view finds its most salient expression in the idea, thoroughly elaborated by Leibenstein, that the criterion is a decision rule granting a veto power to the losers ([60]; further references in Hennipman [43]).

These controversies, on which much ingenuity has been expended, are absent in the positive Paretian theory, which does not presume to lay down a policy norm. The Pareto criterion, strictly interpreted in a neutral sense, certainly does not arbitrate in questions of distribution, including those relating to gainers and losers. They involve interpersonal comparisons, which the criterion is precisely intended to eliminate. So it cannot require compensation or bestow a power of veto.[27] Nowhere does Pareto state his criterion in this sort of form. He concentrates on the situation of maximum ophelimity and points out that, while it is not yet attained, more commodities can be made available for distribution in such a way that everybody's welfare may be increased. He does not add the condition that everyone should actually be made better off.[28]

Another and more serious difficulty which results from foisting the desirability assumption upon the Paretian theory is its dubious validity, even if the usual proviso with regard to income distribution is taken into account. The common argument that Pareto optimality is a universally or at least widely accepted ideal has never been empirically verified. It would be fortuitous indeed if an economic concept, from which ethical considerations are deliberately excluded, should at the same time be an unassailable policy norm. The diversity of values existing in society renders any idea about a unanimously acclaimed end of policy nugatory in advance. Differences of opinion about the political and ethical aspects of Pareto optimality are no more than one would expect. They are surely not lacking among economists. From their writings a startling variety of value judgments on the 'Paretian value judgment' may be culled, which are far from being uniformly favourable. On the whole, economists appear to have grown increasingly sceptical about the Paretian optimum being ethically unquestionable. According to Boulding, for example, 'it rests on an extremely shaky foundation of ethical propositions' ([29], p. 128) and Millward denies that there is 'anything inherently, ethically desirable in having a Pareto efficient solution' ([69], p. 35).

The criticisms are mostly directed against the desirability of consumers' sovereignty, implied in the normative interpretation of the Paretian theory. So it is averred that 'want-satisfaction is not a particularly worthy ideal' (Alexander, [5], p. 28), a statement which may elicit the query whether the thwarting of wants is worthier. As this topic has been extensively discussed it need not be enlarged upon further.[29] The restrictions to which consumers' sovereignty as a norm is subject are not ignored by the ethical school; Samuelson, for instance, points out that 'paternalistic policies are voted upon themselves by a democratic people' ([98], p. 1232). But facts like these considerably weaken the claim to propose definite policy prescriptions. Another factor preventing a general concurrence with Pareto-optimal policies, repeatedly stressed by Boulding, is malevolence, the all too human inclination to begrudge other people their becoming better off ([29], pp. 29–30; [27], p. 126).

So the contention that Pareto improvements are 'unequivocally desirable' (Meade [67], p. 68; also Downs [37], p. 192) cannot be sustained. One also feels obliged to question Buchanan's view that the Pareto optimum may be counted upon to find near-universal assent, because only a 'minimal ethical commitment' is required ([30], p. 194). It follows that the Wicksellian unanimity rule which Buchanan revived, and applied with great acumen to a wide field, is not a sure guarantee of the achievement of Pareto optimality. In passing it may be remarked that this rule should not be confused with Leibenstein's. The Wicksell rule is proposed as a means of realising and testing the realisation of the Paretian optimum, and is therefore not a value judgment, while Leibenstein identifies the unanimity rule with the Pareto criterion in the normative sense.

XII

The above considerations force the conclusion that the desirability assumption is a useless encumbrance. To erect the Paretian theory as a normative system is apparently a hazardous enterprise, aligning it with controversial value judgments and thus making it gratuitously vulnerable to attacks on a variety of ethical and political grounds.

Closely connected with this consequence is a grave danger to which the theory is exposed by this approach. In the alliance of economics and ethics the latter is the dominant partner. The value judgments determine the substantive meaning of the conclusions. So, despite the division into an ascientific and a scientific compartment, normative Paretian welfare economics functions as a seamless whole, entirely committed to a particular set of value judgments. Hence it appears as a system of belief, preaching, for example, the virtues of unrestricted consumers' sovereignty and, at least in one of its variants, the justice of Pareto optimal movements.[30] The claim of its practitioners that it yields definite recommendations suggests that they endorse the 'Paretian value judgments' as being truly valid. Thus they put themselves into the position of true believers. The brilliantly written booklet by Dehem, *L'utopie de l'économiste* [36], propounding the idea that economists owe allegiance to the ideal of Pareto efficiency, is a sign that this role is at times eagerly accepted.[31]

Paretian welfare economics in the shape of an ideological creed is a ready target for damning criticism and even for satire, like Falero's *reductio ad absurdum* [39]. It is an old and common grievance that it favours the maintenance of the *status quo*. Leibenstein added the complaint that it is, on account of its unanimity rule, undemocratic in the sense of rejecting majority rule ([60], pp. 308 f.). These charges may perhaps, even within the normative context, be disqualified as misapprehensions, but if so, they have undoubtedly been fostered by many expositions of the pseudo-Paretian normative doctrine.

In recent years the embroilment with ideological issues has acquired a new dimension, since Sen started the ball rolling with the thesis that the Paretian principle, as understood in the theory of collective choice, is incompatible with liberalism [104]. His contention, which evoked lively discussion, has been developed by Peacock and Rowley into a full-fledged onslaught on what they term the dictatorship of Paretian welfare economics ([87], 95). In their eyes it is a religion, with Samuelson as high-priest, while Buchanan, although an arch-Paretian, is the leader of a heretic fringe. Its catechism supports conservatism and is also a dangerous threat to personal liberty because it sponsors a wide range of coercive government interventions to achieve Pareto optimality. The 'Paretian dogma' does not admit of any compromise when this objective is at stake.

Their depiction may be deemed tendentious, as most adherents of the normative Paretian doctrine are not such narrow-minded fanatics as they are presented here. But the victims, who persistently announce that they proffer normative rules, have only themselves to blame if they are taken at their word. To one who lives by the authentic Paretian theory the tract reads like a saddening libel. It is a wry thought that, of all things, Pareto's brainchild has been struck by the fate of being denounced as an ideological dogma. Most regrettably, the authors do not realise that the normative version they oppose is a distortion, and that the true remedy is to return to the pristine meaning of the theory. On the contrary, they vehemently deny the possibility of a neutral interpretation and do not even shrink from impugning the integrity of those who do not share the normative conception by accusing them of 'a professional misdemeanour' (p. 1).[32] Dogma indeed!

As a matter of fact, the two authors demonstrate in an almost dramatic fashion what the fatal outcome of the normative interpretation is bound to be. It inevitably entangles the theory in ideological quarrels. If this process continues, it threatens to spell the end of the Paretian theory as a useful part of economic science. It is therefore in urgent need of being delivered from the clutches of the so-called Paretian value judgments. As a body of positive knowledge it is available to all comers, whatever their political predilections. It does not prescribe what they ought to do, but it may help them to make rational decisions (cf. Graaff [41], p. 170).

The neutral interpretation is straightforward and clear, while the ethical one is tortuous and obscure. That the positive theory of allocation is limited to providing instrumental advice is nothing to be ashamed of. It has been remarked, apparently with some regret, that this task 'leaves the economist as not much more than a human computer' (Millward [69], p. 96). But the function of attending to the 'deductive mill', allotted to him by the leading figures of the ethical school, is not a more glorious one at all. On the other hand, the recognition of the neutral character of allocation theory by no means bars the economist from partaking in discussions of policy ends and the value judgments underlying them. The presumption, even if qualified to some extent, that Paretian welfare economics has the mission to act as society's ethical guide is hollow, and tends to drag it into a morass of deepening confusion and idle polemics. The sooner this pretension is relinquished, the more fruitful the future history of Pareto's offspring will be.*

Notes

1 In this connection the comments by Burkhead and Miner ([31], p. 36) are pertinent.

2 A corresponding threefold classification of the meanings of the Pareto principle is offered by Van den Haag ([111], pp. 181-2).

3 The terms value judgment and normative will, if unqualified, henceforth be employed in this paper in the ethical as distinct from the instrumental sense, unless otherwise indicated. For this meaning of 'normative' see especially Machlup ([65], pp. 102 f.).

4 Cf. the similar remark relating to this problem by Machlup ([65], p. 100): 'Questions of semantics and methodology are difficult to disentangle'.

5 Machlup ([65], p. 116) also regards the thesis that welfare-economics is normative as 'a rebuttable conclusion'. He accepts it as valid, but views welfare economics as altogether different from Paretian allocation theory.

* I would like to express my gratitude to Mrs. Elisabeth Eybers for purging the text of linguistic errors.

6 E.g., regarding the problem of efficiency, Scitovsky ([102], p. 73), Kafoglis ([54], p. 8), Meek ([68], p. 95), and, on the Paretian optimum, Blaug ([24], p. 552).

7 Elsewhere ([71], p. 14) Mishan calls Archibald's criticism, which he wrongly regards as an opposition to welfare economics, 'not very serious' on account of his interpreting Archibald's 'choice-criterion' as arbitrary instead of, as the intention is, its designation as an 'index of welfare'. Mishan employs a very similar 'index of choice-expansion' himself (p. 24). See also the more extensive comments by Bohnen ([26], pp. 22—23) who concedes to Archibald that welfare economics can be transformed into a positive theory but holds that it is in fact normative. Archibald made at least one convert, viz. Albert ([3], p. 46 footnote) who in other publications [1, 2] depicts welfare economics as implicitly and unredeemingly ideological.

8 Rothenberg ([94], p. 3) describes it thus in the opening sentences of his deeply probing work. One is tempted to say that the highly abstract explorations it contains belie his characterisation. Hicks ([47], pp. 6 f.) regards welfare economics as a part of pure but not of positive economics. Mishan ([75], p. 390) employs the term 'pure allocation theory' without, however, explaining it. The expression 'theoretical welfare economics' is used in the literature in a variety of meanings.

9 See as regards Pigou [88], p. 23) and [89], p. 288—289.

10 Cf. Farrell ([40], p. 378), who calls the concept of a Pareto optimum 'completely objective' and propositions concerning Pareto optima 'a part of positive, not welfare economics'.

11 See for a good formulation of the hypothetical and instrumental treatment of allocation policy Millward, ([69], p. 96). Cf. Martin ([66], p. 127) on the 'hypothetical imperatives of economics (particularly Welfare Economics)'. Schumpeter ([101], p. 1069) also argued that 'all propositions of welfare economics can be formulated in the indicative mood'. The contrary opinion is held by Nath ([82], p. 12).

12 This view is also strongly worded by Oort ([84], pp. 19—20), who argues that without a definite set of ethical norms concerning distribution 'the system of allocative optimum conditions . . . surely has no practical significance whatever'.

13 A notable exception is Tinbergen ([110], p. 270). The question may be raised whether there is a significant difference between Buchanan's view and Samuelson's that 'we can formulate these conditions independently of the interpersonal conditions' ([98], p. 1103), if the social welfare function is left completely empty in this respect. Cf. on this question also Allais ([10], p. 406) and Mishan ([72], p. 974).

14 Klappholz ([57], pp. 102 f.) also subscribes to Archibald's argument. Bergson ([20], p. 72) rejects the view that the persuasive language is responsible for the ethical character of welfare economics. The problem of value-loaded language is, of course, not restricted to welfare economics; the present author agrees with Machlup ([65], p. 119) that it would be a 'vast exaggeration' to deny the scientific objectivity of economics on this ground.

15 See the excellent discussion by Hutchison ([53], pp. 64 f.), who strongly objects, however, to the use of the term welfare in economics. Graaff's point that neutralisation will have no effect on the layman ([41], p. 2) may be true, but his proposal to let the outsiders' impressions determine the methodological character of welfare economics goes too far.

16 Alexander, a stout defender of normative economics, also calls efficiency descriptive ([5], p. 24).

17 Cf. Mishan's observation that if the individual's welfare is defined as being dependent on his relative income position 'all Pareto improvements are ruled out' ([71], p. 35).

18 See for this important distinction Hutchison ([53], pp. 53 f.).

19 An example is Mishan's exclusion of 'illegitimate' external effects like resentment and envy ([71], p. 34).

20 Boulding's statement that many, if not most, economists 'regard the Paretian optimum as almost self-evident' ([29], p. 126) clearly refers to its normative interpretation.

21 This point is stressed particularly by Myrdal [79] and Albert [3].

22 Pareto's views on the ethical neutrality of science are extensively discussed by Tarascio ([107], ch. III). His statement (p. 48) that for Pareto ethical neutrality was an ideal and that in practice he felt the need for some compromise does not distinguish sufficiently between logical neutrality, which he considered to be absolute in pure science, and personal objectivity which, as he realised, is relative. See, however, for a contrary opinion Samuels ([96], p. 58). It has often been observed that Pareto was inconsistent, for his writings, as Aron ([13], p. 471) puts it, are 'heavy with passion and value judgments'.

23 This opinion is not undisputed; see e.g. Little ([64], p. 48: Pareto's treatment 'does not mark a break with utilitarian tradition at all' and 'has no philosophical significance') and Bohnen ([26], pp. 66, 81).

24 The same view is expounded by Cirillo, who calls modern welfare economics 'at best an illegitimate child whose father, Pareto, would find it hard to recognize' ([32], p. 145). See also the interesting remarks by Kolm ([58], p. 170) who calls the use of the expression 'Pareto-optimality' without further qualification a calumny.

25 This view still lives on. So Ferguson ([115], p. 476) states that the object of any society is to maximise the economic welfare of its members.

26 In another paper ([8], pp. 22—23) he argues with great eloquence that economics cannot determine the ends of policy, including efficiency.

27 The payment of compensation has, of course, often been advocated independently of the question of whether it is formally required by the Pareto criterion. An interesting example is Kaldor's recantation ([56], pp. 5—6).

28 The same opinion is stated by Schumpeter ([100], p. 131, footnote 23). The passage in the *Manuel* (pp. 514—515), referred to by Pole ([90], pp. 156—157), also mentions compensation as a possibility and not as a requirement. But Pareto's treatment is admittedly rather obscure (Allais, ([11], p. 385, note 13).

29 The main points are aptly summarised by Millward ([69], p. 89).

30 See e.g. Hochman and Rodgers ([51], p. 755): 'there seems to be no ethical basis for denying that Pareto optimal changes are just.'

31 See also Sohmen ([106], p. 94), who demands the most ruthless possible realisation of optimal allocation.

32 To address this rebuke to Bohm [25] is particularly unjustified.

References

[1] Albert, H.: Der Trugschlusz in der Lehre vom Gütermaximum, *Zeitschrift für Nationalökonomie* 1953 (Vol. XIV, No. 1).

[2] Albert, H.: Wertfreiheit als methodisches Prinzip, in [18].

[3] Albert, H.: *Ökonomische Ideologie und politische Theorie*, 2nd ed., Göttingen 1972.

[4] Alexander, S. S.: Economic Values and Economists' Values, in [52].

[5] Alexander, S. S.: Comment, in: J. Margolis (ed.), *The Analysis of Public Output*, New York 1970.

[6] Allais, M.: *Economie pure et rendement social*, Paris 1945.

[7] Allais, M.: *Economie et intérêt*, Paris 1947.

[8] Allais, M.: L'économique en tant que science, *Revue d'économie politique*, January—February 1968.

[9] Allais, M.: The Conditions of Efficiency in the Economy, *Economia Internazionale*, August 1968.

[10] Allais, M.: Pareto, Vilfredo. Contributions to Economics, *International Encyclopedia of the Social Sciences*, Vol. XI n.d. (1968).
[11] Allais, M.: Les théories de l'équilibre économique général et l'efficacité maximale, impasses récentes et nouvelles perspectives, *Revue d'économie politique*, May—June 1971.
[12] Archibald, G. C.: Welfare Economics, Ethics, and Essentialism, *Economica*, November 1959.
[13] Aron, R.: *Les étapes de la pensée sociologique*, Paris 1967.
[14] Arrow, K. J.: *Social Choice and Individual Values*, 2nd ed., New-Haven—London 1963.
[15] Arrow, K. J. and T. Scitovsky (eds.): *Readings in Welfare Economics*, London 1969.
[16] Barone, E.: The Ministry of Production in the Collectivist State, in: F. A. von Hayek (ed.), *Collectivist Economic Planning*, London 1935.
[17] Baumol, W. J.: *Welfare Economics and the Theory of the State*, 2nd. ed., London 1965.
[18] Von Beckerath, E. and H. Giersch (eds.): *Probleme der normativen Ökonomik und der wirtschaftspolitischen Beratung*, Berlin 1963.
[19] Bergson, A.: *The Economics of Soviet Planning*, New Haven—London 1964.
[20] Bergson, A.: *Essays in Normative Economics*, Cambridge (Mass.) 1966.
[21] Bergson, A.: Market Socialism Revisited, *The Journal of Political Economy*, October 1967.
[22] Bergson, A.: Optimal Pricing for Public Enterprise, *The Quarterly Journal of Economics*, November 1972.
[23] Bergson, A.: On Monopoly Welfare Losses, *The American Economic Review*, December 1973.
[24] Blaug, M.: *Economic Theory in Retrospect*, Homewood (Ill.) 1962.
[25] Bohm, P.: *Social Efficiency*, London 1973.
[26] Bohnen, A.: *Die utilitaristische Ethik als Grundlage der modernen Wohlfahrtsökonomik*, Göttingen 1964.
[27] Boulding, K. E.: Welfare Economics, in: B. F. Haley (ed.), *A Survey of Contemporary Economics*, Vol. II, Homewood (Ill.) 1952.
[28] Boulding, K. E.: The Economics of Knowledge and the Knowledge of Economics, *The American Economic Review*, May 1966.
[29] Boulding, K. E.: *Economics as a Science*, New York etc. 1970.
[30] Buchanan, J. M.: *The Demand and Supply of Public Goods*, Chicago 1968.
[31] Burkhead, J. and J. Miner: *Public Expenditure*, London 1971.
[32] Cirillo, R.: Pareto and Contemporary Welfare Economics, *Revue européenne des sciences sociales. Cahiers Vilfredo Pareto* 1973 (No. 30).
[33] Corden, W. M.: *Trade Policy and Economic Welfare*, Oxford 1974.
[34] Culyer, A. J.: *The Economics of Social Policy*, London 1973.
[35] Dasgupta, A. K. and D. W. Pearce: *Cost-Benefit Analysis*, London—Basingstoke 1972.
[36] Dehem, R.: *L'utopie de l'économiste ou la rationalité économique collective*, Paris 1969.
[37] Downs, A.: *An Economic Theory of Democracy*, New York 1957.
[38] Dupuit, J.: *De l'utilité et de sa mesure* (ed. M. de Bernardi), Paris 1934.
[39] Falero, Jr. F.: The Welfare Implications of Homosexuality, *Journal of Political Economy*, September—October 1971.
[40] Farrell, M. J.: The Convexity Assumption in the Theory of Competitive Markets, *The Journal of Political Economy*, August 1959.
[41] De Graaff, J. V.: *Theoretical Welfare Economics*, Cambridge 1957.
[42] Hartog, F.: *Toegepaste welvaartseconomie*, 2nd ed., Leiden 1973.
[43] Hennipman, P.: Paretiaans optimum en Wickselliaanse eenstemmigheid, in: Haan, R. L. *et al* (eds.), *Model en mogelijkheid*, Groningen 1974.

[44] Hicks, J. R.: The Foundations of Welfare Economics, *The Economic Journal*, December 1938.

[45] Hicks, J. R.: The Rehabilitation of Consumers' Surplus, in [15], reprinted from *The Review of Economic Studies*, 1941.

[46] Hicks, J. R.: Preface—and a Manifesto, *Essays in World Economics*, Oxford 1959, reprinted in [15].

[47] Hicks, J. R.: *Capital and Growth*, Oxford 1965.

[48] Hicks, J. R.: Preference and Welfare, in A. Mitra (ed.), *Essays in Honour of A. K. Das Gupta*, Calcutta etc. 1974.

[49] Hicks, J. R.: The Scope and Status of Welfare Economics, *Oxford Economic Papers*, November 1975.

[50] Hochman, H. M.: Rule Change and Transitional Equity, in Hochman, H. M. and G. E. Peterson (eds.), *Redistribution through Public Choice*, New York—London 1974.

[51] Hochman, H. M. and J. D. Rodgers: Redistribution and the Pareto Criterion, *The American Economic Review*, September 1974.

[52] Hook, S. (ed.): *Human Values and Economic Policy*, New York 1967.

[53] Hutchison, T. W.: *'Positive' Economics and Policy Objectives*, London 1964.

[54] Kafoglis, M. Z.: *Welfare Economics and Subsidy Programs*, Gainesville (Fa) 1961.

[55] Kahn, R. F.: Some Notes on Ideal Output, *The Economic Journal*, March 1935.

[56] Kaldor, N.: *Essays on Value and Distribution*, London 1960.

[57] Klappholz, K.: Value Judgments and Economics, *The British Journal for the Philosophy of Science*, August 1964.

[58] Kolm, S. Ch.: The Optimal Production of Social Justice, in: J. Margolis and H. Guitton (eds.), *Public Economics*, London etc. 1969.

[59] Koopmans, T. C.: *Three Essays on the State of Economic Science*, New York etc. 1957.

[60] Leibenstein, H.: Notes on Welfare Economics and the Theory of Democracy, *The Economic Journal*, June 1962.

[61] Lerner, A. P.: *The Economics of Control*, New York 1946.

[62] Lerner, A. P.: The Economics and Politics of Consumer Sovereignty, *The American Economic Review*, May 1972.

[63] Little, I. M. D.: *A Critique of Welfare Economics*, 2nd ed., London 1957.

[64] Little, I. M. D.: Recent Developments in Welfare Economics, *Zeitschrift für Ökonometrie*, June 1950.

[65] Machlup, F.: Positive and Normative Economics, in: R. L. Heilbronner (ed.), *Economic Means and Social Ends*, Englewood Cliffs (N. J.) 1969.

[66] Martin, A.: Empirical and A Priori in Economics, *The British Journal for the Philosophy of Science*, August 1964.

[67] Meade, J. E.: *Trade and Welfare*, London 1955.

[68] Meek, R. L.: Value-Judgments in Economics, *The British Journal for the Philosophy of Science*, August 1964.

[69] Millward, R.: *Public Expenditure Economics*, London 1971.

[70] Mishan, E. J.: *Welfare Economics, Five Introductory Essays*, New York 1964.

[71] Mishan, E. J.: *Welfare Economics. An Assessment*, Amsterdam 1969.

[72] Mishan, E. J.: The Futility of Pareto-Efficient Distribution, *The American Economic Review* December 1972.

[73] Mishan, E. J.: Welfare Criteria: Resolution of a Paradox, *The Economic Journal*, September 1973.

[74] Mishan, E. J.: Flexibility and Consistency in Project Evaluation, *Economica*, February 1974.

[75] Mishan, E. J.: *Cost-Benefit Analysis*, 2nd ed., London 1975.
[76] Morgenstern, O.: Pareto Optimum and Economic Organization, in: Kloten, N. *et al.* (eds.), *Systeme und Methoden in den Wirtschafts- und Sozialwissenschaften*, Tübingen 1964.
[77] Musgrave, R. A.: *The Theory of Public Finance*, New York 1959.
[78] Myint, H.: *Theories of Welfare Economics*, London 1948.
[79] Myrdal, G.: *The Political Element in the Development of Economic Theory*, London 1953.
[80] Nash, C., D. Pearce and J. Stanley: An Evaluation of Cost-Benefit Analysis Criteria, Scottish Journal of Political Economy, June 9175.
[81] Nath, S. R.: *A Reappraisal of Welfare Economics*, London 1969.
[82] Nath, S. K.: *A Perspective of Welfare Economics*, London—Basingstoke 1973.
[83] Ng, Y.-K.: Value Judgments and Economists' Role in Policy Recommendations, *The Economic Journal*, September 1972.
[84] Oort, C. J.: *Decreasing Cost as a Problem of Welfare Economics*, Amsterdam 1958.
[85] Pareto, V.: *Manuel d'économie politique*, 2nd ed., Paris 1927.
[86] Pareto, V.: *Traité de sociologie générale*. Oeuvres complètes vol. XII, Geneva 1968.
[87] Peacock, A. T. and Ch. K. Rowley: Pareto Optimality and the Political Economy of Liberalism, *Journal of Political Economy*, May—June 1973.
[88] Pigou, A. C.: *The Economics of Welfare*, 4th ed., London 1932.
[89] Pigou, A. C.: Some Aspects of Welfare Economics, *The American Economic Review*, June 1951.
[90] Pole, D.: Pareto and the Compensation Principle—A Note, *The Economic Journal*, March 1955.
[91] Radomysler, A.: Welfare Economics and Economic Policy, in [15], reprinted from *Economica* 1946.
[92] Robbins, L.: *An Essay on the Nature and Significance of Economic Science*, 2nd ed., London 1935.
[93] Robertson, D. H.: *Utility and All That and Other Essays*, London 1952.
[94] Rothenberg, J.: *The Measurement of Social Welfare*, Englewood Cliffs (N. J.) 1961.
[95] Rowley, Ch. K. and A. T. Peacock, *Welfare Economics. A Liberal Restatement*, London 1975.
[96] Samuels, W. J.: *Pareto on Policy*, Amsterdam etc. 1974.
[97] Samuelson, P. A.: *Foundations of Economic Analysis*, Cambridge (Mass.) 1947.
[98] Samuelson, P. A.: *The Collected Scientific Papers* (ed. J. E. Stiglitz), vols I and II), Cambridge (Mass.)—London 1966.
[99] Say J. B.: *Cours complet d'économie politique pratique*, 2nd ed (ed. H. Say), Paris 1840.
[100] Schumpeter, J.: *Ten Great Economists*, London 1952.
[101] Schumpeter, J.: *History of Economic Analysis*, New York 1954.
[102] Scitovsky, T.: *Welfare and Competition*, 2nd ed., London 1971.
[103] Sen, A. K.: *Collective Choice and Social Welfare*, San Francisco etc. 1970.
[104] Sen, A. K.: The Impossibility of a Paretian Liberal, *Journal of Political Economy*, January—February 1970.
[105] Sen, A. K.: The Impossibility of a Paretian Liberal: Reply, *Journal of Political Economy*, November—December 1971.
[106] Sohmen, E.: Bericht, in [18].
[107] Tarascio, V. J.: *Pareto's Methodological Approach to Economics*, Chapel Hill (N.C.) 1968.
[108] Tarascio, V. J.: Paretian Welfare Theory: Some Neglected Aspects, *Journal of Political Economy*, January—February 1969.

[109] Tarascio, V. J.: Pareto: A View of the Present through the Past, *Journal of Political Economy*, February 1976.
[110] Tinbergen, J.: *Selected Papers* (ed. L. H. Klaassen *et al*), Amsterdam 1959.
[111] Van Den Haag, E.: Normative and Analytical Welfare Economics: Arrow's Pareto Principle, in [52].
[112] Weber, W.: Über die wirtschaftsbegrifflichen Grundlagen der älteren 'Welfare Economics', *Zeitschrift für Nationalökonomie* 1952 (Vol. XII. No. 4).
[113] Winch, D. M.: *Analytical Welfare Economics*, Harmondsworth 1971.
[114] Wolfelsperger, A.: *Les biens collectifs*, Paris 1969.
[115] (Addendum) Ferguson, C. E.: *Microeconomic Theory*, 3rd ed., Homewood (Ill.), 1972.

Unionism, Inflation, and Consensus

Lloyd Ulman

The search for consensus, in which Pieter de Wolff has participated with great devotion in the course of his distinguished career, is at once a search for socially acceptable levels of employment and price change and a search for industrial peace and social stability. Achievement of the second objective can be regarded as a necessary condition for achievement of the first; otherwise high levels of employment are likely to be associated with both greater strike activity and inflationary wage settlements. On the other hand, achievement of the social objective may not obviously require fulfillment of the economic one; industrial peace and stability have prevailed in the absence of full employment and/or price stability. Thus the social objective is likely to take precedence over the economic target.

French experience might be regarded as a case in point. The failure of attempts to secure an effective incomes policy in the first half of the sixties was attributed to the weakness of the central organizations of both employers and unions, which in turn was attributed by some to the Government's attempts to restrain wage settlements. It was followed by active official efforts to encourage private negotiations over employment policy and other substantive areas by providing financial and legislative support. However, some of these efforts were held to be sufficiently dirigiste to have contributed to the wave of strikes and sit-ins in 1968. Thereafter, the Government, while hardly relinguishing its initiatives, increased bargaining autonomy in the public and nationalized sectors, encouraged national bargaining generally, and legislated recognition of trade union branches at factory level (see [4], [8], [30] and [39]). Similarly, the German Concerted Action program, begun in 1967, was crippled by the wildcats which occurred in that country in 1969, as a result of which one writer subsequently noted that, 'Just at a time when price increases are reaching heights hitherto unknown in the Federal Republic of Germany, a curtain of silence has been drawn about an institution whose role in global steering was once regarded as both a necessary and an optimal component of an effective policy of stabilization' ([21], p. 49).

The subordinate role to which incomes policy has been consigned during the 'slumpflations' of the 1970's thus reflected in Europe the chilling influence of the industrial unrest which followed the events of May 1968. It also reflected both in Europe and in the U.S. an unexpected degree of public tolerance of high levels of unemployment, but this may be because the unemployment – like the inflation which accompanied it – came unexpectedly and in conjunction with an international crisis, and was perceived as a transient phenomenon. If so, the inflation-unemployment tradeoff problem will come to the fore again; the search for consensus in this area is likely to be resumed with increased urgency; and social policies will increasingly be judged on the basis of their compatibility with the achievement of both industrial peace and wage restraint as well as on other grounds. This paper discusses: first, the prior question concerning both the need for restraint imposed by modern wage-setting institutions and their potential for restraint; second, the institutional requirements of consensus policy; next, the extent to which restraint in collective bargaining can be secured in exchange for tax cuts and for wage indexation; and finally, the import of egalitarian wage policies and of worker participation in management for consensus and restraint.

The Potential for Inflation and Restraint?

Analytically, the search for consensus might start with the consideration of certain characteristics of collective bargaining. Some of these characteristics it shares with pricing under conditions of bilateral monopoly, while others are relatively unique. On the side of management bargaining behavior can be approximated by a conventional investment model. The firm might be assumed to maximize the present value of the difference between a target wage change – i.e., the profit-maximizing wage change which it would put into effect if it did not have to incur a cost of opposition from the other party – and the (greater positive) wage change on which it believes that the union would insist 'to the point of impasse'. The present value of this difference between management target and union demand measures the potential gain to management from incurring a strike. This gain in turn determines the maximum costs of resistance which management would be willing to incur and, therefore, the maximum duration of strike which it would be willing to 'buy'.

Given, therefore, a. that the wage changes demanded are, *cet. par.*, inversely related to the gains from taking a strike, b. that the costs are set equal to the gains, and c. that strike costs and duration are directly related, a Hicks-like employer resistance function, relating strike duration directly to wage change (instead of level), is thus derived. However, it might well prove both profitable and feasible for management to 'buy the union out' of a strike of maximum duration by offering a settlement above the preferred management target.

The labor side presents obvious parallels. There too the gains from striking are greater the larger the difference between (labor's) target and (management's) offer and the costs of a strike to union and members vary directly with its duration. Since wage changes are directly (rather than inversely, as in the case of management) related to union gains from striking, a Hicks-like union demand function, relating strike duration inversely (rather than directly) to wage change, could be derived. Moreover, unions as well as managements have been willing to settle for less than their heart's desire in order to avoid a fight to the finish.

It has also been claimed – or assumed – that parallelism extends to the first stage of pre-negotiation behavior: i.e., that the union's wage-change target results from an exercise in the maximization of some magnitude like the wage bill, in a manner analogous to the selection of a profit maximizing wage target by the employer (see [10], chs. III and V). At this point, however, the case for parallelism with the maximizing model of the firm becomes tenuous. Unionists have indeed been known to moderate their demands when they perceive themselves to be threatened with job loss. Such motivation – which has been attributed to the unions in the Federal Republic of Germany throughout much of the postwar period and to the unions in the manufacturing sector of the United States in the first half of the 1970's – is consistent with unwillingness to exceed a wage increase associated with the maximum attainable increase in net labor income (per capita), or at least to exceed such an increase without limit. On the other hand, there have been many instances of powerful unions demanding and securing wage increases in seeming disregard of adverse impacts on employment; the American coal miners in the 1950's and the American building trades in the late 1960's and early 1970's are cases in point. (Indeed, both groups helped to generate sizable non-union sectors within their respective jurisdictions as a result of large negotiated increases in pay.)

In fact, unions may frequently select as targets wage increases which turn out to be either too small or too big to maximize the discounted value of the net income of their members. A union may seek nothing more or nothing less than to maintain the relative income of its members, whether by aiming at the 'going rate of increase' in wages or by seeking compensation for recent or possible future increases in the consumer price index plus perhaps some 'improvement factor' based on productivity or profitability in the firm, the sector, or the general economy. In any case, the target might either exceed or fall short of the income-maximizing increase. A shortfall might be regarded as underexploitation of a union's current monopoly position.

Moreover, a union's willingness to pursue whatever target it chooses depends critically on the preference and cost functions associated with leaders as well as members and hence with the level at which the bargaining decisions will effectively be made. Thus, to cite one possibility, decision-making by radically motivated shop stewards or delegates could reflect the fact that for them the gains from striking include something in addition to the present value of the monetary difference between target and offer. The excess of strike costs which a union would be willing to incur over the purely monetary gains involved might be regarded as an economic measure of politically motivated 'militancy'.

On the other hand, to the extent that unions are subject to the authority of officers at company-wide, industry-wide, or even more centralized levels and to the extent that these officers exercise stewardship over substantial institutional assets, their strike policies are likely to be more cautious. In the first place, while strike costs to the members are reckoned net of any offsets to wage loss – including strike benefits paid by the union – there are no analogous offsets to loss of dues income by the union. In the second place, if an employer offers a union some premium over his own target in order to 'buy off' a strike, a union leader might not gain much politically from calling a strike if it could yield only a small further incremental gain. And if the incremental gain should not prove comparable to the costs involved on the union side, the political penalties to the leader of losing a strike could be severe indeed. (Following a so-called 'no win' teachers' strike in New York City which he had opposed, the union's militant but businesslike president, Albert Shanker, observed that, 'Since a strike represents a possibility of life and death for a union, you do not call a strike unless not calling it is also life and death' [24]). For such reasons, a conventional union leader is likely to calculate the gains from striking on a more narrowly pecuniary basis than a radical leader at the plant level and to set those gains against a greater volume of costs (membership and institutional) than the membership would probably do. Moreover, he might urge that targets be set according to a rather conservative strategy. Under one such strategy, wage comparability would take precedence over ability-to-pay, when the former would indicate a smaller target increase than the latter, while comparability might be sacrificed to ability-to-pay, when the latter would indicate a markedly smaller target change.

This suggests that conventionally led unions (whatever the political complexion of the leadership) are likely to exploit their current market positions most fully during periods of economic slack. And it further suggests that subsequent upswings in demand, while increasing the potential bargaining power of unions, would be associated for a while with some reduction in the degree of exploitation of that bargaining potential. This would occur as long as unions would be content to settle for increases that would continue 'patterns' which had prevailed in the preceding phase of recession.* In some cases, and especially in the U.S., pattern preservation is institutionalized by the operation of multi-year agreements.

This may be compared with Gardner Ackley's theory of oligopoly pricing which holds that, as the ability of large firms to realize their 'ideal monopoly price' increases in cyclical upswings, it is capitalized on ([1], p. 71). Cost increases incurred and absorbed during the preceding slump could stimulate prompt price action during the upswing. In contrast, if union wage patterns had not been seriously distorted during the recession, unions might be content to maintain them during the upswing. Thus special factors could make for a lag of money wages behind prices. However, lags in negotiated wage incomes – whether behind increases in administered prices, export prices (as stressed in the 'Aukrust Model'), import prices, or wages in 'bottleneck sectors' – tend to break off existing patterns of negotiated increases and set new ones which reflect a greater degree of utilization of (an already cyclically increased) bargaining power.

Such price-wage or wage-wage sequences are consistent with a phenomenon which Keynes dubbed 'semi-inflation', and which he described as a series of discontinuous increases in money wages which follow prior increases in aggregate money demand and which are 'determined by the psychology of the workers and by the policies of employers and trade unions' ([22], p. 301). However, the effects of changes in worker psychology and union policies need not be limited to semi-inflation; and these changes can be caused by things other than prior price and wage increases. Increased expectations, whatever their origin, could generate dissatisfaction by the members of a group with their share of income, whether generated within the industrial sector involved or in a wider segment of the economy; and these expectations could lead to efforts to improve, rather than merely maintain, their collec-

* Thus, as far as at least some unionized labor markets are concerned, one need not postulate information lags on the part of individual workers who, as long as they allegedly mistake general for relative wage increases, help to lag money wages behind productivity and prices and thus to ensure that an increase in money (supply and) demand is converted into an increase in output and employment. In the unionized example the same lags might be generated by the purposeful maintenance of relative wages. ([32], pp. 6—7, 38—39, 40—44; [33], pp. 147—160).

tive position. Passage of decision-making authority from businesslike leadership to 'direct actionists' and/or from centralized levels to more numerous points closer to the grass roots could reinforce (as well as reflect) changed attitudes and expectations held by the membership. The setting of more ambitious targets and a stronger disposition to strike for unsatisfied demands in a larger number of separate and uncoordinated bargains could help to generate inflation on a scale sufficient to absorb entirely (in the extreme case) a given increment of demand, even when the economy is still operating at relatively low levels of capacity utilization. (Such a tendency in the direction of 'inflationary depression' can be imparted when inflation increases the propensity to save while depressing the marginal efficiency of investment.) ([12], p. 73–74). In that case, adoption of more strongly stimulative fiscal or monetary policies would be required to yield higher levels of employment and capacity utilization; but the latter, if achieved, could exacerbate the structural problem by providing firmer market support for decentralized bargaining. On the other hand, adoption – or maintenance – of policies insufficiently stimulative to maintain high levels of capacity utilization could contribute to observed movements away from profits in the functional distribution of income and in the direction of wages (see [26], p. 19, [38], pp. 230–232, [25], [31]). The latter in turn could further raise worker expectations and targets while lowering employer counter-offers.

Nor need an alternation of expansion and contraction ('Stop-Go-Stop') unfold into the indefinite future; instead, the expansions can grow weaker and the contractions more pronounced. Normally, cyclical declines in profits are translated into increased employer resistance to union demands; so that even if the latter should be stimulated by continuing or accelerated price increases – which occurred as a result of sharply adverse movement in terms of trade in the past few years – they could not be entirely gratified (see [37], p. 4, [31], pp. 408–9). However, downward trends in profit shares can – although they perhaps need not [25] – contribute to cash flow problems and liquidity shortages during downswings. And illiquidity during a contraction can severely curtail the ability of a firm to take a strike despite cyclical declines in its other strike costs (e.g., lower net loss in current revenue, smaller expected reduction in market share, smaller extra costs associated with 'making up' lost output at either end of a strike); in the extreme case this could endow some unions in the economy with cyclically perverse bargaining strength. Under such circumstances (which appear to have prevailed in the United Kingdom in the first half of the 1970's and in New York City in 1975), if unions press their advantage – in response, perhaps, to rising prices – restrictive or even moderately expansionary monetary-fiscal policy can be associated with serious

financial liquidations. Financial crisis could be averted by ad hoc rescue operations, but, if carried out on a large scale, this could nullify the attempt to restrain inflation by fiscal-monetary policy. Finally, if rescue also entailed transfer of equity to the rescuing authority or even to the squeezed firm's employees, the objectives of the direct actionists would be secured by a pincer operation involving both the political and bargaining wings of the labor movement. This might be regarded as the completion of an economic model of radical-militant unionism. (It has sometimes been referred to in Britain as 'Socialism by squeeze and seize.')
Key ingredients in this concoction have been in evidence in the recent past, including rank-and-file strikes and even plant seizures followed by sympathetic official response (e.g., Lipp in France and Norton-Villiers-Triumph in the U.K.). Moreover, by opposing deflationary policies trade union movements and their political associates have in effect challenged the autonomy of monetary authorities. Demand management can therefore best be viewed as the resultant of opposing private and official forces. (Thus European inflation in the early 1970's was attributed to 'weak political leadership' by some observers who failed to ask themselves why the leadership was weak – and in particular whether political weakness might not have derived from painfully fresh memories of the explosions of grass-roots militancy which began with the events of May 1968 in France.)

Yet the militancy model in extended form has not been approximated in reality. Nor is it inevitable that it should be. Political contest for control over monetary-fiscal policy need not result in official ratification of local militant activity. If the likelihood is that it will not, it is more likely that union groups will be swayed by fear of imminent job loss and will exercise some self-restraint rather than increased pressure on illiquid employers. If firms in oligopolistic sectors could be induced to raise margins over costs less promptly during upswings, unions would have less incentive to exploit their own improved market positions more fully and thus to break prior bargaining patterns. Finally, if unionists can be restrained from the full exploitation of their monopoly positions by fear of job loss or by relative stability in prices and profit margins, might they not also – or alternatively – be restrained by well designed public policy? The assumption of continuous maximum deployment of bargaining potential, which has induced monetarists to deny the possibility of 'wage-push' inflation (except when union membership is rising in relation to the labor force) has also contributed to their skepticism regarding the possible effectiveness of incomes policies. But if the assumption of continuous maximization does not hold, might not the consequent inflationary potential of unionism for unrest and inflation have as its dual a potential for restraint?

Incomes policy is obviously rooted in the premise that collective bargaining carries the potential for both excess and restraint, and this policy has been marked with success as well as failure. Yet the fact that success has so often given way to failure should make it clear that collective bargaining institutions cannot serve in the capacity of a simple two-way conduit, with one end labeled Militancy and the other, Restraint. This modest proposition (which, however, has been less obvious to makers of economic policy than it might have been) was dramatically demonstrated by recent Australian experience. Because of its economy-wide scope, Australia's system of compulsory arbitration, which originated as a device for raising or maintaining minimum wages for unskilled workers in accordance with criteria based on family need, was later called upon first to reduce (in the depression of the '30's) and subsequently to restrain money wage levels in accordance with the economy's 'capacity to pay'. In deference to that principle, the Commonwealth tribunal eliminated its system of quarterly cost-of-living adjustments to the basic minimum wage in 1953 and later abandoned the basic wage adjustments themselves, after it had become obvious that the latter had inspired comparable increases in all higher classifications. Nevertheless, the tribunal 'tended to place less emphasis on price stability and more on the need to maintain equitable wage relationships and industrial peace even if this aggravates inflation' ([20], p. 132). Even so, when (1967) the tribunal did attempt to reduce wage drift by directing that certain increases awarded in the metal industry be 'absorbed' in other jurisdictions, the unions struck, refused to pay the fines levied against their unlawful strikes, ultimately obliged the Government to amend the law, and also obliged the tribunal to adopt new procedures which, in effect, countenanced strikes against existing awards. This unraveling began in the late 1960's and its effect was to add to upward pressures on wages [5]. J. E. Isaac's absorbing analysis of the Australian experience led him into an interesting exchange with himself. He stated the problem by observing that:

> ... unlike many other countries which have tried or are contemplating incomes policy, Australia does not have to start from scratch. Despite many deficiencies, its wage-fixing machinery has the backing of experience and tradition and could, with a few minor changes in procedure and personnel, provide the basic institutional framework for incomes policy. It is after all a *de facto* central wage-fixing authority before which the central representatives of the unions, both manual and white collar, and employers appear in national hearings ... ([5], pp. 134—140).

But he is obliged to conclude that:

A system of compulsory arbitration, conceived and developed under conditions of chronic under-employment and weak unionism to settle industrial disputes by awarding minimum pay and other standards, but having evolved into a means of managing national wages policy, fits uncomfortably in an environment of full employment and strong unionism ([5], p. 142).

The collapse of the Australian policy was associated with the emergence of new and more aggressive leadership in the central federation (the Australian Council of Trade Unions), which in turn reflected shop floor militancy and hostility to union officials who had helped the policy to operate rather effectively prior to its derailing. Thus incomes policy could undermine itself by weakening the private institutional structures on which its effectiveness depends. The imposition through externally generated public policy of restraint in the exercise of union bargaining power could ultimately help to induce a higher degree of exploitation of market power than the collective bargaining system had permitted when its own institutional checks and balances had been effective.

This perverse effect seems also to have been demonstrated in some countries of Europe, including Britain and The Netherlands, the two countries where, in the early postwar period, incomes policy enjoyed what subsequent experience revealed to be its finest hours. Between the winter of 1948 and the winter of 1950, a British Labour Government successfully ran a policy calling for tight wage restraint on a voluntary basis. The policy's effectiveness was taken as a tribute not only to the leadership and high personal standing of its proponent, Sir Stafford Cripps (who was then the Chancellor of the Exchequer) but also to cooperation by such powerful union leaders of the day as Deakin of the Transport Workers, Lawther of the Mineworkers, and Williamson of the General and Municipal Workers. But the policy was finally blown up in a wage explosion; and in 1956, the TUC rejected a Conservative Government's appeal for wage restraint. Subsequent revivals were credited with varying degrees of effectiveness in restraining money wages, but they were also credited with contributing to a strong upsurge of militancy at the grass roots, often under the leadership of radical shop stewards and national union officers. This militancy helped to generate a strong drift of wages above centrally negotiated rates and a drift of power and authority away from the national unions. History was summarily revised; the union 'statesmen' of the Attlee-Cripps era were now derided as 'Knights of the Round Table' (and worse), and the 'moderation' which had earned them international respect was reinterpreted as a sellout. Prominent among the militants were Communist Party activists whose 'Committee for the Defence of Trade Unions', formed in 1965, owed its considerable success to 'a fight against Government wage control and a call for a return to free collective bargaining' ([13], p. 19). In 1974, a generation after Cripps, a coal strike resulted from an open challenge to a statutory incomes policy which had been carefully designed, after consultation with a 'moderate' President of the union, to buy peaceful acceptance in the mines. The union was offered an increase of 13.5 per cent (plus an additional 3.5 per cent in a productivity bargain) under a policy which was supposed to yield no more than 11.5 per cent. Under Communist and other left-wing prodding, the union demanded 25 per cent; and, after an overtime ban, a 'half-time' shutdown of industry by government order, a 16-week strike, and a General Election – lost by a Conservative Government which had demanded an answer to the question 'Who governs Britain?' – it settled for a 29 per cent raise.

The Dutch experience offered some interesting parallels to the British. In 1951 – 53, the Dutch unions acquiesced in a 'wage stop' which was associated with a reduction of 5 per cent in real wages; and while this occurred under a system of legal wage regulation (the Extraordinary Decree of 1945), the decisive element in its effectiveness was the willingness of the unions to cooperate with Jan Tinbergen (who like Cripps was a revered Socialist) and his program, which assigned priority to investment over consumption in order to rebuild the economy. In the mid-1950's, however, the Dutch unions, unlike the British, continued to heed official pleas for restraint (possibly because the Socialists were still in office). But soon protests from the rank and file, individual unions, and the confessional federations began to mount, and they contributed to the greater decentralization of bargaining which marked the next phase of Dutch incomes policy (see [41], pp. 351 – 354). Meanwhile, the government's wage norms had been set too low, and the country's wage and price levels became depressed relative to those of her competitors. As De Wolff put it, the policy was 'too ambitious and too cautious ([42], p' 68)' The potential for restraint in the Dutch bargaining system was exploited not wisely but too well. The union movement was poorly rewarded when what De Wolff termed 'an adaptation process' in the form of a sharp wage explosion was initiated in 1963 on the employer side and, further, when it was associated with and substantially absorbed by a sharp jump in productivity and real earnings instead of unemployment. This raised some embarrassing questions, as Albeda recalled: 'Had the unions been too cautious throughout the post-war years? Was the relatively low standard of living in the Netherlands a result perhaps of the meekness of the trade unions?' ([2], p. 256). De Wolff pointed out that hasty revision of the policy, which in effect ratified the wage increases, enabled the union federations to regain control over their rank and file, who had uncharacteristically indulged themselves in a wave of grass roots strikes. But the institutions thus repaired were no longer capable of exercising the old restraint; and when, in the inflationary environment prevailing in 1969, a Liberal Government secured the passage of a new law which would have given it emergency powers to intervene in individual bargaining situations, the Socialist and Catholic federations objected vigorously. As a result, an increase won in a wildcat strike in the Rotterdam shipyard area was (as in 1964) generalized throughout the economy, while the new statutory authority remained a dead letter on the books' Even so, the authority of the federations apparently suffered erosion since the Rotterdam pay increase was largely propagated through bargaining by the works councils at plant level. Moreover, restraint by the central federations is held to have contributed to their slow growth in membership since World War II, and to the more rapid growth of the unaffiliated unions and the emergence of radical-led 'action committees' ([41], pp. 171–174, pp. 185–189). These developments, in turn have led some of the affiliated unions (notably the NVV metalworkers) to press for greater union presence on the shop floor and—despite (or because of) legal provision for extension of the terms of agreements to non-signatory firms—to attempts to secure extra benefits or privileges for union members ([2], pp. 262–263).

Institutional Protection; the Consensus of Collective Bargaining

Since wage controls could weaken the more centralized union institutions on which their implementation depends, they might be accompanied by policies designed to protect and strengthen those institutions. This was the approach taken by U.S. policy during the second World War. In exchange for a no-strike pledge and acceptance of stringent wage controls, the unions successfully insisted that President Roosevelt reverse his former position and that the War Labor Board be authorized to award unions (in disputes brought before it) 'maintenance of membership' (whereby employees who were union members had to remain in good standing for the duration of the agreement, subject to the right to withdraw during a fifteen-day 'escape period'). Traditions of intense and uninhibited employer opposition and of union rivalry had combined with a lack of ideological incentives to membership to leave American unions anxious to secure their institutional integrity. Passage of the Wagner Act had gone a long way in affording protection by conferring the status of 'exclusive bargaining representation' upon unions which won 'certification elections' and by obliging employers to bargain with them 'in good faith'. But wartime controls left compliant national unions exposed not only to incursions from rival organizations but also to potential erosion of their internal authority as the result of wildcat strikes called by restive locals and of the indifference of existing and potential members. Hence the extension of 'union security' provisions was an ingrained response to a challenge which in its essentials was not unfamiliar (see [35], pp. 61, 91 – 108, 113 – 114).

Moreover, it was accompanied by extension of the dues check-off by the employer and also of procedures for settling the employee grievances and disputes over the interpretation and application of existing contracts. Although these procedures frequently include arbitration as the final step, they are private arrangements, and their intermediate (and sometimes ultimate) stages frequently include the national union when the latter is designated as exclusive bargaining representative and/or is a signatory to the collective agreement. The procedures thus extended and underwrote the authority of the national unions at plant level, especially in large-scale manufacturing sectors. Their authority and their contractual obligations, which typically include commitments not to strike for the duration of the contract, provide the leadership of the national unions with an incentive to prevent or suppress local wildcat strikes which parallels the interest of management in industrial peace (during the contract period) and labor efficiency. Not infrequently one of the two bargaining parties will come to the aid of the other in opposition to local groups of wildcat strikers.

Mutual aid and bilateral protection of the institutional frameworks within which bargaining and the administration of agreements take place is by no means restricted to the United States and its distinctive system of bargaining. Thus in Sweden where union and management authority and bargaining are highly centralized, the Confederation of Trade Unions (LO) has supported successful attempts to induce reluctant multinational subsidiaries to join the Swedish Employers Confederation (SAF) and the central frame agreement; and the employer side has refused to negotiate separately with a breakaway union of dockworkers. Under both (otherwise quite dissimilar) systems, therefore, each side has helped the other to round up its strays in the interest of defending a 'mature bargaining relationship'. This might be regarded as the tacit consensus of collective bargaining, and it is an important component of any wider social consensus. It does not imply collusion nor does it preclude hard bargaining; but it does strengthen the authority of the more centralized, institutionalized, and, therefore, inherently more restrained union bodies.

Yet the effectiveness of buying increased bargaining restraint with increased institutional protection is limited. In the first place, absent the extraordinarily powerful stimulus to consensus provided by war or other external menace, restraint can reach the point where union membership is no longer worthwhile to the individual, as the stoic Dutch union leaders came to realize. I have referred above to instances in which various Dutch unions have sought to remedy this condition by negotiating somewhat greater benefits for (or certain benefits confined to) union members (including payments directly to unions in some cases). Such 'members-only bargaining' is virtually ruled out in the United States where employers are free to extend any benefits which unions may negotiate for their members to other employees in the bargaining unit and where the union's right to exclusive representation is balanced by a broad duty of 'fair representation' to all employees. It is true that in the U.S. there is no provision for the legal extension of bargaining agreements to non-signatory firms in an industry, as there is in the Netherlands, where it may constitute an additional disincentive to union membership and hence an additional reason to engage in members-only bargaining. Yet in the Federal Republic of Germany, where provision is also made for extension and where, as in the Netherlands, unions showed interest in members-only bargaining, the latter was ruled unconstitutional ([34], p. 477). And in Italy, a combination of members-only bargaining and the dues check-off (in metalworking), failed to establish the unions firmly at plant level and to prevent the outbreak of *delegati*-led wildcat strikes in 1969. As a result, the unions felt obliged to abandon members-only bargaining and to practice a *de facto* form of 'equal representation' in order to gain more support at the grass roots ([19], p. 314 and p. 309). In general, it would appear that in democracies there are practical limits to the extent to which private organizations will either be permitted or will find it rewarding to use their economic power to induce or require employees to join them.

Moreover, even where the national union's job territory is reasonably well secured, excessively 'statesmanlike' leaders might find their personal tenure made insecure by militant political challengers. In the U.S., the public policy which has facilitated the achievement of institutional security through provision for exclusive representation, has been balanced by a legislated 'Bill of Rights of Members of Labor Organizations', which has indeed resulted in considerable increase in electoral challenges and turnovers and, probably, in rejections by membership referendum of agreements negotiated by top leadership. Therefore, just as the purchase price of union restraint was a guarantee against employer discrimination against union members in the first World War and the introduction of membership maintenance in the second World War, so the next official move for restraint might encounter demands for relaxation of some of the more unsettling provisions of the Landrum-Griffin Act.

At this point, if not before, it would pay to consider some other paths to consensus and restraint, which may be viewed as offering compensation to the individual wage earner for gains foregone at the bargaining table. They might serve either as complements to the collective bargaining process or as competitors. To succeed in the first role, they would have to reduce grass roots militancy sufficiently to place bargaining authority more authoritatively under the control of the centralized bodies (national unions or federations), but without killing off interest in collective bargaining as a wage-determining institution. Necessity has mothered many such inventions, but we shall mention only a few: indexation, tax cuts, wage equalization, and worker participation in management.

Indexation

Monetarists, led as usual by Milton Friedman, have been among the most recent champions of the indexation of contracts, including collective wage agreements, but these ranks have also included people who believe in the existence of 'sellers' inflation'—and even in the need for incomes policy. General indexation could damp down bargaining militancy among groups of workers who react defensively out of fear of losing their relative and real income positions, either by seeking to discount expected price inflation (by extrapolating past and current rates) during the negotiation of new agreements or by breaking existing agreements. Thus in Australia, where a system of automatic cost-of-living adjustments had been abandoned in 1953, its revival was urged by the Commonwealth tribunal as a way to reduce drift and enable the tribunal to re-centralize wage determination and once again bring it under control [6]. Indexation also gained some support in West Germany among observers who attributed the wave of wildcat strikes in the autumn of 1969 to an outbreak of unanticipated inflation (see [17], p. 10; [40], pp. 57–59). These strikes threatened the authority of the highly restrained leadership of the national unions—who were reproached for their lack of militancy and for their cooperative participation in the multilateral 'Concerted Action' group which had been established just two years earlier by a Social Democratic Minister for Economic Affairs. Moreover, many employers settled with their local works councils, which are not supposed to deal with wage issues and are legally forbidden to strike ([34], pp. 475, 486–487). The unions abandoned moderation in 1970; then, in the manner of their Dutch colleagues, returned to the defense (of the price level and their party) in 1972, only to be rewarded for their valor with another burst of wildcat strikes the following year. It is not surprising that one of the architects of German concertation, Herbert Giersch, should have supported indexation.

While denying the charge that general indexation would make an economy more inflation-prone by eliminating or reducing contractual lags, its proponents do not advance it as a cure-all (see [15], pp. 34–35). In fact, adverse movements in the terms of trade (which have been experienced so dramatically in this decade by the industrialized countries) reveal a major limitation of a device which is designed to maintain real incomes (including real wage rates) at a time when they must fall. A wage escalator under such conditions operates to squeeze profits and reduce output and employment—if monetary policy holds firm. It has been argued that the adverse real effects would be only temporary, since the profit squeeze would induce employers to bargain more toughly during the next round of negotiations ([17], pp. 10—11). But, thanks to indexation which makes it possible to extend the duration of contracts, the next round might take some time to arrive. In the absence of indexation clauses, real wages would be reduced more promptly. Moreover, indexation may even result in the substitution of increased 'institutional' militancy for diminished membership pushfulness. Many management negotiators, who have been generally opposed to granting or liberalizing 'automatic' cost-of-living adjustments, fear that to do so would simply threaten the union negotiators with technological obsolescence and goad them into new and more costly demands at bargaining time. (That there may be some grounds for this belief is suggested by the willingness of various American unions to 'trade away' escalated protection during periods of relative price stability.) To the extent that this apprehension is justified, the effectiveness of indexation in compensating the membership would have to be reckoned net of its threat to institutional security.

Increased militancy by the leadership could also mean (although it need not) that the membership has not been sufficiently pacified by indexation. Indexation may not succeed in damping down militancy which is motivated less by a defensive desire to maintain shares in a satisfacory distribution of income than by active dissatisfaction with the existing income distribution. 'Offensive behavior' proceeding from each organized group's determination to increase its relative income might be frustrated more effectively with general indexation than without it, but success is by no means assured (see [38], pp. 225, 229). The certain knowledge that other groups will be compensated for any price increase to which one's own wage rise may contribute, even together with the knowledge that profits are excluded from such protection, may not prove a very effective deterrent to wage offensives. The failures of indexation in the U.K. and Denmark can be attributed primarily to refusal by union groups to accept existing income distributions, although it is also true, as has been pointed out, that the forms of indexation actually adopted in those (and other countries) are not well designed to eliminate adjustment lags [6]. In such cases additional forms of 'compensation' for restraint may well be required.

One such form of compensation consists of tax cuts combined with incomes policy. This, indeed, has been closely tied in with indexation when it is proposed that the latter include the indexing of tax deductions and brackets; and it is in any event a method of considerable significance and growing importance. It rests on the assumption that, as inflation has pushed wage earners steadily into higher marginal and average tax categories, they have become less dominated by money illusion and increasingly inclined to take both price changes and taxes into account in their wage bargaining. Thus (in the absence of tax indexation), some governments have attempted to secure moderation in wage demands from unions in exchange for tax reductions (and/or subsidies and price controls). West Germany ([29], pp. 7–8), Sweden ([28], pp. 19, 38, 41), and Norway ([27], pp. 15, 38) followed this approach in 1974, and the OECD Surveys of those countries all indicated the belief that they were probably effective.

This approach to consensus through policy bargaining has the best chance of success, for it combines economic compensation to the individual wage earner with some functional compensation to the central union bodies. (Thus the Swedish tax cut of 1974 might be contrasted with threats of a tax increase made by the Swedish Financial Minister in 1956 and 1957 as a means of obtaining the current wage negotiations.) However, these recent experiments in policy bargaining were not conducted in a clean test tube, for, at least in Germany and also in Sweden, levels of capacity utilization and employment were low in 1974, although rates of inflation were quite high. Moreover, the governments hedged their bets to some extent, for they coupled their tax reductions with increased monetary stringency, which, in the case of Germany, produced a severe profits squeeze and a consequent decline in private investment. Thus the moderation in money wage behavior was due in part to recession. Furthermore, to the extent that the policy bargains were effective, they were effective not merely because wage restraint was compensated, but because it was represented to the unions as a necessary condition of economic recovery (especially in the case of Germany). Added to the carrot of direct compensation was a stick in the form of continued or increased unemployment *due to the choice of stabilization policy* by the authorities.

The credibility of that threat rests on two assumptions. The first is that the fear of job loss is an increasing function of the actual level of unemployment (which opinion polls in the U.S. seem to indicate). Thus proponents of this policy implicitly assign to unemployment an active role in damping down wage inflation, in contrast to monetarists who regard it merely as an unfortunate, although inevitable, by-product, or side effect, of a reduction in the rate of spending.

The second assumption is that the political influence of the trade union movement is sufficiently limited, or that the overall community's commitment to full employment is sufficiently limited. Otherwise, the authorities could not condition the adoption of expansionary policies, including tax reduction on bargaining restraint. These conditions apparently hold in Germany where, as the OECD reported,

> . . . moves towards a more expansionary policy stance were accompanied by explicit warnings to both sides of industry that this policy could only be maintained provided wage settlements in 1975 were substantially below the previous ones. This message was taken seriously by employers and unions as wage increases fell drastically compared to the preceding round ([29], pp. 7, 8).

The alternative would be tax reduction and reflation without any *quid pro quo* from the unions. In the U.S. the Ford Administration, which was opposed to incomes policy, might have responded to some prodding by the Labor-Management Committee whose recommendations for tax reductions were substantially reflected in the President's State of the Union Message in 1975.

Wage Egalitarianism

Long before economic egalitarianism had become a major social force, its cause had been served by the labor movements of the major industrialized countries. And long before the term 'incomes policy' had been invented, emergency programs of wage control had granted the lowest paid groups favored treatment, in tribute to the intuitive interpretation of the doctrine of declining marginal utility of income. Hence it may not be surprising that wage equalization – or at least narrowing of occupational and industrial wage structures – should have been offered as compensation for bargaining restraint in the postwar period. It has been argued (notably in Britain) that without overall restraint the economically weak, low paid groups would be unable to experience improvement in their relative positions. Nor did egalitarian wage policies have to fly in the face of market conditions. The Swedes, to take an outstanding example, had egalitarianism much in mind when they greatly increased the student population of their universities – a move which tends to increase the relative supply of highly trained labor – and when they deployed their celebrated active labor market policy to help transfer labor from low-productivity firms and industries to firms and industries which can better afford to pay the higher wages established as contractual norms ([23], p. 49).

But incomes policies which are intended to serve the cause of wage equalization have not been outstandingly successful in neutralizing the bargaining power of high-paid market groups. To the extent that they have been effective in that respect, they have had to rely more on compulsion than on persuasion. Egalitarian wage policies, combined with the operation of highly progressive income tax systems under inflationary conditions, helped to generate organized resistance in the ranks of the upper salariat in Sweden and the Netherlands; and in the former country strikes in the public sector by SACO and SR in 1971 were countered by strike-breaking legislation. In the blue-collar sector, wage drift testified to the unpopularity of solidaristic settlements among high-wage groups in Scandinavia. This was countered through the inclusion of compensatory increases for low-paid industries by the determined central negotiators; but continued resistance contributed to the wave of wildcat strikes in Sweden and to attempts by unions in high-productivity export sectors to secure greater wage increases for themselves than the central federation was willing to have extended throughout the economy.

More highly paid groups of wage earners may not always have been able to protect their relative incomes, but the resistance which they offer to egalitarian policies and settlements tends to leave its mark on the general levels of money wages and prices. A recent wage-estimating model for Norway reveals a strong negative coefficient for wage differentials during contract years, which means that a narrowing of wage differentials produced significantly bigger central settlements (as well as greater wage drift). Thus, according to the OECD, 'egalitarian wage settlements seem to produce higher contractual increases and subsequently entail stronger wage drift with a tendency towards restoring previous differentials' ([27], p. 18). The same study, incidentally, also indicates that increases in marginal tax rates were significantly associated with increases in contractual wages, although increases in the average tax rate were not. This prompted the suggestion that 'changes in the structure of rates without reducing the average tax burden may have a dampening influence on wage claims ([41], pp. 171–174, 185–187). It is interesting that in Sweden the tax reductions in 1974 and in 1975 (which were credited with exerting a moderating influence on union wage demands) should have included reductions in marginal rates in middle income brackets and that they should have been financed by increases in social security contributions and (in 1975) indirect taxes. Long-run policy significance can hardly be ascribed to changes made under the impact of highly abnormal conditions, but these changes might be regarded as recognition of the limits within which egalitarian wage policies are consistent with social consensus and economic restraint.

Worker Participation

Although worker participation in management has come to rival income equalization in popularity as a social reform (at least in Europe) and although it can claim a long ideological heritage, it has yet to be put into practice on a significant scale and it means many different (and sometimes quite opposite) things to many different people. Nevertheless, it requires some consideration as a potential path to consensus for it has lately gathered support from people who see it in that light. It is looked upon – by policymakers, some managers, some trade union leaders, and even radical reformers – as a potential means of securing industrial peace and of avoiding the threat of anarchy raised by the wildcat strikes and plant seizures which swept across the European continent at the close of the last decade. It is also seen as possessing some anti-inflationary potential. In the latter capacity, it is hopefully regarded – whether in its lowly shop-floor manifestation as 'job enrichment' (whole tasks, job rotation, flexibility in work assignments, etc.) or in its more exalted one as 'codetermination' (participation of worker representatives across the entire range of entrepreneurial decision-making) – as substituting superior non-pecuniary incentives for inferior pecuniary ones. The substitution should result in increased worker satisfaction – and, presumably, in lower rates of increase in monetary costs and higher levels of productivity – for three reasons: (a) declining rates of marginal utility of income generated by postwar growth in real wages; (b) greater intolerance of monotonous and unchallenging jobs and subordinate status, induced by higher levels of educational attainment among workers; and (c) extension to the field of work of a generally decentralizing tendency manifest in many other walks of life. Implicit in the foregoing is greater worker identification with the enterprise and greater sophistication with its economic requirements; the worker would acquire the managerial viewpoint.

In fact, management interest in 'job enlargement' was stimulated by labor shortages in the Netherlands and Sweden (see [9], p. 76 and [36], p. 15). Thus insofar as job enlargement can be a substitute for self-defeating attempts to raise relative wages, it could serve the interests of incomes policies; and insofar as it could be a substitute for effective increases in relative wages it could serve the cause of egalitarian wage policy.

But while worker participation might conceivably facilitate economic consensus and wage restraint as a compensatory device, it is difficult to see how it could contribute to the security and authority of the more centralized and 'restrained' union institutions. Presumably it would accentuate existing trends in the direction of more decentralized bargaining at company-wide level. Indeed, U.S. unionists might fear that it could go even further, for they could read into the implied abandonment of their highly adversary relationship with management something suspiciously like a revival of the effective company-dominated unionism of the 1920's (were it not for the fact that contemporary American management is quite as opposed to worker participation as are American unions). The opposition of the Communist-led C.G.T. in France, while couched in terms of class collaboration, is not too different from the instinctive reaction of American business unionism. Ideological aversion to day-to-day bargaining (along with ideological divisions and plural unionism) contributed to organizational vacuums at plant level in France and Italy and elsewhere as well. These vacuums continued to be filled by paternalistic management at least until the 1960's when autonomous grass roots pressures began to develop, erupting into wildcat strikes at the end of the decade. Managerial paternalism and, later, spontaneous organization did stimulate efforts by national unions and federations in different countries to reach down to the grass roots, but they could be thwarted by company-oriented arrangements for employee participation. (The British TUC's insistence that eligibility to vote in elections for plant committee representatives and for worker directors on company boards be confined to union members, in contrast to 'the Continental model', is illustrative of the potential organizational conflict.) Thus the potential of worker participation for wage restraint depends critically on the readiness of workers to substitute the extra non-pecuniary rewards discussed above for extra pecuniary rewards. This is a subject of considerable current debate, and there is some doubt as to how far the marginal utility of income has in fact declined. An American study finds little basis for attributing such phenomena as declining growth of productivity and increases in strikes and quit rates to increased dissatisfaction with the 'quality' of work [14]. Another study finds that demands for wages, along with demands for union recognition, were much more important than 'qualitative' demands (including demands for worker control) in French strikes, even in those which occured during and after May 1968 ([11], ch. II). Moreover, if the past record of rapid economic growth in Europe has tended to reduce the marginal utility of pecuniary income relative to that of work-associated non-pecuniary income, any marked deceleration of growth in the future should tend to arrest and possibly even reverse that tendency.

If worker participation should leave wage appetites unappeased while contributing towards the decentralizing of wage-setting mechanisms, it could increase the difficulty of achieving effective wage restraint. Obviously, experience offers no close parallels to serve as a guide here. Rough analogies might be found in the Dutch system of wage control (1959 – 63) which sought to restrict money wage increases to increases in sectoral productivity and in later British attempts to allow wage increases under 'productivity bargaining' within enterprises as 'exceptions' to general norms. Both experiments were frustrated by the tendency of the bigger wage increases to 'ripple out' beyond their places of origin and raise unit costs outside their intended boundaries.

Nor would one be justified in holding too strongly the *a priori* expectation that increased productivity would issue from worker participation. Where management enjoys freedom to institute changes in work assignments, job design, production standards, etc. – whether or not subject to subsequent grievance and adjudication – it might well find that freedom circumscribed by the obligation to obtain prior agreement. In upholding management's 'prior duty of negotiation', proposed Swedish legislation explicitly permits the calling of strikes while collective agreements are in force, in the event of deadlock over specific issues.

Moreover, in this as in other proposed schemes, management's obligation to bargain extends to investment decisions (specifically including, in the Swedish bill, 'the transfer or leasing of the firm'). Companion codetermination proposals to give worker representatives numerical equality on boards of directors might also mean that profitability and productivity would be more actively constrained in the interests of job security. How strong that constraint would ultimately prove to be is anyone's guess. In Germany, it has been reported that codetermination has tended to delay managerial decision-making, although unintentionally, and to restrict management's 'scope of action' during cyclical downswings 'by insisting on vested employee interests' ([7], p. 28 – 29). In the Netherlands, on the other hand, the right of the Works' Council to consultation in advance of managerial decision-making may be abridged where 'important interests' of the company would be adversely affected ([9], p. 65).

In general, perhaps, constraints on profitability and productivity would tend to vary inversely with the degree of competition to which the enterprise is exposed and with the overall level of business activity. The strength of the worker-participation constraint on productivity might also vary directly with the political influence of the labor groups involved, so that decisions against closing down unprofitable establishments could be ratified by the availability of public subsidy. Obviously sit-ins as well as wildcats have left their stamp on the movement towards worker participation. Participation would hardly blaze a trail in the direction of job protection, but there is fear that it would reinforce well-established union and government policies in various countries which tend in and of themselves to perpetuate uneconomical employing units and thus to inhibit the mobility and efficient allocation of labor.

On the other hand, there is hope that participation will prove conducive to – or at least consistent with – efficient management by carrying forward the work begun by collective bargaining in defense of the dignity of the individual worker at the workplace. Between fear and hope might lie the possibility that participation will perform roughly the same representational function which collective bargaining performs where it is independently established at the plant level. Linkage between the local and the more centralized organizations, which furnishes an institutional basis for consensus and restraint under collective bargaining, would be weaker; but greater concern for the economic health of the enterprise might possibly constitute an alternative source of institutional restraint.

Conclusion: The Price of Consensus

Although both the need and the potential for restraint are rooted in the nature of contemporary wage-setting institutions, efforts to secure restraint through consensus are constrained in the interest of industrial peace and institutional stability. Efforts to secure wage restraint from national unions or more centralized bodies by helping or permitting them to strengthen their positions of authority have been effective in some instances, but there are both practical and normative limits beyond which institutional compensation of this form cannot be pushed in democratic societies. Therefore public authorities have attempted to find policies which hold out promise of compensating the individual wage earner for wage restraint and to employ them as counters in bargaining for wage restraint with trade union federations. Indeed, social policies in a wide variety of areas – including economic stabilization, income distribution, industrial management, even foreign affairs – may have to be designed or administered with an eye to their impact on labor relations and wage bargaining. Some of the policies on which we have cast *our* eye in this paper – especially negotiated tax reductions – are reasonably consistent with the objectives of wage restraint and industrial peace, but all of them have considerable limitations.

So there is a political price to be paid for the new social contract. Insofar as policy bargaining involves policy tradeoffs, and even to the extent that it reflects the lobbying pressures of private groups, it is a familiar and not uniquely objectionable phenomenon. But if and when the pressure to secure a given objective, social or private, includes potential or actual recourse to the strike – the classic and approved sanction in conventional collective bargaining – policy bargaining threatens representative democracy. It is the 'national emergency dispute problem' writ large.

Inclusion of the integrity of the institutions of representative democracy as an argument in the national welfare function – together with employment, price, labor relations, growth, and distributional objectives – cannot simply go without saying.

References

[1] Ackley, G.: The Contribution of Guidelines, In: G. P. Shultz and R. Z. Aliber, eds., *Guidelines, Informal Controls and the Market Place*, Chicago, 1966.

[2] Albeda, W.: Recent Trends in Collective Bargaining in the Netherlands, *International Labour Review*, 1971.

[3] Albeda, W.: *Participation in Management*, Rotterdam, 1973.

[4] Bonnaud, J. J.: Participation by Workers' and Employers' Organisations in Planning in France, *International Labour Review*, 1966.

[5) Braun, A. R.: Compulsory Arbitration as a Form of Incomes Policy: the Australian Case, *International Monetary Fund Staff Papers*, 1974.

[6] Braun, A. R.: Indexation of Wages and Salaries in Developed economies. International Monetary Fund, Research Department, 1975, Mimeo.

[7] Daheim, H.: The Practice of Co-Determination on the Management Level of German Enterprises. In: [3].

[8] Delamotte, Y.: Recent Collective Bargaining Trends in France, *International Labour Review*, 1971.

[9] Does de Willebois, J. L. J. M. van der: On the Quality of Working Life. In: [3].

[10] Dunlop, J. T.: *Wage Determination under Trade Unions*, New York, 1944.

[11] Durand, C. and P. Dubois: *La grève, enquête sociologique*. Paris.

[12] Economist, The, November 22, 1975.

[13] Elliott, J.: Fishermen in Troubled Waters, *The Financial Times*, February 5, 1974.

[14] Flanagan, R. J., G. Strauss and L. Ulman: Worker Discontent and Work Place Behavior, *Industrial Relations*, 1974.

[15] Friedman, M.: Monetary Correction. In: [18].

[16] Galenson, ed.: *Incomes Policy: What can we Learn from Europe?* New York 1973.

[17] Giersch, H.: Index Clauses and the Fight against Inflation. In: [18].

[18] Giersch, H.: *Essays on Indexation and Inflation*, Washington, D.C. 1974.

[19] Guigni, G.: Recent Trends in Collective Bargaining in Italy, *International Labour Review*, 1971.

[20] Isaac, J. E.: Australian Compulsory Arbitration and Incomes Policy, In: F. Blackeaby, ed., *An Incomes Policy for Britain*, London 1972.

[21] Kern, M.: Wandlungen der konzertierten Aktion, *Wirtschaftspolitische Chronik*, 1973.

[22] Keynes, J. M.: *The General Theory of Employment, Interest and Money*, New York 1936.

[23] Lundberg, E.: Incomes Policy Issues in Sweden, In: [16].

[24] New York Times, The, September 30, 1975.

[25] Nordhaus, W. D.: The Falling Share of Profits, *Brookings Papers on Economic Activity*, 1974.

[26] OECD: *Inflation: the Present Problem*, Paris 1970.

[27] OECD: Economic Surveys, Januari 1975.

[28] OECD: Economic Surveys, June 1975.

[29] OECD: Economic Surveys, July 1975.

[30] Oechslin, J. J.: The Role of Employers' Organisations in France, *International Labour Review*, 1972.
[31] Perry, G. L.: *Determinants of Wage Inflation around the World.*
[32] Phelps, E. S. et al.; *Microeconomic Foundations of Employment and Inflation Theory*, New York 1970.
[33] Phelps, E. S.: The New Microeconomics in Inflation and Employment Theory, *American Economic Association Papers and Proceeding* 1969.
[34] Reichel, H.: Recent Trends in Collective Bargaining in the Federal Republic of Germany, *International Labour Review*, 1971.
[35] Seidman, J.: *American Labor from Defense to Reconversion*, Chicago 1953.
[36] Swedish employers' confederation: *Job Reform in Sweden*, 1975.
[37] Tobin, J.: Monetary Policy and the Control of Credit. In: A. T. Sommers, ed., *Answers to Inflation and Recession: Economic Policies for a Modern Society*, New York 1975.
[38] Ulman, L. and R. J. Flanagan: *Wage Restraint: a Study of Incomes Policies in Western Europe*, Berkeley 1971.
[39] Verdier, J.: Labor Relations in the Public Sector in France, *International Labour Review*, 1975.
[40] Willey, R. J.: Trade Unions and Political Parties in the Federal Republic of Germany, *Industrial and Labor Relations Review*, 1974.
[41] Windmuller, J. P.: *Labor Relations in the Netherlands*, Ithaca 1969.
[42] Wolff, P. de: The Netherlands and Germany. In [16].

Index Number Mutations

P. E. Venekamp

Fisher laid himself out to test various formulas with relation to index numbers, by comparing their construction with some formal requirements [2]. The result of these investigations was poor. Fisher discovered no 'good' formulas; even the 'ideal index number' has defects. Practice, however, did not care about Fisher's conclusions. Imperfect formulas are still in use, because they are efficient and suitable.

Independent of Fisher's efforts the statistical basic-data are improving. Moreover modern theoretically founded formulas become available. Nevertheless the old Laspeyres and Paasche are still alive, only the application of their formulas has been modernised. Some aspects of this application are the subject of this study.

Reality of Index Number Mutations

The changing of index numbers is a consequence of the nature of the phenomena described by these numbers. This statement is based on the experience that alterations with regard to such phenomena find a good expression in the variations of the index numbers. Do these numbers answer the purpose of their construction? In 1957 De Wolff was engaged on this problem [3]. He noticed, that the choice of the weights can affect the just mentioned parallelism of changes. His argument was as follows.

A commodity k, one in the consumption pattern of the group to which the index pertains, has the weight g_k ($k = 1, \ldots, n$). If P_k represents the simple price index of k, the composite index number P can be calculated according to (1):

$$P = \sum_k g_k P_k \; (\sum_k g_k = 1) \tag{1}$$

P has been compared with the composite index P', calculated with new weights g_k':

$$P' = \sum_k g_k' P_k \; (\sum_k g_k' = 1) \tag{2}$$

If $g_k' = g_k + \Delta g_k$ and $P_k = P + \Delta P_k$, we obtain

$$P' - P = \sum_k \Delta g_k (P + \Delta P_k) \tag{3}$$

Since $\sum_k g_k' - \sum_k g_k = \sum_k \Delta g_k = 0$, we have

$\sum_k \Delta g_k P = P \sum_k \Delta g_k = 0$. So

$$P' - P = \sum_k \Delta g_k \Delta P_k \tag{3a}$$

As $\sum_k g_k \Delta P_k = \sum_k g_k P_k - \sum_k g_k P = P - P = 0$, we may write

$$\text{Var}\,(\Delta P_k) = \sum_k g_k (\Delta P_k)^2 \tag{4}$$

We may also write

$$\text{Var}\left(\frac{\Delta g_k}{g_k}\right) = \sum_k g_k \left(\frac{\Delta g_k}{g_k}\right)^2 \tag{5}$$

The differences Δg_k and ΔP_k can be correlated according to the following formula:

$$R = \frac{\sum_k \Delta g_k \Delta P_k}{\sqrt{\text{Var}\,(\Delta P_k)\,\text{Var}\left(\frac{\Delta g_k}{g_k}\right)}} \tag{6}$$

(3a) and (6) give $P' - P = R\sigma(\Delta P_k)\sigma\left(\frac{\Delta g_k}{g_k}\right)$ or

$$\frac{P' - P}{P} = RV_k\sigma_g, \tag{7}$$

where $V_k = \sigma(\Delta P_k) / P$

$$\sigma_g = \sigma\left(\frac{\Delta g_k}{g_k}\right)$$

As $|R| \leqq 1$, the relative change of P caused by changes of the weights g_k, equals at most the product of V_k and σ_g. One of these factors would be zero, if $P' = P$. In this case the weights do not change ($\sigma_g = 0$), or the partial indexes have all the same value ($V_k = 0$). The second possibility does not occur in practice.

If the weighted average must be calculated from the simple index numbers P_k ($k = 1, \ldots, n$), the question arises, whether the weights are realistical ones. The criteria, required to answer this question, depend on the purpose for which an index was made. A small deviation of P' from P does not necessitate alterations in the weighting scheme.

Laspeyres and Paasche Method

In the general formula for the Laspeyres index the weight may be expressed as follows:

$$g_k = p_{ok}\, q_{ok} / \Sigma p_{ok}\, q_{ok} \; (k = 1, \ldots, n) \tag{8}$$

where p_{ok} = price of commodity k in a base period
q_{ok} = quantity of commodity k in a base period

It is desirable to shift the base from time to time. A new weighting scheme may be implied by the new base period. The significance of such a decision depends on the result of the calculation according to (7).

The Paasche formula in which

$$g_k = p_{ok}\, q_{tk} / \Sigma p_{ok}\, q_{tk} \; (k = 1, \ldots, n) \tag{9}$$

implies a new weighting scheme for the non-base period t. Now the question arises how far re-calculations with respect to index numbers preceding t, are needed for comparisons. Strictly speaking the use of current period weights makes period-to-period comparisons of price changes impossible. If g_k in (1) equals $p_{ok}\ q_{lk}\ /\ \Sigma p_{ok}\ q_{lk}$ $(0 < 1 < t)$ and g'_k in (2) is identical with g_k in (9) then the ratio in (7) defines the formation of a revised time series over the periods $0 \ldots t$; these time series are based on the same weighting scheme. A re-calculation can be postponed without objection, if the concerning ratio is small.

Adjusted Weighting Scheme

(8) and (9) can be summarized, if g_k represents the weight g_{ik} $(i = 0, \ldots, t)$. The De Wolff problem is less important in case all periods $0, \ldots, t$ contribute to the size of the weight. Then the Laspeyres-Paasche alternative is out of the question. The data are similar to those applied in the Paasche case. The contribution of a period to the weight in operation would be dependent on the changes of $p_{ok}\ q_{ik}$ $(i = = 0, 1, \ldots t)$, taking place over time. Gradual changes may be assumed. For a limited period of time the following model may be used:

$$p_{ok}\ q_{ik} = \alpha_{i,k} i + \beta_{i,k} + \underline{\delta}_{i,k}\ (i = 0, 1, \ldots, t) \tag{10}$$

The constructing principle with respect to the weights should be accentuated; therefore the regression model (10) may be kept as simple as possible in the present little essay. When necessary more advanced models can be used. According to indications in (10) the estimated coefficients depend on the distance between 0 and t; cf. (11).

The data with respect to i become available at the end of the period i or in $i + 1$. This time-lag is not important when a new formula has been introduced at t, and the data with respect to periods $0 \ldots t$ have been used in this formula. This means that model (10) has been carried on to time t, with new prices p_t, because we want to start with a series based on t. Therefore the model is applied to $p_{tk}\ q_{ik} = Z_{ik}$, assuming that (11) can be calculated:

$$Z^*_{ik} = a_{i,k} i + b_{i,k}\ (i = 0, \ldots, t) \tag{11}$$

We do not want a weighting scheme with a fixed or variable character as in the

Laspeyres or Paasche formulas. Here the following principle proposed:

$$g_{t+i,k} = \frac{\hat{Z}_{t+i,1}}{\sum_1 \hat{Z}_{t+i,1}} \begin{pmatrix} i = 0, 1, \ldots \\ 1 = 1, \ldots, m \end{pmatrix} \tag{12}$$

This formula requires a comment.

Sometimes it has been suggested to use the ratio $\frac{(p_{ok}q_{ok} + p_{ok}q_{tk})}{\sum_k (p_{ok}q_{ok} + p_{ok}q_{tk})}$ as a weight. This, however, cancelled the Laspeyres-Paasche conflict. This case induced the question why not every period 0, 1 . . . t can contribute to the weight in t, e.g. the weight might have been based on the ratio $\sum_i p_{ok}q_{ik}/\sum_k \sum_i p_{ok}q_{ik}$, in which every period has an equal importance with respect to the calculation of the weight of k in t. We note, that the approach to the problem in this procedure differs from the Divisia design. Nevertheless the assumption, basis of the just-mentioned ratio, may be less realistic than the assumption of decreasing influence of previous periods. Therefore $\hat{Z}$ has been introduced in (12); we define:

$$\hat{Z}_{t+i,k} = (1 - \alpha)\, a_{t+i-1,k} + (1 - \alpha)\, \hat{Z}_{t+i-l,k} + \alpha\, Z_{t+i,k} \tag{13}$$
$$(i = 1, 2 \ldots)$$
$$(0 < \alpha < 1)$$

where

$$Z_{t+i,k} = p_{tk}\, q_{t+i,k} \tag{14}$$

and

$$a_{t+i-1,k} = a_{t,k} + \beta\left[\sum_{j=1}^{i-1} \hat{Z}_{t+j,k} - Z^{*}_{t,k} - \sum_{j=1}^{i-1} Z_{t+j,k}\right] (0 < \beta < 1) \tag{15}$$

The result of this more or less mechanistic approach involves the evaluation of the coefficients α and β.

Arbitrary Coefficients

The conditions with respect to α in (13) and β in (15) give incomplete indications in case of fixed coefficients, because a theory is missing. We would have to make a choice, as a matter of fact, with statistical consequences. We briefly discuss these consequences. In Brown's original set-up in this field we write [1]:

$$\alpha = 1 - \gamma^2 \tag{16}$$

$$\beta = (1 - \gamma)^2 \quad (0 < \gamma < 1) \tag{17}$$

Hence

$$\hat{Z}_{t+i,k} = \gamma^2 (a_{t+i-l,k} + \hat{Z}_{t+i-l,k}) + (1 - \gamma^2) Z_{t+i,k} \tag{18}$$

It can be shown that the choice of γ influences the bias in $Z_{t+i,k}$ and the variance of $\underline{\delta}$ with respect to Z^*_{ik}, in the opposite direction; the variance decreases, if γ approaches 1. In this case the effect of the last observation does not dominate in the weight.

For a next period (13) and (18) are applicable, which is an advantage in practice.

De Wolff's Conclusion

The application of (18) requires a confrontation with the results produced by (7), which implies, that g_k in (1) equals $g_{t+i,k}$ in (12). Now De Wolff's question is how long the smoothing process of the weighting scheme can be carried on. Also in this case the length of the process depends on De Wolff's criteria.

The coefficient $g_{t+i,k}$ alters smoothly, because the components of (12) change gradually. The only fixed point is Z^*_{tk}. So we have to compare

$$P = \sum_k g_{t+i,k} P_k \tag{19}$$

with

$$P' = \sum_k Z^*_{t+i,k} P_k \tag{20}$$

According to De Wolff, $RV_k\sigma_g$ is the crucial magnitude again. As soon as it is too large, say $> 5\%$, the smoothing process has to be finished off. By similar arguments as given above, the real-world decisionmaking problem is reduced to the De Wolff statement.

Application: an Example

Use of (19) depends on the object in view. The following case shows an example of this nature.

For a better understanding of P in (19), we think of a so-called costprice-index with respect to a specific good about which De Wolff has elaborated an example in [3]. The partial index numbers P_k, participating in the costprice-index, represents the movement of prices of the separate costcomponents (raw materials, wages, etc.). The weights, added to P_k, are the relative shares of these components in the total costprice of the good which concerns us. In the long run the composition of the costprice will be changed in such a way, that a new weighting scheme must be set up.

A problem arises when a newly produced good was not sold at once, but was in stock first. In this situation the number of goods that were sold during a certain period, can be spread over the periods during which they were produced. Now we are approaching the answer to the practical question, how to calculate the cost-price-index with respect to goods delivered to customers. This case can be considered as a supplement of the example, presented by De Wolff.

The periods of production of the goods sold must be the same. In case the goods are of different production periods, the costprice-index must be an average, in which the sequence of alterations in the costprice composition must be assimilated. This index may then be calculated as a composite index number with weights, resulting from the relevant costprice distributions, according to the method of weighted moving averages we just discussed. However, this method is only applicable under certain conditions, e.g. a relatively long time of production, a low turnover velocity with respect to the stock, or unstable prices of the costprice components.

References

[1] Brown, R. G.: *Smoothing, Forecasting and Prediction of Discrete Time Series*, London 1962,

[2] Fisher, I.: *The Making of Index Numbers. A Study of their Varieties, Tests and Reliability.* Boston 1922.

[3] Wolff, P. de: De invloed van de keuze der gewichten op de hoogte van een gewogen index-cijfer, *Statistica Neerlandica*, 1957.

Disproportional Growth and the Intersectoral Distribution of Income

H. S. Houthakker

Although the construction of growth models is among the principal concerns of contemporary economic theory there are several features of actual growth that have not yet been incorporated into the models. One of the most important of these features is the disparity in the growth rates of different sectors of an economy. It has long been known, for instance, that the agricultural sector tends to expand less rapidly than other sectors, so that in the course of development there is normally a shift of manpower from the farms to the city. Perhaps the first to observe this disparity was Ernst Engel, who connected it with the generalization concerning consumers' behavior that has become known as Engel's law [1]. More recently work along these lines has been done by Herbert Simon and Johansen, and of course there are many incidental references in the development literature [5] [4]. In this paper I propose to examine a simple growth model for a closed economy with two sectors in which labor is the only scarce factor. I shall assume that labor is less than perfectly mobile, in accordance with common observation, and that productivity in each of the two sectors increases at some exogenously given rate. It will then be shown that in the sector whose products have the smaller income elasticity either income per worker will be lower, or productivity will grow less rapidly, or both. These results are useful in the explanation of the farm problem and in the evaluation of certain farm policies [see [3], Ch. 2). Thus it will appear that, under the assumptions of this model, efforts to increase farm productivity will normally have an adverse effect on relative farm income.

The following notation will be used:

N_i = Number of workers in the i-th sector ($i = 1, 2$)

$N \quad = N_1 + N_2$
$Q_i \quad$ = total output of the i-th sector (in physical terms)
$p_i \quad$ = unit price of product i in terms of product 1 ($p_1 = 1$)
$Y_i \quad = p_i Q_i$ = total income of the i-th sector
$Y \quad = Y_1 + Y_2$ = national income
$q_i \quad = Q_i / N_i$ = output per worker in the i-th sector
$x_i \quad = Q_i / N$ = consumption per capita of the i-th product
$y_i \quad = p_i q_i = Y_i / N_i$ = income per worker in the i-th sector
$y \quad = Y/N$ = national income per capita
$w_i \quad = p_i x_i / y$ = share of the i-th product in national expenditure
E_{i2} = elasticity of demand for the i-th product with respect to p_2
E_{io} = elasticity of demand for the i-th product with respect to national income
Derivatives with respect to time will be denoted by a dot over the variable.

In order to concentrate the analysis on essentials it will be assumed throughout that

1. The number of dependents per worker is the same in both sectors and constant over time, so that there is no need to distinguish between population and labor force since they remain proportional to each other.
2. The consumption per capita of each of the two products depends only on the relative price p_2 and on per capita national income y, so that the distribution of income does not affect demand.
3. There is perfect competition in the product markets and in each of the two labor markets taken by itself, but the movement of labor between the two sectors may not respond instantaneously to wage differentials.
4. The market for each product is cleared instantaneously; there is no storage.

Before introducing productivity change and migration explicitly it is convenient to derive some formulas concerning price determination under changing supply conditions. Let the demand functions for the two products be given by

$$x_i = h_i(p_2, y) \quad (i = 1, 2) \tag{1}$$

where h_1 and h_2 are related by the budget constraint

$$x_1 + p_2 x_2 = y \tag{2}$$

Differentiating (1) with respect to time we get

$$\dot{x}_i = \frac{\partial h_i}{\partial p_2} \dot{p}_2 + \frac{\partial h_i}{\partial y} \dot{y} \tag{3}$$

and since

$$\frac{\partial h_i}{\partial p_2} = \frac{h_i E_{i2}}{p_2} \tag{4}$$

with a similar formula for $\delta h_i/\delta y$, we can write, after dividing both sides of (3) by x_i,

$$\dot{x}_i/x_i = E_{i2}\dot{p}_2/p_2 + E_{i0}\dot{y}/y \tag{5}$$

Differentiation of (2) with respect to time gives

$$\dot{x}_1 + \dot{p}_2 x_2 + p_2 \dot{x}_2 = \dot{y} \tag{6}$$

And since, by the definition of w_i,

$$1/y = w_1/x_1 = w_2/(p_2 x_2) \tag{7}$$

this can be written, after division by y, as

$$w_1 \dot{x}_1/x_1 + w_2(\dot{p}_2/p_2 + \dot{x}_2/x_2) = \dot{y}/y \tag{8}$$

Substituting (8) into (5) we can eliminate $\dot{y}/y$. Consequently

$$\dot{x}_2/x_2 = (E_{22} + w_2 E_{20})\, \dot{p}_2/p_2 + w_1 E_{20}\, \dot{x}_1/x_1 + w_2 E_{20} \dot{x}_2/x_2 \tag{9}$$

By a well-known theorem on consumer's behavior the coefficient of $\dot{p}_2/p_2$ is always negative, so we obtain the solution

$$\dot{p}_2/p_2 = (E_{22} + w_2 E_{20})^{-1} \{(1 - w_2 E_{20})\, \dot{x}_2/x_2 - w_1 E_{20} \dot{x}_1/x_1\} \tag{10}$$

By another result from consumption theory we must have

$$w_1 E_{10} + w_2 E_{20} = 1 \tag{11}$$

from which we finally conclude that

$$\dot{p}_2/p_2 = \frac{w_1}{E_{22} + w_2 E_{20}} (E_{10} \dot{x}_2/x_2 - E_{20} \dot{x}_1/x_1) \tag{12}$$

To clarify the implications of this formula we consider the case where per capita consumption of both commodities increases at the same percentage rate, so that $\dot{x}_2/x_2 = \dot{x}_1/x_1$. Since the fractional term is necessarily negative, the sign of $\dot{p}_2/p_2$ then is the opposite of the sign of $(E_{10} - E_{20})$. Thus if the second good is a necessity $(0 < E_{20} < 1)$ or inferior $(E_{20} < 0)$ the first good must be a luxury $(E_{10} > 1)$ by virtue of (11) so that $E_{10} > E_{20}$. The relative price of the second good must then decline. From the same reasoning it follows that if the relative price is to be constant, consumption of the necessary good must be increasing less rapidly than of the luxury good.

These qualitative conclusions are independent of the price elasticities; in fact the compensated own-price elasticity of the second good, which appears in the denominator in (12), serves only to determine the absolute magnitude of the price change (if any). This magnitude is also proportional to w_1, the budget share of the numéraire, and since $w_2 = 1 - w_1$ it will be seen that the change in the relative price will be greatest in absolute value if the second good accounts for a small share of consumers' expenditure.

The basic formula (12) is valid for any static demand functions. For future reference it will be useful to consider also a special case, namely the demand functions that have been described elsewhere as 'direct addilog' [2]. These correspond to a preference ordering with a (direct) utility function

$$\varphi(x_1, x_2) = \frac{a_1}{b_1 + 1} x_1^{b_1+1} + \frac{a_2}{b_2 + 1} x_2^{b_2+1} \tag{13}$$

where the a's and b's are constants. According to the first order conditions for a maximum

$$\begin{cases} a_1 x_1^{b_1} = \lambda \\ a_2 x_2^{b_2} = \lambda p_2 \end{cases} \tag{14}$$

where λ is the marginal utility of income and $p_1 = 1$ as before.
Consequently elimination of λ gives

$$p_2 = (a_2/a_1) x_1^{-b_1} x_2^{b_2} \tag{15}$$

and differentiation with respect to time then leads us to

$$\dot{p}_2/p_2 = -\, b_1 \dot{x}_1/x_1 + b_2 \dot{x}_2/x_2 \tag{16}$$

Comparing (16) with (12) we see that the coefficients of $\dot{x}_1/x_1$ and $\dot{x}_2/x_2$ have now become constants, which simplifies the analysis. The elasticity formulas obtained by equating the coefficients in (12) and (16) can, of course, also be proved directly, but this will not be done here. From an empirical point of view direct addilog demand functions have some claim to consideration; they are essentially the widely used double-logarithmic functions modified to make them satisfy the budget constraint.

We now turn to the supply side. The fundamental assumption here is that the labor force increases at some natural growth rate β (assumed to be the same for the two sectors) and migrates from the low-income to the high-income sector at a rate M that varies directly with the income differential. The migration function will be left unspecified for the time being. We can therefore write

$$\dot{N}_1 = \beta N_1 + M \tag{17}$$

$$\dot{N}_2 = \beta N_2 - M \tag{18}$$

Concerning productivity it will be assumed that output per worker increases at some proportional rate α_1 in each sector:

$$\dot{q}_i = \alpha_i q_i \ (i = 1, 2) \tag{19}$$

where α_i will be treated as a parameter; in fact our main interest is to find the effects of changing productivity on sector income.
For this purpose we note, to begin with, that the definitions of x_i and q_i imply

$$x_i = q_i N_i / N \tag{20}$$

and consequently

$$\dot{x}_i/x_i = \dot{q}_i/q_i + \dot{N}_i/N_i - \dot{N}/N \tag{21}$$

Making use of (17), (18) and (19) we find

$$\dot{x}_1/x_1 = \alpha_1 + M/N_1 \tag{22}$$

$$\dot{x}_2/x_2 = \alpha_2 - M/N_2 \tag{23}$$

where the terms involving β have dropped out.[1] By the same argument we obtain the proportional rates of change of sectoral income per worker

$$\dot{y}_1/y_1 = \alpha_1 \tag{24}$$

$$\dot{y}_2/y_2 = \alpha_2 + \dot{p}_2/p_2 \tag{25}$$

For the last term in (25) we can write, using (12), (22) and (23)

$$\dot{p}_2/p_2 = \frac{w_1}{E_{22} + w_2 E_{20}} \left\{ E_{10}\alpha_2 - E_{20}\alpha_1 - M\left(\frac{E_{20}}{N_1} + \frac{E_{10}}{N_2}\right)\right\} \tag{26}$$

which for subsequent manipulation will be abbreviated to

$$\dot{p}_2/p_2 = R(E_{10}\alpha_2 - E_{20}\alpha_1 - S) \tag{27}$$

Here S has the same sign as M, since the expression in parentheses in (26) is always positive (except possibly if one of the goods is inferior, a case that we shall disregard as uninteresting).

Now we are in a position to discuss changes in the distribution of income between the two sectors. For that purpose we shall consider the difference between the rates of change of income as given by (24) and (25). The distribution of income will remain unchanged if

$$\dot{y}_1/y_1 - \dot{y}_2/y_2 = \alpha_1 - \alpha_2 - \dot{p}_2/p_2 = 0 \tag{28}$$

that is if

$$\dot{p}_2/p_2 = \alpha_1 - \alpha_2 \tag{29}$$

Substituting this into (27) we get

$$R(E_{10}\alpha_2 - E_{20}\alpha_1 - S) = \alpha_1 - \alpha_2 \tag{30}$$

leading to

$$\alpha_2(1 + RE_{10}) - \alpha_1(1 + RE_{20}) = RS \tag{31}$$

Using the definition of R, and multiplying through by its denominator, this becomes

$$\alpha_2(E_{22} + w_2E_{20} + w_1E_{10}) - \alpha_1(E_{22} + w_2E_{20} + w_1E_{20}) = w_1S \quad (32)$$

which, from (11), can be simplified to

$$\alpha_2(1 + E_{22}) - \alpha_1(E_{20} + E_{22}) = w_1S \quad (33)$$

To understand this formula let us first consider the case $S = 0$, (and hence $M = 0$) which can arise in at least two different ways:

a. if migration is impossible; this may be the case, in particular, if the two sectors are really two specialized countries;
b. if the initial situation is one where $y_1 = y_2$ so that no migration is desired.

We see then that

$$\left(\frac{\alpha_1}{\alpha_2}\right)_{M=0} = \frac{1 + E_{22}}{E_{20} + E_{22}} \quad (34)$$

so that the growth pattern which preserves the existing distribution of income depends exclusively on the income and price elasticities of the second good.[2] Suppose that the second good consists of farm products, then we may safely assume that $E_{22} > -1$ (the demand for farm products is relatively inelastic with respect to price) and $-E_{22} < E_{20} < 1$ (Engel's law).[3] Hence the right hand side of (34) is greater than one, so that non-farm productivity must increase more rapidly than farm productivity if the distribution is to be preserved. If farm productivity increases more than is indicated by (34) this will benefit the non-farm sector more than the farm sector. In fact, it is easy to show that

$$\frac{\partial}{\partial \alpha_2}(\dot{y}_1/y_1 - \dot{y}_2/y_2) = -\frac{1 + E_{22}}{E_{22} + w_2E_{20}} \quad (35)$$

which is positive if $E_{22} > -1$. Intuitively the reason is that by increasing their output farmers lose more from the resulting change in the terms of trade than they gain from the value of the additional output. If farmers are to benefit from increased farm productivity some will have to move out of agriculture.
Returning now to (33) we must consider the case $S \neq 0$. Suppose first that $S > 0$,

corresponding to an outflow of labor from the second sector, which in our model is only possible if $y_1 > y_2$. If $E_{22} > -1$ it is clear that, for fixed α_1, α_2 will have to be reduced from its value in (34) if (33) is to hold. In that case, therefore, the distribution-preserving growth pattern is even less favorable to farm productivity than it was for $S = 0$. If farmers are already receiving lower incomes than non-farmers the prospects for improvement through increasing productivity are remote. The reader should have no difficulty in carrying out the analysis for other cases.

Finally it is in order to discuss the long-run behavior of the model here developed. The corresponding system of differential equations, namely (12), (17), (18), (22), (23), (24) and (25), is hard to analyze, except if the demand functions are of the direct addilog type mentioned earlier. As to migration, as a first approximation it may be put proportional to the income differential $(y_1 - y_2)$, but it should also involve some other elements. Since $y_1 - y_2$ is undeflated (that is, it is measured in terms of the first good as a numéraire) it seems appropriate to divide it by per capita national income y. Moreover it appears plausible that migration should be proportional to the number of people in the sector of origin and the sector of destination. This suggests

$$M = \gamma N_1 N_2 (y_1 - y_2)/y \tag{36}$$

where γ is a constant. The model now looks as follows:

$$\dot{N}_1/N_1 = \beta + \gamma N_2 (y_1 - y_2)/y \tag{37}$$

$$\dot{N}_2/N_2 = \beta - \gamma N_1 (y_1 - y_2)/y \tag{38}$$

$$\dot{y}_1/y_1 = \alpha_1 \tag{39}$$

$$\dot{y}_2/y_2 = \alpha_2 + \dot{p}_2/p_2 \tag{40}$$

$$\dot{p}_2/p_2 = -\, b_1 \dot{x}_1/x_1 + b_2 \dot{x}_2/x_2 \tag{41}$$

$$\dot{x}_1/x_1 = \alpha_1 + \dot{N}_1/N_1 - \beta \tag{42}$$

$$\dot{x}_2/x_2 = \alpha_2 + \dot{N}_2/N_2 - \beta \tag{43}$$

$$y = (N_1 y_1 + N_2 y_2)/(N_1 + N_2) \tag{44}$$

where we have made use of the fact that the total population grows at a rate β. It is possible to reduce this system to a single differential equation in N_2. First, substituting (42) and (43) into (41) we get

$$\dot{p}_2/p_2 = -b_1(\alpha_1 - \beta) + b_2(\alpha_2 - \beta) - b_1\dot{N}_1/N_1 + b_2\dot{N}_2/N_2 \tag{45}$$

which can be immediately integrated to

$$p_2 = e^{ct}N_1^{-b_1}N_2^{b_2} \tag{46}$$

where c equals the first two terms on the *R.H.S.* of (45) and t denotes time; there is also a constant of integration which can be put equal to unity by a suitable choice of units. It is also clear that

$$y_1 = y_1^* e^{\alpha_1 t} \tag{47}$$

$$y_2 = y_2^* e^{(\alpha_2+c)t}N_1{}^{-b_1}N_2{}^{+b_2} \tag{48}$$

where the asterisks denote initial values, and that consequently

$$y = (1/N)\{y_1^* e^{\alpha_1 t}N_1 + y_2^* e^{(\alpha_1 - c)t}N_1^{1-b_1}N_2^{b_2}\} \tag{49}$$

Equations (47) – (49) can then be substituted into (38):

$$\dot{N}_2/N_2 = \beta - \gamma N \frac{y_1^* e^{\alpha_1 t} - y_2^* e^{(\alpha_2+c)t}N_1^{-b_1}N_2^{b_2}}{y_1^* e^{\alpha_1 t} + y_2^* e^{(\alpha_2+c)t}N_1^{-b_1}N_2^{b_2}} \tag{50}$$

From the population growth assumptions it follows that

$$N = N^*e^{\beta t} \tag{51}$$

where N^* is again an initial value; also

$$N_1 = N^*e^{\beta t} - N_2 \tag{52}$$

Finally we wind up with

$$\dot{N}_2/N_2 = \beta - \gamma N^*e^{\beta t} \frac{y_1^* e^{1t} - y_2^* e^{(\alpha_2+c)t}(N^*e^{\beta t} - N_2)^{-b_1}N_2^{b_2}}{y_1^* e\alpha_1^t + y_2^* e^{(\alpha_2+c)t}(N^*e^{\beta t} - N_2)^{-b_1}N_2^{b_2}} \tag{53}$$

in which N_2 is the only unknown. This equation is analytically intractable but can be solved numerically.[4]

Table 1

Migration and its Effect over One Century
(for Parameter Values see Text)

t	N_2/N	w_2	M	P_2	y_1	y_2	Q_1/Q_1	Q_2/Q_2
0.	0.8000	0.8163	—0.4082	1.000	90.0	100.0	0.0296	0.0751
5.	0.7657	0.7260	1.0350	0.660	104.6	84,8	0.0900	0.0578
10.	0.7165	0.6704	1.2507	0.593	121.5	97.7	0.0861	0.0557
15.	0.6637	0.6125	1.4621	0.534	141.1	113.1	0.0822	0.0537
20.	0.6087	0.5544	1.6600	0.483	164.0	131.2	0.0784	0.0517
25.	0.5529	0.4976	1.8345	0.437	190.5	152.6	0.0749	0.0499
30.	0.4979	0.4436	1.9788	0.397	221.4	178.0	0.0716	0.0482
35.	0.4447	0.3931	2.0896	0.362	257.2	208.0	0.0687	0.0467
40.	0.3944	0.3468	2.1661	0.330	298.8	243.6	0.0661	0.0453
45.	0.3475	0.3047	2.2103	0.301	347.2	285.7	0.0638	0.0441
50.	0.3046	0.2669	2.2252	0.275	403.4	335.3	0.0618	0.0431
55.	0.2657	0.2331	2.2149	0.252	468.6	393.7	0.0600	0.0423
60.	0.2308	0.2031	2.1839	0.230	544.5	462.4	0.0586	0.0415
65.	0.1999	0.1766	2.1361	0.211	632.6	543.1	0.0573	0.0409
70.	0.1725	0.1532	2.0756	0.193	735.0	637.7	0.0562	0.0403
75.	0.1486	0.1327	2.0056	0.176	853.9	748.4	0.0553	0.0399
80.	0.1277	0.1147	1.9289	0.161	992.1	878.0	0.0545	0.0395
85.	0.1095	0.0990	1.8481	0.147	1152.6	1029.5	0.0538	0.0392
90.	0.0938	0.0953	1.7649	0.134	1339.2	1206.4	0.0532	0.0339
95.	0.0803	0.0734	1.6810	0.122	1555.9	1413.0	0.0527	0.0387
100.	0.0686	0.0631	1.5974	0.111	1807.7	1654.0	0.0523	0.0385

An example is given in Table 1, which shows a 100-year history at 5-year intervals. The assumed parameters, which have no pretention to realism, are $\alpha_1 = .03$, $\alpha_2 = .05$, $b_1 = -4$, $b_2 = -8$, $\beta_2 = .02$, $\gamma = .1$; the initial labor force N^* is put at 100 of which 80 are in sector 2. Initially the per capita income y_1^* in sector 1 is 90 and the corresponding figure y_2^* for sector 1 is 100.
It will be seen that although initially $y_1 < y_2$ this inequality reverses itself almost immediately due to a small migration from sector 1 to sector 2 ($M < 0$). In sector 1 per capita income rises steadily at an annual rate of 3%, but in sector 2 per capita income falls temporarily below the initial value, then rises but never catches up with y_1. For the first 30 years or so y_2 is generally about 20% below y_1 since migration is not large enough to equate per capita income in the two sectors.

Subsequently y_2 does rise somewhat faster than y_1, and by the end of the century y_2 is less than 10% below y_1. Migration reaches a peak at about the half-way mark. The share of sector 2 in total expenditures falls steadily from 81.63% at the start to 6.31% at the end; the price of good 2 in terms of good 1 also declines without interruption. Except in the early years total output in sector 1 is above the assumed growth of productivity because of population growth and migration; in sector 2 the growth of output is well below productivity growth plus population growth. Of the many parameters in the model the most characteristic one is probably γ which controls migration according to (36). Table 2 provides some insight into the effect of varying γ; all other parameters are the same as for Table 1. Since this paper deals with the intersectoral distribution Table 2 relates to the per capita income ratio y_2/y_1 (in %) at 25-year intervals.

Table 2

Per Capita Income in Sector 2 as Percentage of Per Capita in Sector 1, for Selected Years and Values of γ

γ	Years 0	25	50	75	100
0.01	111.1	13.1	3.9	1.0	0.5
0.04	111.1	57.6	60.1	69.2	78.5
0.1	111.1	80.1	83.1	87.6	91.5
0.25	111.1	91.5	93.1	95.0	96.6

In interpreting Table 2 it has to be borne in mind that y_1 does not depend on γ, as can be seen from (47), so that the income ratio reflects only the behavior of y_2. Perhaps the most startling result is that, for γ close to zero, per capita income in sector 2 becomes extremely low; it actually falls in absolute value through most of the period and only rises slightly at the very end.[5] This in turn is a result of a sharply falling price of good 2 – a classic case of overproduction. When γ is relatively large the income ratio stays fairly close to 100%, though it remains below parity.

To conclude, it has been shown that in an economy where the income elasticities of different goods are unequal, and where migration is less than perfectly responsive to income differentials, per capita income in the sector whose product has a low income elasticity is likely to be lower than in the other sector; how much lower depends on the sensitivity of the migration rate to the income differential. An exception to this general statement occurs if productivity grows much more slowly in the sector producing the income-inelastic good. To the extent that agricultural products have a lower income elasticity than industrial products this model helps explain the observed income disparity between farmers and others.

Notes

1. The model is not greatly changed if we assume intersectoral differences in natural population growth, but this refinement seems hardly worthwhile.
2. The apparent asymmetry is due to our using the first good as a numéraire. For direct addilog demand functions the R.H.S. of (34) becomes $(1 + b_2) / (1 + b_1)$, which is more symmetric.
3. For the United States the income elasticity of farm products (excluding processing and marketing) is probably around .2 and the price elasticity around —.1. This would put R.H.S of (34) at about nine.
4. The author is indebted to Dennis Tihansky for programming assistance.
5. When y_1 and y_2 are very different the second assumption on p. 96 becomes questionable. At the expense of more complicated formulae it would be possible to relate each sector's consumption of each good to that sector's per capita income.

References

[1] Engel, E.: Die Produktions- und Consumptionsverhältnisse des Königreichs Sachsen, *Zeitschrift des Statistischen Bureaus des Königlich Sächsischen Ministerium des Inneren*, 1857. Reprinted in: Bulletin de l'Institut International de Statistique, 1895.

[2] Houthakker, H. S.: Additive Preferences, *Econometrica*, 1960.

[3] Houthakker, H. S.: *Economic Policy for the Farm Sector*, Washington 1967.

[4] Johansen, L.: Rules of Thumb for the Expansion of Industries in a Process of Economic Growth, *Econometrica*, 1960.

[5] Simon, H. A.: Effects of Increased Productivity upon the Ratio of Urban to Rural Population, *Econometrica*, 1947.

Modelling the Transition Probabilities of Intergenerational Occupational Mobility

Henri Theil

Recently, De Wolff and Van Slijpe [10] analyzed the relation between social background and certain economic and other non-economic variables. In this note, which is based on work which I am presently doing with Mr. Robert Stambaugh in Chicago, I want to report on the related problem of the relationship between social backgrounds in successive generations. The procedure can be briefly outlined by means of data on seven occupational groups published by Glass and Hall [1]. These groups, which consist of occupations of successively lower social status, are the following:

1. Professional and high administrative
2. Managerial and executive
3. Inspectional, supervisors, and other non-manual (higher grade)
4. Same (lower grade)
5. Skilled manual and routine grades of non-manual
6. Semi-skilled manual
7. Unskilled manual

The first seven lines of Table 1 contain the number of father-son pairs observed by Glass and Hall. For example, the first column shows that there are 50 persons in the top group whose fathers were also in the top group, and 16 in the top group whose fathers were in the second group. The first seven entries in the last column are the row sums, i.e., the total numbers of fathers in the seven groups. By dividing each entry of a row by the corresponding row sum, we obtain (estimates of) the transition probabilities p_{ij}. Specifically, p_{ij} is the conditional probability that a person is in the jth group, given that his father was in the ith. If we assume that these probabilities are constant in successive generations, intergenerational occupational

Table 1

British Data on Seven Status Groups

Father's status group	Subject's status group 1	2	3	4	5	6	7	Row sum
				Numbers of observations				
1	50	19	26	8	18	6	2	129
2	16	40	34	18	31	8	3	150
3	12	35	65	66	123	23	21	345
4	11	20	58	110	223	64	32	518
5	14	36	114	185	714	258	189	1510
6	0	6	19	40	179	143	71	458
7	0	3	14	32	141	91	106	387
				Transition matrix				
1	.388	.147	.202	.062	.140	.047	.016	1
2	.107	.267	.227	.120	.207	.053	.020	1
3	.035	.101	.188	.191	.357	.067	.061	1
4	.021	.039	.112	.212	.431	.124	.062	1
5	.009	.024	.075	.123	.473	.171	.125	1
6	.000	.013	.041	.087	.391	.312	.155	1
7	.000	.008	.036	.083	.364	.235	.274	1
				Exchange matrix				
1	.0088	.0034	.0046	.0014	.0032	.0011	.0004	.0228
2	.0044	.0110	.0094	.0050	.0085	.0022	.0008	.0414
3	.0031	.0089	.0166	.0168	.0313	.0059	.0054	.0879
4	.0027	.0049	.0142	.0270	.0546	.0157	.0078	.1269
5	.0038	.0098	.0309	.0502	.1937	.0700	.0513	.4097
6	.0000	.0024	.0076	.0159	.0711	.0568	.0282	.1820
7	.0000	.0010	.0047	.0107	.0471	.0304	.0354	.1293
				Symmetrized exchange matrix				
1	.0088	.0039	.0038	.0021	.0035	.0005	.0002	.0228
2		.0110	.0091	.0049	.0092	.0023	.0009	.0414
3			.0166	.0155	.0311	.0067	.0050	.0879
4				.0270	.0524	.0158	.0093	.1269
5					.1937	.0706	.0492	.4097
6						.0568	.0293	.1820
7							.0354	.1293

mobility is a Markov process. My objective is to discuss a model for the transition probabilities (the p_{ij}'s) of this process. The observed p_{ij}'s are shown in Table 1 in the form of a transition matrix; they obviously satisfy $\Sigma_j \, p_{ij} = 1$, as indicated by the units in the last column.

The entries in the last column in the next seven rows, from .0228 to .1293, are the limit proportions $\pi_1, \ldots, \pi_7$ of the Markov chain model. These proportions constitute the occupational distribution that will be reached in the limit if each father has one son and if the Markov chain is allowed to do its work generation after generation. Given the definition of the transition probability p_{ij},

$$\pi_{ij} = \pi_i p_{ij} \tag{1}$$

is the probability of finding, in equilibrium, a father-son pair with the father in the ith group and the son in the jth. The matrix $[\pi_{ij}]$ is known as the exchange matrix of the Markov chain model and is shown in Table 1. Both the row and the column sums are equal to the limit proportions, since the occupational distributions of two successive generations are identical in equilibrium.

Notice that the exchange matrix is almost symmetric. When evaluating the degree of symmetry, the reader is advised to look particularly at the larger elements and to take into consideration that the number of decimal places shown is rather large, given the size of the samples (the entries in the last column and the first seven rows). If the exchange matrix is symmetric, $\pi_{ij} = \pi_{ji}$, the Markov chain is reversible in the sense that there exists, in equilibrium, a reverse Markov chain (a 'Vokram chain') which describes the occupations of persons in terms of those of their sons with the same transition matrix. This is further pursued in the last seven rows of Table 1, where the observed exchange matrix is symmetrized by substituting $\frac{1}{2}(\pi_{ij} + \pi_{ji})$ for π_{ij}. Evidently, the approximation to the observed exchange matrix is close.

This symmetry property is not confined to British data. Danish data from Svalastoga [6] and two sets of American data from Rogoff [5] also yield exchange matrices that are close to symmetry. I used this property in ([9], Chapter 5) to model the transition probabilities of intergenerational occupational mobility by means of distances between status groups, based on mean first passage times. But it can be done in a more direct way, as the account which follows will show. Consider the leading element .0088 of the symmetrized exchange matrix in Table 1. This element may be viewed as the probability (in equilibrium) that both the father and the son belong to the top $100\pi_1 = 2.28$ percent of society. Similarly, .0088 + + .0039 is the probability that the father belongs to the top 2.28 percent and the son to the top 2.28 + 4.14 percent. Note that this interpretation is equivalent to the introduction to a status variable for the father as well as the son. Instead of using the seven groups described in the first paragraph, we measure status as a variable which is continuous from the top of society to the bottom.

This approach has several advantages. First, the number of status groups and the cut-off points between the groups tend to be arbitrary. This problem is avoided by the continuous approach. Second, in the distance model referred to in the previous paragraph, it appears that reducing the number of status groups by combining pairs of adjacent groups reduces the average distance between groups. When we use six status groups rather than the seven of Table 1, which can be done in six different ways by combining adjacent groups, there is a distance reduction in each case and the average reduction is about 10 percent. When we use five status groups rather than seven, the average distance reduction is about 20 percent. Given these results, an obvious solution is to avoid this aggregation problem by replacing the seven status groups by a continuous status variable.

We consider the Markov chain in equilibrium and write X for the status of the father and Y for that of his son, both of which are random variables. We write $f(x, y)$ for the density function of (X, Y) and note that the two marginal distributions must be identical because the system is in equilibrium by assumption. The condition for a reversible Markov chain is

$$f(x, y) \equiv f(y, x). \tag{2}$$

One possible specification of the bivariate status distribution is the bivariate normal distribution. Svalastoga [7, 8] postulated such a distribution and estimated status correlations for successive generations, but he made no attempt to verify to what extent this distribution fits the data. His discussion is in terms of a bivariate lognormal status distribution, but what he actually did is equivalent to using a bivariate normal distribution. Since we here apply such a distribution to the equilibrium situation, the two means of this distribution must be equal, and the two variances also, because the marginal distributions are identical. Without loss of generality we can equate the means to zero, so that this zero represents 'median status', with 50 percent of the population of higher status and another 50 percent of lower status. The variances determine the scale of the status distribution and can be put equal to 1 without loss of generality. So we can write the bivariate normal status distribution in the form

$$f(x, y) = \frac{1}{2\pi\sqrt{1-\rho^2}} \exp\left\{-\tfrac{1}{2}\,\frac{x^2 + y^2 - 2\rho xy}{1-\rho^2}\right\} \tag{3}$$

which satisfies (2). We conclude that ρ, the correlation coefficient of the father's status and that of his son, is the single parameter which determines the mobility process.

The implementation of (3) is a matter of using a table of the bivariate normal distribution. Since the marginal distributions associated with (3) are standardized normal, the limit proportion .0228 of the first group (see the last column of Table 1) implies that, if a person is part of this group, his status exceeds 2.00. Hence the bivariate normal distribution implies that π_{11}, the probability that the father and the son are both in the first group, is equal to $P[X > 2,\ Y > 2]$, which depends on ρ as (3) shows. Proceeding in this way, we can find the bivariate normal approximation of the exchange matrix in Table 1 for any given ρ. It appears that the normal approximation is unsatisfactory for any ρ.

But there are other bivariate distributions besides the normal. In fact, it is not even necessary to specify the form of the distribution completely; it is sufficient to express the cumulated bivariate distribution in terms of the cumulated marginal distributions. Specifically, let p be the value of the cumulated marginal status distribution of the father, measured from the bottom of society, so that $p = .1293$ means that the father belongs to the lowest of the seven groups and $p = .1293 + .1820$ that the father belongs to either of the two lowest groups (see the last column of Table 1). Similarly, let q be the value of the cumulated marginal status distribution of the son, also measured from the bottom of society, and $H(p, q)$ the value of the cumulated joint status distribution of father and son. Consider then the model

$$-\log H(p, q) = [(-\log p)^m + (-\log q)^m]^{1/m} \tag{4}$$

where $m \geq 1$.

The model (4) describes the joint status distribution in terms of the two marginal distributions. If $m = 1$, the right-hand side of (4) is the sum of $-\log p$ and $-\log q$, so that $H(p, q) = pq$, which is the case of stochastic independence of the father's status and that of his son. (This is usually referred to as 'perfect social mobility' in the sociological literature.) If m increases beyond bounds, the right-hand side of (4) converges to the larger of $-\log p$ and $-\log q$, which means that the bivariate status distribution degenerates in such a way that the son's status equals that of his father with unit probability. This limit evidently corresponds to a perfect caste system.

Note that the model (4) does not specify the dependence of the cumulated marginal status distributions p and q on the values taken by the status variable. Gumbel [2]

Table 2

The Observed and the Adjusted Exchange Matrices

Father's status group	Subject's status group 1	2	3	4	5	6	7
			Observed exchange matrix				
1	.0088	.0034	.0046	.0014	.0032	.0011	.0004
2	.0044	.0110	.0094	.0050	.0085	.0022	.0008
3	.0031	.0089	.0166	.0168	.0313	.0059	.0054
4	.0027	.0049	.0142	.0270	.0546	.0157	.0078
5	.0038	.0098	.0309	.0502	.1937	.0700	.0513
6	.0000	.0024	.0076	.0159	.0711	.0568	.0282
7	.0000	.0010	.0047	.0107	.0471	.0304	.0354
			Adjusted exchange matrix				
1	.0090	.0047	.0034	.0021	.0027	.0006	.0003
2	.0047	.0081	.0093	.0067	.0093	.0021	.0010
3	.0034	.0093	.0177	.0176	.0292	.0071	.0035
4	.0021	.0067	.0176	.0243	.0537	.0149	.0076
5	.0027	.0093	.0292	.0537	.1918	.0772	.0458
6	.0006	.0021	.0071	.0149	.0772	.0454	.0347
7	.0003	.0010	.0035	.0076	.0458	.0347	.0365

considered (4) for the case in which p and q are logistic distributions, and Gumbel and Mustafi [3] did this for the case in which p and q follow the first asymptotic distribution of the largest values. (See also Mardia [4], p. 78.) However, for our purpose it is sufficient to apply (4) in its present form. In fact, (4) has a straightforward interpretation in terms of information theory, where information is defined as minus the logarithm of a probability. Both the left-hand side of (4) and $-\log p$ and $-\log q$ on the right are minus the logarithm of a probability. Hence (4) may be interpreted in the sense that the joint status information is a generalized sum of the status information of the father and that of his son.

Table 2 contains the observed exchange matrix, reproduced from Table 1, as well as the exchange matrix based on (4) for $m = 1.44$. Table 3 contains the observed transition matrix, also reproduced from Table 1, and the transition matrix which is implied by the adjusted exchange matrix of Table 2; its computation is a matter of dividing the elements of each row of the exchange matrix by the corresponding row sum. Given that only one parameter (m) is adjusted, the fit can be considered reasonably close. The most modest view of the model (4) is that of a naive model

Table 3

The Observed and the Adjusted Transition Matrices

Father's status group	Subject's status group 1	2	3	4	5	6	7
			Observed transition matrix				
1	.388	.147	.202	.062	.140	.047	.016
2	.107	.267	.227	.120	.207	.053	.020
3	.035	.101	.188	.191	.357	.067	.061
4	.021	.039	.112	.212	.431	.124	.062
5	.009	.024	.075	.123	.473	.171	.125
6	.000	.013	.041	.087	.391	.312	.155
7	.000	.008	.036	.083	.364	.235	.274
			Adjusted transition matrix				
1	.393	.208	.151	.091	.118	.026	.013
2	.115	.196	.226	.162	.225	.051	.025
3	.039	.106	.202	.200	.332	.081	.040
4	.016	.053	.139	.192	.423	.118	.060
5	.007	.023	.071	.131	.468	.188	.112
6	.003	.012	.039	.082	.424	.249	.191
7	.002	.008	.027	.058	.354	.268	.282

for transition probabilities of occupational mobility, the fit of which should be exceeded by more sophisticated models. If we adopt the less modest view that (4) is at least approximately correct, we can use it to obtain better estimates of the transition probabilities. For example, the transition probability $p_{17} = .016$ in the first line of Table 3 is obtained as the ratio 2/129 of the relevant entries in the first line of Table 1. There is no need to explain that this ratio is subject to substantial sampling fluctuations. By contrast, the estimate .013 of p_{17} in the lower half of Table 3 is obtained from (4) and all (almost 3500) observations, so that this estimate must be considered more trustworthy if (4) is at least substantially correct.

References

[1] Glass, D. V., and J. R. Hall: Social Mobility in Great Britain: a Study of Inter-Generation Changes in Status. In: *Social Mobility in Britain*, ed. by D. V. Glass, Glencoe 1954.

[2] Gumbel, E. J.: Bivariate Logistic Distributions, *Journal of the American Statistical Association*, 1961.

[3] Gumbel, E. J., and C. K. Mustafi: Some Analytical Properties of Bivariate Extremal Distributions, *Journal of the American Statistical Association*, 1967.

[4] Mardia, K. V.: *Families of Bivariate Distributions*, Darien 1970.
[5] Rogoff, N.: *Recent Trends in Occupational Mobility*, Glencoe 1953.
[6] Svalastoga, K.: *Prestige, Class and Mobility*, London 1959.
[7] Svalastoga, K.: Gedanken zu internationalen Vergleichen sozialer Mobilität. In: *Soziale Schichtung und soziale Mobilität*, ed. by D. V. Glas and R. König. Sonderheft 5 der Kölner Zeitschrift für Soziologie und Sozialpsychologie, Köln 1961.
[8] Svalastoga, K.: Social Mobility: the Western European Model, *Acta Sociologica*, 1965.
[9] Theil, H.: *Statistical Decomposition Analysis with Applications in the Social and Administrative Sciences*, Amsterdam 1972.
[10] De Wolff, P., and A. R. D. van Slijpe: The Relation between Income, Intelligence, Education and Social Background, *European Economic Review*, 1972.

The Effect of Income Redistribution on Consumer Demand

J. S. Cramer

Introduction

Pieter de Wolff was probably one of the first econometricians to recognize that aggregation is a problem. He did so in a characteristically brief note in the Economic Journal of 1941 that deals with the relation between the micro-economic and the macro-economic income elasticity of demand. The former refers to individual households, and the latter to aggregates; to pass from the one to the other one must know what shifts and changes of the income distribution are involved in the movement of aggregate income. In De Wolff's own words, 'in the general case the definition [of the macro-economic income elasticity] refers to a special type of variations of the [income] distribution function, and this type must be carefully specified' ([7], p. 144).

In the present paper we take up the same theme in an attempt to unravel the demand effects of shifts and of changes of shape of the income distribution. In particular we wish to assess the effect of income redistribution on 1. aggregate demand for specific commodities and 2. ownership rates of durable goods. We shall compare this effect to such common characteristics as the traditional income elasticity of aggregate demand – soon to be defined! – or the incidence of durable ownership.

This limited exercise calls for the aggregation of micro-economic relations over the income distribution, and a brief discussion of this wider problem will indicate how we approach the matter.

The micro-economic relations concerned refer to individual households and relate some characteristic of their consumer behaviour c to their income y, while they all face the same supply conditions and prices. We call these relations Engel functions, waiving the usual restriction of this term to relations that have been estimated from budget survey data, and denote them as

$$c = g(y) \tag{1}$$

The variable c will stand for expenditure on a particular commodity or – on a (0,1) scale – for the ownership of a particular durable. These Engel functions are a poor description of household demand since all its determinants other than income, such as household composition, are ignored. The fact that we consider changes in income alone, with everything else constant, is no adequate excuse for this neglect.

Engel functions in the traditional sense of the term can usually be estimated with fair accuracy, and the question then arises what a given micro-economic relation implies for the reaction of aggregate demand to changes in aggregate income. Although there is a strong temptation to establish macro-economic income elasticities by analogy, the correct answer is that the variation of demand will depend on the initial income distribution and on the exact nature of the changes in this distribution that accompany a change in aggregate income. For aggregate demand per household $\bar{c}$ is given by

$$\bar{c} = \int_0^\infty g(y)f(y)dy \tag{2}$$

where $f(y)$ represents the income distribution; and only a further examination of this expression will show how $\bar{c}$ responds to various presupposed changes in $f(y)$. We can then work out the elasticity of demand in respect of an increase of the income level as well as the effect of a redistribution of income, provided that a precise definition is given of either phenomenon.

A simple but tedious way to obtain these results would be to use a computer to simulate $\bar{c}$ for various income distributions; another possibility is to derive an explicit expression for $\bar{c}$ by matching specific Engel functions to specific income distributions, and then to examine their properties. We have opted for the latter, old-fashioned approach, but we shall not present the systematic exploration of pairs of particular specifications of $g(y)$ en $f(y)$ for which it calls. Only a few results of these algebraic exercises will be needed. Our main purpose is to provide practical if coarse evaluations of the effects of redistribution, and to this end we have selected easy Engel functions and restricted the discussion to a single form of income redistribution.

Within these limitations we present approximative numerical illustration that are relevant to present-day Dutch conditions. The emphasis is throughout on applications rather than on theoretical results, and most of the theorems that we shall use are common knowledge.

Three Income Elasticities of Demand

Since we wish to distinguish changes in the aggregate income level from changes in the distribution of income we should first define either phenomenon more precisely in terms of $f(y)$. This function describes the income distribution; a frequency function would be in order, but we shall regard it as the density function of a random variable y. One may think of y as the income of a household taken at random. We may then use the apparatus of statistical distributions in dealing with the income distribution, and characterize the latter by its moments instead of by specially designed measures of inequality.

In this approach aggregate income per household or the arithmetical mean of household income is

$$\mu_a = E(y) \tag{3}$$

and the variance of incomes

$$\sigma_a^2 = D^2(y) \tag{4}$$

We shall also consider $z = \log y$ and define

$$\tilde{\mu} = E(z), \tag{5}$$

$$\tilde{\sigma}^2 = D^2(z). \tag{6}$$

We use natural logarithms throughout.

Most of the functions $f(y)$ that have been put forward as an approximate description of the income distribution are determined by two parameters, and they are equally well characterized by any two of the four moments that we have just defined. We shall use μ_a and $\tilde{\sigma}$ for this purpose. The choice of this ill-assorted pair is prompted by our definition of income redistribution.

To begin with we identify a change in the income level without distributional effects with an equiproportionate change of all incomes. In terms of the moments that we have introduced this corresponds to an increase in μ_a while $\tilde{\sigma}$ remains constant. This definition is in keeping with the traditional view that income differentials are a relative rather than an absolute concept, so that it is an equal percentage rise rather than a flat sum increase of all incomes that leaves the degree of income inequality unchanged. Some authors regard invariance under equiproportionate income changes as a prerequisite of measures of inequality (see [4], p. 149). In recent years this view has been challenged by critics who opt for constant absolute differentials, and it must be conceded that this is a matter of choice, as is any definition of what constitutes a change in income levels that has no distributional effects.

The natural concomitant of this definition is to identify the redistribution of income with a change in $\tilde{\sigma}$. Since the total income that is being redistributed is given, μ_a must remain constant.

The further course of this paper is now clear. We describe the income distribution by μ_a and $\tilde{\sigma}$, and rewrite (2) as

$$\bar{c} = E\{g(y)\} = \int_0^\infty g(y) \cdot f(y \mid \mu_a, \tilde{\sigma}) \cdot dy \tag{7}$$

For certain specified distribution functions $f(y)$ and some easy Engel functions $g(y)$ this leads to an explicit expression of the form

$$\bar{c} = \bar{c}(\mu_a, \tilde{\sigma}) \tag{8}$$

We may then consider the macro-economic *income elasticity of demand*, defined as

$$\eta = \frac{\partial \log \bar{c}}{\partial \log \mu_a}, \tag{9}$$

as well as a *redistribution elasticity of demand*,

$$s = -\frac{\partial \log \bar{c}}{\partial \tilde{\sigma}}. \tag{10}$$

Note that we have here reversed the sign since income redistribution towards greater equality, or a smaller variance, is nowadays usually considered as likely (or as desirable) as a further rise of the income level.
We shall take a particular interest in the ratio of these two elasticities since we wish to compare the demand effect of a likely degree of redistribution to that of the customary increase in the income level. The latter is readily identified as an annual rise of say 2 to 3% of per capita real disposable household income, but the former is hard to define. What annual reduction of $\tilde{\sigma}$ would mean that there is a marked yet feasible trend towards greater income equality? Even the present level of $\tilde{\sigma}$ is hard to establish, since it refers to disposable household income whereas the available statistical tables invariably present tabulations of tax returns by gross taxable income. Very little is known about the actual distribution of household income among the lower income groups. If we put the present value of $\tilde{\sigma}$ at .5, this is nothing more than a fair guess.
With $\tilde{\sigma}$ at .5 and a (log)normal distribution of incomes, the distance from a 'poverty line' delimiting the lower 2.5% and an 'affluence line' exceeded by the upper 2.5% of all incomes equals 1.96 natural logarithms, which corresponds to a ratio spread of 1 to 7. If $\tilde{\sigma}$ were to decline by .01 per annum this ratio would be reduced to 1 to 5 in ten years' time, and to 1 to 3 in twenty-five years. This represents a substantial rate of redistribution that is about four times as high as the long-term trend towards greater equality of the last decades. It has been shown by Tinbergen ([6], p. 19) that the latter leads to a decline of various measures of inequality by about one half of a percent per annum. If we take these measures as linear in $\tilde{\sigma}$, with $\tilde{\sigma}$ at .5, this works out at a reduction by .0025 each year.

These considerations lead us to identify substantial redistribution of incomes with a decline of $\tilde{\sigma}$ by .01 per annum. By (9) and (10) its effects on demand are the same as those of an annual increase in real disposable income by s/η percent.
The empirical generalizations put forward above also lead us to introduce yet a third elasticity of demand, viz. the *historical income elasticity of demand.* This is the apparent income elasticity that is obtained from an analysis of time-series data over the last two decades or so. It is a hybrid, since in fact a steady increase in the income level has been accompanied by a small but persistent move towards greater equality; yet as a rule these distributional changes are ignored in estimating the income elasticity. For the Netherlands we can put the annual increase in per capita real disposable income over the last decades at 2.5%; the trendlike reduction in $\tilde{\sigma}$ has just been set at .0025 each year. If these values are regarded as typical, the estimated historical income elasticity will be approximatively equal to

$$\eta^* = \eta + 0.1s = \eta(1 + 0.1\, s/\eta) \tag{11}$$

In practice, however, we shall find that the ratio of s to η is already quite small so that the discrepancy between η^* and η is negligible.

Two Simple Engel Functions

For current consumer expenditure on non-durable goods we shall consider two extremely simple Engel functions. The first is the semi-logarithmic function that is usually considered appropriate for necessities with typical income elasticities not far exceeding unity, viz.

$$c_1 = \gamma + \beta \log y. \tag{12}$$

It immediately follows that

$$\bar{c}_1 = \gamma + \beta\tilde{\mu}. \tag{13}$$

The second is the iso-elastic Engel function, or

$$c_2 = \delta y^\eta \tag{14}$$

with

$$c_2 = \delta \cdot E(y^\eta). \tag{15}$$

This is again applicable to commodities that are currently consumed but with somewhat higher income elasticities of, say, between 1 and 2. In the case of an iso-elastic Engel function the micro-economic and macro-economic income elasticities are equal, whatever the form of the income distribution. We anticipate this result in the use of η in (14) and (15).

The Lognormal Income Distribution

In order to establish the elasticities (9) and (10) for $\bar{c}_1$ and $\bar{c}_2$ we must express $\tilde{\mu}$ and $E(y^\eta)$ in terms of μ_a and $\tilde{\sigma}$. At first sight we might obtain these expressions quite generally by writing

$$y^{\eta} = e^{\eta z} = e^{\eta\mu} \cdot e^{\eta(z-\mu)}$$

$$= e^{\eta\mu}\left\{1 + \frac{1}{2!}\eta^2(z - \tilde{\mu})^2 + \frac{1}{3!}\eta^3(z - \tilde{\mu})^3 + \ldots\right\} \tag{16}$$

so that

$$E(y^{\eta}) = e^{\eta\mu}\{1 + \tfrac{1}{2} \cdot \eta^2 \cdot \tilde{\sigma}^2 + \tfrac{1}{6}\eta^3 E(z - \tilde{\mu})^3 + \ldots\}. \tag{17}$$

For $\eta = 1$, this will yield μ_a. The higher order central moments of z that occur in (17) are, however, awkward since nothing has been assumed about their behaviour in the definitions of η and s; although it is clear that they will remain constant in the case of the equiproportional income change to which η refers, we simply have not specified the redistribution case in such detail, and whether they are constant or not will depend on the specific density function $f(y)$ assumed. A simple solution is to assume a *lognormal income distribution*, which is often used as a convenient approximation to the actual income distribution. Equ. (17) is then replaced by the expression

$$E(y^{\eta}) = e^{\eta\mu + \frac{1}{2}\eta^2\sigma^2} \tag{18}$$

from which all the higher-order central moments have vanished. For this and other properties of the lognormal distribution see [2].

For $\eta = 1$ this yields

$$\mu_a = e^{\mu + \frac{1}{2}\sigma^2} \tag{19}$$

so that

$$\tilde{\mu} = \log \mu_a - \tfrac{1}{2}\tilde{\sigma}^2 \tag{20}$$

and—upon substitution in (18)—

$$E(y^{\eta}) = \mu_a^{\eta} \cdot e^{\frac{1}{2}\sigma^2(\eta^2 - \eta)} \tag{21}$$

The rest is easy. Substitution of (20) into (13) and of (21) into (15) yields

$$\bar{c}_1 = \gamma + \beta \log \mu_a - \tfrac{1}{2}\beta\tilde{\sigma}^2 \tag{22}$$

and

$$\log \bar{c}_2 = \log \delta + \eta \log \mu_a + \tfrac{1}{2}\eta(\eta - 1)\tilde{\sigma}^2, \tag{23}$$

for the semilog and iso-elastic Engel functions respectively. The elasticities (9) and (10) are then found to be

$$\eta_1 = \frac{\beta}{c}, \qquad s_1 = \frac{\beta}{c_1} \cdot \tilde{\sigma} = \eta_1 \cdot \tilde{\sigma}, \tag{24}$$

and

$$\eta_2 = \eta, \quad s_2 = \eta(1 - \eta)\tilde{\sigma}. \tag{25}$$

The ratio of s to η follows immediately. In the case of a semilog Engel curve it is equal to $\tilde{\sigma}$, or .5, so that the rather drastic redistribution we have envisaged in section 2 has the same effect on demand as an increase of the income level by .5 percent per annum. For iso-elastic Engel functions, the redistribution effect is equivalent to a rise in incomes of .5 $(1 - \eta)$ percent, so that its absolute size will usually be even smaller; moreover it is negative for luxuries, and positive for necessities.

The Gamma Income Distribution

We have also considered alternatives for the lognormal function as a description of the income distribution. The Pareto distribution is as attractive as ever by its neat mathematical properties, but it is inappropriate for present purposes. The density function decreases monotonically towards the right, and it therefore aplies to a part of the income distribution well beyond the modal income only. Income redistribution outside this range cannot be studied with this function, and income redistribution within the upper part of the income range is of limited interest.

Another alternative is the gamma distribution, recently put forward by Salem and Mount [5] who claim that it constitutes a significant improvement over the lognormal as a description of U.S. income distributions. The density function is

$$f(y) = \frac{\lambda^\alpha}{\Gamma(\alpha)} \cdot y^\alpha e^{-\lambda y} \tag{26}$$

and we have

$$\mu_a = E(y) = \alpha/\lambda, \tag{27}$$

$$\sigma_a^2 = D^2(y) = \alpha/\lambda^2, \tag{28}$$

$$\tilde{\mu} = E(\log y) = \frac{\partial \log \Gamma(\alpha)}{\partial \alpha} - \log \lambda, \tag{29}$$

$$\tilde{\sigma}^2 = D^2(\log y) = \frac{\partial^2 \log \Gamma(\alpha)}{\Gamma \alpha^2}. \tag{30}$$

Another result that we need is

$$E(y^\eta) = \lambda^{-\eta} \cdot \frac{\Gamma(\alpha + \eta)}{\Gamma(\alpha)}. \tag{31}$$

The successive derivatives of log Γ are known as the polygamma functions or psi functions. We adopt the latter notations and write

$$\psi(\alpha) = \frac{d \log \Gamma(\alpha)}{d\alpha} \tag{32}$$

and hence

$$\tilde{\mu} = \psi(\alpha) - \log \lambda, \tag{33}$$

$$\tilde{\sigma}^2 = \psi'(\alpha). \tag{34}$$

Aggregate consumption for the two Engel functions considered is now derived by substituting (33) into (13) and (31) into (15). We next substitute

$$\log \lambda = \log \alpha - \log \mu_a, \tag{35}$$

which follows from (27), and obtain

$$\bar{c}_1 = \gamma + \beta \cdot \psi(\alpha) - \beta \log \alpha + \beta \log \mu_a, \tag{36}$$

$$\log \bar{c}_2 = \log \delta + \eta \log \mu_a - \eta \log \alpha + \log \Gamma(\alpha + \eta) - \log \Gamma(\alpha). \tag{37}$$

In deriving the elasticities we use the fact that by (30) $\tilde{\sigma}$ is a function of α alone. Constant $\tilde{\sigma}$ is therefore equivalent to constant α, and the income elasticities defined in (9) follow at once as

$$\eta_1 = \beta/\bar{c}_1, \quad \eta_2 = \eta. \tag{38}$$

For the redistribution elasticity (10) we write

$$s = -\frac{\partial \log c}{\partial \tilde{\sigma}} = -\frac{\partial \log c}{\partial \alpha} \cdot \frac{d\alpha}{d\tilde{\sigma}} \tag{39}$$

and substitute, from (30),

$$\frac{d\alpha}{d\tilde{\sigma}} = 2\tilde{\sigma}\left[\frac{d\tilde{\sigma}^2}{d\alpha}\right]^{-1} = \frac{2\tilde{\sigma}}{\psi''(\alpha)}. \tag{40}$$

This yields

$$s_1 = \frac{\beta}{\bar{c}_1} \cdot \left\{\frac{1}{\alpha} - \psi'(\alpha)\right\} \cdot \frac{2\tilde{\sigma}^2}{\psi''(\alpha)} \tag{41}$$

and

$$s_2 = \left\{\frac{\eta}{\alpha} + \psi(\alpha) - \psi(\alpha + \eta)\right\} \cdot \frac{2\tilde{\sigma}^2}{\psi''(\alpha)} \tag{42}$$

These expressions are not easily evaluated, the less so since standard tabulations of the psi functions like [1] do not cover the values of α that correspond to the selected value of .5 for $\tilde{\sigma}$. A special tabulation of the elasticity ratio s/η has therefore been prepared. It is shown in table 1. I am very much indebted to Mr. J. Kiviet for programming and performing these computations.

Table 1

Elasticity Ratio s/η for Gamma Income Distribution

Value of a	Value of σ	Semi-log case, s_1/η_1	Constant elasticity case, s_2/η_2, by value of η_2: .8	1.0	1.2	1.6	2.0
4.9	.476	.42	.07	0	—.07	—.20	—.32
4.5	.499	.43	.08	0	—.07	—.21	—.33
4.1	.525	.45	.08	0	—.07	—.21	—.33
3.8	.548	.46	.08	0	—.07	—.21	—.34

The first two columns indicate various values of α and the corresponding value of $\tilde{\sigma}$—from (30)—around the selected value of .5 for the latter. The third column shows the elasticity ratio for the semilogarithmic Engel function. As can be seen from (38) and (41) this depends on α only. As it turns out the ratio is even somewhat lower than the value of .5 that was found to hold good in the case of a lognormal income distribution. If we consider constant elasticity Engel functions, the ratio depends on η as well as on α (or $\tilde{\sigma}$), and we therefore give its value for various income elasticities ranging from .8 to 2. As before we find quite small values, which change sign as we pass from necessities to luxuries.

A Conclusion for Non-Durables

So far we have considered the effect of income redistribution on the demand for non-durable goods for current consumption by examining two Engel functions and two income distribution functions. To facilitate comparisons this effect is expressed by an elasticity ratio; by the argument of section 2, this indicates an annual percentage increase in real income that in terms of demand effect is equivalent to a reasonable yet substantial rate of income redistribution. The results of section 3 and 4 are set out together in table 2.

Table 2

Summary of Results: Elasticity Ratios s/η

Income distribution	Semi-log Engel function	Constant elasticity Engel function, *by* value of η		
		.8	1	1.6
lognormal	+.50	+.10	0	—.30
gamma	+.44	+.88	0	—.21

Within the limits of this exercise, the outcome is quite clearly that the demand effects of income redistribution are almost negligible.

The Case of Durable Ownership

Apart from the two Engel functions of section 3 there is a third case we wish to consider, namely the case of a (0,1) variable like durable ownership that tends to a definite upper limit as income increases indefinitely. The point is once more that there are some limited advantages in using certain results from mathematical statistics, but that we can only solve the problem if certain specific assumptions are made.

In the case we have in mind the household demand variable c refers to an *attribute* like the ownership of a particular durable or a habit as, e.g., 'taking holidays abroad'. The demand variable is therefore restricted to the values 0 and 1, and it follows that the influence of income on the individual household values cannot be represented by a deterministic function $g(y)$ as before. The common procedure is of course to consider relative frequencies of $c = 1$ at various income levels, or – what comes to the same thing – to treat the individual value of c for any single household as a random variable with a bivariate distribution

$$P(c = 1 \mid y) = g(y), \quad P(c = 0 \mid y) = 1 - g(y). \tag{43}$$

A close analogue to (1) is established by writing

$$c = E(c \mid y) = g(y). \tag{44}$$

We now consider the particular (but fairly common) case in which demand for this attribute does not show saturation at finite incomes, so that $g(y)$ increases monotonically with income and asymptotically approaches a saturation level k as y increases beyond all limits. For common attributes – like car ownership – k can safely be put at 1, but in special cases like the ownership of musical instruments a lower value is in order. The upshot of these restrictions is that $g(y)/k$ increase monotonically from 0 to 1 as y increases indefinitely, so that it has the usual properties of a distribution function. We bring this out by writing from now on

$$g(y) = k \cdot H(y) \tag{45}$$

Upon returning to equ. (2) we now obtain the expression

$$c = k \int_0^\infty H(y) f(y) dy \tag{46}$$

We integrate over positive y only, as in equ. (2); but as long as $f(y) = 0$ for $y < 0$ this involves no restriction on H. The interest of this expression is that one may find a transformation $x = x(y)$ such that upon its substitution (46) turns into the *convolution formula*

$$\int F_1(m - x)f_2(x)\mathrm{d}x = \int F_2(m - x)f_1(x)\mathrm{d}x = F_3(m), \tag{47}$$

in which F_1 and f_2 stand for the distribution function and density function of two independent random variables, and F_3 is the distribution function of their sum (see [3], p. 190). It is necessary to reverse the sign of the argument in either of the two functions involved; one way of handling this is to strive for a symmetrical transformed distribution, so that we have, say, $f_2(x) = f_2(-x)$.
Equ. (46) then is simplified to

$$\int F_1(+x)f_2(-x)\mathrm{d}x = F_3(0). \tag{48}$$

The practical application of this formula depends of course on the chance that it refers to two random variables that are readily summed in the case of independence so that F_3 is obtained at once. We have sketched its derivation to show how far we can go without loss of generality, but when it comes to examples the only one we can offer at present is once more the ubiquitous lognormal distribution.
In this case the income distribution is lognormal, and upon the transformation

$$x = \log y \tag{49}$$

we have

$$f(y)\mathrm{d}y = \mathrm{d}N(x; \tilde{\mu}, \tilde{\sigma}^2) \tag{50}$$

$$= \mathrm{d}N(-x; -\tilde{\mu}, \tilde{\sigma}^2)$$

where the right-hand side denotes the normal density function. We now specify the Engel function as a lognormal distribution function with parameters of its own, or

$$H(y) = N(x; \mu_2, \sigma_2^2) \tag{51}$$

When we substitute these two expressions into (48), and recall that the normal distribution is reproducible, we obtain for (46)

$$\bar{c} = k \cdot N[0; (\mu_2 - \tilde{\mu}), (\tilde{\sigma}^2 + \sigma_2^2)] = k \cdot N(t; 0, 1) \tag{52}$$

with

$$t = \frac{\tilde{\mu} - \mu_2}{\sqrt{\tilde{\sigma}^2 + \sigma_2^2}}. \tag{53}$$

It remains to evaluate the elasticities connected with this expression. Omitting the parameters of the standard normal distribution we rewrite (52) as

$$\bar{c}/k = N(t), \tag{54}$$

and obtain – using equ (20) –

$$\eta = N'(t)/N(t) \tag{55}$$

and

$$s = N'(t)/N(t) \cdot \tilde{\sigma} \cdot \left\{ \frac{t + \sqrt{\tilde{\sigma}^2 + \sigma_2^2}}{\tilde{\sigma}^2 + \sigma_2^2} \right\} \tag{56}$$

so that

$$s/\eta = \tilde{\sigma} \left\{ \frac{t + \sqrt{\tilde{\sigma}^2 + \sigma_2^2}}{\tilde{\sigma}^2 + \sigma_2^2} \right\} \tag{57}$$

By (54) t is a function of $\bar{c}/k$; $\tilde{\sigma}$ has been put at .5; σ_2 is usually found to range between, say, .6 and 1. We may therefore evaluate equ (57) as a function of $\bar{c}/k$ for these two limiting values of σ_2. The result is shown in figure 1.

Since the income elasticity is always positive the curves of figure 1 imply that the redistribution elasticity itself changes sign at values of $\bar{c}/k$ well below one half. Inspection of (56) confirms that the change of sign occurs at $t = -\sqrt{\tilde{\sigma}^2 + \sigma_2^2}$, so that – at the usual values of $\tilde{\sigma}$ and σ_2 – the redistribution effect is negative only for attributes with an effective overall penetration rate $\bar{c}/k$ of, say, 20% or even less. It might be thought that the change in sign occurs at the same point where the income elasticity in its monotonic decline towards zero equals unity. This, however, is not the case; the value of t just indicated corresponds to income elasticities of 1.61 and 1.37 for σ_2 at 1 and .6 respectively. Once the critical penetration rate

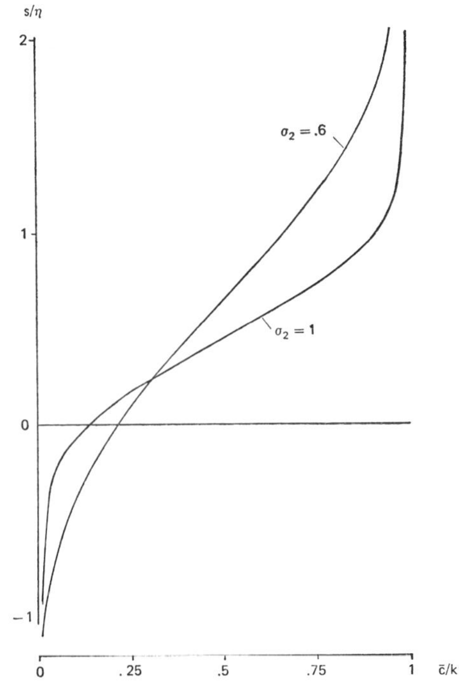

Figure 1. Lognormal Ownership Function — the elasticity ratio s/η as a function of the effective penetration rate $\bar{c}/K$.

of about 20% has been passed, redistribution has a positive effect on demand. Thus under present conditions any redistribution of income would lead to an increase in the number of one-car households but reduce the number of two-car households.

The second conclusion from figure 1 is that the effect of redistribution is of limited scope. The elasticity ratio rarely exceeds 2 in absolute size, so that the degree of redistribution we have introduced above is equivalent to an annual change in the income level of plus or minus 2 percent at most. This value may be exceeded at either extreme of the penetration rate $\bar{c}/k$, but if this is close to 1 the income elasticity itself is quite small so that the redistribution effect is still moderate even though the elasticity ratio increases steeply. The only case in which a sizeable effect of income redistribution can be expected is that of extreme luxuries that are as yet owned by only a tiny minority. They will virtually disappear.

References

[1] Abramowitz, M., and I. A. Stegun: *Handbook of Mathematical Functions*, New York 1965.

[2] Aitchison, J., and J. A. C. Brown: *The Lognormal Distribution*, Cambridge 1957.

[3] Cramèr, H.: *Mathematical Methods of Statistics*, Princeton 1945.

[4] Centraal Plan Bureau: *De personele inkomensverdeling, 1952—1967*, Den Haag 1975.

[5] Salem, A. B. Z., and T. O. Mount: A Convenient Descriptive Model of Income Distribution —the Gamma Density, *Econometrica*, 1974.

[6] Tinbergen, J.: *Income Distribution—Analysis and Policies*, Amsterdam 1975.

[7] de Wolff, P.: Income Elasticity of Demand, a Micro-Economic and a Macro-Economic Interpretation, *Economic Journal*, 1941.

On the Relative Strength of Sentiments and Intentions*

A cross-section study of Dutch data

A. Pais

Introduction

By now, the relevance of attitudinal variables to consumer behavior no longer constitutes a source of major controversy.[1] Time and again, the impact of variables such as attitudes, sentiments and intentions has been established. Still, at this stage at least two points are to be noted. For, although much econometric work has shown that 'psychological' variables – defined in one way or another – most often do contribute to the explanation of economic processes, the question has been asked if, after all, economists really need to incorporate these variables into their models.[2] Can't we do without them by reducing variables of this type to 'objective' ones? If attitudes, expectations and the like are generated via some stable mechanism by a number of objective variables – such as income or the rate of unemployment – it might be superfluous to go into the routine of regularly holding surveys in order to obtain attitudinal data about the respondents. Suitably constructed models, dealing with objective variables only, then would suffice in explaining consumer behavior. This would, furthermore, entail the additional benefit that no need would arise to saddle economists with psychological theory or to have them dabble in fields where their footing is less secure.

The well-known Index of Consumer Sentiment (ICS) has been cited as a case in point.[3] As a matter of fact, some indications point to the existence of a more or less stable relationship between objective variables and the ICS, at least for the United States during the post-war period up to 1970.[4] And so the position has been defended that this obviates the necessity of survey research aimed at gathering the sentiments, intentions etc. of the populace that are used in constructing this index.

But we feel that this position should not be generalized into a rejection of all surveying directed at finding out about consumer intentions and feelings. Several arguments may be advanced in this connection. For one thing, the question may be raised how stable over time a relationship between objective and subjective variables really is: extrapolation may be dangerous. For another, psychological variables may still yield a specific contribution to analysis, even if combined with objective variables that, to a certain extent, give rise to them. Furthermore (and apart from their usefulness as a means of procuring psychological data) surveys can quickly produce detailed data also on many objective variables. And finally, how could we get to micro-economic cross-section analysis without those surveys? So let them continue.

The last-mentioned argument in favour of consumer surveys brings us to the second point of contention, i.e. the level of aggregation at which psychological variables of one kind or another can be fruitfully used. Until now, macro-economic time-series analyses have carried the day. And much of the consensus that exists on the applicability of psychological variables pertains to the macro-level. Applications at the micro-level have been rather few and their results sometimes contradictory.

Tobin, for instance, investigated reinterview data from a 1952–53 survey sample of U.S. households in order to find out which role subjective variables play in explaining net expenditure on cars, appliances and furniture; change in personal non-mortgage debt; and change in liquid asset holdings. He reached the conclusion that 'the more diffuse attitudinal questions are strikingly less succesful as predictors than the buying intention questions . . . Buying intentions have predictive value; other attitudinal questions do not.' He leaves open, however, the possibility that 'other evidence, based on different survey data or different techniques of analysis, may point to different conclusions' [11].

Different outcomes have indeed been obtained at several occasions. As an example, which will serve us as a frame of reference throughout much of the following analysis, we may mention the study of U.S. reinterview data from the 1967–68 period by Dunkelberg [3]. Apart from the time periods, the material used by Tobin and Dunkelberg is in many ways similar. Both studies, e.g., have dealt with data collected under the program of Surveys of Consumer Finances, conducted by the Survey Research Center of the University of Michigan. Moreover, in both cases a one-year period has been analyzed: respondents have been reinterviewed twelve months later. So, it has been possible to establish to what extent sentiments, opinions and intentions, expressed at the start of the one-year period, have been relevant to actual behavior during the next twelve months.

Dunkelberg, however, states as one of the conclusions from his analysis that 'used jointly, both attitudes and intentions make significant contributions to the explanation of spending variations, both at the micro-level and in time-series equations." Buying intentions 'tend to be oriented toward a particular type of expenditure', while attitudes, on the other hand, 'are more diffuse in their orientation', which prompts to as broad a specification as possible of the dependent variable. For, if at all, attitudes can be expected to be relevant – primarily – to discretionary expenditure which may take many forms.

The attitudinal variables, used in the analyses, should not be specified too narrowly either. In the Gestalt-psychological view, prevalent in most Katona-inspired psychological economic studies, human attitudes are taken to be multi-faceted. For this reason, comprehensive indices of consumer sentiment are to be preferred as explanatory variables over single-faceted approaches to consumer sentiment. So, usually answers to several questions on consumer sentiment and expectations are condensed into an attitudinal index. We too shall adhere to this convention.

In this study a micro-economic investigation will be made into the predictory power of consumer attitudes and buying intentions with respect to spending on motor-cars in the Netherlands during 1974 and 1975. The choice of the dependent variable will be explained in the next section. There also, a description will be given of data and variables used in the analysis. In the section thereafter this analysis will be discussed.

Data and Variables

Since 1972 consumer surveys are being conducted on a regular basis in most member-countries of the European Community. This is a program initiated by and carried out under the auspices of the Community. Three times a year a representative sample of the househould population is interviewed. In addition to the usual demographic data, the respondents are being asked about expectations and realizations, both regarding the personal and the general economic situation. Furthermore, buying intentions are probed with respect to a number of consumer durables. As to motor-cars, these intentions are being asked referring to periods of 3 months and one year, respectively.

Each sample consists of two halves, which are being reinterviewed in a later survey. Denoting these moieties by A, B, C and D, the following scheme has prevailed for the May 1974 – May 1975 period. (The actual number of interviewees has been put between brackets).

May 1974	A (1775)	B (1827)		
October 1974			C (1784)	D (1919)
January 1975	A (1384)		C (1501)	
May 1975		B (1353)		D (1464)

We have investigated the survey groups B and C, which means that both a twelve and a three months period have been analyzed. It will be obvious that the total number of observations in the analysis is determined by the smaller of the two amounts referring to a certain survey group. So, the maximum number of cases in the 12-months analysis is 1353 and in the 3-months one 1501.

Actually, for a variety of reasons many more had to be dropped. As stated above, these surveys refer to the household population. The interviewee, however, may be any member of the household over 18 years of age. Although parental authority certainly is on the decline, we felt that still, in many respects, the head of the household and his/her spouse are the most influential ones when it comes to purchasing major household items. Therefore, all those interviewees other than husband or wife have been left out of account.

Then, there is the complication with reinterviewing that the respondent the first and the second time may not be the same person. Only those cases have been studied where the same person had been interviewed twice. (On this account 357 out of 1353 have been left out from the B-group; with the C this number has been 343).

For the detection of interaction effects we have made use of the AID-program (which we will come to in the next section). This entailed the necessity to leave out all those observations which were defective on one or more of the following aspects: age, occupation, education and income.

Two more groups have been deleted from the samples. In the first place those whose answers on the dependent variable (motor-car expenditure) were defective in one way or another. And then, because we have endeavoured to enhance as much as possible the comparability between our study and Dunkelberg's, people of sixty years of age and older have not been taken into account either. (No families whose household head exceeded sixty years in age were included in the Dunkelberg study). After all, this left us with 635 cases in the B-group and with 751 in the C-group.

We have already indicated that much is to be said in favour of a broadly defined dependent variable in assessing the predictive power of attitudinal factors. In the Dunkelberg study, e.g., total net outlay on cars, durables, additions and repairs to the house, vacations, and sports and hobby equipment (during 1967) figured as such. Our data, however, yield insufficient quantitative information in this respect. True, with respect to all articles for which buying intentions are gauged, a question is inserted from which may be deduced whether or not these goods have actually been bought in the preceding months, so that at the time of the reinterview intentions and realizations can be compared. But no information is gathered on the amounts spent, let alone on net outlay.

For motor-cars the picture is somewhat different. Respondents are not only asked if the car bought was a new one or second-hand, but also the price of the motor-car comes into the picture. The interviewee has to indicate in which of seven price classes his purchase is to be put. This, of course, yields no exact information on the amount spent.

To each of the seven classes we have assigned a central value:

price class (in guilders)	*central value*
– 4500	3036
4500 – 5500	5000
5500 – 6500	6000
6500 – 7500	7000
7500 – 9000	8250
9000 – 11000	10000
11000 and over	14100[5]

Furthermore, no direct information can be obtained from the surveys on the exchange of old cars for new ones, or the amounts involved. However that may be, when it comes to household outlay on durables, the data on gross motor-car expenditure constitute the only more or less specified value category. Therefore, in our regression analysis the amounts spent on cars (as indicated above and regardless of whether a new or a second-hand car was involved) have been taken as the dependent variable.

The explanatory variables fall into one of two classes: subjective or objective. The first category is constituted by sentiments and intentions. The U.S. ICS, as it is in use today, is constructed on the basis of answers to five questions regarding the evaluation of general and personal economic circumstances. These questions are nowadays also being asked in the Common Market surveys. (See appendix A). At the micro-level construction of this index has been to allot two points to each positive answer to a question, one point to 'no change'-answers (or the like, plus 'don't know'), whereas no points are given for a negative answer.

For each respondent, the points thus scored are added up and so yield the individual ICS-value. Thus, the interviewee may score from zero up to ten points on the ICS. As, however, one of the five sentiment questions was not yet included in the May 1974-questionnaire, the individual ICS for the 12-months analysis can only take on values from zero to eight. For the sake of comparability, the ICS for the 3-months period has thereupon also been based upon the same four questions.[6]

The change in this sentiment-index between the two interviews has been measured in a straightforward way by subtracting the value of the ICS at the first interview from the value at the second interview. This variable will be indicated by ΔICS. (Note that this variable relates to one year in the 12-months and to one quarter in the 3-months analysis).

With respect to buying intentions of motor-cars the answers to two questions have been included in our analyses. First there is the question whether the respondent plans to buy a car within three months. If he proclaims to be (reasonably) certain to do so, the corresponding variable (denoted by INT) takes on the value one; if not, the value zero. Secondly, there is the same question but with respect to one year. Here too, the corresponding variable (denoted by INT2) will get the value = 1 when the respondent answers to be (reasonably) sure of purchasing a car during that period, otherwise zero. (INT and INT2 will be alternatively used in the regression analysis referring to the three months period).

The objective variables to be identified at this stage are income, income change and age. Net disposable household income (Y) has not been asked directly but, again, the respondent was requested to indicate to which of seven income classes his/her household belongs. For each of these seven classes a central value has been computed:[7]

Y (in guilders)	*central value*
– 10,000	5,758
10,000 – 13,000	11,350
13,000 – 17,000	14,652
17,000 – 21,000	18,725
21,000 – 25,000	22,772
25,000 – 35,000	28,917
35,000 and over	52,850

The values for income change (ΔY) have been computed in the same way as ΔICS. In the interviews the age of the head of the household (variable denoted by AGE) is also taken down in classes. Under sixty, nine classes are distinguished, which we gave the following central values:

age	*central value*
under 20	18
20 – 24	22
25 – 29	27
30 – 34	32
35 – 39	37
40 – 44	42
45 – 49	47
50 – 54	52
55 – 59	57

Other variables will be defined as they are introduced into the analysis.

Regression

Next to the definition of the variables, the specification of the relationships between them is of paramount importance to the results. In [3] four rather obvious specifications yielded significant results. We have investigated whether similar outcomes can be derived for the Netherlands. Table 1 summarizes the results.

For the sake of comparison, column 5, taken from the Dunkelberg study, has been added. Measured by the value of the correlation coefficient, there too this equation is the most successful one. It should be recalled that the dependent variable in that investigation encompassed a wide variety of discretionary expenditures, whereas the ICS-variables were based upon five sentiment questions. Still, apart from the ΔICS-variable, the patterns emerging from columns 4 and 5 do not differ too much.

Equation 1 indicates the extent to which the objective income variables contributed to the prediction of gross motor-car expenditure. Both income and income change are positively – and significantly – correlated with the dependent variable. The signs are right. Furthermore, it is to be noted that the order of magnitude (and significance) of the coefficients hardly changes over the various specifications of the explanatory equations.

Equation 2 shows that the addition of attidudinal variables significantly improves the predictory power of equation 1. This, however, is to be attributed to the ICS-variable

Table 1

The Influence of Sentiments and Intentions Upon Consumer Expenditure

Predictor	Equation number				
	1	2	3	4	5
Y	.0683 (.0133)	.0644 (.0133)	.0639 (.0134)	.0616 (.0131)	.07677 (.00462)
ΔY	.0386 (.0150)	.0375 (.0150)	.0375 (.0150)	.0399 (.0147)	.04597 (.00834)
ICS		240.576 (103.485)	248.551 (105.829)	219.116 (101.636)	62.9050 (20.2730)
ΔICS		72.415 (92.985)	76.341 (93.667)	60.516 (91.274)	42.2830 (18.2470)
AGE			4.262 (11.658)		
INT2				2037.641 (405.246)	632.22 (91.11)
multiple correlation coefficient	.202	.223	.224	.294	.429

The dependent variable in equations 1-4 has been gross outlay by Dutch households on motorcars, May 1974-May 1975. The numbers between brackets indicate the standard errors of the partial regression coefficients.

only; the regression coefficient pertaining ΔICS does not attain statistical significance in this, or the other two, equations. In this respect we may offer the following reasoning. Leaving out all explanatory variables other than consumer sentiment, an equation of the type Expenditures $= b_1 \cdot \text{ICS} + b_2 \cdot \Delta\text{ICS} +$ constant, may be rewritten as: Expenditures $= b_1 \cdot \text{ICS}_1 + b_2(\text{ICS}_2 - \text{ICS}_1) +$ constant $= \text{ICS}_1(b_1 - b_2) + + b_2 \cdot \text{ICS}_2 +$ constant (with obvious interpretation of ICS_1 and ICS_2). If then $b_2 \approx 0$, this implies that the influence of ICS_2 upon spending behavior during the time in between the two interviews has been negligible, which is another way of saying that, obviously, ICS_2 did not cast its shadow before it. The time-shape of ICS-development during the interval period clearly must have possessed the characteristics necessary to secure this result. The ICS-values at the start and the end of the period are, as a matter of fact, proxies for this development: its time-shape determines to what extent ICS_1 and ICS_2 may serve as indicators of the mood in between.

On the other hand, the finding that $b_1 \approx 0$ implies that ICS_1 and ICS_2 influence purchasing behavior in opposite directions. Normally, one would expect a higher level of ICS to stimulate household buying. However, in this case (of which we will see an example in the 3 months analysis), ICS_1 will induce contrary reactions (provided b_2 is positive).[8] This calls for a specific explanation. We shall return to this topic below.

Equation 3 adds the age variable to the variables of equation 2. This does not have any impact. Dunkelberg, who met with a similar result, points to non-linear effects of age (being a proxy for the life-cycle stage of the family) as an explanation. (Cf. also the results of the *AID*-and the short-term analyses, below, equations 6 and 10).

In equation 4 buying intentions are introduced. This appears to be a variable with strong explanatory power. Although it somewhat reduces the statistical significance of the regression coefficient of ICS, the latter remains thoroughly significant at a level of about 3 per cent. So, both sentiments and intentions appear to contribute significantly to the explanation of consumer spending behavior, also in the Netherlands.[9]

In order to make sure that no hidden underlying factors may account for the relationship as has been found to exist between attitudes and household expenditure, the ICS has been subjected to an AID-analysis.[10] This is a stepwise type of analysis (without linearity or additivity assumptions) which explains a dependent variable by means of a number of other variables. Starting from the total sample all possible dichotomizations of each predictor are tried out so as to find the binary split that provides the largest reduction in the unexplained sum of squares. This amounts to finding the partition which maximizes the Between Sum of Squares (BSS) for the relevant sample group over all possible dichotomizations on all predictors.

This procedure may be repeated with respect to the subgroups thus formed until one or more of the following limits is reached:

a. the number of observations in the subgroup(s) becomes too small for further analysis. (In our analysis this minimum number has been put at 50);
b. the BSS, after a binary split of the last subgroup, falls below a specified fraction of the sample Total Sum of Squares (TSS). (In our program the 'eligibility' criterion has been .01);
c. the TSS for every subgroup no longer meets a specified fraction of the sample TSS. (In our program the 'reduction' criterion has been put at .006).

In the AID analysis nine predictors have been used, namely

1. age (as specified above);
2. sex of the interviewee;
3. education; three levels have been distinguished: primary, secondary, and higher;

4. life-cycle stage of the household; the age of the head of the household (under 45 or 45 and over) and the presence of children (under six years) have been used to differentiate between families;
5. occupational status of head; five groups have been distinguished, namely the liberal professions, farmers, employees and civil servants, skilled labourers, and unskilled labourers. In addition, attention has been given to whether or not people are fully employed;
6. civil status of head, t.w. unmarried, married, widow(er), or divorced;
7. income in May 1974, as defined above;
8. income in May 1975, same as 7;
9. ΔY, as defined above.

From this analysis it appears that those who – on the average – score highest on the ICS-scale are to be found among the younger households, where the head of the family is a civil servant or an employee, in the primary and secondary education

Our AID-tree shows the following branches:

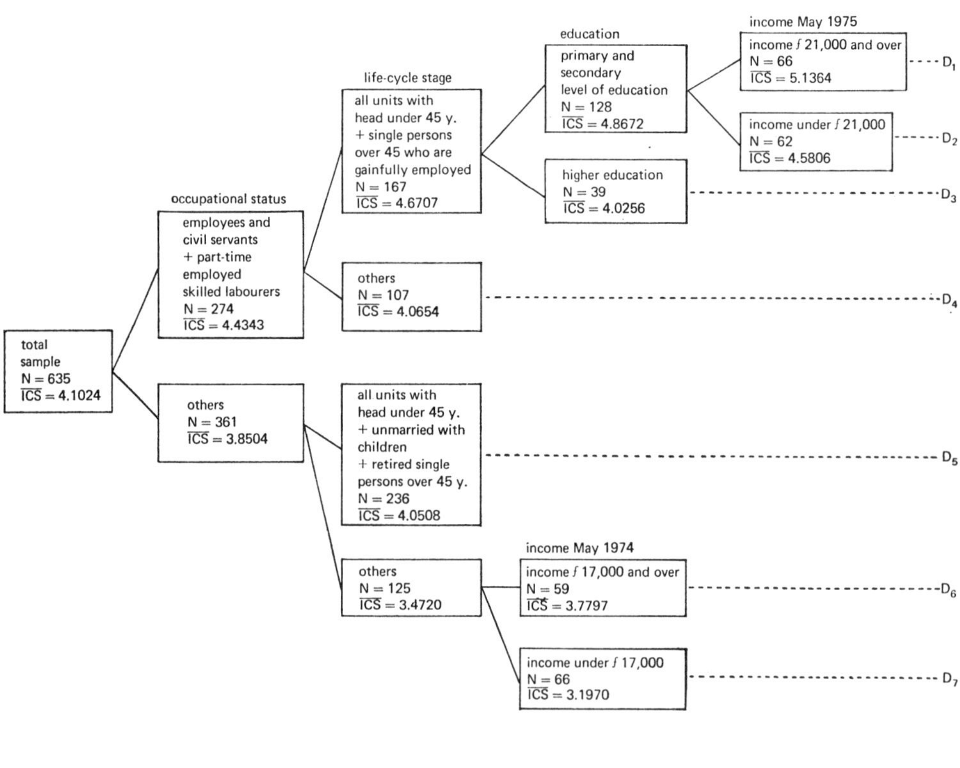

group, and (in May 1975) belonging to the upper half of the income pyramid. Whereas the bleakest ICS-view is taken by those labourers and self-employed, who belong to the older households and (in May 1974) found themselves in the lower part of the income pyramid.[11]

There exists a tendency for younger households, still being more or less in the formative stage, to be relatively active with respect to buying durable goods.[12] It may, therefore, be advisable to incorporate the AID-findings—together with attitudes and intentions—into equation 4 which, from those in table 1, offered the best explanation of our dependent variable. This has been done in equation 6 below.

Belonging to one of the seven AID-subgroups may be indicated by means of dummy variables, *D*1 to *D*7. For instance, those in the first subgroup score one on *D*1 and zero on the other dummy variables. To avoid overdetermination we have deleted the group covered by the fifth dummy. Therefore, parameter estimates have to be interpreted in deviation from subgroup 5. We obtained the following estimates of regression coefficients:

Equation 6

Predictor	Regression coefficient	(Standard error)
Y	.0492	.0152
ΔY	.0320	.0157
ICS	206.980	107.070
ΔICS	49.377	93.522
INT2	2035.194	406.875
*D*1	1028.131	503.559
*D*2	— 167.910	488.380
*D*3	1298.525	621.394
*D*4	— 14.701	435.098
*D*6	954.479	513.042
*D*7	236.391	489.092
multiple correlation coefficient	.321	

The dependent variable has been the same as for the equations 1—4.

It is interesting to observe that inclusion of the dummy variables hardly detracts from the explanatory power of the ICS: its regression coefficient still remains statistically significant (though here at a level of about 5 per cent, against around 3 per cent in equation 4).

From the definition of the *D*-variables it is understandable that their introduction has – also – somewhat diminished the statistical significance of the income coefficients; both however remain clearly significant. Buying intentions are not affected at all. Of the dummy variables *D*1, *D*3 and *D*6 carry significant weight. All signs of the respective coefficients are plausible. In all, equation 6 confirms the usefulness of taking both objective and subjective variables as predictors of consumer expenditure.

Replacement demand certainly plays an important role in generating (gross) car expenditure. An estimate has been made of the trade-in value obtained by car buyers. If, from the answers to the questionnaire, the number of cars in the family after the car purchase did not exceed the number before this purchase, we have taken this as an indication that a trade-in has taken place. This had been taken care of by assigning a value = 1 to a dummy variable *T* in the affirmative case (a trade-in has been effectuated) and zero in the opposite case. Inserting this *T* variable into equation 4 yields the following regression coefficients:

Equation 7

	Y	ΔY	ICS	ΔICS	INT2	T
	.0604 (.0130)	.0380 (.0146)	207.243 (101.206)	69.083 (90.858)	2035.857 (403.163)	1404.847 (512.327)
R = .312						

The 95 per cent confidence interval for the *T* coefficient is from 399 to 2411.

Then there is the question to what extent buying intentions and actual purchasing behavior are related to the necessity or desirability of replacing existing stocks. An approach to this problem will be discussed in appendix B. Our finding, however, remained inconclusive.

In the following table results from our analysis of the three months period from October 1974 – January 1975 are given.

Table 2

The Influence of Sentiments and Intentions upon Consumer Expenditure

Predictor	Equation number				
	8	9	10	11	12
Y	.0300 (.0073)	.0297 (.0073)	.0318 (.0074)	.0275 (.0072)	.0262 (.0072)
ΔY	.0086 (.0092)	.0079 (.0092)	.0087 (.0092)	.0068 (.0091)	.0063 (.0090)
ICS		33.654 (57.812)	1.647 (61.129)	37.532 (57.418)	27.040 (56.983)
ΔICS		108.562 (56.233)	98.644 (56.517)	107.254 (55.840)	103.956 (55.419)
AGE			—13.009 (8.143)		
INT				1318.950 (387.584)	
INT2					1073.409 (222.299)
multiple correlation coefficient	.149	.166	.176	.206	.239

The dependent variable has been gross outlay in guilders on motor-cars by Dutch households, October 1974—January 1975.

Comparison of the results from table 2 and table 1 yields some similarities and some striking differences. Again, from the equations in table 2, net household income appears to be a highly significant predictive variable with respect to car expenditure. Income change during the period under study, however, does not have any impact. It seems reasonable to suppose that the shorter the time period under consideration, the more transitory the character of income change tends to be in the minds of the economic subjects. Additionally (or alternatively) it may be mentioned that a time-lag of at least several months is to be expected between income change and spending.

The relative importance of ICS and ΔICS now shows a reversal of the positions that were found to hold for the 12-months period. Changes in sentiment appear to contribute significantly to the explanation (although the 5 per cent level of statistical significance is at best barely attained). ICS itself, on the other hand, remains utterly insignificant throughout. As elucidated above, this implies contrary spending reactions with respect to the Index of Consumer Sentiment: those with a relatively high ICS-score hesitating to spend, whereas those who score rather low on ICS prefer to buy now (see also note 8).

As a tentative explanation for this phenomenon, one may point to the fact that shortly before the October 1974 interviews were held, the Government Budget had been presented, to the accompaniment of all kinds of dire predictions about coming unemployment and the like, which to many may have come as a rather unpleasant surprise. Two types of reaction, then, are conceivable to account for our findings: one, fearing worse or the worst, may lead to making hay while the sun still shines. The other, hoping for better days in the future, may lead to postponement of purchases until the dark valley has been passed through. So, in reaction to rather disturbing official views, those with a low ICS-score (in October 1974) may have bought, while the more 'optimistic' ones may have decided to wait a while.

According to equation 10 age now exerts a weak negative influence on motor-car expenditure. The regression coefficient does not significantly differ from zero, its significance level being 11 per cent. Buying intentions, however, again appear to be important predictors of purchasing behavior. As a comparison of equations 11 and 12 shows, the level of statistical significance for INT2 is even somewhat more pronounced than for INT.[13]

Compared with the objective variables, the subjective ones did not appear to carry more weight in the short-run three months period than in the longer one year stretch. Still, also this study of the three months period again confirmes the predictive value of 'psychological' variables.

Conclusion

The foregoing cross-section analyses of Dutch household data have shown that both sentiments and (buying) intentions play a predictive role with respect to consumer spending. The explanatory power of intentions appeared to be stronger and also more systematic than that of sentiments. But this conclusion should be qualified. In the first place, the period studied (1974–75) showed some unique features. During the fall of 1974, for instance, to many it must have become clear that unemployment and less buoyant times might be more persistent than thought before. This view may have influenced the relationship between attitudes and spending, as indicated in the foregoing section.

Then, in comparing our results with those obtained for the U.S. [3], it should be borne in mind that the questionnaires used in the Dutch (and European Community) consumer surveys yield – on many financial topics – less precise data than their U.S. counterparts. This too may have influenced the strength of the outcomes.

Furthermore, there is the most important consideration that consumer attitudes are likely to exert their influence upon a broad field of expenditure categories. Due to the fact that only for gross outlay on motor-cars some quantitative financial data were collected in the consumer surveys we have analyzed, we have had to concentrate our study upon this important but still rather narrow category.

All this notwithstanding, our analyses have shown that in addition to objective factors, 'psychological' variables contribute significantly to the explanation of consumer behavior. A conclusion which is unaffected by the observation that, after all, but a modest percentage of the variance of the dependent variable could be explained even by our most successful specification of the relationship between spending on motor-cars and the explanatory variables.

Sentiments and intentions do matter. Also on the micro-economic level the predictive value of subjective variables appears to be beyond doubt.

Notes

1 See, e.g., Ferber [4], who notices that this does not imply the absence of all controversy. For one thing, there is still doubt of the forecasting value—in macro-models—of attitudinal indexes. For another, the great importance of buying intentions as it appears from cross-section studies, is not readily translated into macro-relationships.

2 In many publications George Katona, the founder of psychological economics, has advanced his theories on the importance of subjective factors, especially in highly developed economies. See of his more recent publications, e.g., [5], [6], [7].

3 See for a discussion of this index: Curtin [2], who deals with the macro-ICS only.

4 In this respect we may refer to [1], [9].

5 The averages for the lowest and highest class have been estimated on the basis of an internal study at the Faculty of Economics, University of Amsterdam.

6 Regression of motor-car expenditure on the single variables that constitute the ICS proved unsatisfactory.

7 From the 1967 distribution of (net disposable) personal income the Pareto-constant was found to be 2.96. This value has been applied to our data relating to net household incomes. In 1967, the modal income class was the one between 7 and 8 thousand guilders. The C.B.S. index of

* The author wishes to express his gratitude to the European Commission for kind permission to use survey data collected in the Netherlands under supervision of the European Community. He also wants to thank the Dutch Central Bureau of Statistics for its cooperation. This study could not have been written without the assistance—over and above the call of duty—given by Mr. M. H. Kolk, at the present time graduate student at the Faculty of Economics, University of Amsterdam, who did all the computer work connected with this article.

contractual wages rose from 261 in 1967 to 528 in 1974 (1954 = 100). So, we have made the assumption that the Pareto-constant is applicable to the 1974-distribution of net household income from 17 thousand guilders upward. The central value for the highest income class has been computed as 35,000(2.96/1.96). For the income classes (in f 1,000) from 17—21, 21—25 and 25—35, the central value has been computed according to the formula:

$$\frac{a}{a-1}\left\{\frac{\left(\frac{1}{b^{a-1}}-\frac{1}{c^{a-1}}\right)}{\left(\frac{1}{b^{a}}-\frac{1}{c^{a}}\right)}\right\}$$

where a is the Pareto-constant, b the lower and c the upper limit of the income class.

The central values for the three lower income classes have been computed by taking the arithmetical average per corresponding 1967-income class and multiplying those averages by 528/261.

8 Regression of gross motor-car expenditure from October 1974—January 1975 on ICS_1 and ICS_2 yields

$$\text{Expenditure} = -\underset{(51.280)}{73.566}\, ICS_1 + \underset{(54.876)}{113.683}\, ICS_2 + 431.520 \text{ guilders.}$$

So, b_2 is positive and significant at around 4 per cent, b_1 negative (and its estimate, at any rate, does not rule out the same absolute value as b_2).

9 It is germane to point out that the majority of purchases often are made by non-planners, although the fraction that does buy is much higher with the planners than with the non-planners. This feature can also be observed in our data.

10 See [10] for a description of this technique.

11 The AID-analysis in [3], where income, educational level, head of househould age and occupation have served as relevant variables to dichotomization led to the formation of six subgroups. Looking again at the most optimistic and pessimistic groups, the split between low and high incomes appeared to work in much the same way as in our analysis. But there the similarity largely stops.

12 See [8] for Dutch data on this topic.

13 Due to the different role of ICS in the three months equations no AID-analysis of the one-quarter-ICS has been incorporated here.

References

[1] Adams, F. G. and L. R. Klein: Anticipations Variables in Macro-Econometric Models. In: *Human Behavior in Economic Affairs*, Amsterdam 1972.

[2] Curtin, R. T.: Index Construction: An Appraisal of the Index of Consumer Sentiment. In: *Surveys of Consumers 1971—1972*, Ann Arbor (USA) 1973.

[3] Dunkelberg, W. C.: The Impact of Consumer Attitudes on Behavior: a Cross-Section Study. In: *Human Behavior in Economic Affairs*, Amsterdam 1972.

[4] Ferber, R.: Consumer Economics, a Survey, *The Journal of Economic Literature*, 1973.

[5] Katona, G.: Theory of Expectations. In: *Human Behavior in Economic Affairs*, Amsterdam 1972.

[6] Katona, G.: Cognitive Processes in Learning: Reactions to Inflation and Change in Taxes. In: *Surveys of Consumers 1971—72*, Ann Arbor (USA) 1973.

[7] Katona, G.: *Psychological Economics*, Amsterdam 1975.

[8] Pais, A.: *Consumer Credit in The Netherlands*, Rotterdam 1975.

[9] Shapiro, H. T.: The Index of Consumer Sentiment and Economic Forecasting—a Reappraisal. In: *Human Behavior in Economic Affairs*, Amsterdam 1972.
[10] Sonquist, J. A., and J. N. Morgan: *The Detection of Interaction Effects*, Ann Arbor (USA) 1964.
[11] Tobin, J.: On the Predictive Value of Consumer Intentions and Attitudes, first published in *The Review of Economics and Statistics*, 1959; reprinted in *Essays in Economics*, vol. 2, Amsterdam 1975.

Appendix A

Questions Used in Constructing the ICS

Question 4 was not asked in May 1974, so our ICS variables have been based upon the answers to questions 1—3 and 5. All five questions are used to construct the U.S. index.
The options for answering the first four questions are identical. Therefore, a listing of possible answers is only given following the first question.

1. Will, according to your opinion, the general economic situation in the Netherlands, during the next 12 months:
   — improve markedly
   — improve somewhat
   — remain unchanged
   — deteriorate somewhat
   — deteriorate markedly
   — don't know
2. Did the financial position of your household during the past 12 months:
3. Will, according to your opinion, the financial position of your household during the next twelve months:
4. Do you believe that, on the whole, economic conditions over the next five years will:
5. Do you feel that people are right in making major purchases now?
   — yes, it is rather the right time for that
   — it is not especially the right or wrong time for that
   — no, it is rather the wrong time for that
   — don't know.

Appendix B

The Stock of Motor-Cars

Does the discrepancy between the actual value of the household car stock and the value this household 'ought' to have, influence buying intentions and purchasing behavior? From our data it has not been possible to obtain significant or plausible indications to that effect.
In order to be able to determine the value of car stock per household, the following assumptions have been made.

1. For newly bought cars, purchased during the 3 months preceding the May 1974 interview, the value has been put at 100 per cent of the price paid (which—by the way—is not exactly known but put at the central value of a price class; see section p. 143).
2. Depreciation of older, newly bought cars, has been computed on the basis of a scheme, provided by the Dutch tourist organization ANWB. A car usage of 15,000 km per year has been assumed with a one percentage point depreciation for each 5000 kms. Furthermore, the car price index numbers (as provided by the Dutch Central Bureau of Statistics) have been taken into account. Eventually this amounts to the following schedule:

year of purchase	*value, as a percentage of the price paid at the time of the purchase*
1973/74	78
1971/72	56
1969/70	34
1967/68	10
before 1967	value uniformly put at *f* 250,—

3. For second-hand cars, the difference L between the year of purchase and the year of construction has been determined. The following depreciation scheme (with respect to the price paid) has been adopted: (in percentage points)

car bought	$L = 1$	$L = 2$	$L = 4$	$L = 6$	$L \geqslant 8$
during the past three months	0	0	0	0	0
1973/74	14	20	$32\frac{1}{2}$	59	r.v.
1971/72	49	59	r.v.	r.v.	
1969/70	$92\frac{1}{2}$	r.v.			
before 1969	r.v.				

(r.v. = residual value, again uniformly put at *f* 250,—).

The depreciation percentages given above have been computed along the same lines as those for new cars. Note, that the questions as to year of purchase and year of construction, according to the survey questionnaire, are not to be answered exactly but by indicating the appropriate class of two (and, for the period before 1965, more) years.

For the subgroup A (May 1974) a regression of the value of household car stock, V, on income, educational level, occupational status and a residence variable has been computed. The following dummy variables have been used:
E_1, E_2, E_3, denoting primary, secondary, and higher level of education (of the interviewee); 0_1, 0_2, 0_3, 0_4, 0_5, denoting the liberal professions, farmers, employees and civil servants, skilled labourers, and unskilled labourers, respectively;
R_1, R_2, R_3, R_4, R_5, R_6, denoting residence by classification of municipalities, based upon the number of inhabitants, namely (in thousands of people):
over 100, 50—100, 20—50, 10—20, 5—10, and under 5, respectively.

For 1133 (out of 1775) households with head under sixty years of age—for which all relevant data were available—the following relationship was established:

$$\underset{(.0096)}{V = .0913\,Y} - \underset{(232.737)}{144.953\,E_2} + \underset{(340.698)}{577.321\,E_3} + \underset{(377.177)}{1942.220\,O_1} + \underset{(473.581)}{450.128\,O_2} + \underset{(316.897)}{740.780\,O_3} +$$

$$+ \underset{(301.738)}{572.714\,O_4} + \underset{(274.905)}{318.820\,R_2} + \underset{(255.031)}{394.031\,R_3} + \underset{(259.443)}{461.319\,R_4} + \underset{(304.772)}{352.762\,R_5} +$$

$$+ \underset{(328.946)}{529.670\,R_6} - \underset{(290.71)}{469.28} \text{ guilders.} \quad \text{(multiple correlation coefficient} = .409).$$

On the basis of this equation we have computed the 'normative' value of car stock, V^*, for the households studied in the 12-months analysis, i.e. 635 cases. For each household $(V^* - V)$ has been determined. The following tabulation illustrates the lack of systematic association with buying intentions (and actual buying among the 'planners').

$(V^* — V)$ in f 1000 (May 1974)	Total number of households	Number of households for which INT2 = 1	Number of households for which INT2 = 1 and that actually bought a car
— 3 to — 12	86	11	3
— 1 to — 3	92	17	6
0 to — 1	47	7	4
0 to + 1	88	16	11
1 to 2	184	13	5
2 to 3	86	12	5
3 to 7	52	6	3
	635	82	37

Inclusion of $(V^* — V)$ into equation (4), predicting the outlay on motor-cars, also did not meet with success: the sign of the regression coefficient relating to $(V^* — V)$ being negative, which means that the greater the value of actual car stock (as compared with the 'normative' value), also the greater the gross outlay on cars, and vice versa. Which is not what might be expected. Differentiating between owners and non-owners of a car in May 1974 did not markedly improve the results.

Developing the Rijnmond Model

D. van der Werf

Introduction

A first report on the existing Rijnmond medium term interindustry model has been published in 1972 [9]. This model was produced by a research group of Rijnmond public authority led by E. D. J. Kruijtbosch and C. J. van Eijk during the years 1967 up to 1972. The merits of this model preponderantly lie in the application of theory in a concrete situation, the development in a congested area like the Rhine estuary. Especially for this model regional input-output tables were constructed for the years 1960 and 1965 in close cooperation of the Rijnmond staff and the Central Bureau of Statistics.

After the model had been completed and made ready for forecasting and the computation of policy alternatives Prof. Van Eijk stopped his advisory activities and Mr. Kruijtbosch left Rijnmond service. After their departure a new team was charged to extend and improve the basic model. A forecast of the economic structure of the Rhine estuary up to 1980 as well as the computations of a number of policy alternatives, made by the basic model were published in a political memorandum of the Rijnmond executive committee [10].

The basic model is of the input-output type. Interindustry deliveries and labour demand are linear functions of output. Private and public consumption and exports are exogenous. Private investments are endogenous and determined by marginal capital-output ratio's. Labour supply bottlenecks were dealt with by lowering final sales in those sectors where capacity problems are most likely. The outlines of the basic model will be sketched first. In the two sections that follow we show how the model has been used for previsions and policy scenarios.

Since its publication in 1972 the model underwent a number of modifications. The basic model was designed as a demand model with one possible constraint on the supply side: availability of manpower. A congested area like Rijnmond has become congested by the working of more bottlenecks than labour alone. Accounting for more bottlenecks restricting production, in particular land and the environment, transformed the linear forecasting model into a classical linear programming model. Bottlenecks in supply and restrictions on emissions tend to constrain the free working of the demand multiplier. In congested situations a 'constrained multiplier' is the more appropriate. It can be read off from the dual solution, together with 'shadow prices' for the constraining factors.

A further problem concerns the changes in labour, land and emission coefficients in response to policy and additional investment for those purposes. This has led to the design of a layered version of the model, by which it is hoped to compute endogenous changes in these coefficients. The possibility of such a layered model was first suggested to Rijnmond by A. R. G. Heesterman, who acted as a consultant to the Rijnmond staff in the years 1973 to 1975.

To bring the model up to date the interregional input-output table for 1970 has been calibrated starting from regional input-output data for 1965 and using the national table 1970 as well as very partial regional data for 1970.

A very nasty question in this context always remains the reliability of technical and regional input-output coefficients. Apart from that, the input-output tables contain a lot of data on small industrial activities that is of no avail for forecasting and planning compared with the scarce information on important activities like the chemicals and oil refinery industries or retail and wholesale trade. The more technical criteria of official classifications do not form a good base for economic models. This led to a regrouping of industries, according to important criteria from an economic point of view, such as demand and price elasticities of products, or the elements of the production function.

This regrouping makes it possible to redesign the model into a smaller but more comprehensive system, in which demand restrictions are adapted in successive iterations to income and unit labour costs, as produced by the previous primal solutions. In the feedback process effective use will be made of labour-productivity functions and demand and price elasticities for sectors, as well as a regional consumption function. This model, discussed below, is still in its implementation stage.

A preliminary appraisal concludes this article. A practical conclusion to be mentioned here, is that comprehensiveness has to be paid for, and in this instance it is paid for by reducing the number of sectors in our model.

Last, but not least, I mention those members of the Rijnmond staff that cooperated in this project. They are Mr. P. Bal, who did most of the statistical work and the preparation of data, Mr. P. C. M. Elderman, who did a lot of work in converting the model into the layered linear programming system, Mr. B. C. van der Weide, who had the task of implementing the model into the machine and who calibrated the 1970 table, and Mr. J. Unk who assembled emission coefficients. And I thank in particular also those who did the typing of the manuscript especially Mrs. Van der Hor and Messrs. Van der Mey and Goor who did the drawing of the charts.

The Shape of the Model

The original version of the Rijnmond medium term model has been designed for extrapolation of growth and industrial composition of regional production and employment, in different circumstances and policy scenarios. It is an interindustry model based on the regional input-output structure. Official regional input-output tables are available for the base years 1960 and 1965, for some 14 districts in the Netherlands [2]. The tables are on a national-regional base, as they give inter-industry deliveries from national origin to regional destination. These input-output tables were converted into tables on regional-regional base before they were used for the Rijnmond model. Conversion was done in close cooperation between the Rijnmond staff and the Central Bureau for Statistics. The resulting tables give the intermediate and final sales for each of 30 industries of the Rijnmond area:

$$X_{i,1} + X_{i,2} + \dots X_{i,n} + C_i + I_i + E_i + N_i = X_i \qquad (1)$$

X_i = total output of industry i

$X_{i,j}$ = intermediate deliveries of industry i to industry j within the region

C_i, I_i, E_i, N_i = consumption, investments, exports abroad and exports to the rest of the country from industry i.

Analogous to the Leontief-approach of fixed technical coefficients the model uses fixed regional input-output coefficients:

$$X_{ij} = a_{ij}X_j \tag{2}$$

The assumptions implied in (2) are basically different from those of the fixed Leontief coefficients. In the Leontief case deliveries from other industries are used in fixed proportions in relation to technological coefficients, and it does not matter from where deliveries are shipped. For a regional analysis based on Leontief we would have needed a world-regional base table. In the regional-regional base analysis deliveries from within the region are used in fixed proportions. This implies fixed trade flows and fixed technological coefficients. Of course much of the working of the model depends on the stability of regional input-output coefficients a_{ij}. This topic will be touched upon later.
Substitution of (2) into (1) gives (in matrix form):

$$Ax + f = x \tag{3}$$

or:

$$x = (I - A)^{-1}f \tag{4}$$

where:

x = 30 × 1 vector of industry output (X_i)

A = 30 × 30 matrix of regional input-output coefficients a_{ij}

f = 30 × 1 vector of final demand

and:

$$f = c + j + e + n \tag{5}$$

where

c = 30 × 1 vector of private and public consumption

j = 30 × 1 vector of investment in structures and equipment, by origin

e = 30 × 1 vector of exports abroad

n = 30 × 1 vector of interregional exports.

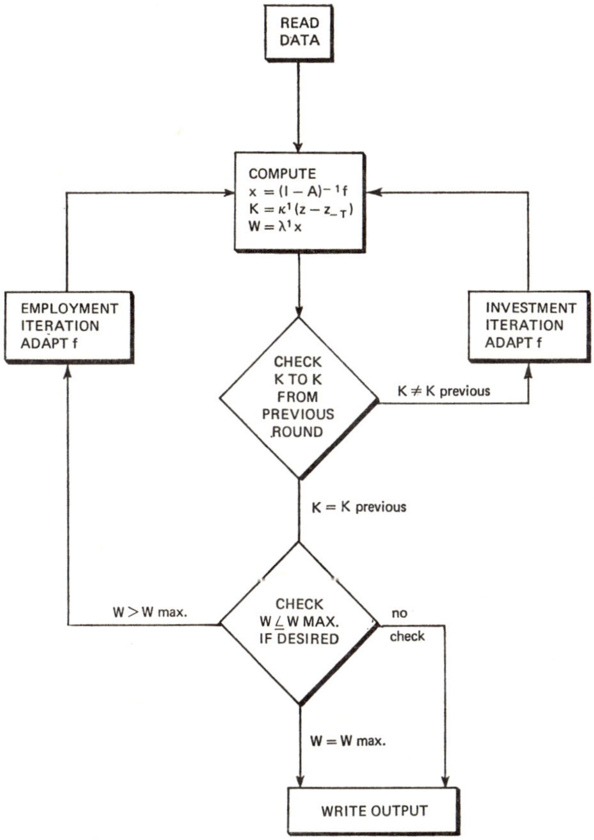

Figure 1. Flow scheme of iterative solution.

The regional forecasting model deviates in two important respects from the conventional input-output model as represented in (4) and (5) (see also figure 1):

a. investments are endogenous
b. there is a labour constraint

Ad a. The Rijnmond model is designed to forecast structural changes in the economy, in particular where they deviate from national trends.
A first problem is that changes in the growth rate may have considerable influence on the pace of investment, and for that matter on the development of the industrial structure. To bring this feedback into the model, it has been extended with a number of equations. In this long-term analysis cyclical movements in activity are left

out of account and the level of capital utilisation is kept unchanged. Investments by destination are determined by means of capital coefficients per industrial activity. As no reliable figures for total capital stock exist, the investments function makes use of incremental capital output ratio's (*ICOR*'s). Investments by destination are transformed into investments by origin before they can be used as final demand sector. For this the investment vector j is expressed as a linear transformation of output x after assumption of a number of linear relations which we shall now briefly describe.

I. Regionally produced investments are distributed over respective origins by multiplying by a 30 × 2 matrix of industries of origin quotas for structures and equipment as known from the input-output table:

$$j = \Lambda \bar{j} \tag{6}$$

where:

Λ = 30 × 2 matrix of industries of origin quotas for structures and equipment

$\bar{j}$ = 2 × 1 vector of total investments produced within the Rijnmond area, distributed over structures and equipment.

The investments contained in vector j are fed into final demand after each successive round of the investment iteration procedure (see fig. 1).

II. Not all investments required by industries in Rijnmond are produced by Rijnmond industries. For structures they are (by definition) but for equipment only a minor part of investment goods are produced in the home region. In determining $\bar{j}$ from investment demand fractions of 1.0 and .15 were applied:

$$\bar{j} = \hat{\varphi}\bar{k} \tag{7}$$

$\hat{\varphi}$ = 2 × 2 diagonal matrix of fractions of regionally produced investment

$\bar{k}$ = 2 × 1 vector of total investment requirements distributed over structures and equipment.

III. Investment requirements of structures and equipment respectively are derived from investment demand per industry by multiplying by a quota matrix B:

$$\bar{k} = Bk \qquad (8)$$

in which:

$B = 2 \times 30$ matrix of structures equipment quota of investment demand per industry of destination

$k = 30 \times 1$ vector of investment demand per industry of destination.

IV. Investment demand is related by a set of incremental capital output ratios to the contribution of capital to production increases, or

$$k = \hat{\kappa}(z - z_{-T}) \qquad (9)$$

where:

$\hat{\kappa} = 30 \times 30$ diagonal matrix of *ICOR*'s

$z = 30 \times 1$ vector of capital's contribution to production;
the subscript $-T$ indicates a five years' lag.

The *ICOR*'s of the matrix $\hat{\kappa}$, shown in table 1, were computed by the Central Planning Bureau from the ratio of k_i to Δz_i by industry. These coefficients include a correction for the contribution of labour to growth of production. This contribution of labour equals the additional number of employed multiplied by their average wage-level during the observation period, the latter as a proxy for the marginal labour productivity. These coefficients are applied to the five years' differences in the vector z representing capital's contribution to production.

V. The correction of the capital-output ratio for that part of production growth that cannot be attributed to capital, but only to labour, is nicely founded theoretically, but turns out to be of little quantitative importance, as in most cases the increase in the labour force is quite small. It makes the Rijnmond model unduly complicated, however, as the average wage-level $\bar{P}$ is derived from the average increase in labour productivity, using forecast years weights instead of base years

Table 1

Data Used in Forecasting 1970 and 1975 from 1965 Base Year

		Incremental capital-output ratio's	Annual growth of labour productivity
1.	Agriculture etc.	2.5	6.0
3.	Non-coal mining	2.5	20.0
4.	Animal food	5.5	3.0
5.	Other food	4.0	4.0
6.	Beverages and tobacco	1.0	6.0
7.	Textiles	4.0	3.0
8.	Shoes and clothing	3.0	3.0
9.	Wood, furniture etc.	3.0	3.0
10.	Paper	4.0	3.0
11.	Printing, publishing	3.0	6.0
12.	Leather, rubber	3.0	3.0
13.	Chemicals and oil	2.0	11.0
14.	Earthenware, glass etc.	3.0	3.0
15.	Metal products, machinery	4.0	3.0
16.	Transport equipment	3.0	5.0
17.	Other manufacturing	2.5	5.0
18.	Construction	2.5	3.0
19.	Public utility	7.0	8.0
20.	Wholesale and retail-trade	2.5	3.0
21/22.	Banking, insurance	6.5	2.0
24/26.	Transport and communication	6.0	7.0
27/31.	Other services	6.5	—

weights. The *ICOR*'s are defined with respect to value added, so in deriving investments from the increase in production (after corrections for labour's contributions) value added should be used as well. It is defined:

$$y = (I - A' - \hat{\mu})x \tag{10}$$

y = 30 × 1 vector of value added by industry

$\hat{\mu}$ = 30 × 30 diagonal vector of complementary import quota

Starting from value added by industry and the average wage-level $\bar{P}$, capital's contribution to production vector z is computed by:

$$z = y - \bar{P}w \tag{11}$$

where

z = 30 × 1 vector of contribution of capital by industry

$\bar{P}$ = scalar variable representing marginal labour productivity (average wage-level)

w = 30 × 1 vector of numbers employed by industry.

Form (11) contains the only non-linearity of the equation system, and makes it necessary to solve the model by iteration. As the increases in labour productivity for branches that are weighted in $\bar{P}$ are predetermined, not much harm is done by substituting base years weights for forecast years weights. Predetermined $\bar{P}$ renders the model completely linear.

VI. Finally the numbers employed are linearly related to output by labour requirement coefficients λ, or

$$w = \hat{\lambda}x, \tag{12}$$

but for a complication described below.

If we now combine (6) with (12), the result is:

$$j = \Lambda\hat{\varphi}B\hat{\kappa}[I - A' - \hat{\mu} - \bar{P}\hat{\lambda}](x - x_{-T}) \tag{13}$$

or

$$j = C(x - x_{-T})$$

where

$$C = \Lambda\hat{\varphi}B\hat{\kappa}[I - A' - \hat{\mu} - \bar{P}\hat{\lambda}] \tag{14}$$

Labour coefficients are no invariable data, but change in response to labour productivity increasing investments. In the Rijnmond model they are forecast from estimates made by the Central Planning Bureau (table 1).

Ad b. The manpower constraint. If the constraint is not binding, total manpower employed equals labour demand as computed by (12).
If the constraint becomes binding, i.e. if

$$\lambda' x > W_{max} \tag{15}$$

which means that if unconstrained labour demand exceeds the labour supply constraint (W_{max}), labour demand is brought in line with supply by intuitively lowering demand where bottlenecks are most likely to occur. It was assumed that regional consumption and exports to the rest of the country would be maintained, but that export demand would be proportionally reduced in all sectors (employment iteration). The way of solving the model with both iterations will be easy to follow from the solution's flow scheme in figure 1.
If $\bar{P}$ is predetermined, the system of equations (3) and (5) to (10) can be solved for x by substitution and elimination of j. The solution gives:

$$x = (I - A - C)^{-1}(c + \mathrm{e} + n - Cx_{-T}) \tag{16}$$

The employment iteration reduces to the simple linear programme:

$$\text{maximize } E = i'e \tag{17}$$

subject to (16) and

$$E \leq i' e_{max}$$

$$e - \Phi e_{max} = 0 \tag{18}$$

$$\lambda' x \leq W_{max} \tag{15}$$

where

E = sum of exports abroad
e = 30 × 1 vector of export demand constraints
Φ = proportional reduction factor (scalar variable)
i = 30 × 1 unit vector
This problem can be solved straightforwardly by adding (18), which is linear in the endogenous variables, to the linear system. A solution with $\Phi > 1$ will be rejected.

Table 2

Forecasts of Total Output and Employed Labour and of Main Items on the Expenditure Side

Item	In mln. guilders of 1965				Volume index		
	1965	1970	1975	1980	1970 /65	1975 /70	1980 /75
Regional expenditure *(predetermined)*							
Government investment	312	359	415	504	115	116	121
Housing	262	266	257	294	102	97	114
Private consumption	2055	2483	3001	3326	121	121	111
Government consumption	74	94	124	161	127	132	130
Stock formation	117	131	138	138	112	105	100
Forecast without labour constraint							
Output of industries	17027	24084	33000	41705	141	137	126
Employment in industries (1000 man-years)	410	433	450	438	106	104	97
Investment of industries	1616	2262	2682	2579	140	118	96
of which structures	320	381	443	409	119	116	92
Equipment	1296	1881	2239	2170	145	119	97
Investment produced in home region	624	663	779	735	106	118	94
Forecast with labour constraint							
Output of industries	17027	24060	31834	42504	141	132	134
Employment in industries (1000 man-years)	410	433	438	444	106	101	101
Investment of industries	1616	2255	2385	2765	140	106	116
of which structures	320	380	404	431	119	106	107
Equipment	1296	1875	1981	2334	145	106	118
Investment produced in home region	624	661	702	781	106	106	111

Previsions

In 1972 the model was ready for use. An ex-post comparison was made of input-output coefficients of the 1960 and 1965 tables, from which it was concluded that shifts over time were not to be expected to disturb forecasts. *ICOR*'s were applied to 1960–65 and 1965–70 data and seemed to behave quite well. From comparisons (see figures 2 and 3) the model was found suitable for previsions.
In 1972–1973 normal previsions were published for the five years' periods 1965–1970, 1970–1975 and 1975–1980. The ex-post forecast for 1970 was made because

Table 3

Forecast of Industry Output 1970, 1975, 1980 (Volume Index)

	1965 actual mln.	Without labour constraint			Labour constraint		
		1970/65	1975/70	1980/75	1970/65	1975/70	1980/75
Agriculture etc.	152	126	115	105	126	111	111
Non-coal mining	47	173	159	143	172	152	152
Animal food	429	121	118	107	120	115	111
Other food	1.117	130	118	100	130	115	104
Beverages and tobacco	391	115	120	116	115	119	118
Textiles	37	104	112	108	104	110	111
Shoes and clothing	112	106	110	102	106	109	103
Wood, furniture etc.	80	123	127	120	123	126	123
Paper	115	138	132	125	138	130	128
Printing, publishing	262	133	132	124	133	130	127
Leather, rubber	31	154	128	125	154	125	131
Chemical and oil	4.715	179	162	144	179	155	154
Earthenware, glass, etc.	60	130	124	121	129	122	125
Metal products, machinery	532	124	130	118	124	126	124
Transport equipment	782	124	123	109	124	118	117
Other manufacturing	371	141	144	129	141	139	137
Construction	1.243	117	117	113	117	113	118
Public utility	243	159	160	123	159	157	126
Wholesale and retail-trade	1.870	130	130	117	130	128	121
Banking	180	132	124	121	132	121	126
Insurance	271	116	115	114	116	113	116
Housing	277	115	112	102	115	112	102
Sea and air transport	1.581	128	113	109	127	107	119
Other transport	1.102	141	130	117	141	125	125
Communication	103	126	125	118	126	122	123
Medical services	180	108	107	108	108	107	108
Business services	263	123	120	116	123	117	120
Recreation	29	122	114	115	122	112	118
Hotels, cafés, restaurants	158	115	114	115	115	112	119
Other personal services	130	117	115	114	117	114	115
Total output	17.027	141	137	126	141	132	134

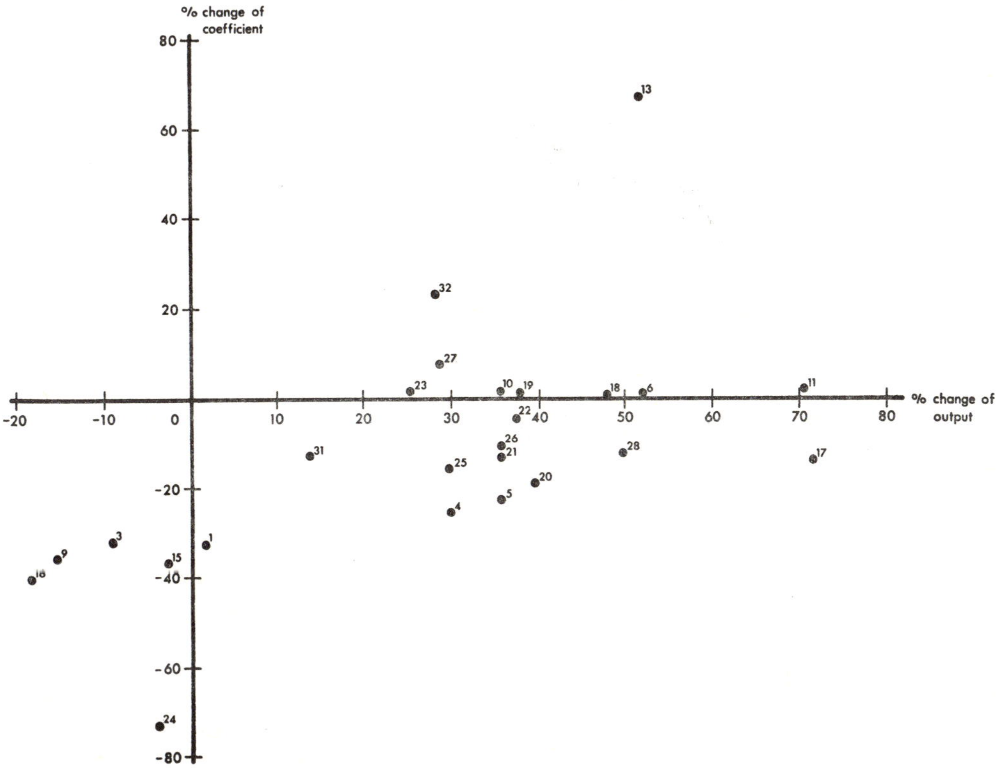

Figure 2. Changes in regional input-output coefficients 1960—1965.

no statistics were yet available. Only recently a comparison of these ex-post forecasts with official figures for that year became possible. For this comparison the constant prices figures of the forecast had to be inflated to the 1970 price-level. Forecast and realisation for output of industries are compared in figure 4.

In table 2 the forecasts for 1965 – 1970 are given together with those for 1970 – 1975 and 1975 – 1980 for the main items on the expenditure side, as well as output and employed labour, both with and without manpower constraint. Index numbers for output by industry are given in table 3. These figures should give a fairly complete description of economic developments within the area, especially if completed with information on labour employed by branch of industry, a supplementary output of the model, not given here for reasons of space. However not all this information actually is computed by the model. Point of criticism of the model is that it really gives little output if compared to the extent of input necessary to run it. The inputs of the model are:

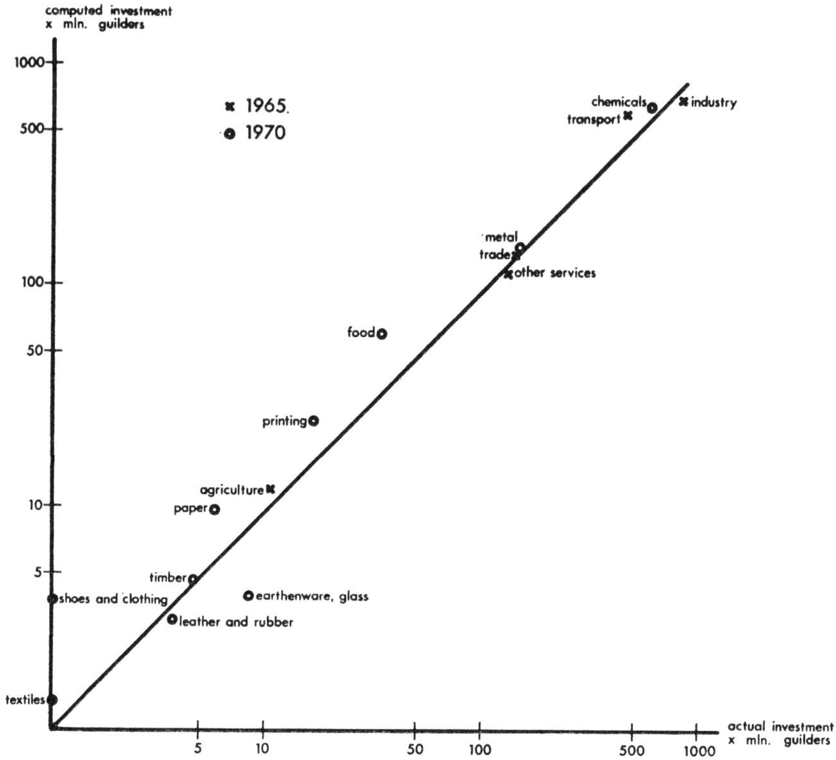

Figure 3. Expost comparison of computed investment by branch of investing industry, 1965 and 1970.

1. The regional input-output table; tables officially published have to be converted to regional-regional base for use in the model.
2. A set of capital-output ratio's per sector; these are generally furnished by the Central Planning Bureau but have to be adapted to the specific base period of the model.
3. Construction quota for investments contained in matrix B; these are also furnished by the Central Planning Bureau.
4. Fractions of investments produced in Rijnmond region; these can be derived from the available interregional input-output table for 1965.
5. Manpower constraint. This item has to be estimated from conflicting information from the Central Bureau of Statistics and regional labour offices.
6. Forecasts of final demand:

   a. private consumption; forecasts by the Central Planning Bureau of national consumption are corrected for differences in population growth;

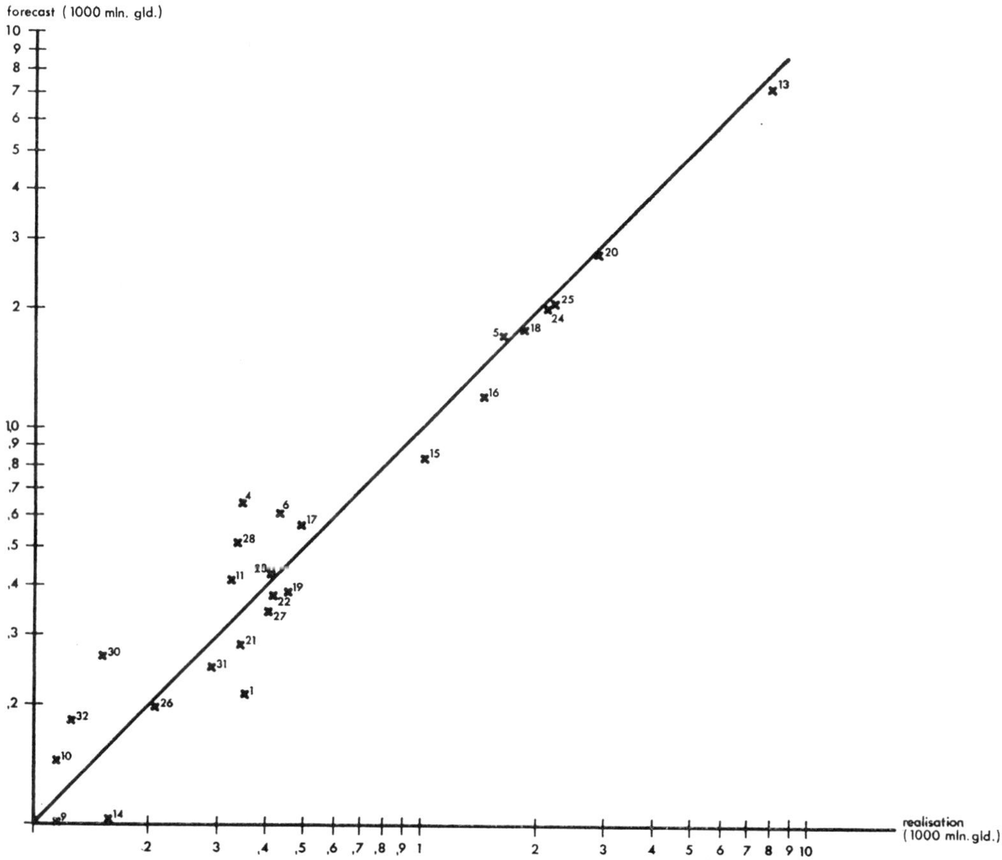

Figure 4. Forecast and realisation of output by industry 1970 (current prices).

b. exports abroad are forecast proportional to C.P.B. forecasts of national exports;

c. government expenditure and exports to the rest of the country are estimated in proportion to national consumption, government expenditure, exports; this is the weakest component of final demand forecasting; a good solution of the weighting problem is only possible with an interregional input-output table.

This quite considerable amount of data is fed into the model in order to return:

1. gross output and value added per industry;
2. employment per industry;
3. final investment demand per industry.

From a viewpoint of forecasting the model is not very efficient in the use of data. A questionable point is also the dominance of the main diagonal in the inverse matrix of input-output coefficients, making for an output that closely resembles final demand estimates. Would it not have been possible to make equally good estimates without any model by reweighting national demand or output estimates? Table 4 tries to answer this criticism. The reader may judge for himself whether the answer is affirmative. As for the model, it may be considered

a. that the model is still in a build-up phase and should be further developed;
b. that the model should also be used for the evaluation of different policy scenarios.

Scenario Analysis

The region Rijnmond covers only 1.7% of national territory, but produces 12% of national product. Stronger still, this production is concentrated in a narrow strip along the river mouth of about 5 km wide and 40 km long, partly close to the urban areas of Vlaardingen, Schiedam, Rotterdam (see map). Fast development of heavy port industries, especially oil- and petrochemical industries, caused severe problems of labour shortages, congested infrastructure and air pollution. It became clear that the expansion rhythm had to be kept in check, and that probably industrial activities had to be selected for their impact on the labour market, infrastructure and the environment. In order to obtain some clearer view on possible consequences of policies a number of alternative solutions was run by the model. We will cite here two scenario runs.

Scenario I. A Blast Furnace and Steel Plant on Maasvlakte.
In 1969 and following years central and local governments negotiated a possible blast-furnace and steel plant on Maasvlakte, an artificial peninsula for industrial use jutting out into the sea just south of the main port-entrance. The existing Maasvlakte having insufficient space for this project, an extension would be necessary causing public investment to rise after the projects start in 1975 by an amount of of Dfl 575 mln of 1965 during the five years 1976–1980.
Apart from land reclamation as such these investments include costs of harbour construction and bridges and roads. The annual investments outlay by 1980 would amount to Dfl 120 mln (in prices of 1965). This figure could not be computed with the model, but is fed into it as autonomous investments to be produced by the building industry. The model could be used for the computation of private invest-

Table 4

Comparison of Naive and Model Forecasts

	Bench mark 1965	Volume index 1970/65		
		Output model without labour constraint	Estimated output C.P.B.	Final Demand estimate
Agriculture etc.	0.9	126	113	127
Non-coal mining	0.3	173	349	132
Animal food	2.5	121	118	120
Other food	6.6	130	117	130
Beverages and tobacco	2.3	115	115	114
Textiles	0.2	104	124	103
Shoes and clothing	0.7	106	114	105
Wood, furniture etc.	0.5	123	134	124
Paper	0.7	138	129	138
Printing, publishing	1.5	133	134	131
Leather, rubber	0.2	154	134	159
Chemicals and oil	28.0	179	162	181
Earthenware, glass, etc.	0.4	130	134	136
Metal products, machinery	3.2	124	136	128
Transport equipment	4.6	124	141	127
Other manufacturing	2.2	141	145	146
Construction	7.4	117	140	119
Public utility	1.4	159	170	170
Wholesale and retail-trade	11.1	130	132	130
Banking	1.1	132	114	123
Insurance	1.6	116	114	111
Housing	1.6	115	115	115
Sea and air transport	9.4	128	127	128
Other transport	6.5	141	132	144
Communication	0.6	126	114	110
Medical services	1.1	108	114	108
Business services	1.6	123	114	123
Recreation	0.2	122	114	123
Hotels, cafés, restaurants	0.9	115	114	114
Other personal services	0.8	117	114	111
Total output	100.0	141	137	143

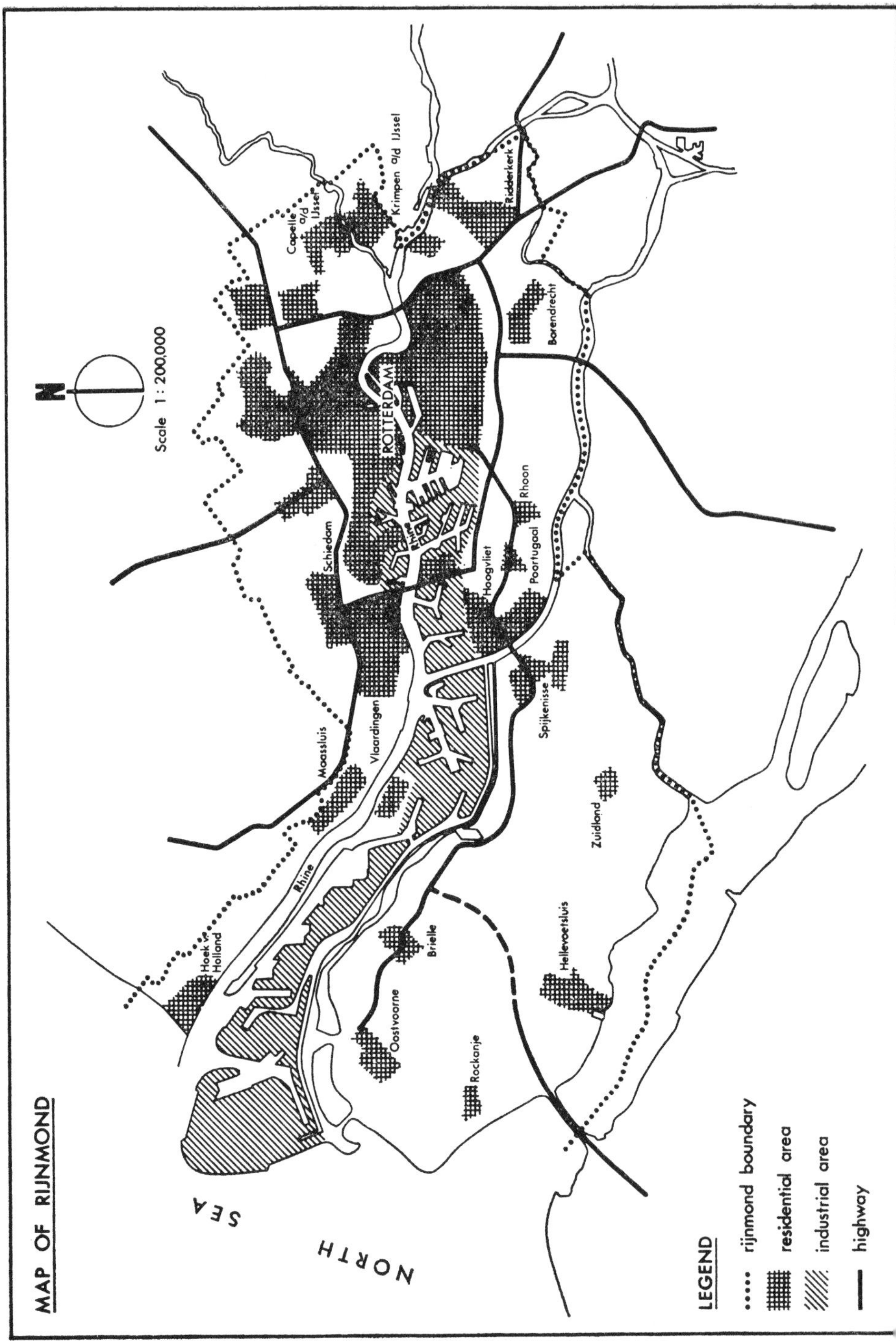

MAP OF RIJNMOND
Scale 1 : 200,000
N
ROTTERDAM
Rhine
Rhine
Hoek v. Holland
Maassluis
Vlaardingen
Schiedam
Capelle a/d IJssel
Krimpen a/d IJssel
Ridderkerk
Barendrecht
Rhoon
Poortugaal
Hoogvliet
Spijkenisse
Zuidland
Hellevoetsluis
Brielle
Oostvoorne
Rockanje
NORTH SEA
LEGEND
rijnmond boundary
residential area
industrial area
highway

ments of the steel industry, as the project's first stage should be concluded in 1980 with a production of 2.5 mln tons of steel. For this computation a special row of input-output and capital coefficients for the steel industry was inserted, as no such industry at present exists in the area. Meanwhile in 1980 the second stage of the project would be under construction, implying investments of some 43 mln. These latter investments again have to be fed into the model exogenously, as no capital-output connection with 1980 production exists. Finally steel shipments are likely to stimulate port handling of regional exports, good for an additional 9% increase in exports of the port handling industry, to be specified exogenously as well.

The procedure results in the following output (without restriction on employment)

additional in	*employment (men)*	*value added (Dfl mln)*
all sectors	6500	731
construction industry	3050	55
port handling industry	850	33
steel industry	1500	617

Not long before these calculations were made, the project was practically turned down for two main reasons:

1. additional demand for labour was expected to cause difficulties in housing and commuting facilities, in particular because the Maasvlakte is very unfavourably situated from the viewpoint of labour supply. One of the fears was also an overstrain of the labour market causing a drainage of labour employed in less paying industries in the area, and the inflationary consequences of such a reallocation process, not in the least after 1980 when the plant would reach completion;
2. emissions of in particular dust and toxic materials such as fluor became an unsurmountable obstacle. Government agencies recognized that these problems could ultimately be solved from a technical point of view, but public opinion was not convinced of this.

Scenario II. Abatement Investment Policies

This second scenario is a case study of extra investments needed to abate air pollution. Most industries cause air pollution but in the Rijnmond area the chemical industry, oil refineries and electricity generation cause most of the trouble. Reduction of air pollution is of course dependent on the state of the technology,

but can only be implemented by investments. The scenario excludes special non-productive abatement investments. Investments reducing air pollution are supposed to be incorporated in investments for replacement and expansion, and are specified as an increase in the marginal capital output ratio of 20% for the main polluting sectors (chemicals, oil refinery, port handling, electricity generation). When the scenario was run no knowledge on the efficiency of these additional investments in terms of emission was available, and no suppositions were made. Cost increases caused by investments will at least partly be shifted onto the customer. Increased prices mean less final sales of polluting industries, to be specified exogenously because the model contains no price equations. These reductions of final demand lead indirectly to a reduction of production and employment in supplying industries, partly or wholly compensated by final demand increases for investment good producing sectors (in particular in the construction industry) and possibly also by surplus capacity reactions.
The abatement investment scenario resulted in the following output:

additional in	*employment (men)*	*value added (mln Dfl)*
all sectors	– 5550	– 691
chemicals and oil	– 1350	– 527
port handling industry	– 3250	– 124
construction industry	500	8

For both scenarios quite complicated suppositions had to be made as the model does not cover price and surplus capacity reactions and does not say anything about environmental restrictions, important conditions in the real world.
In the steel plant run not only additional sales were projected, but technical coefficients had to be specified autonomously as no such industry is actually in existence in the area. In the abatement run suppositions had to be fed into the model as to the extent of investment increases, and also price reactions had to estimated exogenously. Most of the essential information was compiled separately and in fact put into the model. The model in this stage cannot do much more for us than some redistributing work, and is in fact as inefficient in scenario analysis as it is in forecasting.
Comparable problems were encountered when in January 1974 the effects of the oil crisis had to be estimated. The consequences of raw-material shortages had to be fed into the model translated into a reduction of final demand. The time had come for a transformation of the model to deal with the most important economic

reactions such as price reactions on the demand side, as well as to deal with the most pressing restrictions on supply of raw materials, energy, land for industrial use, manpower and room for emissions.

Conversion to Linear Programming

Clearly more supply bottlenecks are likely to exist than total supply of manpower, as included in the original Rijnmond model. First, within the field of labour various categories may be distinguished, as to schooling, profession, age and sex, each of which has its specific supply position relative to demand. Further scarcity of land for industrial purposes was touched upon in relation with extension of Maasvlakte. Here also a distinction may be made between agricultural and industrial use, and seaport and non-seaport premises. And finally it was quite strongly felt that industrial expansion may conflict with the pollution absorbing capacity of the environment and the supply position of energy and raw materials.

A greater number of restrictions makes it necessary to leave the intuitive way of adapting the model's solution to the supply restriction by lowering exports across the board, and to turn to a decision model as sketched in fig. 5. As the model is almost linear in the equations, it seemed obvious to choose for linear programming.[1]

Before this method can be used a number of problems has to be solved, partly of a technical, partly of political nature. Meanwhile some progress has been made in solving the technical problems. The political questions still wait for solutions. Here follows a short summary of the main problems and of what we did about them.

a. For linear programming a linear system is needed. In previous sections it was described how the investment equations were made linear and incorporated in the linear model.

b. Next to regional $I-O$ coefficients, total labour and capital coefficients, a number of additional coefficients have to be specified for land use, emissions and effluent, use of energy and raw materials. We could compute some of these coefficients, but the basic statistical material was found to be quite shaky.

c. The linear programming model needs an objective function, for instance total sales or total output to be maximized. For the Rijnmond model gross value added was chosen as the objective. In many models growth of value added or output is considered to be an objective of the policy maker(s). For the Rijnmond model no such supposition is made. Gross value added to be maximized is considered an aggregate objective of all individual economic subjects in the

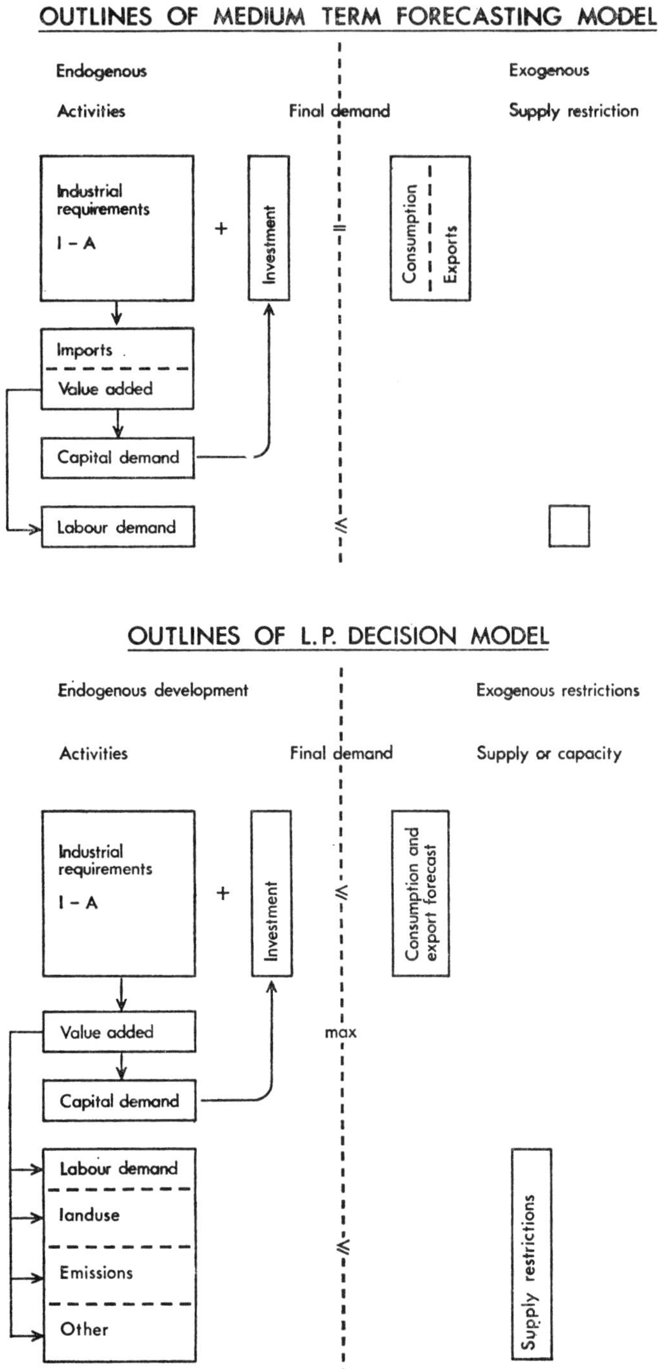
OUTLINES OF MEDIUM TERM FORECASTING MODEL
Endogenous
Exogenous
Activities
Final demand
Supply restriction
Industrial requirements
I – A
+
Investment
=
Consumption
Exports
Imports
Value added
Capital demand
Labour demand
≤
OUTLINES OF L.P. DECISION MODEL
Endogenous development
Exogenous restrictions
Activities
Final demand
Supply or capacity
Industrial requirements
I – A
+
Investment
≥
Consumption and export forecast
max
Value added
Capital demand
Labour demand
landuse
Emissions
Other
≤
Supply restrictions

Figure 5.

region. This is only a behavioural hypothesis and does not anticipate any government's policy views. One might criticize the objective function in a sense that depreciation or investments should be deducted. It certainly is true that gross value added is no impeccable criterion, but neither is deduction of investments, and moreover this is not likely to affect the solution very much.

d. The objectives of the policy makers are represented in the restrictions on labour, land, pollution, energy and raw materials use. Only in a few instances the policy making authorities specified their constraints, namely in the fields of foreign labour and land use. Even in a pressing field like pollution no constraints could be specified.

One of the difficulties that this model has in common with many others is that it does not fit all problems of the real world. If environmental policy was confined to across the board restrictions of emission for all emitters in the area, realistic specifications of environmental side conditions would be possible. However, the area is not homogeneous, pollution from different sources affects the air in the cities differently according to location, environmental policy often has the character of negotiated best practicable means reductions. It will thus remain difficult to force reality into a model like this. Still industrial expansion is restricted by environmental bottlenecks, and if we want to make a realistic forecast and realistic scenarios of possible situations we will have to take them into account one way or the other.

The information going into the re-formulated model consists of two classes of constraints, the original demand estimates and the newly introduced supply restrictions. The programme gets the shape:

$$\text{maximize } Y = i'(I - A' - \hat{\mu})x \tag{10}$$

subject to

$$(I - A - C)x + Cx_{-T} \leq \delta_{max} \tag{19}$$

$$S'x \leq \sigma_{max} \tag{20}$$

where

$\delta_{max} = 30 \times 1$ vector of demand restrictions $c + e + n$.

$\sigma_{max} = 30 \times 1$ vector of supply restrictions W_{max} etc.

S = 30 × 13 matrix of employment coefficients (λ), land use coefficients, pollution coefficients etc.

On the demand side, the forecasts of final demand (consumption and exports in each sector) form the upper limit of sales. These upper bounds are undershot if capacity or other restrictions on supply become binding. As long as demand is fully met by sales, the linear programming solution is identical to the solution of the traditional model (except for the restriction on labour). As soon as restrictions on the supply of labour and/or on environment factors become binding sales undershoot demand. For every binding supply restriction one demand restriction will become not binding and total value added will be reduced compared to the original non-l.p. solution. The distribution of cuts in production is unproportionate, being a function of reductions in sales and interindustry deliveries.

Shadow-Prices and Restricted Multipliers

The dual solution of the linear programming model gives shadow-prices for both demand and supply restrictions. These shadow-prices are the changes in the objective function, i.c. total value added, connected with marginal changes in each of the restrictions:

$$p_i = \frac{\Delta Y}{\Delta R_i} \tag{21}$$

where

Y = total value added
R_i = restriction i
p_i = shadow-price of restriction i.

If a restriction is not binding, no change in Y is connected with a marginal change in this restriction, and the shadow-price is zero. For binding restrictions the model should give positive shadow-prices, as any binding restriction is bound to reduce Y. Shadow-prices of restrictions on *demand* may be interpreted as multiplier effects of final demand in a particular sector. Bottlenecks in supply and restrictions on emissions tend to restrict the free working of the demand multiplier. If for supply reasons demand in some sector cannot be fully met by sales, increases in demand

do not affect total sales and the demand multiplier in that sector is zero. If sales equal the demand restriction, the multiplier may be positive, but still restricted by bottlenecks affecting supplying industries. Multiplier analysis based upon this linear programming model fully accounts for restrictions on supply.
With known multipliers for final demand in every sector, it is also possible to compound multipliers for final demand categories such as consumption, exports etc. by weighting with relative shares in consumption, exports etc. For instance if:

$$e = \varepsilon' E, \tag{22}$$

ε = 30 × 1 vector of industry export shares
E = total exports

then

$$M_e = \varepsilon' m_e \tag{23}$$

M_e = multiplier of export demand
m_e = 30 × 1 vector of industry export multipliers

These restricted multipliers may turn out to be considerably lower than unrestricted multipliers. Much depends also on which model is used in evaluating a multiplier and how binding restrictions are. If a consumption function is incorporated in the model, the unrestricted multiplier will be much higher than if no consumption function is part of the model. As soon as supply restrictions become binding, differences between the two approaches (with and without consumption function) are likely to diminish, though multipliers will remain different. In one of the next sections we will consider the possibility of incorporating a consumption function in this model.
For negotiations with industries considering location in the area as in the past the blast furnace and steel plant, as well as for important expansions, a clear picture of their possible positive contribution to total production may be of much practical use. Besides this the primal solution of the linear programming model may complete the picture of the impact of other industries.

Shadow-prices of restrictions on *supply* or capacity can be interpreted as marginal productivity of the production factor concerned. Take, for example the shadow-price for labour:

$$p_W = \frac{\Delta Y}{\Delta W_{max}} \tag{24}$$

where:

P_W = shadow-price for labour
Y = total value added
W_{max} = restriction on labour supply

Here p_W is the marginal labour productivity. Other possibly restricted factors as land, environmental factors such as tolerable levels of solid waste disposal, air, water and land pollution, energy supply etc. also should be considered as scarce production factors. Shadow prices obtained from a linear programming model of this type give a global indication of the scarcity value and social cost of certain factors, not a precise costing of the factors as actually required by a particular firm or industrial process.

For factors which have market prices e.g. labour, this point may be illustrated by referring to the two major elements of abstraction in the linear programming approach. There is the assumption of homogeneity which overlooks actual differences in quality and local scarcity; and there are market imperfections. However, for rational decisions at least some impression of opportunity costs would be highly desirable, for land and labour as well as for restrictions in other fields.

The shadow-price of any restriction is dependent on

a. the restriction itself,

b. other restrictions, either supply or demand restrictions.

Shifts in restrictions may involve all other shadow-prices. With a linear model like this one not every shift should bring about a change in the set of shadow-prices, even if its starting position is binding. In most cases shifts in restrictions, outwards or inwards, should cover certain intervals, before shadow-prices are affected. Reactions go with leaps and bounds. From a view-point of interpretation the size of these intervals is quite important, and also in what sectors reactions appear and how sharp they are. Therefore we analysed the dual by means of parametric adjustments of the right hand side.

As no exact data are available for all of the restrictions, and in particular not for the emissions, for this sensitivity analysis, emission restrictions were provisionally put at levels of 90% and 95% of computed emission levels without restrictions. Some results of this analysis are given in table 5.

Table 5

Survey of Shadowprices for Different Kinds of Labour, Land, Emissions as Calculated with the L.P.-Model with Alternately Binding Restrictions

Item in restriction	Shadowprice in gld.
Workers and employees:	
Unskilled, skilled	20,000 / man
Schooled, vocational	20,000 / man
Secondary level	80,000 / man
Higher level	unrestricted
Land for industrial use	1.0 / m^2
Sulfurdioxyde (SO_2)	4.9 / kg
Carbon monoxyde (CO)	10.0 / kg
Oxydes of nitrogen (NOx)	14.0 / kg
Fluor (HF)	4,000.0 / kg
Flying dust	24.0 / kg
Solid waste	5,100.0 / kg
Water pollution	200.0 / kg

Most of the shadow-prices are more or less in the line with a priori expectations. Quite remarkable is the position of solid waste disposal in this table. It would mean a shadow-price of Dfl. 15 mln for the contents of a 3 ton's van. This impossible conclusion stems from the fact that every activity produces solid waste with the effect that no substitution of activities can eliminate solid waste to such extent that the restriction is met. If the authority does not want to relax restrictions and does not want any total reduction of activity in order to meet them, the only way out of the dilemma is the creation of a waste disposal industry. By coincidence local authorities in the Rijnmond area do exploit a waste disposal industry. To take this into account a waste disposal sector of the Leontief type can be inserted in the model (see [7]). The Rijnmond staff is actually assembling data to construct a column in the $I-O$ table from data of this industry.

A Layered Model for Abatement Analysis

Industrial labour requirements tend to diminish, being the inverse of labour productivity. The increase in labour productivity is a function of:

a. absolute scarcity factors, requiring a general increase in efficiency (increasing returns to scale, technological change);

b. relative scarcity factors, requiring substitution by other factors of production, in particular by improved and more expensive equipment (capital deepening).

The increasing trend in labour productivity is accounted for in the original Rijnmond model by dividing labour requirements through exogenous estimates of productivity, derived from those made by the Central Planning Bureau for the country as a whole.
Comparable reductions in requirements are probable in other fields. Interindustry deliveries will obviously feel the impact of this fact but this problem will be provisionally left out of the picture. Attention will be concentrated on reductions in requirements of other production factors, in particular the use of available room for emissions and land for industrial use.
Of course productivity trends may be estimated exogenously as well, and fed into the model when forecasts are made. The general trends in requirements (if known!) are then accounted for, but the specific conditions in the area under review do not enter the picture. And as the Rijnmond problem is actually the scarcity of land and room for emissions, we will try to adapt the model in order to get some impression of the necessary reductions in requirements for a full employment and maximum sales solution.
For this purpose total production for each activity is split into three additive components (see also figure 6):

1. Normal production with labour and other production factor requirements (as specified in the linear programming model);
2. Production with zero labour requirements, with increased capital output ratios, but with normal requirements for other production factors; (unclean production without labour);
3. Production with zero requirements for land and environmental factors, with increased capital output ratios, but with normal labour requirements (clean production with labour).

If sufficient degrees of freedom were available, such a layered model could be run with 3×30 activities (30 being the number of activities in the input-output table) to give a solution from which the necessary reductions for each activity could be derived.
However, only 30 final demand restrictions and 13 supply restrictions could be placed against the 3×30 activities (four different types of labour, industrial and non-industrial land, emissions of SO_2, NO_x, dust, HF, CO, solid waste, water pollution). This means that no unique and stable solution is obtained in this way.

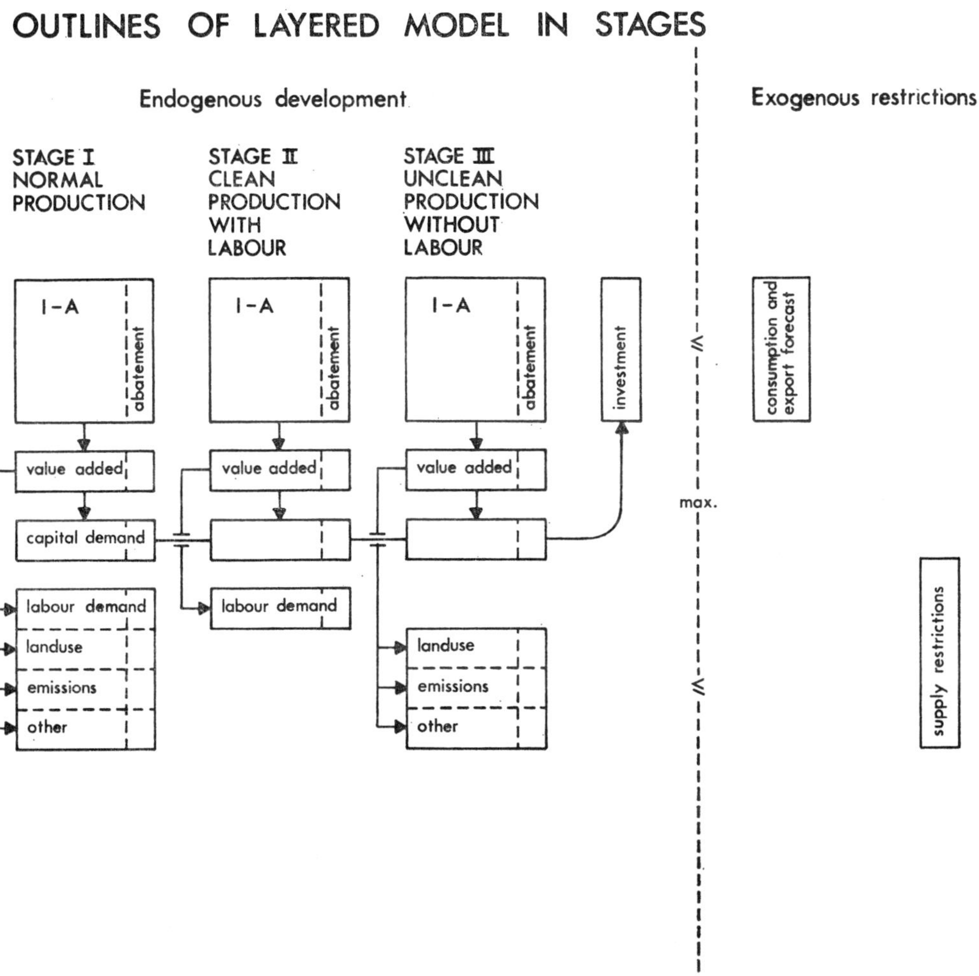

Figure 6.

The author now suggests a solution in three stages in the following sequence:

First stage. The linear programming model is run as described in the previous sections, including a priori estimates for the increase in labour productivity; productivity increases for other factors are not specified. The first stage model in which production levels x_1 are reached becomes:

$$\text{maximize } Y = i'(I - A' - \hat{\mu})x_1 \tag{25}$$

subject to:

$$(I - A - C)x_1 - Cx_{-T} \leq \delta_{max} \tag{26}$$

$$S'x_1 \qquad \leq \sigma_{max} \tag{27}$$

The systematic feature of this first stage model is the limitation of production and value added by the imposed requirement that land for economic use and the various environmental emissions do not exceed their base year values. With constant land and environment productivity the only way to effectively use the increased labour productivity is to re-allocate scarce land and environment factors from 'dirty' and land-using activities like oil refinery and other port-related activities to 'clean' products and services which provide employment and production at lower environmental costs. As there are limits to the demand for such 'clean' products, even with the projected increase in demand, the main outcome of this stage is likely to be unemployment of labour, coupled with non-attainment of the projected demand levels in some sectors.

Second stage. As the causes of not attaining demand levels in particular industries can be traced to emission-levels and land use per unit of output the obvious solution of the unemployment problem lies in reduction of unit-emission and unit land-use levels. By putting emission and land-use at zero levels, the second stage solution gives the necessary conditions for full employment. Previously dirty industries may expand, if only their emissions do not increase. In the second stage model all slacks of the previous solution (excess demand, unused capacity) are substituted into the restrictions; where slacks are non-existent restrictions are put at zero level. The second stage model in which production levels $x_1 + x_2$ are reached becomes:

$$\text{maximize } Y = i'(I - A' - \hat{\mu})x_2 \tag{28}$$

subject to

$$(I - A - C)(x_1 + x_2) - Cx_{-T} \leq \delta_{max} \tag{29}$$

$$S_\lambda'(x_1 + x_2) \qquad \leq \sigma_{\lambda max} \tag{30}$$

$$S_v'x_1 - N'_{min}(x_1 + x_2) \qquad \geq 0 \tag{31}$$

where S is partitioned into

S_λ $= 30 \times 4$ matrix of labour requirements
S_v $= 30 \times 9$ matrix of land use coefficients, pollution coefficients etc.
$N_{min} = 30 \times 9$ matrix of lower bounds for land, pollution etc. coefficients

Third stage. When labour becomes binding the model enters its last stage, either directly after the first stage, or after the second stage (the sequence of the model can be followed from the flow scheme in figure 7). The economic meaning of the labour restriction becoming binding is that there is still unsatisfied demand that can only be reached if labour productivity is sufficiently increased. The slacks of the previous solution are again substituted into the restrictions. Instead of emission and land use coefficients, which are again put at their normal levels, now labour coefficients are put at zero. The third stage model in which production levels

$$x = x_1 + x_2 + x_3 \tag{32}$$

are reached, is as follows:

$$\text{maximize } Y = i'(I - A' - \mu)x_3 \tag{33}$$

subject to:

$$(I - \mathrm{A} - C)x + Cx_{-T} \leq \delta_{max} \tag{19}$$

$$S_v'(x_1 + x_3) \leq \sigma_{v\,max} \tag{34}$$

$$S_\lambda'(x_1 + x_2) - L_{min}'x \geq 0 \tag{35}$$

where

$L_{min} = 30 \times 4$ matrix of lower bounds for labour requirements.

This three stages solution for the linear programming model is still in a phase of implementation. The sum of the three stages solutions should give the integral solution, including the necessary reduction of requirements and emissions to obtain maximum production and employment within predetermined bounds. Necessary increases in productivity follow from the average requirements of the three productions. To prevent lower requirements in the solution than are feasible for a priori reasons, lower bounds for requirements should be specified beforehand. If such lower bounds become binding in the second stage, more than three stages may be needed to obtain a final consistent solution.

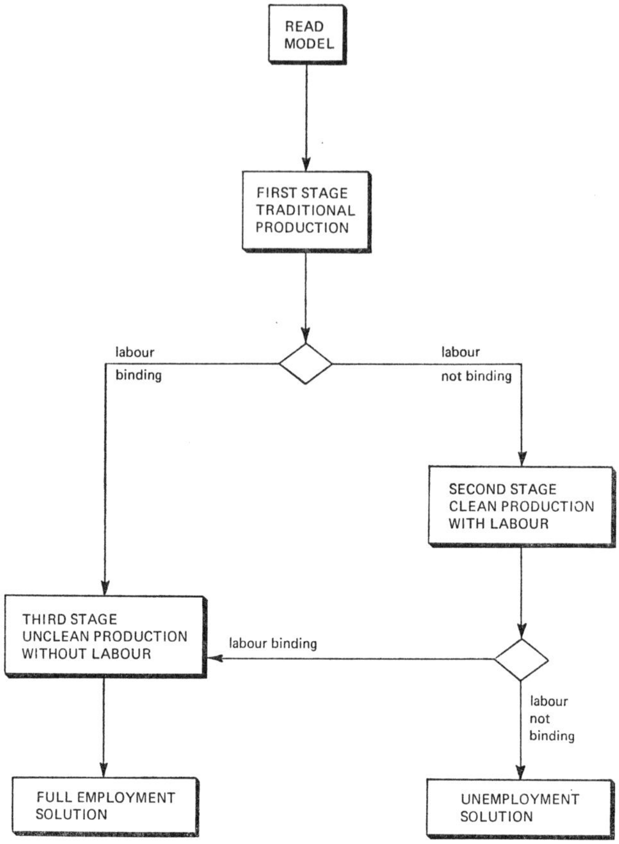

Figure 7. Flow scheme of three stages model.

The reason to continue with production with labour in the second stage and to end with production without labour in the third stage instead of the other way round lies in full utilisation of labour being a policy target, whereas full coverage of tolerable room for non-labour factors such as land for industrial purposes or polluting emissions obviously is not. The third stage is useful in particular to get to know what it would mean for production in every sector if demand is satisfied up to market restrictions and what supply restrictions become ultimately binding. It is interesting to compare this layered model for abatement evaluation with the more traditional approach of special abatement sectors as cited in the last section with respect to solid waste disposal. Abatement sector analysis essentially is a cost analysis. The input-output linear programming model will choose for the abatement sector, if the cost per unit of pollution abated is lower than the reallocation of production to less polluting activities and/or reducing total production.

The layered model may be used to evaluate reductions in requirements or emission coefficients to be obtained for a full employment solution. These reductions in requirements are entirely to be obtained by investments. Both models apply to different abatement systems. A separate abatement activity like for instance solid waste disposal can be more realistically described by adding a sector for abatement. The layered model may be superior for abatement problems that mainly call for investments to adapt existing processes, without affecting interindustry requirements to any significant extent. A combined cost analysis by the two approaches calls for more information on investment costs for abatement purposes, which is needed to make the comparison complete. Costs of capital use should be included in the objective function. Abatement alternatives may then be explored in the second stage model.

Such a layered model might give a fair picture of limiting factors in regional growth. The approach has the advantage of being straightforward, and for that reason likely to be comprehensible for lay decision-makers. The disadvantages lie in the heavy data requirements and in the reliability of data. This applies as well to forecasts of sectoral final demand, as to the statistical data material.

The Input-Output Table for 1970

For administrative reasons the Central Bureau of Statistics is late in computing 1970 regional accounts and input-output tables. Only data on regional production and primary inputs have yet become available. The last regional input-output table refers to 1965.

However, important changes in the industrial structure, in particular the development of seaport industries, made their way in the second half of the sixties. A reliable forecast should be based upon a benchmark that is updated at least up to 1970.

Meanwhile the Rijnmond staff made a bold attempt to compile a provisional 1970 table from available statistics. A great advantage was that for 1965 a two-region interregional table exists, a result of close cooperation of the C.B.S. and the Rijnmond staff [9]. This table gives the input-output relations inside and between two regions: 'Rijnmond' and 'rest of the country'. The table is consistent with the national input-output table for the same year. This consistency is a basic element in the computation of the provisional 1970 table. The reasoning is that given

a. regional data on production and primary costs for 1970 and
b. the national input-output table for 1970 [1]
   and starting from
c. the interregional input-output table for 1965

it should be possible to calibrate the 1970 table by the RAS-method [11].

Stating the broad outlines of a computing policy does not do justice to the infinite number of details and difficulties to be mastered in the computing process. I will name some of them.

1. Existing differences between the national table and the sum of regional tables, due to
   – administrative or secondary activities of a company that in a national table are classified according to the main activity of the company, but in the regional table according to the main activity of a regional branch;
   – activities that do no belong to any subnational territory like e.g. shipping and military services, but have either to be classified somewhere, or to be eliminated from the national table.
2. Introduction of the new 'Standard industrial classification of all economic activities' (SIC) in all C.B.S.-statistics since 1969, and for that matter in the 1970 table. The 1965 interregional table had to be transformed from ISIC into SIC before computations could start.
3. The calibrating procedure appeared only to converge to sensible results for the block of interindustry deliveries. The items regional imports from abroad and components of regional final demand had to be estimated cell by cell directly by applying regional ratios to 1970 national figures:
   – for imports regional ratios of imports to sum of interindustry deliveries from the 1965 table;
   – for final demand by origin regional production figures for 1970;
   – for final demand by destination regional ratios from the 1965 table.
4. In calibrating an interregional interindustry matrix with small figures in the off-diagonal interregional blocks, at least compared to the intra-regional deliveries, there is a chance of cell-explosion in off-diagonal block cells. To prevent such explosions regional subtotals had to be imposed.

In short: after adapting the statistical data to a new classification and correcting for statistical differences between regional and national figures, and after preliminary estimation of regional imports and final demands, interindustry deliveries have been calibrated by the RAS-method under some additional restrictions. The procedure can be followed from figure 8. A condensed version of the interregional table for 1970 is presented in the annex.[2]

In the sequel some points of criticism of this model will be discussed, and possible solutions will be suggested. These solutions have not been definitively or even provisionally implemented in the model and are partly still in a stage of philosophy. The input-output-theory of this model is founded on the assumption of stable and reliable input-output coefficients. In so far as these are technical coefficients they can by definition only remain unchanged over time and over space as long as technology remains unchanged. It is clear that this can never be the case, at least over time. Moreover for economic reasons, such as changes in relative prices, a company may alter its production process even with unchanged technology or will apply different processes for the same product in different plants.

The input-output tables available for this model lead the user to forget more and more of his theoretical scruples. Every branch of industry in this table is an aggregate of companies of sometimes quite different character and production fields, and each company counts a number of incomparable production processes. Sometimes very distinct subsectors are combined to great aggregates as for instance oil refinery and chemical industries, wholesale and retail trade, sea and air transport. These three combined sectors accounted for 28%, 11% and 9% of total gross private output of Rijnmond in 1965, against 13 out of 30 sectors with gross output of 1% each or even less. Such differences can only be accepted in the exceptional case of great homogeneity of grouped industries. In the Rijnmond case this homogeneity clearly does not exist.

For so called technical coefficients all this may result in shifts over time (and over space) that have nothing to do with technology, but everything with differences in growth, related to price and demand developments. Apart from this, there is the question of relative prices, which is important as long as technical coefficients are expressed in money terms. Even with an analysis in constant prices, as is commonly made, changes in relative prices may affect coefficients and impair their stability over time.

Some years ago Tilanus investigated the stability of input-output coefficients from an empirical point of view [12]. In practice I – O coefficients for the Netherlands seem to be quite stable over time in nominal terms because of the working of substitution effects, and for that reason usable for I – O analysis.

In regional input-output analysis the coefficients problem is probably still more pressing. Regional input-output coefficients reflect the interindustry deliveries of Rijnmond industries to Rijnmond industries, in our example. We cannot call for technology any more as evidence for stability over time. The only reason why

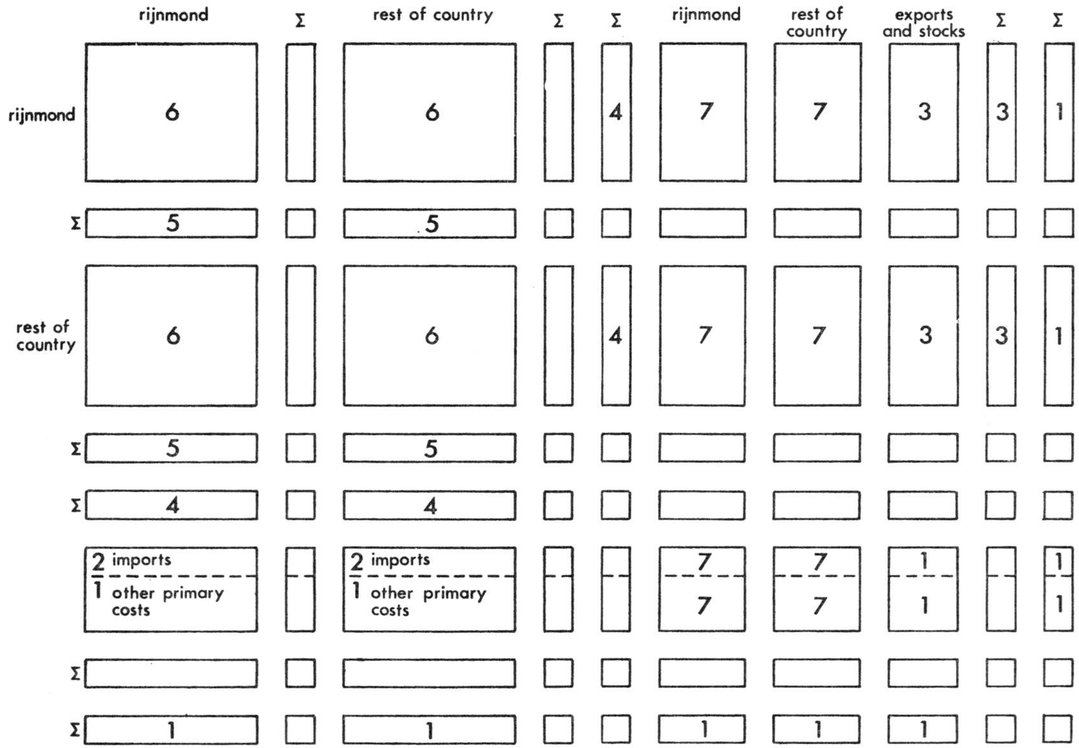

Steps

1 total output and primary costs (data)

2 imports (ratio analysis of 1965 table)

3 final sales by origin (ratio analysis of regional output)

4 sums of interindustry deliveries (by deduction)

5 additional restrictions (ratio analysis 1965 table)

6 calibrating by R.A.S.-method

7 final sales by destination (ratio analysis of 1965 table)

Figure 8. Computation of the interregional table for 1970.

Rijnmond to Rijnmond deliveries follow a constant pattern are existing producer-client relations, that apparently are quite stable. This does not preclude that differences in supply prices or supply-conditions like delivery delays may cause shifts to other suppliers, either from inside to outside the region or vice versa. However, according to Kruijtbosch and Van Eijk empirical evidence over the period 1960–1965, based on both tables in 1965 price level, did not produce shifts of sufficient size to impair the making of reasonable forecasts.[3]
Even after the bigger changes in the Rijnmond economy during the expansion period 1965–1970 the model seems to behave quite sensibly. It is not unlikely that the inverse matrix being dominated by the main diagonal played a major role in the good behaviour of this model.
Meanwhile the input-output table with about 30 branches of industry contains a lot of spurious information:

a. on branches that are unimportant as such for an over-all analysis of the economy like e.g. hardware production, or paper and editing, or medical and health services;
b. on branches for which reliable statistical information is hard to get, or even impossible, in particular in the services sector;
c. on technical coefficients that suffer from problems of aggregation.

To overcome these problems at least partially, the author suggests further aggregation of industrial branches into broader sectors, but upon economic considerations. This would also meet a general drawback of input-output and most other economic statistics, namely, that classification is based upon technical criteria, and that economics play no part in it.

Economic Classification of Industries

In recent years a number of activities has shown considerable decline in growth, in Rijnmond as well as elsewhere in Western Europe, some industries even an absolute decline, especially if measured in numbers employed, if not in output. Well known examples on a national scale are the textiles, clothing and leather industries. On the other hand industries like the chemical industry or the manufacturing of electronical equipment show considerable expansion. This does not imply that all companies in declining sectors are actually in decline and all companies in so-called growth sectors in buoyant expansion. Industrial life shows a great variety of developments, and any classification is bound to distort reality. In this sections

ANNEX INTRA- AND INTERREGIONAL INPUT-OUTPUT TABLE 1970 (CONDENSED)

	1	2	3	4	5	6	7	8	9	10	11	12	13	14	15	16	17	18
1	243.9	13.5	2.1	.0	.1	10.3	26.4	0.7	62.0	.0	359.0	274.2	5.3	3.6	.0	.0	1.8	16.4
2	6.4	8.2	2.0	0.5	1.6	11.0	27.1	0.3	0.3	0.2	57.5	10.3	17.8	13.3	1.0	1.0	3.8	53.4
3	5.8	4.2	65.5	2.8	13.1	27.8	45.9	72.0	0.3	1.7	239.1	7.9	2.8	28.3	4.1	3.5	7.3	25.1
4	9.9	1.5	4.3	180.2	100.6	51.7	33.2	66.7	2.7	1.3	451.8	11.5	0.9	2.2	129.8	14.8	5.5	7.4
5	6.7	2.3	3.4	15.3	67.9	91.9	92.1	18.3	1.2	1.1	300.2	14.1	4.6	7.7	16.4	34.8	27.5	27.1
6	17.8	10.6	28.9	7.3	77.0	864.0	677.4	45.0	4.8	7.6	1740.3	172.8	45.4	58.4	59.2	362.1	513.1	773.7
7	36.9	18.0	21.5	16.8	47.9	175.5	452.8	48.9	7.6	9.6	835.3	126.4	29.2	39.8	41.9	22.6	93.0	99.9
8	7.5	2.9	5.6	8.0	19.9	44.1	41.3	120.7	7.2	75.0	332.2	0.1	.0	0.1	0.8	0.3	.0	0.2
9	136.6	1.0	0.6	.0	.0	0.8	2.9	.0	37.8	.0	179.7	63.7	1.1	0.8	.0	.0	0.2	2.7
10	3.1	1.1	9.2	1.1	3.4	23.0	57.1	6.1	1.0	1.6	106.6	2.3	0.8	4.7	0.8	0.6	2.6	13.8
11	474.6	63.2	143.0	231.9	331.4	1300.1	1456.2	378.7	124.8	98.0	4601.9	683.3	108.0	158.9	254.0	439.8	654.8	1019.9
12	282.3	31.5	6.7	0.1	0.6	18.3	20.6	1.1	32.3	.0	393.6	3053.6	72.7	133.5	0.9	6.4	39.6	363.5
13	28.0	48.4	25.5	2.7	8.6	32.3	49.8	4.0	1.7	0.1	201.0	461.3	1101.6	295.2	49.8	72.8	176.0	586.8
14	7.2	8.9	55.6	7.9	80.3	51.4	55.6	182.0	2.8	1.0	452.5	168.1	116.1	1439.7	155.2	203.3	274.5	679.3
15	5.2	4.0	3.2	184.1	87.9	80.1	31.6	61.2	2.5	0.3	460.2	263.4	39.6	100.2	5030.9	1028.7	222.7	334.9
16	4.7	2.1	2.2	10.9	43.3	86.2	46.3	14.4	1.2	0.1	211.4	174.6	109.0	142.8	473.6	1015.1	551.3	660.1
17	19.3	9.1	13.9	7.7	49.6	245.8	369.7	28.7	8.1	1.2	753.1	296.1	196.0	253.8	183.8	960.2	859.1	3155.1
18	38.6	27.7	23.0	27.0	58.6	203.8	112.6	47.1	9.8	1.0	549.2	1028.1	566.0	587.6	653.3	570.8	963.7	2092.7
19	0.3	0.1	0.1	1.8	2.6	1.4	0.5	1.8	.0	1.5	10.1	96.1	54.0	83.2	141.4	165.1	199.4	270.0
20	287.9	5.5	2.0	.0	.0	0.4	5.1	.0	7.8	.0	308.8	7883.7	26.4	27.5	.0	.0	5.7	50.4
21	0.7	0.4	1.9	0.3	0.9	6.1	7.7	1.4	0.6	0.1	20.1	68.9	33.7	174.3	33.7	41.1	140.3	523.3
22	674.3	137.7	134.2	242.4	332.4	725.8	699.6	341.6	66.9	5.3	3360.2	13493.9	2315.1	3237.9	6722.7	4063.4	3432.3	8716.2
23	1148.9	200.9	277.2	474.3	663.8	2025.9	2155.8	720.3	191.7	103.3	7962.1	14177.1	2423.1	3396.8	6976.7	4503.2	4087.1	9736.1
24	1.1	.0	.0	1.3	0.6	0.7	9.0	0.7	0.4	0.5	14.3	11.7	.0	1.5	11.2	5.3	8.6	82.6
25	493.8	90.0	62.4	282.7	380.9	3911.9	975.8	332.8	18.9	1.4	6550.8	5702.4	3026.0	1267.1	3644.8	4325.2	3278.1	3843.3
26	21.7	231.3	2.0	10.0	11.1	1232.2	258.4	7.4	9.1	57.8	1841.4	110.3	1147.7	27.0	-43.0	-53.1	345.6	1713.8
27	-26.5	-1.8	.0	-14.6	-17.8	.0	0.5	.0	-5.0	-32.7	-97.9	-939.5	-5.2	-89.0	14.6	11.8	-147.0	2.5
28	174.7	111.8	164.8	287.0	458.0	1162.5	1824.8	541.1	14.8	162.1	4901.6	2606.3	1623.2	2480.2	3218.0	3521.0	4380.4	12817.3
29	41.9	25.7	35.0	60.6	105.3	281.8	367.6	147.8	2.6	33.8	1102.1	578.1	362.3	581.0	719.4	818.7	986.5	2675.4
30	163.7	116.6	58.7	161.0	348.4	1733.7	1639.3	84.5	118.9	420.7	4845.5	1697.3	808.4	1347.3	2085.0	3299.6	4783.3	9804.7
31	.0	.0	.0	.0	.0	.0	-273.1	.0	.0	.0	-273.1	.0	.0	.0	.0	.0	.0	-2173.9
32	871.0	573.6	322.9	788.0	1286.5	8322.8	4802.3	1114.3	159.7	643.6	18884.7	9766.0	6962.4	5615.1	9650.0	11928.5	13635.2	28765.7
33	2019.8	774.5	600.1	1262.3	1950.3	10348.7	7002.2	1834.6	351.4	746.9	26846.8	23943.2	9385.5	9011.9	16626.7	16431.7	17722.3	38457.8

Explanation of column and row numbers

row/column number	industry (Rijnmond/non-Rijnmond)
1/12	animal food, other food, leather and rubber, shoes and clothing, non coal mining;
2/13	textiles, beverages and tobacco, paper;
3/14	coal mining, wood and furniture, printing and publishing earthenware and glass;
4/15	metallurgy, metal products and machinery;
5/16	electrical equipment, transport equipment, public utilities, other manufacturing;
6/17	chemicals and oil, communication, other transport;
7/18	sea and air transport, wholesale and retail trade, banking, insurance, other services;
8/19	construction;
9/20	agriculture;
10/21	housing;

row number	row totals/subtotals
11	sum of rows 1 to 10, intermediate and final deli veries from Rijnmond industries;
22	sum of rows 12 to 21, intermediate and final deli veries from non-Rijnmond industries;
23	sum of rows 11 and 22;
32	sum of rows 24 to 31, total primary input;
33	sum of rows 23 and 32, total inputs;

column number	column totals/subtotals
11	sum of columns 1 to 10, inputs of Rijnmond industries;
22	sum of columns 11 to 21, inputs of non-Rijnmond industries;
23	sum of columns 11 and 22;
35	sum of columns 24 to 34, total final demand;
36	sum of columns 23 and 35, total output;

ANNEX INTRA- AND INTERREGIONAL INPUT-OUTPUT TABLE 1970 (CONDENSED) CONTINUED

	19	20	21	22	23	24	25	26	27	28	29	30	31	32	33	34	35	36
1	.7	160.1	.0	462.2	821.2	235.9	1.3	.0	.0	432.0	1.5	.0	.0	.7	.9	526.3	1198.6	2019.8
2	1.3	.5	.1	102.5	160.0	52.2	1.6	.0	.0	407.7	3.8	.0	.1	3.5	.6	145.0	614.5	774.5
3	69.5	1.4	4.2	154.1	393.2	22.9	10.7	1.2	2.9	88.9	8.7	1.2	2.9	4.5	7.8	55.3	206.9	600.1
4	30.6	1.6	.4	204.8	656.7	6.6	5.1	3.3	60.4	33.4	5.1	5.9	60.4	29.1	10.1	386.3	605.6	1262.3
5	10.6	1.3	0.5	144.6	444.7	209.0	16.6	1.6	111.0	102.3	9.1	3.3	90.8	114.5	30.0	817.4	1505.6	1950.3
6	187.2	57.0	19.0	2247.8	3988.1	356.7	20.3	.0	.0	783.5	38.2	.0	.0	109.7	115.3	4937.0	6360.6	10348.7
7	64.1	21.0	6.0	544.1	1379.4	1945.6	-46.5	12.2	76.9	615.2	19.7	.9	72.3	-33.7	75.7	2840.5	5578.8	6958.2
8	.5	.2	.0	2.3	334.5	55.6	62.2	372.0	943.8	1.8	.1	.2	.8	.0	29.6	33.9	1500.1	1834.6
9	.0	2.5	.0	71.0	250.7	22.4	.5	.0	.0	9.6	.5	.0	.0	4.8	.2	62.6	100.7	351.4
10	3.7	1.7	.8	31.7	138.4	464.2	3.3	1.9	40.6	4.7	3.6	2.8	61.0	.0	21.6	4.8	608.5	746.9
11	368.2	247.2	31.0	3965.0	8566.9	3371.0	75.2	392.1	1235.6	2479.2	90.3	4.4	288.2	233.1	291.8	9809.0	18279.9	26846.8
12	21.5	3286.6	.0	6978.2	7371.8	549.1	2.3	.0	.0	8573.0	41.9	.0	18.0	-210.7	12.1	7585.7	16571.4	23943.2
13	44.4	32.5	5.6	2826.0	3027.0	322.9	4.5	.5	.9	2836.2	49.4	1.4	10.1	51.5	17.2	3054.0	6358.5	9385.5
14	2117.6	67.5	53.1	5274.3	5726.8	145.2	35.8	.9	14.2	1515.0	232.5	-4.9	100.0	61.5	95.4	1039.7	3285.1	9011.9
15	1046.5	107.2	15.0	8189.1	8649.3	48.7	26.9	1.8	182.8	477.4	108.6	19.6	1407.4	382.9	132.5	5088.7	7977.4	16626.7
16	295.7	61.2	13.2	3496.8	3708.3	61.6	12.8	3.8	287.5	2734.9	222.0	36.4	1559.7	928.5	248.4	6627.6	12723.4	16431.7
17	418.2	381.2	38.2	6741.7	7494.8	114.7	1.4	.0	.0	1982.1	117.0	.0	196.0	144.3	255.8	7416.0	10227.4	17722.3
18	841.9	590.6	103.4	7998.3	8547.5	261.1	2.9	1.8	121.9	19627.1	-85.8	99.2	981.0	-249.3	612.9	8581.5	29954.2	38501.8
19	1220.0	145.6	659.6	3034.4	3044.5	3.1	1.3	.0	4.4	519.5	565.5	3388.2	8594.0	.0	269.8	308.1	13653.9	16698.4
20	.0	964.9	.0	8958.5	9267.3	93.9	1.7	.0	.0	1082.1	38.4	.0	-49.0	178.2	7.6	2301.4	3654.3	12921.6
21	113.8	75.8	21.5	1226.5	1246.6	7.2	.0	1.4	44.5	4217.9	61.8	-0.9	870.9	.0	194.7	43.2	5482.5	6729.1
22	6119.5	5713.1	909.7	54723.9	58084.1	1607.6	89.5	10.2	656.2	43565.2	1351.4	3740.6	13688.0	1286.9	1846.4	42046.0	109888.0	167972.2
23	6487.7	5960.3	940.7	58688.9	66651.0	4978.6	164.7	402.3	1891.8	46044.4	1441.8	3755.0	13976.2	1520.0	2138.2	51855.0	128168.0	194819.0
24	8.2	10.0	8.3	147.4	180.1	5.3	.0	.0	.0	36.3	.0	.0	.0	.0	.0	.0	41.6	221.7
25	2900.3	414.7	24.9	28426.5	34958.9	992.2	302.5	14.6	803.1	9416.2	674.5	75.4	5221.9	1396.0	.0	2098.0	20993.4	55952.3
26	63.6	185.9	463.2	3960.6	5802.0	401.6	36.8	52.6	254.2	3714.4	347.5	492.4	1831.8	.0	.0	137.0	7268.0	13070.0
27	.0	-44.0	-223.3	-1419.1	-1517.0	.0	.0	.0	.0	.0	.0	.0	.0	.0	.0	.0	.0	-1517.0
28	4734.9	865.2	1332.9	37579.4	42481.0	.0	511.5	9.8	.0	.0	5527.9	59.5	.0	.0	3941.3	.0	10050.0	52531.0
29	1293.2	152.4	276.2	8442.9	9545.0	.0	184.3	.0	.0	.0	1903.2	.0	.0	.0	1343.5	.0	3431.0	12976.0
30	1210.5	5377.1	3906.3	34319.5	39165.0	.0	44.5	.0	.0	.0	592.7	.0	.0	.0	157.8	.0	795.0	39960.0
31	.0	.0	.0	-2173.9	-2447.0	.0	.0	.0	.0	.0	.0	.0	.0	.0	.0	.0	.0	-2447.0
32	10210.7	6961.3	5788.5	109283.3	128168.0	1399.1	1079.6	77.0	1057.2	13166.9	9045.5	627.3	7052.8	1396.0	5442.6	2235.0	42579.0	170747.0
33	16698.4	12921.6	6729.1	167972.2	194819.0	6377.7	1244.3	479.3	2949.0	59210.9	10487.3	4382.3	21029.0	2916.0	7580.8	54090.0	170747.0	.0

Explanation of column and row numbers

column number	final demand components (Rijnmond / non Rijnmond)	row number	primary inputs
24 / 28	private consumption	24	imports from extraterritorial government
25 / 29	government consumption	25	imports from abroad
26 / 30	government investment	26	indirect taxes
27 / 31	private investment	27	subsidies
32	stockbuilding	28	wages and salaries
33	exports to extraterritorial sector	29	social security contribution by employers
34	exports abroad	30/31	gross profit / interest income of banks

we shall try to find a classification of industries that accounts for economic causes of differences in sectoral development. Official statistical classifications in use like ISIC or SIC are preponderantly based on product or process affinity. This kind of classification is not directly related to important circumstances from an economic point of view like market structure or the production function. Regrouping will be based on economic criteria, though necessarily ISIC or SIC will have to be ultimately used as bench mark, no other data source being available.

Thanks to extensive econometric research of the Dutch economy by the Central Planning Bureau the main behavioural relationships such as income and price elasticities for consumption, sales and price elasticities for exports, determinants of labour demand and investments, are available for 23 branches of industry. These branches have been regrouped into 7 sectors: 4 sectors of manufacturing and mining, further agriculture, services and the building industries. The selecting criteria for the 4 manufacturing and mining industries are based upon differences in behaviour. It is for that reason a representative grouping, and in view of the existing variety of companies it is quite possible that particular companies from a behavioural standpoint appear in the wrong grouping.

As starting points for regrouping of manufacturing and mining industries were available:

1. on the supply side: derived productivity functions for labour, based on Cobb-Douglas production functions;[4]
2. on the demand side: sales and price elasticities for consumption and exports.[5]

After some research it was possible to distinguish a significant criterion in the influence of the ratio of wages and capital user costs on demand for labour, higher relative labour costs calling for capital deepening with less employment of labour and more employment of capital. The elasticity of demand for labour in industry i with respect to the labour-capital user cost ratio appeared to be clearly clustered around an unweighted mean of $-.23$ and $-.48$ respectively. From a demand point of view a comparable dichotomy is possible into sectors with a sales elasticity of over and under unity. The sales elasticity of consumer expenditure in each sector is defined with respect to total consumer expenditure. They are related to income elasticities, but the latter coefficients are not directly available as the latest consumer surveys do not give income data. The sales elasticity of exports in sector i is defined in the same way with respect to total exports. Data have been investigated to find out whether other criteria could be used as well, however, without any significant result.

Table 6

Selection Criteria for Industry Grouping

Sales elasticity	Elasticity of the labour-capital user cost ratio < .4	> .4
< 1	animal food other food clothing non-coal mining	textiles beverages and tobacco paper
> 1	machinery transport equipment other manufacturing	chemicals and oil metallurgy electrical equipment public utilities

In table 6 manufacturing and mining industries are grouped into their respective classes.[6] This not very conspicuous table touches the very root of recent industrial development. For what are the reasons industries decline and companies fail:

– they are stuck in markets that do not show expansion (low sales elasticity), and/or
– they are trapped in a relatively bad competitive performance (slow reaction to increased labour-capital cost ratio).

In the best of cases the management of the company failed to react on new circumstances, but is yet in a position to improve the product mix or to introduce new technology. In the worst of cases activity should be stopped in the present location and transplanted to places where high relative labour costs are not such a pressing problem, at least not for the time being. On the other hand industries with a relatively strong position (high sales elasticities, more possibilities to react to the production factors price ratio) could stay and expand in their present location.
However, in both cases developments have their impact on the labour market. Of course transfer of activities to other regions directly involves employment. But also in cases of maintained or expanded industries a reduction of employment is probable as they maintain their position by substituting capital for labour. The non-industrial sectors will absorb surplus labour, but it depends on the production function and their sales and price elasticities whether total absorbtion of surplus labour is possible.
The model that is to describe these processes must be quite comprehensive as it should allow for estimates of demand taking income and prices into account, as well as labour demand functions allowing for the substitution process of capital

for labour. In the next section the author will try to get some of these elements in the linear programming Rijnmond model, at the same time attempting a solution of the pollution factor.

Towards a More Comprehensive Analysis

In this section the elements of previous sections are combined in a model with a smaller number of sectors, but fit for a more comprehensive analysis of regional development from an economic point of view.

These elements are

1. the linear programme with demand and supply restrictions from p. 179 – 182;
2. the layered model for the evaluation of necessary changes in labour and land requirements and emissions from p. 185 – 191;
3. the inclusion of an abatement sector for solid waste disposal, in accordance with Leontief (see p. 185);
4. reduction of the number of industries by regroupment for economic analysis; this reduction of the number of industries will make it possible to do without the multistage solution of the layered model;
5. inclusion of the 1970 interregional table and extension of the model over both regions, to reach consistent estimates of interregional transactions (exports to rest of the country, fractions of regional investment and consumption supplied by the home region);
6. inclusion of a regional macro-consumption function, now the geographical distribution of expenditure is known from the interregional input-output table; only with respect to income flows from region to region some hypothesis will have to be worked out;
7. endogenous labour productivity functions for normal production by applying derived Cobb-Douglas functions as specified by the Central Planning Bureau [4].
8. relative prices for sectoral products, based on mark up of unit labour costs hypothesis and if possible also of unit capital costs;
9. endogenous determination of demand per sector by applying price and sales elasticities to macro-estimates of regional consumption and exports;
10. as a last suggestion may be added that the geographical distribution of demand also may be influenced by regional differences in unit production costs; compare the regional price elasticity of –.75 applied by the Central Planning Bureau in its regional investment tax study [6].

Exogenous variables for this model will be:

1. estimates of national exports and government outlay;
2. determinants of labour productivity in normal production according to derived Cobb-Douglas labour productivity functions; labour-capital user cost ratio, length of working time, technological productivity trend; increases by returns to scale can be derived endogenously from production;
3. lower bounds for requirements and emissions to be specified for each of sectors from a priori knowledge of what is technically feasible in the forecast period;
4. restrictions on supply of production factors, other input or emissions; these are scenario values to be set according to political attitudes;
5. capital output ratios:
   a. for normal productions according to C.P.B. estimates;
   b. for unclean production without labour; these could be normal c/o ratios, only without correction for labour's contribution;
   c. for clean production with labour; generally higher than for normal production, but no evidence available.

A sketch of the most likely shape of the model is given in figure 9. Since the model contains a number of non-linearities, in particular in the determination of demand per sector by income and price elasticities, it will probably have to be solved in an iterative way.

Conclusions

Recently a newly manned working group under chairman P. Nijkamp has been charged to conduct continued research on the Rijnmond model. In this working group several possible ways of developing the model are discussed. Two of these may be mentioned here:

1. Substitution of regular input-output coefficients by attraction coefficients of the Klaassen-Van Wickeren type, by which supply-factors in regional development may better be accounted for. Such attraction coefficients have already been implemented into the Rijnmond model by Van Wickeren [13].
2. Multiple goal programming, as employed by Van Delft en Nijkamp to the Maasvlakte choice problem [6].

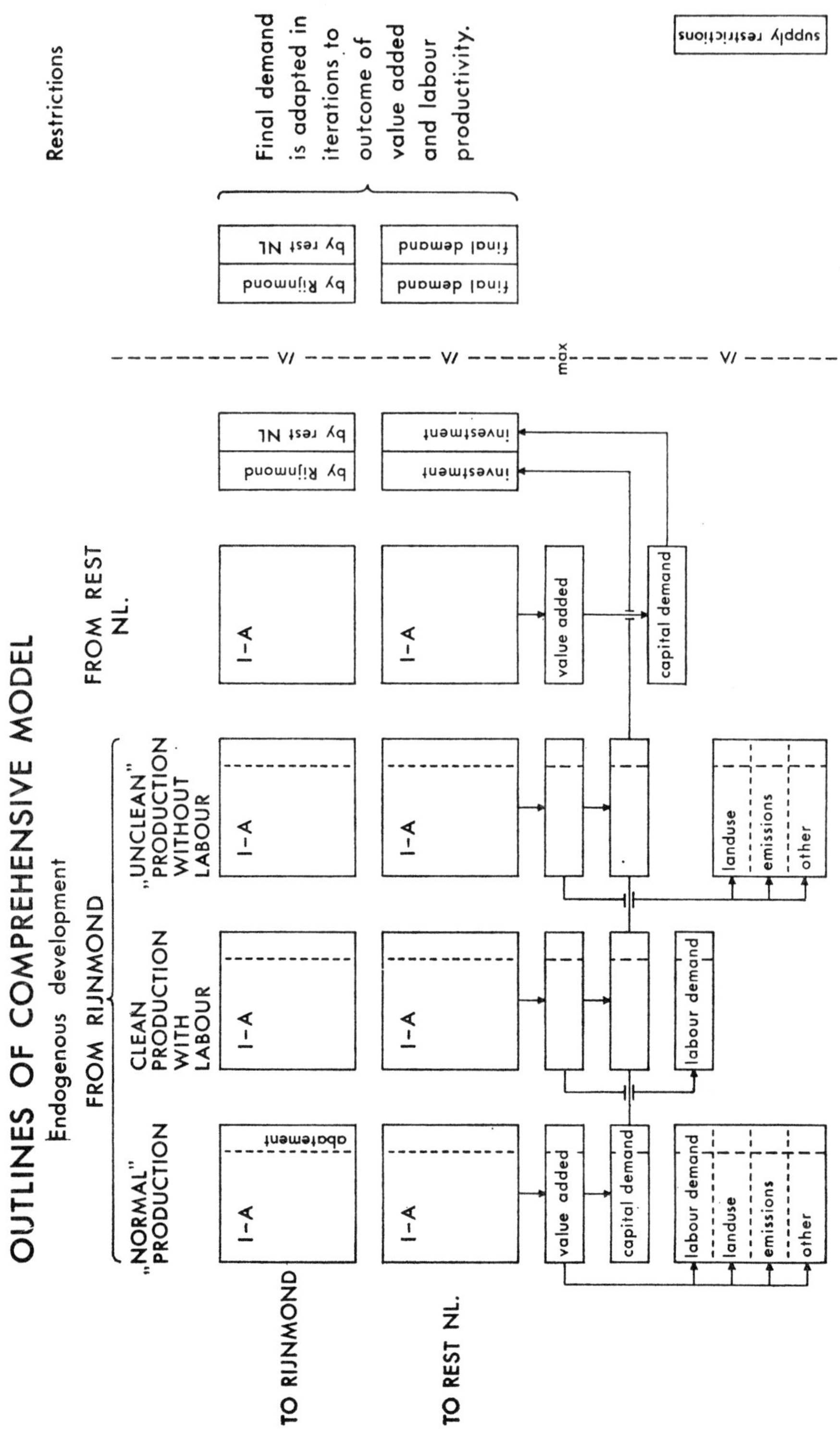
OUTLINES OF COMPREHENSIVE MODEL
Endogenous development
Restrictions
FROM RIJNMOND
FROM REST NL.
„NORMAL" PRODUCTION
CLEAN PRODUCTION WITH LABOUR
„UNCLEAN" PRODUCTION WITHOUT LABOUR
TO RIJNMOND
TO REST NL.
I–A
abatement
value added
capital demand
labour demand
landuse
emissions
other
by Rijnmond
by rest NL
investment
final demand
max
Final demand is adapted in iterations to outcome of value added and labour productivity.
supply restrictions

Figure 9

To both alternatives now are added:

3. The layered model with its multiple stage solution as presented on p. 178 – 183, and
4. The comprehensive interregional l.p. model with reduced number of activities, as sketched in the preceding section.

It may be stressed that the four approaches are only in part mutually exclusive. Attraction coefficients for example, might be used in each of the three other possibilities. Each of the alternatives has its stronger and weaker points. Only a detailed model, either of the attraction or of the regular input-output type, can give answers to questions regarding specific industries; but such models have great data requirements, and reliable data are not always easy to get. A less detailed, but more comprehensive approach may give a more consistent overall picture and can do with much less data requirements, but of course it is not in a position to furnish detailed information. As long as we do not want to go in for probably unmanageable great models, comprehensiveness has to be paid for by reducing the amount of detail. Whether the one or the other model will be the more successful depends for a great deal on the purpose of the user. This would mean that different models for the same area can very well be used in alternation for different purposes.

Notes

1 A comparable l.p. model for the Rijnmond area was designed earlier by Muller and Pelupessy, to evaluate the scarcity of pure air in Rijnmond. See [7].

2 The complete table is available on request at Rijnmond Public Authority, Postbox 23073, Rotterdam.

3 Het economisch structuurmodel van Rijnmond [9] p. 14.

4 Source: Central Planning Bureau [4] Table V.1, p. 131.

5 Source: Central Planning Bureau [3] Tables 4.1, p. 73; 4.2, p. 74; 4.7, p. 88; and unpublished updated figures.

6 The classification in the new Rijnmond table uses a somewhat different grouping in the metal industries sector, which makes it hardly possible to give the exact grouping of table 6 in the condensed I-0 table.

References

[1] Centraal Bureau voor de Statistiek: *De productiestructuur van de Nederlandse volkshuishouding* (The production structure of the Dutch economy), in particular part V.; 's-Gravenhage 1964—1975 (Dutch).

[2] Centraal Bureau voor de Statistiek: *Regionale rekeningen* (Regional accounts) 1960, 1965 's-Gravenhage 1968, 1970 (Dutch).

[3] Centraal Planbureau: *De Nederlandse economie in 1970*; 's-Gravenhage 1966 (Dutch).

[4] Centraal Planbureau: *De Nederlandse economie in 1973*; 's-Gravenhage 1970 (Dutch).

[5] Centraal Planbureau: *Mogelijke consequenties van een investeringsheffing op gebouwen in het Westen.* Bijlage van de memorie van antwoord no. 8 Ontwerp Wet selectieve investeringsregeling. Zitting 1972—1973—12045 (Dutch).

[6] Van Delft, A. and P. Nijkamp: *A Multi-Objective Decision Model for Regional Development*, Environmental Quality Control and Industrial Land Usė. Paper prepared for the European Meeting of the Regional Science Association 1975.

[7] Leontief, W.: Environmental Repercussions and the Economic Structure: an Input-Output Approach. *The Review of Economics and Statistics*, 1970.

[8] Muller, F. and W. Pelupessy: Economische waardering van de schaarse lucht in Rijnmond (Economic Valuation of Scarce Air in Rijnmond). *Economische Statistische Berichten*, 1971 (Dutch).

[9] Rijnmond Public Authority: *Het economisch structuurmodel van Rijnmond* (The Model of Rijnmond Economic Structure); Rotterdam 1972 (Dutch).

[10] Rijnmond Public Authority: *De Rijnmond-economie in de jaren zeventig; schets van een beheerste ontwikkeling.* (The Rijnmond economy in the seventies; Outline of a Controlled Development); Rotterdam 1973 (Dutch).

[11] Slater, L. J.: *More FORTRAN Programs for Economists.* Cambridge 1972.

[12] Tilanus, C. B.: *Input-Output Experiments: the Netherlands 1948—1961*; Rotterdam 1965.

[13] Van Wickeren, A. C.: Rijnmond Attraction Analysis versus Rijnmond Input-Output Analysis. Paper prepared for the *Annual Meeting of the Dutchspeaking Section of Regional Science Association 1974.*

The Cambridge Controversy and Welfare*

A. Heertje

Introduction

This article, which is meant to honour my teacher of mathematical economics, deals with an aspect of the so-called Cambridge controversy in capital theory that has been rather neglected. I refer to the welfare theoretical aspects of the choice of techniques within the framework of a simple two sector model of production. Without much discussion it is stated that from the set of wages-profit curves, which form a one to one correspondence to the possible alternative techniques, the element is chosen with the property that the rate of profit is maximised, given the real wage rate. It is demonstrated that this is either the outcome in equilibrium of perfect competition based on maximising behaviour of a large number of individual producers or it is the equilibrium solution with the property that prices are set in such a way that the system will be reproduced.

A question may be raised with respect to the movement from technique A to technique B along the envelope ignoring efficiency rules in making marginal adjustments of technique. Here, a problem of dynamic welfare theory is encountered, in so far as the new equipment substitutes capital goods which are installed recently or rather long ago. Important welfare theoretical problems also emerge from the influence of a change in technique on the level and composition of demand for labour. It is not our intention to go into these problems here. We restrict our analysis to a purely static context, in which the choice of the optimal technique is treated as a rather technical problem, the solution of which can be made explicit through the introduction of a social welfare function.

As is well-known, the relationship between consumption per head (c) and the growth rate of the system (g) for each technique is the dual of that between the real wage rate (w) and the rate of profit (r). Hence, the counterpart of the maximisation of the real wage rate, given the rate of profit, is the maximisation of consumption per head, given the rate of growth of the system. It is common practice when introducing a social welfare function to relate utility to consumption per head (c). Therefore, we consider it to be more promising to confront the concept of a social welfare function with the relationship between consumption per head and the growth rate. It is then one step to conceive of social welfare as a function of (c) and another step to broaden the welfare function and to include other arguments in it.

In this article we shall assume that the income distribution is also a determinant of social welfare. It will be shown that the set of optimal techniques to maximise social welfare, differs from the set that corresponds to the choice of technique in models of production, where the envelope is derived on the basis of a simple maximisation of the consumption per head (c) or the wage rate (w), given the growth rate (g) or the rate of profit (r). The next paragraph develops the model on which the analysis rests.

The Model

Let us assume a two sector model of production in which there is a capital good sector and a consumption good sector. Capital goods are denoted by K and consumption goods by Y. Both sectors employ labour (L) as a primary input and the same homogeneous capital good as an input.

For a given technique there is no substitution between capital and labour and we characterise a given technique by the set of four coefficients (a_1, a_2, b_1, b_2), where (a_1, a_2) are the capital-output coefficients and (b_1, b_2) are labour output-coefficients. The rate of depreciation of the capital goods is d and the price of the capital goods relative to that of consumption goods is denoted by p. We will consider only steady state situations which are characterised by full employment. The system may experience growth according to an exogenously given rate of growth (g). If we denote capital per head K/L by k, labour in sector 1 in proportion to total labour by $l_1(t)$, so that $l_1(t)$ and $l_2(t)$ add up to unity and consumption per head Y/L by (c), we arrive at the following system of equations:

$$k_1(t) = a_1(d + g)\, k(t) \qquad l_1(t) = b_1(d + g)\, k(t) \tag{1}$$

$$k_2(t) = a_2 c(t) \qquad\qquad l_2(t) = b_2 c(t) \tag{2}$$

$$\text{where } \; k_1(t) + k_2(t) = k(t) \; \text{ and } \; l_1(t) + l_2(t) = 1 \tag{3}$$

If we assume that wage earners are being paid at the end of the period of production, the price relations are:

$$p = a_1(d + r)p + b_1 w \tag{4}$$

$$1 = a_2(d + r)p + b_2 w \tag{5}$$

The wage-profit curve, which can be derived from (4) and (5) through elimination of p, is written as:

$$w = \frac{1 - a_1(d + r)}{(d + r)m + b_2}, \text{ where } m = a_2 b_1 - a_1 b_2 \tag{6}$$

The consumption per head-growth curve, which can be derived from (1), (2) and (3) through elimination of $k(t)$ now reads:

$$c(t) = \frac{1 - a_1(d + g)}{(d + g)m + b_2} \tag{7}$$

The price of the capital goods (p) equals:

$$p = \frac{b_1}{(d + r)m + b_2} \tag{8}$$

The value of capital per head (pk) is:

$$pk = \frac{b_1}{(d + r)m + b_2} \times \frac{a_2}{(d + g)m + b_2} \tag{9}$$

National income per head is equal to $y = c + pk\, g = w + p\, kr$.

Now, in order to describe a continuous technology, introduce a parameter that varies continuously across the techniques (a_1, a_2, b_1, b_2) [3, 4]. We only deal with the case in which the technical coefficients are a function of one parameter (λ).

Furthermore, we assume that the rate of depreciation in general also depends on λ and therefore is not exogenously given. So we have:

$$\begin{aligned} a_1 &= a_1(\lambda) \\ a_2 &= a_2(\lambda) \\ b_1 &= b_1(\lambda) \\ b_2 &= b_2(\lambda) \\ d &= d(\lambda) \end{aligned} \tag{10}$$

The traditional approach in the literature is to maximise (r) for a given real wage rate (w) or to put it in terms of the twin problem, the choice of the optimal technique is based on the maximisation of (c) for a given rate of growth (g). The solution of this optimal problem consists of the wage-profit frontier or its dual, the consumption per head-rate of growth frontier. Both frontiers are from a mathematical point of view pure envelopes. For a clear understanding of the economic character of these envelopes it seems appropriate to observe that the duality breaks down if one assumes a relation between (g) and (r), such as $g = \sigma r$ $(0 < \sigma < 1)$. If then the choice of technique is based on the maximisation of (w), given (r), this procedure also determines (g) and therefore the optimal value of (c). Only if $\sigma = 1$ each envelope is the other's dual.

The formal structure of the maximisation of (c), given a set of side conditions, now takes the following form:

$$\begin{aligned} &\text{Maximise } c(t) \\ &a_1(\lambda)\,[d(\lambda) + g]k(t) + a_2(\lambda)\,c(t) + k(t) \\ &b_1(\lambda)\,[d(\lambda) + g]k(t) + b_2(\lambda)\,c(t) = 1 \\ &d(\lambda) \leq 1 \\ &a_1(\lambda)[d(\lambda) + g] < 1 \\ &c(t),\ k(t),\ \lambda \text{ and } d(\lambda) \geq 0 \end{aligned} \tag{11}$$

A function $F(c, g) = 0$ can be derived, the main step being the elimination of λ from the Kuhn-Tucker-set of equations, which form the basis of the solution.

The form of the function $F(c, g) = 0$ depends on the specification of the technology parameter λ. For each value of λ there exists a consumption-rate of growth curve and also its dual the wage-profit curve. In the literature discussion arose about the the characteristics of the collection of wage-profit curves, of which the wage-profit frontier $G(w, r) = 0$ can be derived. In particular, there is the possibility that a technique, which is optimal at relatively low levels of the rate of profit, is again optimal at higher levels of the rate of profit, although other techniques are most profitable at rates in between. This possibility destroys the neoclassical belief that there is a simple one-way relationship between mechanized techniques and the rate of profits. This discovery of the possibility of the reswitching of techniques is often considered to be the main victory of English economists in the Cambridge controversy [1, p. 7].

This paper, however, suggests the view that the crucial difference between the two approaches to economic reality lies in the role that is attributed to the income distribution. In the neoclassical view the rate of profit and the wage rate are determined from the supply side by the productivity of the factors of production, capital and labour, given the methods of production in use. The income distribution then is a consequence of these possibilities and the structure of demand. Now, according to the other view the chain of events is just the other way round. The distribution of income is a social choice and is as such the starting point for the type of technical methods which will be employed in the process of production. In particular, the rate of profit is not a consequence of the productivity of capital, but rather the factor that determines the choice of technique from the set of available technical possibilities. In one way or another, capital as an aggregate depends on the ruling rate of profit, if we neglect the very special case that the wage-profit curves are linear, so that the price of capital is independent of (r). Hence, capital is a result of the solution and not its determinant.

A special topic in the literature deals with the relationship between the consumption per head-rate of growth frontier and the wage-profit frontier on the one hand and the economic system on the other hand. In a well-known contribution by D. M. Nuti [2], it has been stated that the choice of technique in a capitalist economy in fact boils down to the maximisation of (w), given the rate of profit (r) and in a fully planned socialist economy is determined by the maximisation of (c), given (g). In a capitalist economy one remains in the (w, r)-domain and in a socialist economy one operates in the (c, g)-domain. The Golden Rule of Accumulation establishes a link, in so far as the technique which maximises consumption per head at a given rate of growth $\bar{g}$, is the same that maximises the wage rate at a given rate of profit $\bar{r}$ if $\bar{g} = \bar{r}$. This formal result breaks down if $\bar{g} \neq \bar{r}$ and capitalist and socialist economies then each go their own way.

Our approach of introducing a social welfare function may throw some light on this topic, if for the time being the use of a social welfare function is not considered to be in contradiction with a capitalist economy.

A Social Welfare Function

Let us start with the simple assumption that social welfare is only a function of consumption per head (c). Utility (U) then is a function of (c) : $U(c)$, with $\frac{\partial U}{\partial c} > 0$ and $\frac{\partial^2 U}{\partial c^2} < 0$. The traditional approach on which the derivation of the envelope $F(c, g)$ is based, corresponds to the assumption that the social welfare function reads $U(c) = c$. The same result with respect to the envelope may be derived if we use the more general social welfare function $U = U(c)$.

Consider now the wage share $\alpha = w/y$ $(0 < \alpha < 1)$ as a measure for the functional income distribution. As a second specification of the social welfare function, we assume for illustrative purposes, that social welfare only depends on the functional distribution of income, in such a way that social welfare is higher if α increases. It needs no emphasis that this is a very special normative judgment of a political nature, which cannot be derived from pure economic considerations. Now we have:

$$U(w/y) = U(\alpha) \text{ with } \frac{\partial U}{\partial \alpha} > 0 \tag{12}$$

A more general social welfare function conceives of utility as a function of the wage share (α) and consumtpion per head (c). The significance of the maximisation of social welfare in this sense for the set of optimal techniques is then studied. If we apply the social welfare function $U(c, \alpha)$, not only the functional income distribution is determined in an optimal way by choosing a certain technique, but also consumption per head.

For a clear understanding of the economics of the model the assumption that the rate of growth (g) is exogenous should be underlined. The rate of growth does not depend on the technology parameter λ, but it appears that the choice of technique depends on (g). This exogenous role of (g) may be compared with the position of (r)

in the open system we deal with. The rate of profit (r) is not determined by the productivity of the capital goods, but it is just the other way round: a certain level of r determines the optimal technique. The question that may be raised with respect to the influence of the functional distribution of income on (g), shall be dealt with in section 6.

Mathematical Aspects

From a mathematical point of view, we are concerned with a rather simple Kuhn-Tucker problem. We have to maximise an objective function which is assumed concave and differentiable under a set of side conditions, which are also assumed and differentiable, and may be either equalities or unequalities. The Kuhn-Tucker optimum conditions are necessary in order to ensure the existence of an optimum. If we start from the general social welfare function, used in this article, the problem may now be stated as follows:

$$\text{Maximise } U(\alpha, c), \tag{13}$$

subject to

$$\{1 - a_1(\lambda)\,(d(\lambda) + g)\}k(t) - a_2(\lambda)\,c(t) = 0 \tag{14}$$

$$1 - \{b_1(\lambda)\,(d(\lambda) + g)\}k(t) - b_2(\lambda)\,c(t) = 0 \tag{15}$$

$$w - \alpha(c(t) + g\,p\,k\,(t)) = 0 \tag{16}$$

$$c(t) > 0,\ 0 < \alpha < 1,\ k(t) > 0,\ \lambda > 0 \text{ and } 0 < d(\lambda) < 1 \tag{17}$$

In order to facilitate the description of the change in technology, we consider the special case $a_1 = \lambda$, so that $a_2 = a_2(a_1)$, $b_1 = b_1(a_1)$, $b_2 = b_2(a_1)$ and $d = d(a_1)$. The Lagrange function L now is, apart from the multiplicators, a function of $c(t)$, $k(t)$, α and a_1 (all > 0) and one obtains the set of optimum conditions by differentiating L to c, k, α and a_1 and putting the results equal to zero.
From the optimum conditions the following final equation may be derived:

$$\frac{\partial U}{\partial c} \cdot \frac{dc}{da_1} + \frac{\partial U}{\partial \alpha} \cdot \frac{d\alpha}{da_1} = 0 \tag{18}$$

Now, this result implies that the optimum solution is an interior point in the induced topology of the feasible set. It appears that the side conditions do not play the role they normally do in these kind of problems. The structure of the problem at hand, in particular the production system with respect to which the maximisation of social welfare is carried out, is such that the side conditions are always fulfilled from the start. In other words the optimum solution is no boundary point in the induced topology of the feasible set.

In order to arrive at a verbal interpretation of this rather straightforward result, let us first assume that social welfare U only depends on consumption per head (c), so that $\dfrac{\partial U}{\partial \alpha} \equiv 0$. We then have:

$$\frac{\partial U}{\partial c} \cdot \frac{dc}{da_1} = 0 \tag{18a}$$

It follows that the optimal technique in this case is just the same as the one that is depicted in the literature on the Cambridge controversy, where in fact $U(c) = c$. Given the rate of growth (g), (c) or U is maximised by choosing an appropriate value of a_1. It should be pointed out that the derivation of the envelope $F_1(c, g) = 0$ does not oblige us to quit the (c, g)-domain. Now consider the other case in which $\dfrac{\partial U}{\partial c} \equiv 0$, so that social welfare only depends on the wage share α. We then have:

$$\frac{\partial U}{\partial \alpha} \cdot \frac{d\alpha}{da_1} = 0 \tag{18b}$$

We now face a different but interesting situation. It is easy to express α as a function of (a_1, r, g). According to (18b) this function should be differentiated to a_1 and the result put equal to zero. The optimal technique $\hat{a}_1$ then is a function of (r) and (g), $f(r, g)$ which leads to the quasi-envelope: $G_2(\hat{w}, g, r) = 0$.

The essential feature is that the optimal value of $\hat{w}$ is no longer determined as soon as we assume a specific value for the rate of growth (g), but it also depends on the rate of profit. In order to derive $F(c, g) = 0$ we remain in the (c, g)-domain, but the derivation of $G_2(\hat{w}, g, r) = 0$ is based on calculations that refer to the (c, g)-domain and the (w, r)-domain. One can also determine the optimal value of consumption per head ($\hat{c}$) and derive the quasi-envelope $F_2(\hat{c}, r, g)$.

Both F_2 and G_2 are now functions that describe the behaviour of consumption per head and the real wage rate if a technique is chosen that maximises social welfare from the point of view of the wage share α.

If we consider the more general case, according to which an optimal technique is chosen that maximises welfare $U(c, \alpha)$, it is also the form of the social welfare function that matters. With the aid of (7) and the expression for α, it is possible to derive from (18) the optimal technique $\bar{a}_1$ as a function of the rate of profit (r) and the rate of growth (g). Now we are able to determine $\bar{c}$ and $\bar{\alpha}$ in such a way that social welfare is maximised through a suitable choice of technique. Again quasi-envelopes $F_3(\bar{c}, r, g)$ and $G_3(\bar{w}, g, r)$ may be derived, that describe the behaviour of consumption per head and the wage rate as functions of (g) and (r), if a technique is chosen that maximises social welfare from the point of view of consumption and the wage share.

Economic Aspects

Let us concentrate now on the general case, where a technique $\bar{a}_1$ is chosen in such a way that social welfare U as a function of c and α is maximised. Now, the interesting result is that if we assume that the rate of growth (g) is exogenously given, the optimal technique still depends on the rate of profit (r). This underlines the crucial role of the rate of profit, with respect to the choice of techniques, even if the rate of growth is given. The goals of society as expressed by the social welfare function give rise to another distribution of income depending on (r), the optimal technique then leading to another optimum of the wage share. It should be pointed out that the absolute level of the optimal wage rate $\bar{w}$, is in general lower and at most equal on the basis of the maximisation of $U(c, \alpha)$ than it would be in case of simply maximising the wage rate, as it is done in the traditional set-up. If (w) is a function of (r) only the technique that maximises the wage rate may lead to such a higher level of national income y that α, being the quotient of w and y, may reach a higher level with another technique. This latter technique may then be better from a point of view of social welfare, if the role of the wage share in the social welfare function is more important than that of consumption per head. These kind of statements can be made more precise if specific assumptions are made with respect to the form of the social welfare function.

Technology is able to adjust itself to social preferences, one of the consequences being that a more fair distribution of income from the point of view of labourers may lead to a relatively low level of national income. This tendency, of course, is counteracted by the preference for more consumption as expressed by the social welfare function.

It should perhaps be made clear that the quasi-envelope may reveal a generalisation of the reswitching-phenomena in so far as techniques which are chosen at certain levels of the rate of profit and the rate of growth with the property to maximise social welfare, are again the best choice at other levels after being replaced at intermediate levels of (r) and (g).

Now, we have come to what is perhaps the most interesting feature of our analysis, the fact that it – contrary to Nuti's analysis – depends on the specification of the social welfare functions, whether or not consumption per head is determined by (g) or by (g) and (r). It is no longer possible to associate capitalism with the (w, r)-domain and socialism with the (c, g)-domain. Even in a capitalist society the criterion of a just distribution of income may play a fundamental role in the conception of social welfare. As soon as this is the case the discussion can no longer be framed in terms of fixing (g) of (r) and consequently choosing an optimal technique but it is a matter of knowing (g) *and* (r) in order to determine the best technique in view of social welfare.

Let us now come back to the question raised in section 4 with respect to the exogenous character of the rate of growth (g). It has been made clear that the optimal income distribution depends on (r) and (g) through the optimal technique $\bar{a}_1$. If it is assumed that only the capitalists save, a higher value of the wage share would imply a lower value of the savings ratio. Assuming the relation $g = \sigma r (0 < \sigma < 1)$, it follows that σ depends on α and therefore on $\bar{a}_1$. The introduction of the postulated savings behaviour makes the ratio of growth g an endogenous variable. The system then looses one degree of freedom, but due to the rate of profit it remains open. Such a procedure, therefore, only underlines the significant role of the rate of profit in the choice of technique and it supports again the opinion of the English economists in the Cambridge controversy.

Conclusion

The modest piece of analysis presented here, may be elaborated in various directions. It is possible to refine the idea about the distribution of income and one may also wish to bring in the possibility of less than full employment. More specific results may be obtained by introducing special assumptions about the involved functional relationships. The idea that the choice of technique is in fact a welfare theoretical problem, so that technical change is to a lesser extent an autonomous process than is often thought seems to be made clear sufficiently. The exogenous character of the rate of profit does not exclude the determination of an optimal wage share through a suitable choice of technique from the set of technical possibilities.

References

[1] Harcourt, G. C.: *Some Cambridge Controversies in the Theory of Capital*, Cambridge 1972.

[2] Nuti, D. M.: Capitalism, Socialism and Steady Growth, *The Economic Journal*, 1970; reprinted in *Capital and Growth*, Harmondsworth, 1971, edited by G. C. Harcourt and N. F. Laing.

[3] Sato, K.: The Neoclassical Postulate and the Technology Frontier in Capital Theory, *The Quarterly Journal of Economics*, 1974.

[4] Thomas, E. A. C.: On Technological Implications of the Wage-Profit Frontier, *Journal of Economic Theory*, 1975.

* This article has been written during my stay at the Netherlands Institute for Advanced Study in the Humanities and Social Sciences. I am indebted to my colleague at Wassenaar, Robert H. Haveman for helpful comments during the preparation of this paper.

Toward a Unified Theory of Individual Economic Behavior*

C. Robert Wichers

Neoclassical theory depicts the individual as alternating between the consumer role and the producer role. The individual's behavior is described in terms of two objective functions, one for each role, and two constraints – again, one for each role. The purpose of this essay is to describe the individual's behavior by means of a single, unified theory, with only one objective function and only one constraint. The chosen objective function is, but for interpretation, very nearly a utility function. It plays a minor part, unlike the constraint.

As constraint is chosen a pointed, convex, polyhedral cone, called the *attainable set*. Figures 1, 2 and 3 provide illustrations. (As shown, each of the three cones is truncated by the coordinate planes.)

The individual is viewed as taking *actions* such that the objective function is maximized over the attainable set. 'Actions' encompass both production activities and transactions, as well as some other activities that have an economic aspect but are not usually considered in economic theory. Actions are defined as vectors. Their positive elements represent quantities added to the individual's endowment – through production, purchase, and so on – and their negative elements represent quantities subtracted – through sale, free disposal, use as input in a production process, and so on. As this description suggests, the constraint is identical with the attainable set of production theory, in its activity-analytical version, except for interpretation. The attainable set of this paper is not a set of production activities alone; it also represents the constraints that the individual must face in his consumer role. Our attainable set is thus seen to be a substitute for the familiar budget constraint, as well.

The sequel is divided into six sections. Section 1 describes the objective function

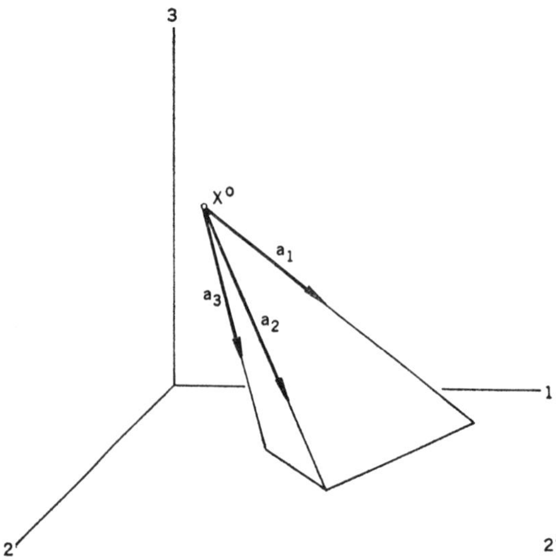

Figure 1. A three-dimensional attainable set.

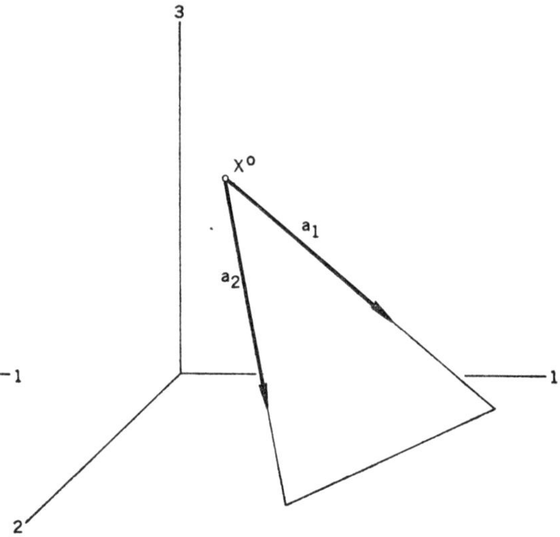

Figure 2. A two-dimensional attainable set.

and the attainable set in non-mathematical detail. As the description proceeds, it becomes clear that construction of a unified theory creates a host of questions – about utility, money, supply, interactive behavior, and many other topics. Answers to some of these questions are attempted in Section 2.

Sections 1 and 2 lay the economic-theoretical groundwork for Sections 3, 4, and 5, which form the business end of the paper.

In section 3, the attainable set is mathematically defined, and its relation to the familiar budget constraint established. The relationship is found to throw unaccustomed light on the nature of prices.

Section 4 develops a general reaction function. Among this function's special cases are the individual's demand and supply functions, as well as certain production-theoretical analogues of those functions.

A matching, generalized Slutsky relation is derived in Section 5. This Slutsky relation provides answers to such questions as: after a suitably compensated price change, will the individual buy more milk or less? Sell more milk or less? Spend more money on milk or less? Receive more money from the sale of milk, or less? And: after a suitably compensated change of a production process, will the individual produce more or less? And: after a suitably compensated wage change, will the individual work more or less? Earn more or less? More generally: what will be the effect of a compensated change of some action (which is a vector) on the individual's behavior?

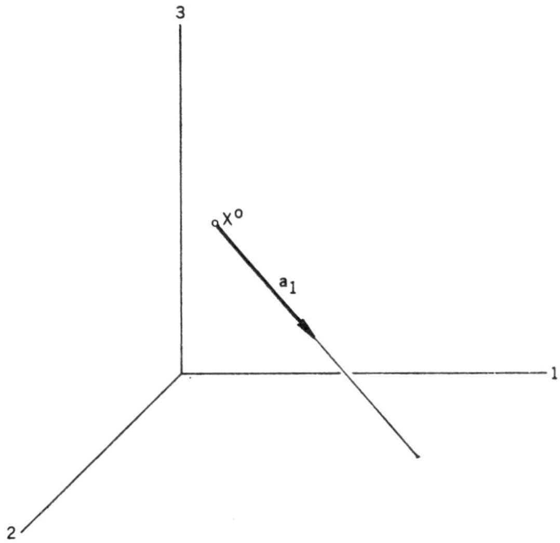

Figure 3. A one-dimensional attainable set.

Section 6, finally, lists some of the questions that remain. One of these questions, concerning the introduction of continuous time into the model, is dealt with in some detail.

Although the material of Sections 1 and 2 deviates substantially from neoclassical theory, the presentation is in the neoclassical spirit of, *e.g.*, Hicks [5]. Special efforts have been made to ensure that the relations between traditional micro-economic analysis and the model below are clear at all times.
Sections 3, 4 and 5 have an activity-analytical flavor; appropriate references are Dantzig [3], Gale [4], and, especially, Koopmans [6].
In a sense, the literature on household production functions can be viewed as aiming to construct a unified theory of individual economic behavior. An intellectual debt to, in particular, Becker [1] and Muth [10] is accordingly acknowledged.

Because of the use of linear algebra, the sequel might occasionally remind one of Lancaster [7, 8]. The relationship is tenuous, however. Lancaster's purpose is to construct an alternative to neoclassical consumer theory, not a unified theory of individual economic behavior. Also, Lancaster combines an orthodox budget constraint with a utility function defined on characteristics space, whereas this essay combines an unorthodox attainable set with an objective function defined on commodity space.

1. *The Objective Function and the Attainable Set*

A unified theory of individual economic behavior does not distinguish between producers and consumers; it only recognizes individuals – who, of course, act sometimes as consumers, sometimes as producers. By the same token, no distinction is made between consumer goods and producer goods. There are only goods (or commodities: the terms will be used synonymously throughout). Whether a commodity serves as a producer good, or as a consumer good, or as both, it is still called a commodity.[1]

A unified theory of individual economic behavior has room for only one objective function and only one constraint. This section sketches both, in a preliminary manner. More precise descriptions are given in subsequent sections.

The single objective function, which plays a rather minor role in what follows, is denoted by f, and taken to be single-valued, once-differentiable, strictly quasi-concave, and defined over the set of *endowments*. Endowments are non-negative vectors x. Their elements, which represent commodity quantities, will be interpreted as stocks, rather than flows. That is to say, the elements of x will be interpreted as commodity quantities *possessed*.

All of the individual's economic behavior can be described, assumedly, in terms of the objective function f and its maximization over the attainable set. If the individual acts as a consumer, the objective function replaces the traditional utility function. If the individual acts as a producer, the objective function replaces profit (or stockholder happiness, or anything else producers are thought to maximize). Substituting objective-function maximization for *profit* maximization is not a very large step, nor is it entirely novel. A much more drastic change, although it may not seem so, is the substitution of the objective function for *utility*. The difference between the two is that the objective function is defined over the set of endowments (stocks), whereas utility is usually assigned to quantities purchased (flows). A detailed discussion of the implications is given in the next section.

We now turn to the single constraint that characterizes a unified theory of individual economic behavior. The objective function will not be needed until the penultimate section, 5.

The constraint – the attainable set – is a pointed, convex, polyhedral cone. Being pointed, it has a vertex. This vertex, denoted by x^0 (see Figures 1, 2 and 3), is the *initial endowment*. Every point of the attainable set is an *attainable endowment*. Any vector affixed at the initial endowment and ending at an attainable endowment is an *action*. Actions represent both production activities and transactions, as well as some other activities with an economic aspect. Illustrations follow shortly.

Of particular interest are the principal edges of the attainable set. These edges are spanned by vectors called *basic actions*. Some are sketched in Figures 1, 2, and 3. Every action is a non-negative linear combination of the basic actions, as is easy to see.[2]

An action, being a vector, has elements – as many as there are goods. Positive elements represent quantities acquired, negative elements, quantities relinquished. Buying a toothbrush, for example, is an action in which the element pertaining to toothbrushes is positive, and the element pertaining to money is negative. It is not essential that the remaining elements of the action 'buying a toothbrush' be zero. If the toothbrush seller, in an attempt to boost sales, gives away one tube of tooth paste with every brush, it is convenient to say that the action 'buying a toothbrush' has yet another positive element, namely, the element pertaining to tooth paste. The action is then a joint purchase. It is further possible that, to get the combination of toothbrush and tooth paste, one needs more than just money – the buyer may have to give up a number of coupons, say. We could, of course, put a money value on the coupons and add the result to the amount of money to be paid for the toothbrush-tooth paste combination. But it is more convenient not to do so; it is more convenient to say that the action 'buying a toothbrush' has yet another negative element, namely, the element pertaining to coupons. The action is then not only a joint purchase, but a joint sale as well.[3]

Continuing the example, we consider the toothbrush seller. From his point of view, too, the action – now called 'selling a toothbrush' – is a joint purchase, for he acquires both coupons and money. The action is also a joint sale to him, for he gives up both a toothbrush and a tube of tooth paste.

The pointedness of the attainable set requires some comment. Pointedness implies irreversibility: an action, once undertaken, cannot be undone. Irreversibility is clearly plausible when imposed on actions associated with producer behavior. For example, after Jones has painted Smith's house, Jones cannot return the house and the paint to their former state. Neither can Smith, but that has less relevance here.

When it comes to actions associated with consumer behavior, irreversibility appears less plausible. In real life, it is clearly possible to buy a thing and then sell it for exactly the same price – anyone who returns a purchase to a store does just that. Yet the postulated pointedness of the attainable set seems to rule it out.

The problem is readily resolved by introduction of the good 'labor'.[4] Since many actions – in the everyday sense – require effort, it is reasonable to say that in many actions – now in the formal, mathematical sense – the element pertaining to the good 'labor' is negative. With this convention, the action 'buying a necktie' has a positive necktie element, a negative money element, and a negative labor element; 'selling a necktie' has a positive money element, a negative necktie element, and, like 'buying a necktie', a negative labor element. It follows that these two actions, regarded as vectors, are *not* collinear. To some extent then, the notion of labor-as-a-good legitimizes our stipulating that the attainable set be pointed.[5]

At this stage, it becomes necessary to digress with some comments on utility, money, and the producer-consumer dichotomy. Section 2, next, has details. The analysis of the attainable set is continued (in a more mathematical vein) in Section 3.

2. *Utility, Money, and the Producer-Consumer Dichotomy*

A unified theory, such as it is our purpose to construct, has room for only one objective function. As mentioned, the objective function is defined over the set of endowments or stocks. As also mentioned, the *utility* function is usually defined over the set of quantities purchased, which are flows. The difference between stocks and flows being substantial, a closer investigation is called for. It will be seen that the choice of whether to assign utility to stocks or to flows amounts to a choice between two entirely different economic theories.

The practice of assigning utility to flows, although widespread, is not universal. General-equilibrium theorists, for example, tend to assign utility to stocks, witness the Edgeworth Box diagram. It is easy to see that the interpretation of this diagram makes sense only if the carriers of utility are taken to be stocks. Among the general-equilibrium theorists who assign utility to stocks is Pareto: '. . . [the] commodity quantities that appear in the formulas of pure economics . . . are no longer the quantities consumed, but the quantities the individual has *at his disposal*.'[6] Marshall held, similarly, that the 'total utility of a thing to anyone increases with every increase in the amount of it *he already has*,' thereby showing that he, like Edgeworth and Pareto, assigned utility to stocks.[7]

The modern custom of assigning utility to flows, to quantities purchased, appears restricted to the theory of consumer behavior, and is recent. It seems to have been first put into words by Hicks: '. . . the consumer derives from the goods he *purchases* so much 'utility', the amount of utility being a function of the quantities of goods *acquired* . . .'[8] Such has been Hicks's influence that all leading consumer theorists currently assign utility to purchases.

Why does all this matter? It matters because, once utility is assigned to purchases, one cannot assign it to sales as well. Consequently, sales (or seller behavior) cannot be regarded as guided by utility considerations – whatever the seller's objective function, it is not utility. More affirmatively put, all selling becomes producer behavior.[9]

As the preceding paragraph shows, once utility is assigned to purchases, one needs more than just a theory of consumer behavior – one must also have a theory of producer behavior, to deal with supply. The construction of a unified theory of individual economic behavior then becomes impossible. In the light of our goal, therefore, it is essential to examine, and if possible refute, the arguments of those who maintain that utility may not be assigned to stocks.

As it turns out, there is only one argument. It is that possessions have only 'indirect utility', whereas purchases have 'direct utility'. We met this observation before[1] and found it to be merely semantic. When 'utility' is replaced with 'objective function', the argument evaporates.

There is, then, nothing against assigning utility to stocks (after which it is but a small step to define the objective function f over the set of endowments, as was done earlier). On top of that, there are at least two arguments that actually favor the decision to assign utility to stocks. First, we saw that assigning utility to stocks is standard practice in general-equilibrium theory, and this constitutes a powerful precedent. Second, an individual's purchases are plausibly held to depend on and vary with the quantities he already owns; such dependence can only be expressed in theoretical terms by assigning utility to stocks. In the light of these arguments, it will be taken for granted that assigning utility to stocks is both permissible and desirable. This, in turn, will be considered sufficient justification of our defining the objective function f over the set of endowments.

The title of this section is 'Utility, Money, and the Producer-Consumer Dichotomy.' Utility has been discussed; money is next.

As it turns out, a unified theory of individual economic behavior must treat money as a commodity, must give money and (other) commodities the same theoretical treatment. Many authors consider this objectionable; several of their arguments are briefly reviewed below. Afterwards, some implications of equal treatment for money and commodities are listed. It will then be seen that whether or not money is regarded as a commodity is considerably more than a mere epistemological exercise.

Of the arguments against equal treatment for money and commodities, probably the most familiar is that money is wanted not for its own sake but for what it can buy. This is, once again, the indirect-utility argument, confusing usefulness with the function called 'utility'. The argument loses most of its force when utility is assigned to stocks instead of flows; it loses whatever force remains when 'utility' is replaced with 'objective function'.[10] Besides, if a thing were to become a non-commodity by being wanted only for what it can buy, it would follow that the farmer's wheat and the druggist's aspirin are non-commodities too. The farmer grows wheat, not because he wants it for its own sake, but for what it can buy (assuming there is a difference), and the druggist stocks aspirin with the same purpose. Indeed, if the indirect-utility argument were taken strictly, no thing would be a commodity to its seller.

Money is also said to be different from other commodities because of its role of medium of exchange. To say that money is a medium of exchange does not mean, presumably, that money changes hands in *every* transaction; the existence of barter belies that. Apparently then, money is a medium of exchange because it plays a role in *many* transactions. But that does not make money qualitatively different from other commodities, no more than that used pipes form a non-commodity on the ground that they play a role in so very *few* transactions. Or, to borrow an example from another science: Newton's theory treats the sun and the earth, despite their pre-eminent importance in our daily lives, just as it treats all other bodies. In sum, what is essential in practice is not necessarily essential in theory.[11]

A variation on the medium-of-exchange theme is found in an ingenious construction by Clower [2]. If a good can be traded directly for every other good, Clower defines it as money; otherwise, the good is a commodity. At first glance, this appears to separate money from commodities, thereby justifying the (common) practice of treating money and commodities differently. But a closer look reveals that the set of commodities (in Clower's sense) is likely to be empty: every good can probably be traded directly for every other good, meaning that every good is money (in Clower's sense). To prove the set of commodities non-empty, one would have to find two goods that could not possibly be directly exchanged for one another, in any quantities whatever. No such goods appear to have yet been found, and we shall continue under the assumption that none exist.

There are many more arguments against equal treatment for money and commodities, but the most persuasive ones have now been discussed, and found unconvincing. Negative though this finding may be, it is all the justification we need. For, since a unified theory does not have the freedom of traditional theory to regard any thing as either a consumer good or a producer good, a unified theory can only treat money as a commodity, or fail; consequently, it is essential that arguments against such treatment be shown wanting. But *more* than that is not necessary.

Treating money as a commodity has numerous implications, some of which are described below.

a. When money is viewed as a commodity, one of the variables $x_1, x_2, \ldots$ in the objective function must represent a quantity of money. In the light of our assumption that the objective function is defined over the set of endowments (stocks, possessions), the quantity of money appearing in the objective function represents so-called cash balances. These are nominal balances, not real cash balances. One might, of course, define them to be real balances, but equal treatment for money and other commodities implies that, then, *all* quantities in the objective function be real – the individual's stock of peanuts, say, would have to be corrected for price level before it could enter the objective function. We will not do this.[12]

b. When money is viewed as a commodity, the budget constraint may not be written as $\Sigma p_i x_i = m$; for this would put money (m) in a role of exception. An acceptable budget constraint would be $\sum p_i x_i = \sum p_i x_i^0$, where $\{x_1, x_2, \ldots\}$ is any attainable endowment, $\{x_1^0, x_2^0, \ldots\}$ is the initial endowment, and $\sum p_i x_i^0$ is the individual's wealth. Suppose money is good n; then x_n represents a quantity of money, and x_n^0 is the quantity of money initially held. The price of money, p_n, is identically equal to one, assuming, of course, that money serves as the numéraire.

The budget constraint $\sum p_i x_i = \sum p_i x_i^0$, or, in vector notation, $p'x = p'x^0$, will reappear later, when the relation between our attainable set and the budget constraint is established.

Figures 4 and 5 serve to clarify points (*a*) and (*b*). In both diagrams, the objective function is taken to be the utility function, except that it is a utility function defined over the set of endowments, not purchases. This setup, admittedly unusual, provides the clearest illustration.

In Figure 4, money is *not* treated as a commodity, so that endowments are vectors with two elements instead of three, the individual's possessions consist of an endowment and a quantity of money, and the objective function is maximized subject to the constraint DE, which is a segment of a line. In Figure 5, money *is* regarded as a commodity, so that all endowments have three elements; the objective function is maximized subject to the constraint BDE, which is a segment of a plane.

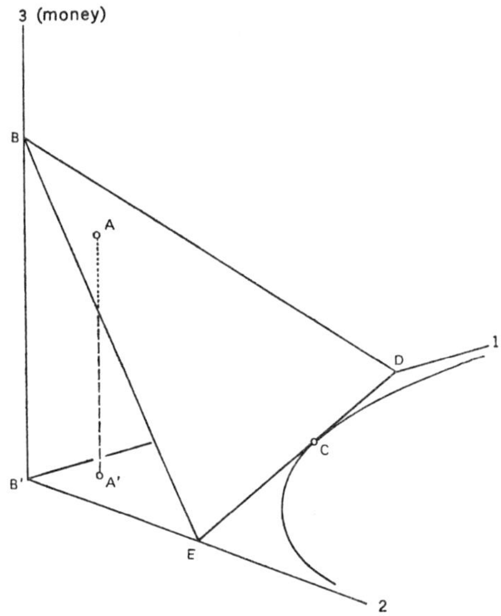

Figure 4. When money is not a commodity, equilibrium is at C.

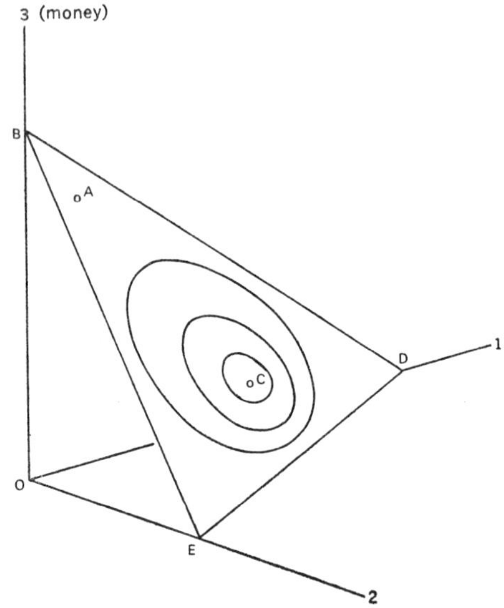

Figure 5. When money is a commodity, equilibrium is at C.

We return to Figure 4. Initially, the individual is at A. The projection of A onto the commodity plane is A′, with coordinates $(x_1^0, x_2^0, 0)$. Thus, the initial endowment is $\{x_1^0, x_2^0\}$, and the value of the objective function at that point is $f(x_1^0, x_2^0)$. What happens next? Assume, with Hicks, that the individual exchanges his commodity stocks for money.[9] The individual's endowment then moves to B. At B, the endowment is $\{0, 0\}$, the first two coordinates of B, and the objective function has the value $f(0, 0)$.

Since f is (temporarily) identified with utility, f has positive first-order partial derivatives, reflecting that more is better than less. Clearly then, the individual's trading from A to B has lowered the value of the objective function. This is contrary to postulate. We thus see that Hicks's suggestion, already found to be epistemologically unacceptable, introduces a logical inconsistency as well.

Eventually, the individual of Figure 4 trades his way to C. The first two coordinates of C constitute the final endowment or equilibrium endowment. The third coordinate is zero, signifying that all money is spent. This makes intuitive sense, considering that, in Figure 4, money is not among the arguments of f. The constraint DE has equation $p_1x_1 + p_2x_2 = p_1x_1^0 + p_2x_2^0 + m$, where $m = AA'$ is the amount of money initially held. All through trading, the individual's endowment never leaves triangle B′DE.

In Figure 5, money is regarded as a commodity. The constraint, BDE, contains the initial endowment (A). The final endowment (C) meets the constraint, as it did in Figure 4. But as Figure 5 shows, C is no longer necessarily a point of DE: not all money is necessarily spent.[13] The constraint, BDE, intersects the contour surfaces of f, not shown, along convex, closed curves, some of which are shown. At C, the curve of intersection is reduced to a point of tangency. If the initial endowment is denoted by $\{x_1^0, x_2^0, x_3^0\}$, the constraint BDE has equation $p_1x_1 + p_2x_2 + p_3x_3 = p_1x_1^0 + p_2x_2^0 + p_3x_3^0$. If money is chosen as the numéraire, p_3 will be identically equal to 1. All through trading, the individual's endowment never leaves triangle BDE. It is not necessary that the endowment, on its path from A to C, ever reach B.

This completes the illustration of points (*a*) and (*b*) by means of Figures 4 and 5. We return the objective function to its original definition, and continue with the list of implications of equal treatment for money and commodities.

c. When money is viewed as a commodity, exchange involving money becomes theoretically indistinguishable from barter. It is sometimes held that any theory of barter is of little practical value so long as money is not 'integrated' into it. (General-equilibrium theory has been occasionally criticized on this score.) But when money is regarded as a commodity, integration is automatically achieved.

d. When money is viewed as a commodity, spending money becomes a form of selling, obeying the same economic-theoretical laws as, say, the selling of oranges. By the same token, the acquisition of money comes to obey the same laws as the acquisition of any other commodity. For an example, suppose the price of tobacco – in terms of money – goes down, so that the price of money – in terms of tobacco – goes up. The Slutsky equation now implies that tobacconists will, following suitable compensation, demand (buy, receive) less money. What is suitable compensation? The Slutsky equation is formulated under the assumption that compensation be made in terms of the supplied good. For the tobacco buyer, the supplied good is money; for the tobacconist, it is tobacco. Thus, the tobacconist is compensated for the price change by being given a quantity of tobacco.[14]

e. When money is viewed as a commodity, earning money becomes a form of (effective) demand. For an example, similar to the preceding one, suppose a wage increase occurs. The wage is the price of labor ('energy') in terms of money, so that the price of money in terms of labor goes down. After compensation, the wage earner now demands (earns, buys, receives) more money. Compensation is again taken to be made in terms of the supplied good, which is labor. Thus, the wage earner should give up labor, by doing some unpaid work, for instance. He may not want to, but that is not the point – what matters is that this is a testable result. In both this and the preceding example, compensation was assumed to be made in terms of the supplied good. It will be shown in Section 5 that compensation in this form is suboptimal. There are, more often than not, sizable theoretical advantages to compensating in terms of several goods at once. Also, some of those goods may be demanded goods.

Of the three topics mentioned in the title of this section – 'Utility, Money, and the Producer-Consumer Dichotomy' – two have now been dealt with. Utility was discussed, and so was its successor, the objective function; it was found that the objective function may be justifiably defined over the set of endowments, rather than over the set of purchased bundles. Money has also been discussed; it was found that money may be justifiably treated as a commodity. That leaves the producer-consumer dichotomy.

A unified theory of individual economic behavior does not distinguish between producers and consumers, has no room for the producer-consumer dichotomy. By the same token, there is no room for the distinction between consumer goods and producer goods.

Discarding the producer-consumer dichotomy has several advantages. For one, simplicity is served. For another, if there are no consumers or producers, but only individuals, it is unnecessary to decide which of a person's acts constitute producer behavior, and which are consumer behavior. Such a decision is not always easy, as the following two examples may show.

The first example concerns working, which is the same as selling the good 'labor' (or 'energy'). Is this producer behavior or consumer behavior? The question is difficult to answer, unless we follow Hicks and assign utility to purchases [5]. All selling then becomes producer behavior; this includes the selling of labor. But now an inconsistency arises – the complement of selling labor is the demand for leisure time, and this demand is traditionally considered consumer behavior. It appears that the inconsistency can be removed only by discarding the producer-consumer dichotomy. Only then will it be unnecessary to classify an individual's actions as either producer behavior or consumer behavior.

The second example concerns the spending of money, which is a form of selling. Is this producer behavior or consumer behavior? Again, it is hard to say, unless we follow Hicks and assign utility to purchases. Spending, being an act of selling, is then not governed by utility considerations, hence must be producer behavior.

But spending money is traditionally considered consumer behavior, at least if the money is spent on consumer goods, and so we have another inconsistency. Again it appears that the inconsistency can be removed only by discarding the producer-consumer dichotomy.[15]

The disappearance of the producer-consumer dichotomy entails not only advantages. It creates some problems, too. In macro-economic theory, for example, many conclusions rest on the distinction between households and businesses, between consumers and producers. Many macro-economic processes are thought to result from the interaction of consumers and producers. Clearly then, if consumers and producers are lumped into one category, as they are in a unified theory, macro-economics is substantially affected. Similar remarks can be made, and a similar conclusion drawn, for general-equilibrium theory. Presumably, both macro-economic theory and general-equilibrium theory can be modified so that the producer-consumer dichotomy is no longer needed in either theory. But the task is obviously big, and no attempt will be made here. More generally, the present piece ignores all interactive behavior.[16]

3. *Attainable Set and Prices – Mathematical Aspects*

So far, the attainable set has been described only sketchily. This section presents a more thorough treatment, first defining the attainable set, then relating it to its two predecessors, *viz.*, the attainable set of production theory and the budget constraint of consumer theory. The discussion prompts some questions about the nature of prices; these questions are considered in the last half of the section.

Let $a_1, \ldots, a_k$ be n-vectors, columns of the $n \times k$ matrix A. Of primary interest are the non-negative linear combinations of these vectors, $a_1c_1 + \ldots + a_kc_k$ or, more briefly, Ac, with $c \geqq 0$. (We write $c \geqq 0$ for non-negative c, and $c \geq 0$ for semipositive c.) For a given matrix A, the set of all such non-negative linear combinations is a convex, polyhedral cone, said to be spanned by A's columns. The cone is called pointed iff $Ac = 0$ has only one non-negative solution c (which is then $c = 0$). Some definitions follow.

A matrix A is an *action matrix* if its columns are linearly independent and are so that $Ac \geq 0$ has no non-negative solution c. (The two defining conditions have a ready economic interpretation, given in the next paragraph.) A vector is a *basic action* if it is a column of an action matrix. A vector is an *action* if it is a non-negative linear combination, Ac, of basic actions; the (non-negative) elements of

c are *levels* or *action levels*. The *attainable set*, denoted by S, is the truncated cone $\{x: x = x^0 + Ac, c \geqq 0, x \geqq 0\}$, where x^0 is the initial endowment. The elements of S are *attainable endowments.* Every attainable endowment can obviously be written as the sum of the initial endowment and some action.

By the just given definition, the columns of an action matrix – the basic actions – must meet two requirements: they must be linearly independent, and they must be so that $Ac \geq 0$ has no solution $c \geqq 0$. The latter condition can also be read as: there may not exist a semipositive action, or: every action must have at least one negative element, or: every action will, if continued long enough, exhaust the stock of at least one good. This implies that the attainable set is bounded. The attainable set is also closed, as its definition shows. By a familiar theorem, we now find that the (continuous) objective function takes on a maximum over the attainable set. This is precisely the purpose of our ruling out the existence of a semipositive action: it guarantees existence of an equilibrium endowment. (The equilibrium endowment is also unique, as a geometrically obvious consequence of the strict quasiconcavity of f and the convexity of the attainable set S.)

The other condition imposed on the action matrix is that its columns, the basic actions, must be linearly independent. This ensures that the individual's behavior is uniquely determined at all times.[17]

We return briefly to the first condition on basic actions, according to which there exists no semipositive action. This condition blocks the way to instant riches, to the 'Land of Cockaigne', in Koopmans's phrase [6]. Nothing is acquired without something (labor, for example) being given up. By contrast, free disposal *is* possible, as is easy to see.[18]

Now that the attainable set has been defined, its relation with standard microeconomic theory must be clarified. The connection with production theory is obvious: our attainable set differs only terminologically from that of linear-activity analysis. But the connection with consumer theory – more particularly, the budget constraint – could stand illumination.

Let the budget constraint be $p'x = p'x^0$, where x^0 is the initial endowment, p is an n-vector of prices, good n is money, $p_n \equiv 1$. The attainable set S is at once a generalization and a particularization of this budget constraint. It is a particularization in that actions are irreversible, and transactions are not. We temporarily remove the irreversibility requirement, solely to facilitate the comparison of the attainable set and the budget constraint. The attainable set, $S = \{x: x = x^0 + Ac, c \geqq 0, x \geqq 0\}$, is thereby turned into $\{x: x = x^0 + Ac, x \geqq 0\}$.

When the identity matrix of order $n - 1$ is bordered by an nth row with elements $-p_1, \ldots, -p_{n-1}$, the result is

$$A = \begin{bmatrix} 1 & & & \\ & \cdot & & \\ & & \cdot & \\ & & & \cdot \\ & & & 1 \\ -p_1 & \cdots & & -p_{n-1} \end{bmatrix} \text{(Blanks are zeros)} \tag{1}$$

This is an action matrix, as is easy to see: the columns are linearly independent, and there is no semipositive vector among the linear combinations of those columns. (There is, even, no semipositive vector among the non-negative linear combinations of A's columns, but that has little relevance now that irreversibility has been temporarily dropped.) By taking the ith basic action to the level 2, the individual acquires 2 units of good i, and gives up $2p_i$ units of money. Similarly, by taking the ith basic action to the level -3 (this is possible, without irreversibility), the individual gives up 3 units of good i and acquires $3p_i$ units of money. It is apparent that the ith basic action may be interpreted as 'buying good i' or 'selling good i', depending on the sign of the associated level.

Continuing with the illustration, let $x = x^0 + Ac$, with A as in (1), be some attainable endowment. Then

$$\begin{aligned} x_1 &= x_1^0 + c_1 \\ x_2 &= x_2^0 + c_2 \\ &\vdots \\ x_{n-1} &= x_{n-1}^0 + c_{n-1} \\ x_n &= x_n^0 - \sum_1^{n-1} p_i c_i \end{aligned}$$

(It is worth noting that the numbers $c_1, \ldots, c_{n-1}$ do double duty here: they are action levels, and they represent the purchased or sold quantities of goods $1, \ldots, n-1$.) We multiply the first equation by p_1, the second by $p_2, \ldots$, the nth by p_n ($\equiv 1$), and add. This gives $p'x = p'x^0$, the budget constraint. It follows that $\{x\colon x = x^0 + Ac,\ x \geqq 0\}$, which is the attainable set without irreversibility, contains the budget constraint. The opposite is also true: the set $\{x\colon x = x^0 + Ac,\ x \geqq 0\}$, with A as in (1), has dimension $n - 1$, and is therefore contained in the budget hyperplane. Consequently, $\{x\colon x = x^0 + Ac,\ x \geqq 0\}$, with A as in (1), is merely another representation (parametric representation) of the budget constraint.

The parametric representation emphasizes actions—or transactions, in this context—, whereas the budget constraint emphasizes prices.

It is now clear how attainable set and budget constraint are related. First, we write the budget constraint in parametric notation, using the action matrix A in (1). Then that matrix is generalized: its columns are permitted to have more than one positive element, and more than one negative element. (At this point, the numbers $c_1, \ldots, c_{n-1}$ cease to do double duty.) As a further generalization, the condition that there be exactly $n - 1$ columns is relaxed. (Figures 1, 2, 3 illustrate that an action matrix may have any number of columns, up to n, provided actions are defined as irreversible. When actions are reversible, the conditions defining action matrices imply that there are at most $n - 1$ columns. This is easily verified.) Further insight issues from the observation that a basic action with more than one positive element represents either a joint purchase or joint output—'joint product'—, depending on whether that basic action has the nature of a transaction or of a production activity. Similarly, a basic action with more than one negative element represents a joint sale or a production process with several inputs.

A characteristic feature of the action matrix in (1) is that the prices of goods $1, \ldots, n - 1$ can be read off immediately. (It is not possible to read off the price of good n. Then again, there is no need for it either, since good n is money and $p_n \equiv 1$.) Once the generalization of (1) begins and basic actions are allowed to have more than one positive element and more than one negative element, prices can no longer be read off. They can still be found, however—up to a point. Prices *can* be found after the first stage of generalization of the matrix A in (1), that is, after basic actions are allowed to have several positive elements and several negative elements. But prices cease to be unambiguously definable after the second stage of generalization, that is, after we discard the requirement that there be exactly $n - 1$ basic actions. Proofs follow, after a preparatory paragraph.

If the budget constraint, $p'x = p'x^0$, is written as $p'(x - x^0) = 0$, it becomes clear that the price vector p is orthogonal to every vector joining the initial endowment x^0 to an attainable endowment x. It follows that p is orthogonal to the budget hyperplane. For a different proof, observe that p is orthogonal to each column of the matrix in (1). (Verification requires use of $p_n \equiv 1$.) But the columns of the matrix in (1) span the budget hyperplane, and the conclusion that p is orthogonal to the budget hyperplane follows again.[19]

It will now be shown that prices continue to exist even when the matrix in (1) is generalized, to the point where its columns are allowed to have several positive elements and several negative elements. It will also be shown that prices cease to exist, or are at least no longer unambiguously definable, once we complete the generalization and drop the requirement that there be exactly $n - 1$ basic actions. First, let A be halfway generalized, so that A has $n - 1$ columns, each of which may have several positive elements and several negative elements. If M is any matrix, Farkas's Lemma implies that either $Mz \geq 0$ has a solution z or $M'y = 0$ has a positive solution y ([4], p. 49). Applied to the halfway generalized matrix A, the statement becomes: either there exists a semipositive action, or there exists a positive vector y orthogonal to all of A's columns. Existence of semipositive actions has been ruled out, by the definition of action matrices. It follows that there exists a positive vector y orthogonal to all of A's columns. Furthermore, since A's columns are linearly independent and are at this point still $n - 1$ in number, they span a hyperplane—the budget hyperplane, obviously. The positive vectors y orthogonal to A's columns are orthogonal to the budget hyperplane, and hence collinear. Exactly one of these y has unit nth element. This y can serve as a vector of prices. Those prices are imputed prices, of course, but at least they exist.

Next, let A be completely generalized, so that A's columns may have several positive and several negative elements *and* there need not be $n - 1$ columns. Since we are still going under the temporary, simplifying assumption that actions may be reversible, A has either $n - 1$ columns or fewer. Not more than $n - 1$ columns —more than $n - 1$ columns would span all of R^n, and so make every endowment attainable. (If actions are irreversible, the number of basic actions can go up to n, as Figure 1 illustrates.)

We have already seen that prices—possibly imputed prices—exist if A has exactly $n - 1$ columns. Suppose, then, that A has fewer than $n - 1$ columns, a case illustrated in Figure 3. It is easy to see that positive vectors orthogonal to all of A's columns continue to exist, by Farkas's Lemma. But it is also easy to see that those positive vectors are no longer collinear: when A has fewer than $n - 1$ columns, those columns span (not a hyperplane but) a linear manifold of dimension less than $n - 1$, and the positive vectors orthogonal to this manifold are not all multiples of one another. In this case, then, even imputed prices cease to be unique. This was to be shown.

A numerical example may be useful. A restaurant offers a choice of two breakfasts. The first breakfast, which consists of three slices of toast, two slices of bacon, one cup of coffee, two eggs, and a glass of orange juice, costs four dollars. The second breakfast, which consists of two slices of toast, two slices of bacon, two cups of coffee, one egg, and no orange juice, costs two dollars. Six goods are involved, namely, toast, bacon, coffee, eggs, orange juice, and money, in that order. The action matrix A has two columns, representing 'buying the first breakfast' and 'buying the second breakfast', respectively. Thus,

$$A = \begin{bmatrix} 3 & 2 \\ 2 & 2 \\ 1 & 2 \\ 2 & 1 \\ 1 & 0 \\ -4 & -2 \end{bmatrix} \begin{matrix} \text{(toast)} \\ \text{(bacon)} \\ \text{(coffee)} \\ \text{(eggs)} \\ \text{(orange juice)} \\ \text{(money)} \end{matrix}$$

It is easy to verify that A is, indeed, an action matrix.

The example continues with a search for a price vector. This means we must find a positive vector orthogonal to all of A's columns. Or again: we must find a positive y satisfying $A'y = 0$.

Solving $A'y = 0$ for y by conventional methods gives $y = k_1\{1, 0, 0, 0, 1, 1\} + k_2\{0, 1, 0, 0, 2, 1\} + k_3\{0, 0, 1, 0, 3, 1\} + k_4\{0, 0, 0, 2, 0, 1\}$, where the weights k_i are arbitrary. In searching for a price vector, one would naturally consider only the positive y's – only the y's with six positive elements. Now, as is easy to see, a solution y is positive iff the four weights k_i are chosen positive. This means there are ∞^4 potential price vectors. Even if these vectors are normed by the requirement that the last element, y_n, be unity (reflecting that $p_n \equiv 1$), there are still ∞^3 vectors left. All are equally acceptable as price vectors; therefore, none is.

The just-completed numerical example illustrates that prices, even imputed prices, are not under all circumstances uniquely definable. It is therefore appropriate that the definition of the attainable set does not refer to prices, does not presuppose that prices exist. It is also reassuring, because the actions appearing in our unified model must reflect producer behavior, too; and it would seem undesirable to have a description of producer behavior rely totally on the existence of prices.

Where the existence of prices is not required, there would seem to be no need for a numéraire, either. Considering this remark, we inspect again the 'neoclassical action matrix' in (1), and its nth row in particular. The nth row, which pertains to the nth good, is so different from the other rows that good n is immediately recognized as exceptional. Indeed it is, for good n plays the role of numéraire. But when the generalization of the matrix in (1) begins – when, in particular, the basic actions are permitted to have any number of positive elements and any number of negative elements – the nth row ceases to be exceptional. With that, the numéraire, too, ceases to be exceptional. No longer does any good stand out as an obvious candidate for the numéraire role. This is just what one would expect, in a theory that does not presuppose the existence of prices.

All this adds up to one conclusion: essential as money and prices may be in economic practice, they are of subordinate importance in economic theory (premises granted, of course). There is, more particularly, no need to choose a numéraire, and there is no need to use price as an action-defining characteristic.[20]

In the later parts of this section, actions were temporarily assumed reversible, to facilitate comparison between the attainable set and the budget constraint of consumer theory. Comparison having been made, we now restore irreversibility. This further weakens the position of prices, as the following may show.

When actions are irreversible, an action matrix may have up to n columns, as in Figure 1. Consider first an action matrix with exactly n columns. It is geometrically obvious that there exists no positive vector orthogonal to all those columns. There is, in consequence, no consistent way of defining prices, even imputed prices. Next, consider an action matrix with (*a*) $n - 1$ colums or (*b*) fewer than $n - 1$ columns. We saw before that prices, or imputed prices at least, are uniquely definable in case (*a*), not uniquely definable (but at least definable) in case (*b*). Now that irreversibility has been restored, there may no longer exist a positive vector orthogonal to all basic actions, and positive prices, imputed or otherwise, may become undefinable. This can be seen as follows.

Figure 6 sketches the situation of an individual with two basic actions ($k = 2$) in a three-goods world ($n = 3$). The vectors a_1 and a_2, shown, are indeed basic actions: they are linearly independent, and there is no semipositive action among their non-negative linear combinations. At the same time, there is no positive vector orthogonal to both a_1 and a_2, as is geometrically obvious. (Thus, $A'y = 0$ has no positive solution y. By Farkas's Lemma, $Az \geq 0$ then has a solution z, suggesting that there does exist, after all, a semipositive action. The suggestion is false, however. Although, in the situation of Figure 6, $Az \geq 0$ has many solutions z, it has no solution $z \geqq 0$. And unless $z \geqq 0$, Az is not an action.)

A brief review concludes this section.

The construction of a unified theory of individual economic behavior requires that all such behavior be described in terms of one objective function and one constraint. So far, the single objective function has been hardly needed. The objective function is defined as a single-valued, once-differentiable, strictly quasi-concave function on the set of all endowments (possessions, stocks), as opposed to the set of all purchased quantities (bundles, flows). The single constraint, called

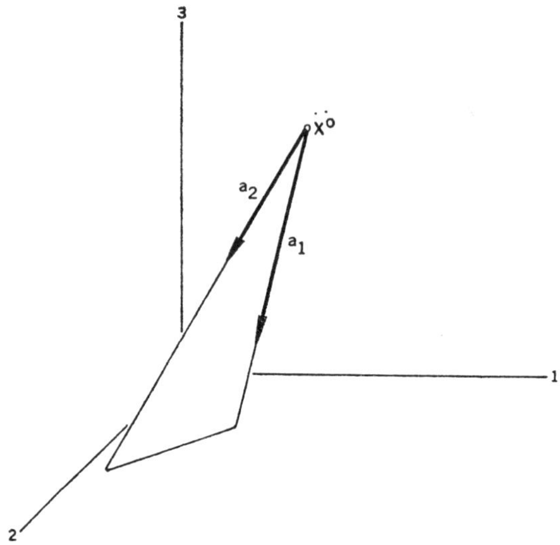

Figure 6. A situation in which there exists no positive vector orthogonal to the basic actions.

the attainable set, is a pointed, convex, polyhedral cone, truncated by the coordinate hyperplanes of R^n, and denoted by S. The elements of S are the attainable endowments; the vertex of S is the initial endowment, x^0. The principal edges of S are spanned by basic actions, columns of the action matrix A. Actions are non-negative linear combinations of the basic actions, and can therefore be written as Ac, with $c \geqq 0$. The non-negativity of c expresses that actions are irreversible.

The matrix A is an action matrix iff A has full column rank and there is no $c \geqq 0$ such that Ac is semipositive. Equivalently, the columns of A must be linearly independent, and a semipositive action may not exist. The Land of Cockaigne is thus closed off, but free disposal is possible.

Non-existence of an action $Ac \geq 0$ renders the attainable set bounded; this helps ensure that the objective function will assume a maximum over the attainable set. In neoclassical consumer theory, boundedness is achieved by assuming existence of a vector $p > 0$ orthogonal to the attainable set. This is more demanding, because it implies, by Farkas's Lemma, that $Ac \geq 0$ has no solution c, while all we need is that $Ac \geq 0$ have no solution $c \geqq 0$. (In Figure 6, for example, $Ac \geq 0$ does have a solution c, but no solution $c \geqq 0$.) Besides, if there are exactly $n - 1$ basic actions, the positive vectors—if any—that are orthogonal to those basic actions will all point in the same direction, so that one of them can be interpreted as a vector of (imputed) prices; but if there are fewer than $n - 1$ basic actions, the positive vectors – if any – that are orthogonal to the basic actions will point in infinitely many different directions, and so cannot be given a plausible economic interpretation.

Special attention has been given to the commodities labor ('energy') and money. The notion of labor played an important role in justifying the irreversibility of seemingly reversible actions, such as buying and selling. Buying and selling are irreversible because both require effort, that is, both use up a quantity of labor. As for money, it proved essential for the construction of a unified theory that money be treated as a commodity.

4. *The Reaction Function*

Purpose of this section is to define a reaction function, a relation describing, among other things, how a price change affects the individual's demand and supply, and how a change of a production process (in the form of a change of a technical coefficient or a technical ratio) affects the output quantities produced and the input quantities used up. Evidently, to define the reaction function, it is sufficient to choose a dependent variable and an independent variable. We begin with the latter.

The reaction function's independent variable is taken to be an entire basic action, a_i, with i arbitrary but fixed. Realistically, no more than one or two elements of a_i are likely to vary, but it is mathematically simpler to define the reaction function in terms of the entire vector a_i. In applications, one can always treat any number of a_i's elements as constant, if that seems desirable. The following examples provide illustration.

For a first example, suppose that Exxshell Oil Company sells gasoline for 60 cents per gallon. Measuring gasoline in gallons and money in cents, we write the action 'selling Exxshell gasoline' as $\{-1, 60, 0, 0, \ldots, 0\}$, in obvious notation. Now the company raises the price to 65 cents per gallon, so that 'selling Exxshell gasoline' becomes $\{-1, 65, 0, 0, \ldots, 0\}$. This illustrates that, in practice, action changes may well be confined to changes of a single element, the other $n-1$ elements remaining constant.

For a second example, suppose a glue manufacturer discovers that he can lower production cost by using a little more of ingredient A and a little less of ingredient B, for every pound of ingredient C. The action 'making glue' then has two varying elements, $n-2$ constant elements. (Assuming that glue sales remain the same, the basic action 'buying ingredient A' will be taken at a greater level than before, but that basic action does not itself change. Similarly, 'buying ingredient B' will be taken at a smaller level, without changing.)

For a third example, consider the action 'earning money', with a positive money element and a negative energy element. If the wage rate changes, this action changes, but only in one element; the other $n - 1$ elements are constant.

Turning now to the dependent variable in the reaction function, we define this to be *any action element*. Illustrations follow, after we borrow some terminology from Koopmans [6].

Koopmans defines production and consumption this way: an activity produces good j if its jth element is positive, and consumes good j if its jth element is negative. This definition will be adopted here, but with 'action' instead of 'activity'. Thus,

– an action with positive jth element produces good j;

– an action with negative jth element consumes good j.

It is worth noting that consumption and production are attributed to actions, not to individuals.

If some action is interpretable as a transaction, its positive elements are interpretable as quantities purchased, its negative elements as quantities sold. From Koopmans's definition it now follows that *a purchased quantity is a quantity produced, and a sold quantity is a quantity consumed.* Buying tea adds to the stock of tea, and so constitutes production; indeed, the action 'buying tea' produces tea. The same action also consumes money. The tea drinker does not consume tea, but 'drinking tea' does. 'Borrowing tea' and 'stealing tea' produce tea, whereas tea is consumed by such actions as 'selling tea' and 'throwing tea into the harbor'. To continue the examples: income is an amount of money produced by the action 'earning money' (or some other action, similarly named. How actions are named is, for theoretical purposes, immaterial). The reader is asked to note that income is here regarded as endogenously determined; in a unified theory, there is no other choice (except, trivially, the choice of assuming that all income is received through bequest). Profit is an amount of money produced by a linear combination of 'buying inputs', 'transforming inputs into outputs', and 'selling outputs', or perhaps by a linear combination of 'buying bonds' and 'selling bonds'. (It seems logical that bonds be regarded as a commodity, considering that money is being regarded as a commodity.) Profit after taxes is profit plus the (negative) amount of money consumed by the action 'paying taxes'. Depositing money in a savings account is an action; it consumes money, and produces the intangible good 'title to the account'. And so on.

The preceding examples make it clear that 'any action element' – the dependent variable in the reaction function – is the same as 'any quantity produced or consumed'. The reaction function therefore describes how any produced or consumed quantity varies with changes of a basic action. To express this dependence in exact, functional form is probably the most important problem to be found in a unified theory of individual, non-interactive, economic behavior. The next section explores the matter further.

5. *Some Properties of the Reaction Function*

The reaction function describes how changes in some basic action will affect any action element. To find the analytical form of this relationship, one would have to specify the analytical form of the objective function (or find some other way – assuming, with Cassel, that there is one). Barring that, the best one can do is to establish *properties* of the reaction function.

This section establishes three properties of the reaction function. The first of these is of Slutskian lineage, and requires that f be defined to have positive first-order partial derivatives (in addition to the conditions on f imposed earlier). The other two properties hold regardless of what the objective function looks like. From now on, the reaction function is denoted by $q(a_i)$.

To formulate and prove the first property, assume that the strictly-quasi-concave objective function f has positive first-order partial derivatives. The vector of these derivatives is denoted by grad $f(x)$ or grad f. Thus, grad $f > 0$. Next, let the basic action a_i change, to become $a_i + da_i$. No other basic action changes. The addition da_i is a vector, with unspecified numbers of positive, negative, and zero elements. (In applications, one could specify that all but a few elements of da_i are zero – see last section's examples.) The elements of da_i are assumed so small, in absolute value, that, throughout the change from a_i to $a_i + da_i$, the basic actions remain basic actions. In other words, $a_1, \ldots, a_i + da_i, \ldots, a_k$ are linearly independent, and cannot be linearly combined – using weights $c \geqq 0$ – to form a semipositive action; and the vectors $a_1, \ldots, a_i + h \,.\, da_i, \ldots, a_k$ have those properties too, for all h in (0, 1). This is a simplifying assumption – four others follow.

Let x^1 be the final endowment or equilibrium endowment prior to the change, and let Ac be the action transforming the initial endowment, x^0, into x^1. Since Ac is a non-negative linear combination of the basic actions, the elements of c are positive or zero. If they are all zero, x^1 and x^0 coincide. This possibility will be ruled out – the second simplifying assumption.

Let c_0 be the vector obtained from c by eliding all zero elements, if any, from the latter. Then c_0 is a positive vector, with k_0 elements, say, and $k_0 \geqq 1$. (The vector c has k elements; $k_0 \leqq k$.) The basic actions corresponding to the elements of c_0 form a submatrix, A_0, of A. Clearly, $Ac = A_0 c_0$. It is convenient to call a basic action 'attractive' if it is a column of A_0, 'unattractive' otherwise. The final endowment x^1 is then attained by taking all attractive basic actions and no unattractive ones.

The columns of A_0 span a facet of the attainable set, of dimension k_0. Let this facet be F_0. By construction, F_0 contains the final endowment, x^1, as an interior point. If, for example, F_0 is spanned by two basic actions, x^1 lies inside the angle or cone formed by those basic actions, and not on the boundary. If F_0 is spanned by one basic action, x^1 lies on the ray spanned by that basic action, but x^1 is not the beginpoint of the ray (that is, $x^1 \neq x^0$).

A qualification is necessary. The facets of the attainable set are not ordinary cones, but truncated cones. It is therefore possible for x^1 to be interior to F_0 in the sense just described, and yet to lie on the boundary of F_0. This occurs if x^1 lies in one of the coordinate hyperplanes of R^n. The third simplifying assumption is that such corner solutions are ruled out.[21]

If a_i, the changing basic action, is not attractive, the final endowment is generally not affected by the change. For instance, someone who never buys sugar will not, as a rule, start buying sugar when its price drops a little. The fourth simplifying assumption is that 'something will happen', that the change of a_i will have some effect on the equilibrium endowment.

It is possible for a_i to be so marginally unattractive as to become attractive when changing to $a_i + da_i$. In that case, the post-change A_0 has one more column than the pre-change A_0. By the same token, a marginally attractive a_i may become unattractive; A_0 then loses a column. Although these complications are not particularly difficult to handle, ignoring them will shorten the exposition considerably. The fifth simplifying assumption is, accordingly, that the collection of attractive basic actions remains the same throughout. Collecting assumptions,

a. basic actions remain basic actions;
b. the equilibrium endowment differs from the initial endowment;
c. the equilibrium endowment is positive (no corner solutions);
d. the equilibrium endowment changes when a_i changes;
e. the collection of attractive basic actions remains the same.

(Only the first assumption is essential. The other four can be done without, given a little effort).

Following standard reasoning, we take the change of a_i to be compensated in some way. Compensation is usually made in terms of money, but in this essay it may take the form of an entire commodity bundle, not necessarily containing money. This should not come as a surprise – money, here regarded as merely one of many commodities, does not deserve the position of pre-eminence that compensation in terms of just money would imply.

Also standard is that compensation should be so as to make the individual exactly as well off, in terms of utility, as before. Our objective function, f, is not utility, but we might demand, analogously, that compensation allow the individual to reattain the old (pre-change) value of f. Then again, it is not certain that this requirement would have operational meaning. No interpretation has been attached to f, and so it cannot be said that the individual is 'indifferent' between any two endowments carrying the same f-value. Besides, compensation in the neoclassical manner has another drawback: it asks that the individual be able to assay indifference. This is so demanding a requirement that it all but robs the Slutsky equation of its empirical content.

To avoid the difficulties described, we shall ask that compensation enable the individual to reattain his old (pre-change) *equilibrium endowment*. This form of compensation (known as overcompensation, except that overcompensation is usually defined as allowing reattainment of the pre-change equilibrium *bundle*, rather than equilibrium endowment) – this form of compensation has the advantage of being empirically feasible. It does not require that the individual engage in introspection and announce his preference ordering.

As is well-known, compensation of the type described does not appear to lead to the familiar, Slutskian, symmetry property. This is no great loss, because the symmetry property has limited empirical content: its verification requires that equality of two differential quotients be established, which appears empirically impossible. Equality of difference quotients *is* possible, but that translates into no more than approximate equality of differential quotients.

Where convenient, pre- and post-change magnitudes are distinguished by the absence or presence of a bar. Thus, the new initial endowment is $\bar{x}^0$. Writing the compensation as dx^0, one has $\bar{x}^0 = x^0 + dx^0$. The matrix A becomes $\bar{A}$ (so that A and $\bar{A}$ differ only in their ith columns, which are a_i and $\bar{a}_i$, respectively); the new action levels are $\bar{c} = c + dc$ (which defines dc); the new equilibrium endowment, $\bar{x}^1$, lies in the facet $\bar{F}_0$, which is spanned by the columns of $\bar{A}_0$; the columns of $\bar{A}_0$ – the *new* attractive basic actions – are the same as those of A_0, except that $\bar{A}_0$ has a column $\bar{a}_i$ where A_0 has the column a_i; and so on.

The compensation dx^0 renders the old equilibrium endowment reattainable, by definition. Otherwise, dx^0 is as yet completely unspecified. For the moment, then, the only restriction on dx^0 is that x^1 must be expressible as the sum of the new initial endowment, $\bar{x}^0$ or $x^0 + dx^0$, and some linear combination of the new basic actions, $a_1, \ldots, \bar{a}_i, \ldots, a_k$, columns of $\bar{A}$. Put differently, the new facet $\bar{F}_0$, which is spanned by the columns of $\bar{A}_0$, must contain both x^1 and $\bar{x}^0$. Any point of $\bar{F}_0$ can therefore serve as the new initial endowment, because x^1 can be reached from any point of $\bar{F}_0$. No point outside $\bar{F}_0$ can serve as the new initial endowment, because x^1 cannot be reached from any point outside $\bar{F}_0$.

It is easy to see that the compensation *may* be chosen equal to $- c_i da_i$; for the initial endowment then becomes $\bar{x}^0 = x^0 - c_i da_i$, and addition of $\bar{A}c$ (which is a linear combination of the new basic actions) yields $x^0 - c_i da_i + \bar{A}c = x^0 + Ac = x^1$. But $x^0 - c_i da_i$ is merely one point of $\bar{F}_0$. Our purposes are served just as well if we add, to the tentatively chosen compensation $- c_i da_i$, *any* linear combination of the vectors that span $\bar{F}_0$—say $\bar{A}_0\theta_0$, with θ_0 arbitrary.

Definition. The compensation is the n-vector $dx^0 = \bar{A}_0\theta_0 - c_i da_i$, where θ_0 is an as yet unspecified k_0-vector.

It would be imprudent to specify θ_0 at this early stage.

The property to be proved concerns the effect of the compensated change of a_i on the elements of $c_i a_i$. Four preliminary results are needed.

The first preliminary result:

$$A_0' \operatorname{grad} f(x^1) = 0 \tag{2}$$

Proof. The equilibrium endowment is an interior point of the facet F_0 in which it lies. At the equilibrium endowment, therefore, grad f is orthogonal to F_0, and hence to the vectors that span F_0. This is what (2) says.[22]

The second preliminary result:

$$(\bar{x}^1 - x^1)' \operatorname{grad} f(x^1) > 0 \tag{3}$$

Proof. This follows directly from one of the definitions of strict quasi-concavity (*Cf.* [12], p. 378).

The third preliminary result:

$$\bar{x}^1 - x^1 = \bar{A}_0(\theta_0 + dc_0) \tag{4}$$

Proof. By definition, $\bar{x}^1 = \bar{x}^0 + \bar{A}_0\bar{c}_0 = (x^0 + dx^0) + \bar{A}_0(c_0 + dc_0)$. Subtracting $x^1 = x^0 + A_0c_0$ gives $\bar{x}^1 - x^1 = dx^0 + (\bar{A}_0 - A_0)c_0 + \bar{A}_0dc_0 = dx^0 + c_ida_i + \bar{A}_0dc_0$. By definition, $dx^0 = \bar{A}_0\theta_0 - c_ida_i$, and (4) follows.[23]

Let the columns of A be ordered so that the *first* k_0 columns form A_0. It is then certain that a_i is not only the ith column of A, but the ith column of A_0 as well. The ith element of $\theta_0 + dc_0$ is, similarly, $\theta_i + dc_i$. We now have the fourth preliminary result:

$$(\theta_i + dc_i)da_i'\text{grad}\, f(x^1) > 0, \text{ for every } \theta_i \tag{5}$$

Proof. Combining (3) and (4) gives $(\theta_0 + dc_0)'\bar{A}_0'\text{grad}\, f(x^1) > 0$, and subtracting (2) gives $(\theta_0 + dc_0)'(\bar{A}_0 - A_0)'\text{grad}\, f(x^1) > 0$. All rows of $(\bar{A}_0 - A_0)'$ are null except the ith, which is da_i'. Thus, $(\theta_0 + dc_0)'(\bar{A}_0 - A_0)' = (\theta_i + dc_i)da_i'$, and (5) follows.

This concludes the preliminaries. We can now formulate and prove the first property of the reaction function. The property takes the form of two theorems. Between the two theorems, some numerical examples are inserted.

Theorem 1. If the semi-inequality $\mu da_i + A_0\mu_0 \geq 0$ (μ is a scalar, μ_0 a vector) has a solution μ, μ_0, the compensation can be so chosen that it is possible to predict, for each element of c_ia_i, whether it will increase, decrease, or remain the same. (The proof will show which choices of the compensation are suitable.)[24]

Proof. Let the given semi-inequality have a solution μ, μ_0, and therefore infinitely many solutions. We multiply both sides of the semi-inequality into grad $f(x^1)$, recall that grad $f(x^1)$ is assumed positive and that $A_0'\text{grad}\, f(x^1) = 0$, and get $\mu da_i'\text{grad}\, f(x^1) > 0$. (Because $da_i'\text{grad}\, f(x^1)$ is a fixed quantity, we find that, in all solutions μ, μ_0 to the semi-inequality, μ has the same sign—always positive, or always negative, and never zero.) Comparison of what was just found with preliminary result (5) shows that sign (μ) = sign ($\theta_i + dc_i$), for every θ_i. Since da_i and the columns of A_0 may be regarded as known, sign (μ) is empirically obtainable. So, then, is sign ($\theta_i + dc_i$).

The compensated change turns c_ia_i into $c_ia_i + d(c_ia_i)$, where $d(c_ia_i)$ is readily seen to equal $dc_i\bar{a}_i + c_ida_i$. Hence

$$d(c_ia_i) = (\theta_i + dc_i)\bar{a}_i + c_ida_i - \theta_i\bar{a}_i \tag{6}$$

The right-hand side is the sum of three vectors. The first is the product of the vector $\bar{a}_i$, which is known, and the constant $\theta_i + dc_i$, of which the sign is known, as we just saw. In other words, the first term on the right is a vector whose non-zero elements are known in sign, but not in value. The second vector on the right, $c_i da_i$, is known. The third vector, $-\theta_i \bar{a}_i$, is the product of the known vector $\bar{a}_i$ and the ith element of θ_0, which is still ours to choose. It is asserted that θ_0 can be so chosen that each element of $d(c_i a_i)$ is sign-determinate.

For each j such that the jth element of $\bar{a}_i$ is zero, the choice of θ_0 is immaterial. As (6) shows, for every such j one has $d(c_i a_{ij}) = c_i da_{ij}$, a quantity known in sign as well as in value.

Consider, then, the indices j for which $\bar{a}_{ij}$ is not zero. If $\theta_i + dc_i$ is *negative*, a sufficiently large, *positive* value of θ_i will, for each of the given j considered, swamp the fixed quantity $c_i da_{ij}$, and give $d(c_i a_{ij})$ the (known) sign of $\bar{a}_{ij}$. The largest of these sufficiently large numbers will then achieve the desired sign-determinacy for all elements of $d(c_i a_i)$. This completes the proof for the case $(\theta_i + dc_i) < 0$. If $(\theta_i + dc_i)$ is *positive*, one must choose θ_i *negative*, and sufficiently large in absolute value; otherwise the proof is the same.

It is noted that the choice of the vector θ_0 is still largely unconstrained: only θ_i must meet certain requirements.[25]

Two numerical illustrations follow.

Example 1. Consider the simplest neoclassical case – one (attractive) basic action ($k_0 = k = 1$) and two goods ($n = 2$). Let the single basic action be $a_1 = \{1, -2\}$: one unit of good 1 is obtainable in exchange for two units of good 2. (See Figure 7.) The price associated with a_1 is thus 2. The individual usually buys three units, say, of good 1: $c_1 a_1 = \{3, -6\}$. Let $da_1 = \{0, -1\}$, so that $a_1 = \{1, -2\}$ becomes $\bar{a}_1 = \{1, -3\}$, signifying an increase of the price from 2 to 3.

The semi-inequality $\mu da_1 + \mu_1 a_1 \geq 0$ has a solution (it always does when $k_0 = n - 1$; see footnote 24), for instance, $\mu = -1, \mu_1 = 0$. Because μ is negative, $\theta_1 + dc_1$ is negative, too, for any choice of θ_1. Representing 'a positive number' by (pos) and 'a negative number' by (neg), one has, from (6), that

$$\begin{aligned} d(c_1 a_1) &= (\theta_1 + dc_1)\bar{a}_1 + c_1 da_1 - \theta_1 \bar{a}_1 \\ &= (neg)\{1, -3\} + \{0, -3\} - \theta_1\{1, -3\} \\ &= \{(neg) - \theta_1, (pos) - 3 + 3\theta_1\}. \end{aligned}$$

The first element of $d(c_1 a_1)$ is sign-determinate (negative, in fact) if we choose

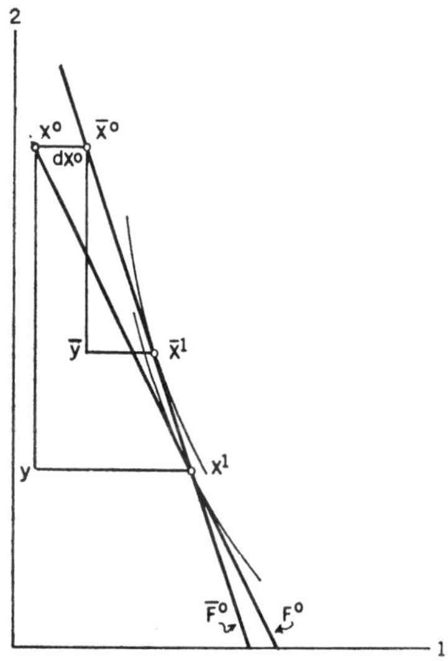

Figure 7. Compensation, dx^0, changes x^0 to $\bar{x}^0$, and x^1 to $\bar{x}^1$. The individual now acquires less ($\bar{y}\bar{x}^1 < yx^1$) and gives up less ($\bar{y}\bar{x}^0 < yx^0$).

$\theta_1 \geqq 0$. The second element of $d(c_1 a_1)$ is sign-determinate (positive, in fact) if we choose $\theta_1 \geqq 1$. Setting $\theta_1 = 1$ will satisfy both conditions, and so render $d(c_1 a_1)$ entirely sign-determinate.

The compensation, $dx^0 = \bar{A}_0 \theta_0 - c_1 da_1$, is, in this case, $\{1, -3\}(1) + - \{0, -3\} = \{1, 0\}$: the individual receives one unit of good 1. Compensation is thus seen to take place, not in terms of the good supplied (money), but in terms of the good demanded. Were the individual compensated in terms of money, it would be impossible, as Hicks has shown, to determine the sign of the second element of $d(c_1 a_1)$. Hicks concluded that there exists an essential difference between demand and supply;[26] we find, however, that the difference is due to the definition of compensation, and disappears when compensation is allowed in terms of a good (or several goods) other than money. With compensation as defined, demand and supply are treated with complete symmetry, and the only difference between them is one of algebraic sign.

As Figure 7 shows, after the compensated change of a_1 – which is in this example a compensated price change –, the individual acquires less of good 1 and gives up less of good 2. This confirms what was just found by analytical methods: the first element of $d(c_1 a_1)$ is negative (less of good 1 is bought), and the second element of $d(c_1 a_1)$ is positive (the negative number $c_1 a_{12}$ increases, 'becomes less negative', so that supply, $|c_1 a_{12}|$, decreases).

We note yet that the calculated compensation, one unit of good 1, is worth three units of money, because the new price of good 1 is 3. The traditional definition of overcompensation would have the individual receive, not three dollars' worth of good 1, but three dollars.

Example 2. An individual, living in a four-goods economy, $n = 4$, has two basic actions, both attractive, at his disposal ($k_0 = k = 2$). Let $a_1 = \{1, 1, 0, -3\}$, $a_2 = \{0, -1, 1, 5\}$, $c_1 = 2$, and $da_1 = \{0, 0, 1, -1\}$. Then a_1 becomes $\bar{a}_1 = \{1, 1, 1, -4\}$.

The semi-inequality $\mu da_1 + A_0\mu_0 \geq 0$ has a solution, for instance, $\mu = 1$, $\mu_0 = \{1, 1\}$. It follows that sign $(\theta_1 + dc_1)$, being equal to sign (μ), equals $+1$, for every choice of θ_1. So, from (6),

$$\begin{aligned} d(c_1a_1) &= (\theta_1 + dc_1)\bar{a}_1 + c_1 da_1 - \theta_1\bar{a}_1 \\ &= (pos)\{1, 1, 1, -4\} + \{0, 0, 2, -2\} - \theta_1\{1, 1, 1, -4\} \\ &= \{(pos) - \theta_1, (pos) - \theta_1, (pos) + 2 - \theta_1, (neg) - 2 + 4\theta_1\}. \end{aligned}$$

Choosing $\theta_1 \leqq 0$ as well as $\leqq 2$ as well as $\leqq \frac{1}{2}$ will make all elements of $d(c_1a_1)$ definite in sign. Setting $\theta_1 = 0$ will do; the first three elements of $d(c_1a_1)$ are then positive, and the fourth is negative.

The compensation is $dx^0 = \bar{A}_0\theta_0 - c_1da_1$, with the vector θ_0 still partly unspecified: $\theta_1 = 0$, but θ_2 is a free parameter. Choosing the simplest possibility, we set $\theta_2 = 0$. Then $dx^0 = -c_1da_1 = \{0, 0, -2, 2\}$: the individual is 'taxed' two units of good 3, and he receives two units of good 4. Afterwards he buys more of goods 1 and 2, the first two elements of $d(c_1a_1)$ being positive; he buys good 3, which he did not do before (at least not via the first basic action – he did buy good 3 via the second basic action); and he sells more of good 4 (the negative number c_1a_{14} becomes 'more negative').

It is observed that the conclusions reached in this example do not require that prices exist, nor that any good be designated as numéraire.

According to Theorem 1, the vector $d(c_ia_i)$ is entirely sign-determinate if $\mu da_i + A_0\mu_0 \geq 0$ has a solution. What if the semi-inequality has no solution? Theorem 2, next, provides the answer.

Theorem 2. If $\mu da_i + A_0\mu_0 \geq 0$ has no solution μ, μ_0, it is impossible to predict the sign of any element of $d(c_ia_i)$, unless, trivially, the corresponding element of $\bar{a}_i$ is zero.

Proof. It will be shown that, if the given semi-inequality has no solution, the sign of $da_i'\text{grad} f(x^1)$ cannot be empirically determined. The sign of $\theta_i + dc_i$ can then not be empirically determined either, considering that $(\theta_i + dc_i)da_i'\text{grad} f(x^1)$ is known to be positive – see preliminary result (5). A glance at (6) suffices to show that the sign-determinacy of the elements of $d(c_i a_i)$ stands and falls with the sign-determinacy of $\theta_i + dc_i$, except, trivially, for those elements of $d(c_i a_i)$ corresponding to zero elements of $\bar{a}_i$. (If $\bar{a}_{ij} = 0$, one has $d(c_i a_{ij}) = c_i da_{ij}$, a quantity known in sign as well as value.) Thus, proving that the sign of $da_i'\text{grad} f(x^1)$ is indeterminate will prove Theorem 2.

All that is known about grad $f(x^1)$ is that it is a positive vector, orthogonal to A_0's columns, and not orthogonal to da_i. (The last assertion is implied by the fourth preliminary result, $(\theta_i + dc_i)da_i'\text{grad} f(x^1) > 0$.) Consequently, every vector with these three properties is empirically indistinguishable from grad $f(x^1)$. If we construct a vector v with the three properties and assert that this v is just grad $f(x^1)$, no amount of empirical evidence can disprove that statement.

Let $\mu da_i + A_0\mu_0 \geq 0$ have no solution. Then, by Farkas's Lemma, the system $da_i'y = 0$, $A_0'y = 0$ has a positive solution y. Let the two vectors v_1 and v_2 be defined through

$$v_1 = y - h(\text{grad} f(x^1) - y)$$

$$v_2 = y + h(\text{grad} f(x^1) - y),$$

where $h > 0$ is so small that both v_1 and v_2 are positive. It is easy to see that v_1 and v_2 have the three properties grad $f(x^1)$ is known to have. First, v_1 and v_2 are positive, by construction. Second, v_1 and v_2 are orthogonal to A_0's columns. (For example, $A_0'v_1 = A_0'y - hA_0'\text{grad} f(x^1) + hA_0'y$, a sum of three terms that are all zero.) Third, $da_i'v_1 = -hda_i'\text{grad} f(x^1) \neq 0$, and $da_i'v_2 = +hda_i'\text{grad} f(x^1) \neq 0$, so that neither v_1 nor v_2 is orthogonal to da_i. Stronger, $da_i'v_1$ and $da_i'v_2$ have opposite signs.

One of $da_i'v_1$ and $da_i'v_2$ is positive – say $da_i'v_1$. If it is asserted that $v_1 = \text{grad} f(x^1)$, a statement impossible to disprove, then $da_i'v_1 = da_i'\text{grad} f(x_1) > 0$. If it is asserted that $v_2 = \text{grad} f(x^1)$, another statement impossible to disprove, it follows, likewise, that $da_i'\text{grad} f(x^1) < 0$. Neither inequality can be refuted, meaning that the sign of $da_i'\text{grad} f(x^1)$ cannot be empirically determined. This is what we wanted to prove.

Theorem 2 has no implications for the neoclassical case ($k_0 = k = n - 1$), because, as was shown earlier, the semi-inequality $\mu da_i + A_0\mu_0 \geq 0$ always has a solution when $k_0 = n - 1$.[24]

This concludes our discussion of the effect of a_i's compensated change on $c_i a_i$. The assumption grad $f > 0$ is no longer needed, and hence dropped.

Purpose of this section, it may be recalled, is to establish properties of the reaction function, $q(a_i)$. Theorems 1 and 2, taken together, describe the first property. It is a striking one, in part because it generalizes the Slutskian negative-definiteness result, and in part because its wide applicability (a_i may represent not only a transaction but also a production process) underscores the breadth of scope of a unified theory. But it is a narrow property, too. Theorems 1 and 2 describe the effect of a compensated change of a_i on all elements of the action $c_i a_i$, and on no other action elements; the reaction function, on the other hand, relates changes of a_i (not necessarily compensated) to artibrary action elements. An example may illustrate the difference.

Suppose the objective function were quadratic. Then, as some straightforward manipulations may show,

(1) arbitrary action elements depend on a_i according to $q(a_i) = a_i'Ma_i/a_i'Na_i$, the quotient of two quadratic forms in a_i;

(2) the matrix M is determined by one's choice of dependent variable, so that different matrices M are associated with different action elements; and

(3) the matrix N is always the same matrix, regardless of which element of which action serves as dependent variable.

Suppose, further, that a_i is 'buying shoes', and that a_i has only one variable element, namely, the price p of shoes. The reaction function $q(a_i)$, above, is thereby simplified, and becomes the quotient of two quadratic polynomials in p. Denoting this quotient by $q^*(p)$, one then has

$$q^*(p) = (m_1 p^2 + m_2 p + m_3)/(n_1 p^2 + n_2 p + n_3), \tag{7}$$

say, where m_1, m_2, m_3 are parameters, and n_1, n_2, n_3 are constants. For instance, the individual's demand for coffee, written as a function of the price of shoes, is given by (7). Similarly, the individual's output of playing cards, written as a function of the price of shoes, is given by (7), and so is his demand for shoes. Whether (7) is interpreted as describing the individual's demand for coffee, or his output of playing cards, or his demand for shoes, the constants n_j hold their values. Only the parameters m_j change.

Equation (7) is valid regardless of the choice of dependent variable, but it still makes a difference whether the dependent variable is or is not an element of $c_i a_i$. Dependent variables that are not elements of $c_i a_i$ are the individual's demand for coffee, and his output of playing cards. Dependent variables that are elements of $c_i a_i$ are the individual's demand for shoes (a_i is 'buying shoes'), and his expenditure for shoes. Expenditure for shoes is an element of $c_i a_i$, a quantity of money consumed by the action 'buying shoes'.

The expenditure for shoes, being an action element, obeys (7). At the same time, the expenditure for shoes equals p times the demand for shoes, and the demand for shoes *also* obeys (7). Apparently, when (7) is used to represent the individual's demand function for shoes, m_1 is zero. Any other value of m_1 would immediately give a contradiction. Another useful conclusion is that, when (7) is used to describe the individual's expenditure for shoes as a function of the price of shoes, m_3 is zero. Were this not so, the righthand side of (7) would not be a multiple of p.

The contents of the last paragraph illustrate that the elements of $c_i a_i$ depend on a_i in a simpler way than do arbitrary action elements.[27] This brings us back to the starting point: the Slutskian property, described in Theorems 1 and 2, is a narrow property, because it pertains to only a relatively simple form of the reaction function. That simple form is the one in which the dependent variable is an element of $c_i a_i$. Since Theorems 1 and 2 have nothing to say about the reaction function whenever the dependent variable is *not* an element of $c_i a_i$, their scope is regrettably restricted.

This section presents two more properties of the reaction function. These, unlike the first property, hold with complete generality; that is, they hold also if the dependent variable is an element of an action other than $c_i a_i$. Of interest is yet that both properties below are valid for all specifications of the objective function. They would hold, in other words, even if f were not differentiable, or not strictly quasi-concave.

The first of the remaining two properties is

$$q(ka_i) = q(a_i) \text{ for all } k > 0. \tag{8}$$

This says that whether cigarettes are fifty cents per pack or two packs for a dollar does not affect the individual's cigarette consumption; and whether the wage rate is quoted as four dollars per hour or two dollars per half hour makes no difference in the individual's working habits. The condition $k > 0$ is necessary because of the irreversibility postulate. For $k < 0$, only one of the members of (8) would have economic meaning.

Property (8) is closely related to what is known as the absence of money illusion. Like the absence of money illusion, property (8) is quite plausible in a perfectly divisible world, but only there. Its significance is therefore slight, and (8) is presented here only for the sake of completeness.
It is clear that the validity of (8) does not depend on the specification of f, as asserted.

A third property of the reaction function, and the last one to be given here, requires that the reaction function be generalized first. *In the rest of this section, the dependent variable in $q(a_i)$ is taken to be (not just any action element but) any linear combination – with constant weights – of action elements.* Some examples follow.
The caloric value of an individual's food purchases is a linear combination of action elements, with constant weights, so that its dependence on a_i (whatever a_i may represent) is given by the reaction function.
The weight of all fruit, bought, borrowed, and stolen by the individual in various places, is a linear combination of action elements, with constant weights, so that its dependence on a_i is given by the reaction function.
If the individual has both money income and income in kind, the total (money) value of his income is a linear combination of action elements, and so depends on a_i according to the reaction function.
If the individual makes both brooms and doormats, production costs depend on a_i according to the reaction function. Since production costs form an action element, this last example illustrates the old definition of reaction function as well.[28]
It is useful to distinguish between the reaction function, singular, and the reaction functions, plural. The reaction function, singular, is a function with parameters unspecified; specifying the parameters – that is, giving them numerical values – yields reaction functions, plural. A similar distinction exists between the linear function, $y = a + bx$, and linear functions such as $y = 3 + 4x$ and $y = 2 - 5x$. Using this convention, one has from the new definition of reaction function that *the set of all reaction functions is a vector space.*

This is the promised third property of reaction functions. In all likelihood, only some reaction functions in the vector space have actual significance, have an actual, economic interpretation.
It is evident that the vector space property holds regardless of the specification of f, as asserted.
For an illustration of the third property, we briefly return to the quadratic

objective function. As mentioned earlier, if f is quadratic, action elements depend on a_i according to $q(a_i) = a_i'Ma_i/a_i'Na_i$. Here, M is different for different action elements, *but N is always the same matrix.* It follows that the indicated class of functions, $a_i'Ma_i/a_i'Na_i$, is closed under addition and scalar multiplication. Were N different for different action elements, the vector space property could not hold.

We conclude this section with a summary. Initially, the reaction function was taken to describe how arbitrary action elements – equivalently, arbitrary quantities produced or consumed – depend on the basic action a_i. Eventually, this definition was generalized; the dependent variable, until then an arbitrary action element, became an arbitrary linear combination (with constant weights) of action elements. The reaction function has numerous properties, three of which were presented. The first property says that, iff a certain semi-inequality has a solution, a change of a_i can be compensated so that all elements of c_ia_i change in a predictable direction. The proof used the strict-quasi-concavity of f, and also the temporarily postulated positivity of f's first-order partial derivatives.
The second property says that the length or norm of the basic actions is immaterial, does not influence the equilibrium endowment. This is true regardless of how f is specified.
The third property says that the set of all reaction functions is a vector space. This, too, is true regardless of the specification of the objective function.

6. *Continuous-Time Dynamics and Some Other Issues*

The development of our unified theory began with definitions of an objective function and an attainable set, definitions that prompted remarks on, in particular, money. After that, the reaction function was defined, and a few of its properties derived. We now turn to some of the remaining issues.
A theory of individual economic behavior should not be considered complete until it incorporates time, uncertainty, and indivisibility. This final section treats primarily, although sketchily, of time. Little will be said about uncertainty, nothing at all about indivisibility.
A convenient starting point is found in the action 'eating'. This action consumes food; more important, it produces labor ('energy'). The action 'eating' is therefore just what our model needs to turn individual economic behavior into an endless cycle: the individual works to earn money, spends the money on food, eats the food to gain energy, spends the energy by performing work.[29] Traditional microeconom-

ic theory is interested in only part of that cycle—how we work to earn money is described by the theory of producer behavior, and how we spend the money earned is described by the theory of consumer behavior. But how we create energy by eating is generally considered outside the province of economics.

By locking itself out of the dining room, microeconomics breaks up the endless behavioral cycle into segments, each with a clear-cut beginning and a clear-cut end. The segmentation is reflected in the familiar trichotomy of goods into primary, intermediate, and final goods. Primary goods are prominent at the beginning of the cycle segment, intermediate goods, in the middle, final goods, at the end.

The just-sketched arrangement derives its justification, such as it is, from the fact that eating is, by intuitive interpretation, neither consumer behavior nor producer behavior. Neoclassical theory is therefore not equipped to take eating into account. A unified theory of individual economic behavior is different in this respect, for it does not have the producer-consumer dichotomy, and so cannot classify the individual's actions as being consumer behavior, producer behavior, or neither. A unified theory treats actions as just that—actions. And since eating is, by intuitive interpretation, an action, a unified theory cannot ignore it.

To avoid misunderstanding, it should be stressed that the culinary aspects of eating are of no concern here. What matters is that there exists an energy-producing action. Existence of an energy-producing action closes the gaps in the behavioral cycle—it places the individual under the theorist's constant surveillance, so to speak. And existence of an energy-producing action does more. It renders illegitimate the distinction between primary, intermediate, and final goods, entailing a drastic change of the microeconomic perspective. Elaboration follows.

The traditional description of individual economic behavior emphasizes goods and their evolution. Goods, starting out as raw materials, are gradually perfected into final goods; as final goods, they find their way into the household, from which time on they are, according to traditional thinking, of no further interest. The story is thus given a natural ending. But once eating is legitimized as an object of economic-theoretical scrutiny, and the gaps in the cycle of individual economic behavior are filled, goods can no longer be justifiably divided into primary, intermediate, and final goods. A different way of thinking is then needed, a different picture. In this picture, emphasis is on actions rather than on goods. Whether a particular piece of gold, say, lies in a jeweler's vault or rests one mile underground is of no interest in our model. What is of interest is that the miner digs for gold, and that the jeweler works his gold. What is of even greater interest is that these two actions have the same structure, are on equal theoretical footing, and should receive the same theoretical treatment.

By filling the gaps in the behavioral cycle, we have lost a natural starting point and a natural endpoint for our investigations. The notions of initial and final endowment, in particular, have been rendered meaningless. But there is an obvious substitute, *viz.*, $x(t)$, the *endowment at time t*. This is where time comes in.[30]
Attention now shifts to S, the pointed, convex, polyhedral cone that is the attainable set. Which point of S should be taken to represent $x(t)$, the endowment at time t? As some reflection shows, the vertex of S is the logical candidate. Since the individual's endowment presumably changes over time, so that the vertex of S changes over time, it follows that S itself, the entire attainable set, changes over time. Just as light shines out from a miner's headlamp, so does the attainable set S—now better denoted $S(t)$—emanate from the point $x(t)$, at all times. It will be assumed, in the interests of simplicity, that the principal edges of the attainable set (the basic actions) remain parallel to themselves, throughout. In other words, the action matrix is taken to be independent of t. The same is assumed for the objective function f.
Consider now the point at which the objective function is maximized over the attainable set. Let this equilibrium point be denoted by $e(t)$. Writing $e(t)$, rather than just e, serves flexibility: it is the right notation if the equilibrium point happens to change over time, and no harm is done if this should not be the case.
The point $e(t)$ is an endowment in that its elements represent stocks. But $e(t)$ is not the endowment at time t, unless, trivially, $e(t)$ coincides with $x(t)$. It seems best to describe $e(t)$ as the *endowment desired at time t*.
The obvious next step is to postulate some relationship between the actual endowment $x(t)$ and the desired endowment $e(t)$. Among the many possible postulates, two stand out in that they have a more traditional flavor than the others. One is the postulate that the rate of change of $x(t)$, that is $\dot{x}(t)$, be proportional to $e(t) - x(t)$, and the other is that $\ddot{x}(t)$ be proportional to the same vector, $e(t) - x(t)$. Discussion follows.
If $\dot{x}(t) = \alpha[e(t) - x(t)]$, for some scalar $\alpha > 0$, it is easy to see that the point $e(t)$ is fixed and that, as t increases, $x(t)$ gets arbitrarily close to this fixed equilibrium point. For large t, then, $x(t)$ is virtually constant, implying that the individual does virtually nothing.
To make this more precise, let $A\dot{c}(t)$ be the *action taken at time t*, and let its integral, $Ac(t_2) - Ac(t_1)$, be the *action taken between times t_1 and t_2*. (Thus, $x(t) = x(0) + Ac(t)$, which, upon differentiation with respect to t, shows that $\dot{x}(t)$ just equals $A\dot{c}(t)$, the action taken at time t.) Now, if $x(t)$ approaches constancy, as it does, one has $\dot{x}(t) \to 0$; and since $\dot{x}(t) = A\dot{c}(t)$, one has $A\dot{c}(t) \to 0$ as well. By the linear independence of A's columns, the statement $A\dot{c}(t) \to 0$ is equivalent

to $\dot{c}(t) \to 0$. If actions were reversible, this would mean that the individual acquired approximately as much of every good as he gave up – if he bought a hundred apples, he would use up approximately a hundred apples, by selling, eating, throwing away, and so on. But actions are irreversible, and $\dot{c}(t) \to 0$ means something else. The meaning of $\dot{c}(t) \to 0$ is that, in the end, the individual becomes wholly inactive. He stops buying, selling, eating, producing (in the traditional sense). This being too unrealistic to be acceptable, we turn to the alternative postulate, $\ddot{x}(t) = \alpha[e(t) - x(t)]$.

If $\ddot{x}(t) = \alpha[e(t) - x(t)]$, for some scalar $\alpha > 0$, it is again easy to see that the point $e(t)$ is fixed. Furthermore, if actions were reversible, the individual's endowment would oscillate around this fixed point, approaching it as t increased. But actions are irreversible, and $x(t)$ does not oscillate. Instead, $x(t)$ shoots past the fixed equilibrium point, slows down, and stops. Irreversibility of actions keeps $x(t)$ from 'falling back' toward equilibrium.

It is apparent that the alternative postulate is, if possible, even more unrealistic than the first. With the first postulate, the individual would hardly act, but at least he would act, at all times. With the second postulate, $x(t)$ comes to a standstill at some finite t, and the individual is totally inactive from then on.

Some reflection shows where the difficulty lies. A real individual who is totally inactive will soon become hungry. Once hungry, he will want to earn money for food; and so the behavioral cycle starts. Consider now the individual appearing in our model. He is a fictitious individual. His behavior cannot be observed, because it is not the behavior of a real person. Naturally, his behavior is meant to resemble that of a real person. As it now turns out, the resemblance is not good enough. For, unlike a real person, the fictitious protagonist of our model *has no reason to do anything, once he has reached his equilibrium endowment.* Real people continue to act, because the very business of living calls for such an effort. But there is no analogue in our model that can explain why a 'theoretical person' should similarly remain on his toes.[31]

To correct the lack of realism, we note again that real people become hungry even if they do not act. This suggests that the individual's endowment be assumed subject to an exogenously determined loss of energy. Such an assumption is efficacious, since it causes the individual of the model to act incessantly, just as a real individual would. At the same time, the assumption is epistemologically unsatisfactory, since it gives a role of exception to one good, namely, energy. This defect is easily remedied, however. It suffices to assume that *all* elements of the individual's endowment are subject to autonomous losses and gains. (By including autonomous gains, we capture the situation of the farmer, the orchard owner, and anyone else who owns things that grow.) It is not excluded that some of the losses and gains may be zero.

Let the vector $r(t_2) - r(t_1)$ represent the autonomous losses and gains between times t_1 and t_2, so that $\dot{r}(t)$ represents the rate at which autonomous losses and gains occur at time t. The endowment change at time t, $\dot{x}(t)$, is then the sum of two vectors. One is $\dot{r}(t)$, the other is $A\dot{c}(t)$, the individual's action taken at time t. The model equation, adjusted for the new assumption, might be $\dot{x}(t) = \alpha[e(t) - x(t)] + \dot{r}(t)$, or $\ddot{x}(t) = \alpha[e(t) - x(t)] + \dot{r}(t)$, or something similar. Whether or not $\dot{r}(t)$ varies over time is unimportant here. What matters is the very presence of $\dot{r}(t)$ in the model. It is the presence of $\dot{r}(t)$ that keeps the individual of our model going, keeps him acting at all times; and this, in turn, makes the individual resemble the real person he is meant to represent.

Introduction of $\dot{r}(t)$ influences the form of the reaction function. Details will be omitted, but the main line of argument is as follows.

Let the model equation be specified as $\dot{x}(t) = \alpha[e(t) - x(t)] + \dot{r}(t)$, and suppose the objective function f is known, up to (but not necessarily including) the values of its parameters. Maximizing f over the attainable set $S(t)$ yields $e(t)$. This $e(t)$ will be a function of the things that determine f and $S(t)$, *viz.*, the parameters of f, the vertex $x(t)$ of $S(t)$, and the vectors $a_1, \ldots, a_k$ spanning the principal edges of $S(t)$. Substituting for $e(t)$ into the model equation, one gets, say, $\dot{x}(t) = \phi(x(t), \dot{r}(t), A)$. Assuming solution possible, it follows that $x(t) = \psi(\dot{r}(t), A)$, say. This completely describes the time path of the individual's endowment, and so leads directly to the (now time-dependent) reaction function.

It is of interest to note that $e(t)$, as described in the last paragraph, is quite likely to vary; the endowment desired at time t is likely to be different from the endowment desired at time $t + \Delta t$. Traditional microeconomics accommodates the existence of such taste changes by letting the objective function – utility – vary. In the present model, taste changes are dealt with differently, through $\dot{r}(t)$. The objective function is assumed not to vary with time.[32]

In the models $\dot{x}(t) = \alpha[e(t) - x(t)]$ and $\ddot{x}(t) = \alpha[e(t) - x(t)]$, discussed earlier, $x(t)$ would eventually become stationary. Now that exogenously determined influences, $\dot{r}(t)$, have entered into the model, stationarity is no longer certain. *If* $x(t)$ becomes stationary, it means that, in the end, the individual's actions just offset the influences summarized in $\dot{r}(t)$. Equivalently, stationarity of $x(t)$ means that there exists an action that, when added to $\dot{r}(t)$, gives null, for all sufficiently large t; or again, it means that *minus* $\dot{r}(t)$ lies in the attainable set $S(t)$, for all sufficiently large t (and ignoring that $S(t)$ is truncated). If this condition is not met, the individual's actions may still be capable of offsetting *part* of the exogenous influences. But the remaining part of $\dot{r}(t)$ then goes unopposed. It is this unopposed component that pulls and pushes the endowment every which way, thereby preventing the attainment of a stationary state. (In fact, the endowment may drift off toward infinity. To get there will take an infinitely long time, though.[18])

Models such as the one here used for illustration completely describe the time path of the individual's endowment. This may seem to run counter to intuition, because it does not leave the individual any choice. On the other hand, utility theory presents the individual as 'choosing' the utility-maximizing bundle, which does not leave him any choice either. The continuous-time approach (and, more particularly, the fact that the individual is now 'under constant surveillance' by the theory) merely emphasizes that there is no such thing as choice, except as a figure of speech.

This completes the discussion of time, and of its introduction into our model of individual economic behavior. The treatment has been sketchy, but our purpose in this section is merely to formulate a language with which to approach various problems of model construction. Solution of those problems is not attempted.

Introduction of $\dot{r}(t)$ provides a convenient opportunity of bringing uncertainty into the model. It suffices to allow $\dot{r}(t)$ to vary irregularly, for instance by regarding $\dot{r}(t)$ as a stochastic process. (Actually, $\dot{r}(t)$ is only a single time function, not an entire stochastic process. Treating $\dot{r}(t)$ as a stochastic process is, however, mathematically more convenient.) The model equation $\dot{x}(t) = \alpha[e(t) - x(t)] + \dot{r}(t)$ now becomes a stochastic differential equation. If f is known, $e(t)$ can be expressed in terms of $x(t)$, the basic actions, and the parameters of f, and the model equation can be solved. The solution, $x(t)$, depends on the parameters of f, on the basic actions, and on $\dot{r}(t)$. Since $\dot{r}(t)$ is random, $x(t)$ is random. Specifying the process $\dot{r}(t)$ will determine the process $x(t)$. Of course, f is not known, the given model equation may prove unrealistic, and it may not be possible to specify $\dot{r}(t)$ in a way that is both realistic and mathematically tractable. The preceding analysis should therefore be regarded as merely an illustration of the structure of the problem described, and not as a feasible method of solving that problem.

It is evident that the construction of a unified theory of individual economic behavior requires a great deal more work. The first task is, probably, to obtain the analytical form of f.[33] Once f is known, the analytical form of the reaction function – the simple, non-dynamic, non-random reaction function of Sections 4 and 5 – is readily found. Reliance on mere properties of f, such as those of Section 5, will then no longer be necessary.

The second task, it would appear, is to find an acceptable behavioral equation – not necessarily $\dot{x} = \alpha[e - x] + \dot{r}$ or $\ddot{x} = \alpha[e - x] + \dot{r}$, of course – as well as an acceptable stochastic specification of the process $\dot{r}(t)$.

Even if all this could be done, the list of remaining problems would be impressive. Some of those problems have been mentioned – how to deal with interactive behavior, for instance, and how to deal with indivisibility. Some have not yet been mentioned – how to incorporate learning, for instance, and the concept of information.[34]

There are also some epistemological questions, likely to prove quite thorny: How does one tell which of an individual's acts are actions, which are basic actions? And: the reaction function presumes that a_i, changes, *e.g.*, because of a price change; could it be that 'changing a price' and, more generally, 'changing an action' are themselves actions? If so, what is their mathematical representation? At this point, could it be advantageous to interpret the elements of $x(t)$ as something other than commodity quantities?

And, finally, there are the truly grand issues – is there, beyond a unified theory of individual economic behavior, a unified theory of *all* individual behavior? If so, will it be possible, next, to combine the various theories of behavior into one social science? And, going further, will it be possible to combine that social science with the physical sciences to form a single science?

Notes

1 It is sometimes observed that producer goods may not be lumped with consumer goods, because the former are essentially different from the latter. Producer goods, the reasoning goes, have no place in the individual's scale of preference, and consumer goods do. Consumer goods have 'direct utility', production goods, 'indirect utility'. Plausible though this argument may seem, it rests wholly on semantics, and collapses when 'utility' (or 'scale of preference') is replaced with 'objective function'. *Cf.* the once-held position that opium and prostitution are immoral and so cannot have utility. That argument, too, was semantic; Pareto refuted it by replacing 'utility' with *ophélimité*.

2 A non-negative linear combination is here understood to be a linear combination with non-negative weights. Only the weights need be non-negative; the linear combination itself may very well be a vector with negative elements.

* Many thanks go to my friends and colleagues, Marjorie B. McElroy, Michael B. McElroy, and D. Michael Nienhaus, for frequent, stimulating comments and discussions. Special thanks go to Professors P. de Wolff and J. S. Cramer, for supervising the thesis out of which this essay grew.

[3] It is by now difficult to say what is the price of a toothbrush. Then again, the described (trans)-action is obviously well-defined, and its further characterization by means of a price is not vital. A detailed discussion of the existence and role of prices is given in Section 3.

[4] Labor is sometimes called a 'bad', and said to have 'disutility'. This confuses labor, a good, with performing labor, an act. Labor, as used by most economists, is identifiable with *energy*. Working, for example, is an action in which a quantity of energy—a quantity of the good 'labor'—is given up.

[5] According to often-heard reasoning, the effort needed to buy two neckties is less than twice the effort needed to buy one necktie. Were this so, it would vitiate our example. But the argument, quite valid in the imperfectly divisible world in which we live, is quite implausible in the perfectly divisible world of microeconomics, as some reflection may show.
To a general-equilibrium theorist it may be of some interest that, in transacting, buyers as well as sellers give up quantities of the good 'labor', and neither receives what the other relinquishes. It is therefore not plausible that the traders' endowments before and after the trade add up to the same vector. The matter will not be pursued; to limit the paper's size, all interactive behavior is left undiscussed. (Interactive behavior conceivably includes behavior of the firm. Only if a firm is organized under a single will, as the Olympian phrase goes, may we identify the behavior of the firm with the economic behavior of the entrepreneur. The model of this paper then applies. In all other cases, firm behavior has interactive elements. The model of this paper then does not apply.)

[6] *Manuel* [11], p. 250. (Emphasis and translation provided.)

[7] *Principles* [9], p. 93. (Emphasis shifted.)

[8] *Value and Capital* [5], p. 11. (Emphasis supplied.) According to Hicks, the quoted passage reflects Marshall's point of view, but Marshall's just-quoted words show otherwise.

[9] Hicks suggests a different conclusion: 'We may suppose, if we like, that (the individual) exchanges his whole stock into money . . ., when he will find himself in exactly the same position as our consumer whose income was fixed in terms of money' ([5], p. 36). This is unacceptable, however. We may not assume that sellers behave in a certain way, because behavior is the very thing we wish to explain; it is not amenable to assumption.

[10] In connection with this point, it is of interest to examine Samuelson's reasons for treating money and commodities differently. Samuelson ([13], p. 117) points out that the usefulness of having cash balances is categorically different from the usefulness of consuming tobacco, food, and the like; he concludes that money is different from commodities. The conclusion does not follow, however. Samuelson's observation is that cash balances are a stock, that consumed quantities of tobacco and food are flows, and that stocks are categorically different from flows. This implies nothing concerning the absence or presence of differences between money and (other) commodities.

[11] This observation paraphrases Sayers, one of the few advocates of equal theoretical treatment for money and other commodities [14].

[12] With a reason. The literature on the real-balance effect favors putting real money balances into the utility function. The main justification appears to be that a price increase makes the individual better or worse off (depending on whether he is a seller or a buyer of the good with the increased price); hence, the reasoning goes, prices belong in the utility function. But that conclusion does not follow. The price change affects the budget constraint, thereby the final endowment, thereby the value of the attainable utility maximum. In other words, the price change affects utility. There is no reason to assume that it also affects the utility *function*—or, for that matter, the objective function.

[13] *Why* the individual might wish to take some money home is not our concern. The individual's intentions, or rather what we perceive those intentions to be, may lead us to prefer one assumption

over another, and so influence the construction of the theory; but in the theory proper, intentions play no role. The only things that play a role are things that can be mathematically expressed.

[14] As this example shows, every transaction is being regarded as a double purchase and a double sale: the tobacconist buys money and sells tobacco, his customer does the opposite. This is the classical viewpoint, deserving of revival ([16], p. 14).

[15] For a third example see [15], p. 142-7.

[16] *Cf.* footnote 5.

[17] Behavioral theories, it is sometimes argued, need not require that behavior be uniquely determined. Whenever the individual finds himself indifferent between two actions (and so indifferent between all non-negative linear combinations of those actions), he will—so goes the argument—choose an action at random. This is a misapplication, it would seem, of Von Neumann and Morgenstern's recommendation that, under certain circumstances, individuals randomize their strategies. Von Neumann and Morgenstern suggested this in the context of their theory, which is prescriptive. Ours is a descriptive theory, however, and recommendations have no place in it. We seek to describe how individuals behave, not to prescribe how they should behave.
To look at it another way, consider that choosing between actions-with-an-economic-aspect is *itself* an action with an economic aspect. The idea of randomized choice is thus seen to imply, in a descriptive theory, that at least one type of action is *not* governed by objective-function maximization, namely, the action 'choosing'. Obviously, that does not leave much.

[18] It is generally held that free disposal is possible and production *ex nihilo* is not. Our definition of the attainable set is in accord with this view (including even the irreversibility requirement: a theory that permits free disposal but not production *ex nihilo must* assume irreversibility). It may be observed, however, that production *ex nihilo*—or its equivalent in the realm of consumer behavior—is not necessarily implausible. To be sure, a comparative-static model must rule it out, or introduce a bliss point; otherwise, the individual marches off to the Land of Cockaigne, if, indeed, he does not run, and the model itself loses whatever realism it has. In a dynamic model, however, this need not be so. A dynamic model may very well permit the individual to attain infinite riches, *provided the endeavor takes an infinitely long time.* For further details, see Section 6.

[19] Since the vectors in or parallel to the budget hyperplane are actions and p is not an action, it is, strictly speaking, illegitimate to call p orthogonal to the budget hyperplane. But the more accurate phrase 'p belongs to the annihilator of the budget hyperplane' seems overly fussy, in the rather elementary context of the present piece. We shall therefore stick to the comfortable familiarity of 'orthogonal'.

[20] The concept of price is, as a theoretical notion, suspect for yet another reason. Neoclassical consumer theory asserts that no good can have two prices, so that, if a jar of Nescafé sells for \$ 1.25 in store I and for \$ 1.30 in store II, neoclassical consumer theory regards store-I-Nescafé and store-II-Nescafé as different goods. Suppose store III sells Nescafé for \$ 1.30, just like store II. Is store-III-Nescafé then the same good as store-II-Nescafé? We usually take for granted that it is, but there is no reason why it should be. If different prices mean different goods, it does not follow that same prices mean same goods. Same prices *may* mean different goods.
The worst is yet to come. If same prices may mean different goods, it is impossible to tell whether one jar of store-I-Nescafé at \$ 1.25 is or is not the same good as another jar of store-I-Nescafé at \$ 1.25. More generally, it is impossible to tell, for *any* two objects of identical appearance and identically priced, whether they are one good or two. Thus, if the neoclassical argument —'no good can have two prices'—is taken to its logical conclusion, 'good' proves undefinable.
The preceding suggests that price is not needed (and, indeed, should not be used) as a commodity-defining characteristic. It is much simpler to regard Nescafé as a single good, regardless of its price, and to make a distinction between 'buying Nescafé at store I' and 'buying Nescafé at store II'. This is a distinction between actions, not between goods.

[21] In consumption theory, absence of a corner solution is usually taken to mean that all goods are *bought* in positive quantities. Here it means that all goods are eventually *possessed* in positive quantities. The reason is that the objective function is defined over the set of endowments, not over the set of purchases.

[22] Iff the dimension of F_0 is just $n - 1$, the positive vectors orthogonal to F_0 are all collinear. One of those positive vectors can be interpreted as a price vector, p. By (2), grad $f(x^1)$ is another such positive vector. Thus, iff F_0 has dimension $n - 1$, grad $f(x^1)$ is a positive multiple of p. If f were a utility function, this would be the traditional form of the first-order condition for a utility maximum at x^1.

[23] Neither $\bar{x}^1$ nor x^1 depends on the choice of θ_0, so that, apparently, $\theta_0 + dc_0$ is a vector of *constants*. This implies, in particular, that the elements of dc_0 need not be 'small'. If the initial change of a_i is slight, $\bar{x}^1$ will be close to x^1; it follows that, then, $\theta_0 + dc_0 \approx 0$, or $dc_0 \approx - \theta_0$. The vector θ_0 is ours to choose, and we may find it convenient to choose θ_0's elements 'large', in absolute value. If so, the elements of dc_0 will also be 'large' in absolute value.

[24] If $k_0 = n - 1$, and a fortiori in the neoclassical case, the semi-inequality always has a solution. For suppose it does not. By Farkas's Lemma, there then exists a positive vector orthogonal to the n vectors $da_i, a_1, \ldots, a_{n-1}$, implying that $da_i, a_1, \ldots, a_{n-1}$ span a space of dimension $n - 1$ at most. In the neoclassical case, this means that da_i is a linear combination of A_0's columns. It follows that the new facet, $\bar{F}_0$, is the same as the old one, F_0, whence $\bar{x}^1 = x^1$. This contradicts assumption (*d*), above.

Theorem 1 holds several other implications for the neoclassical case, illustrated by example after the theorem's proof, next.

[25] The contents of the last few paragraphs have a simple geometric interpretation. All elements of $(\theta_i + dc_i)\bar{a}_i$ are known in sign, meaning that we know the orthant R^* *of* R^n in which this vector lies. If the sign of θ_i is chosen correctly, $- \theta_i\bar{a}_i$ also belongs to R^*. If the absolute value of θ_i is chosen correctly (that is, large enough), the direction of $c_i da_i - \theta_i\bar{a}_i$ will be arbitrarily close to that of $- \theta_i\bar{a}_i$, whence $c_i da_i - \theta_i\bar{a}_i$, too, comes to lie in R^*. But then $d(c_i a_i)$ will be in R^*—see (6)—, implying, in particular, that all elements of $d(c_i a_i)$ are known in sign.

[26] [5], pp. 32-6.

[27] In applications, some action elements *not* in $c_i a_i$ may turn out to give rise to still simpler forms of the reaction function. If, for example, the output of playing cards proves insensitive to changes of the shoe price p, the relation between the output of playing cards and the shoe price p is given by (7) with m_1, m_2, m_3 proportional to n_1, n_2, n_3. But there is no theoretical necessity for this, and therein lies the difference. The simpler form referred to in the text is one that can be deduced *in advance*, on theoretical grounds.

[28] In the old definition, the dependent variable of the reaction function could be called either an action element or, interchangeably and equivalently, a quantity produced or consumed (in Koopmans's sense). In the new definition, this is no longer so. The dependent variable of the reaction function is now 'a linear combination, with constant weights, of action elements', which is rather a mouthful. (An abbreviation I have found convenient is 'balance'. In this paper, however, we can get by without that term, or any other abbreviation.)

[29] Whether the cycle creates more energy than it uses up, or less, does not influence the argument that follows.

[30] Throughout, t is taken to be continuously variable. We could also take the period-analytical approach, in which t takes on integer values only, and the unit interval corresponds to a period of arbitrary, positive length Δt. On the other hand, applications of period analysis are acceptable only if all obtained results remain meaningful when Δt becomes arbitrarily small. It is therefore simplest to let $\Delta t \rightarrow 0$ immediately.

No particular significance attaches to the (arbitrarily chosen) origin of the time axis, nor, then, to the endowment at time zero, $x(0)$; nor, then, to endowments at 'negative times', $x(t)$ with $t < 0$. Some authors regard time as a commodity, and use 'time' as approximately equivalent to our 'energy'. This practice will not be followed here; time is treated as a parameter, throughout.

[31] The just-observed lack of realism vitiates not only our model. Traditional microeconomics suffers from it, too, only less noticeably so. Specifically, the postulate of utility maximization implies that the individual will not change the equilibrium endowment, once it is reached. A change would only lead to a suboptimal endowment. Microeconomic theory deals with the problem by assuming that the individual is but a part-time utility maximizer—only on Hicksian Mondays—which is not an attractive solution.

[32] Dynamic versions of utility theory usually have the objective function (which is then utility) depend on time. Time enters in the form of a discount factor, introduced to reflect the intuitive notion that every bundle is more utilitous now than in the future. The argument does not work in our model, since the objective function is not utility. Besides, it may be questioned that one's actions are influenced by the future. They are influenced by one's ideas of what the future will be, certainly; but those ideas are themselves of the present. Altogether, there appears to be no need to let f depend on t.

[33] It can be shown that the analytical form of f is derivable from the time path of $x(t)$. A linear time path, for example, implies a quadratic objective function. Details are given in 'The Demand and Supply Functions When Trading Is Efficient.' presented by this writer to the Econometric Society (Dallas, 1975).

[34] One problem that has not yet been mentioned is the familiar but unsolvable problem of finding the analytical form of the Engel function. The Engel function relates the expenditure for a good (which is an action element) to income (which is another action element). The Engel function is not a function, for it is not single-valued; this is why there is no such thing as the analytical form of the Engel function. But there exist some useful substitutes.

One substitute for the Engel function is the relation between an expenditure for a good and the *wage rate*. This relation obeys the reaction function. (The wage rate is an element of the action $a_i =$ 'working'.) Another substitute for the Engel function is the relation between a *budget share* and a_i. A budget share is the quotient of an expenditure and income, each of which depends on a_i according to the reaction function. It follows that the dependence of budget shares on a_i is governed by the quotient of two reaction functions.

References

[1] Becker, G. S.: A Theory of the Allocation of Time, *The Economic Journal*, 1965.

[2] Clower, R. W.: A Reconsideration of the Microfoundations of Monetary Theory, *Western Economic Journal*, 1967.

[3] Dantzig, G. B.: The Programming of Interdependent Activities: Mathematical Model. In: *Activity Analysis of Production and Allocation*, Tj. C. Koopmans, ed., New York 1951.

[4] Gale, D.: *The Theory of Linear Economic Models*, New York 1960.

[5] Hicks, J. R.: *Value and Capital*, 2nd ed., Oxford 1965.

[6] Koopmans, Tj. C.: Analysis of Production as an Efficient Combination of Activities. In: *Activity Analysis of Production and Allocation*, Tj. C. Koopmans, ed., New York 1951.

[7] Lancaster, K. J.: A New Approach to Consumer Theory, *The Journal of Political Economy*, 1966.

[8] Lancaster, K. J.: *Consumer Demand: A New Approach*, New York 1971.

[9] Marshall, A.: *Principles of Economics*, 9th (variorum) ed., London 1961.
[10] Muth, R. F.: Household Production and Consumer Demand Functions, *Econometrica*, 1966.
[11] Pareto, V.: *Manuel d'Economie Politique*, 2nd ed., Paris 1927.
[12] Roberts, B. and D. L. Schulze: *Modern Mathematics and Economic Analysis*, New York 1973.
[13] Samuelson, P. A.: *Foundations of Economic Analysis*, Harvard 1965.
[14] Sayers, R. S.: Monetary Thought and Monetary Policy in England, *The Economic Journal*, 1960.
[15] Scitovsky, T.: *Welfare and Competition*, Homewood 1951.
[16] Wicksteed, P. H.: The Scope and Method of Political Economy, *The Economic Journal*, 1914.

The Individual Welfare Function of Income and its Offspring

Bernard van Praag

Introduction

It is no exaggeration to say that Pieter de Wolff has influenced my scientific life to a great extent. First is has to be remembered that he was the founder of the econometrics curriculum at the University of Amsterdam. Although already in the fifties the Amsterdam Faculty left room for students of econometrics *avant la lettre* with Henri Theil and Hendrik Houthakker as the outstanding examples, it was due to De Wolff that in 1962 an official curriculum in an official department of econometrics was created. This offered a very complete catalogue of optional courses provided by the Faculty of Economics and that of Mathematics which made it possible at a rather early date for students of econometrics to acquire a thorough mathematical background including a measure-theoretical foundation of probability theory. It was when studying that branch of mathematics together with the theory of consumer behaviour, taught by Pieter de Wolff, that I was inspired to my main line of research in the years to come which led to my Ph.D. thesis 'Individual Welfare Functions and Consumer Behavior' in 1968 when Pieter de Wolff acted as my supervisor and chairman of the Ph.D. committee. This was the second way in which he exerted his influence on me.

Although I still remember the stimulating conversations we had, I am also still hearing his warnings against theory without empirical basis. Being himself a scholar in the old Dutch tradition, he was (and is) rather aloof of 'theorizing into the sky' juggling with non-operational concepts. His final appraisal of my thesis was: 'Si non è vero, è ben trovato', leaving the young doctor with a lasting feeling of uneasiness. And so we come to the third influence, which lasts to this very day and

of which the person we honour certainly does not know. His rather critical attitude imprinted on me the idea that theory should go hand in hand with empirical applications as much as possible, not the one without the other. In the sequel, being a progress report, we shall see how this scientific *credo* (evidently not to be obeyed too rigorously) has materialized up to now.
In this report I shall concentrate on my own work, while neglecting nearly all references to the literature. For a more serious consideration of the subjects in economic literature we refer to the basic papers mentioned in the list of references.

The research on which this paper reports resulted for the greater part from the joint effort of the present author and Arie Kapteyn, Abraham Kouwenhoven, Joop Linthorst, Theo Goedhart and Floor van Herwaarden, all of them members of the Economic Institute at Leyden University. This research has been made possible by the financial and material support of the State University of Leyden, the Belgian Consumer Union, the Dutch Consumer Union, the Netherlands Organisation for the Advancement of Pure Research, the Central Bureau of Statistics at the Hague, and the Ministries of Social Affairs, of Culture, Recreation and Social Assistance and of Interior Affairs.
The responsibility for this paper solely rests with the author.

The Concept of Individual Welfare

In the days of Gossen, Edgeworth and their contemporaries everything was simple. Goods were bought for their utility value. Samuelson [13] uses the immortal phrase: 'For Edgeworth utility was as real as his morning jam'. But it proved difficult to find a suitable definition of utility, and still more difficult to specify a utility function or to measure it. Fortunately Pareto [11] demonstrated that static consumer demand theory did not need a basis in a cardinal utility concept, but that an ordinal concept would suffice. This started a long chain of literature which ended in the most sophisticated general equilibrium theories. Houthakker [7] called this evolution 'the erosion of the utility concept'.
However, this brought no consolation to the empirical demand analyst who had to specify the functional form of his demand curves on more or less intuitive grounds, although the ordinal model revealed that a number of specifications were impossible because they did not satisfy a number of basic requirements like homogeneity, adding-up-to-income and the Slutsky conditions. In the old days individual utility was considered not only as a basis for consumer demand theory, but it was

also the cornerstone for taxation theory, savings theory, the construction of family equivalence scales and all other problems which had something to do with income redistribution. For a cardinal utility function defined on the commodity space assigns a utility value to various income levels, if prices are fixed, *the utility function of income*.

As a consequence of the erosion of the utility concept cardinalism became unfashionable, although time and again there were authors like Tinbergen [15], Frisch [3], Robertson [12] but also Aumann [2]—to mention a few—who confessed their belief in or their longing for a cardinal utility concept. We observe that Pareto did not show nor attempt to show that cardinal utility did not exist, but only that it was not necessary as a basis for static demand theory. At this moment cardinal utility functions are used at an increasing rate outside demand theory, e.g. in savings theory, portfolio theory, the theory of taxation, social welfare theory, but they are mainly specified on the basis of their convenience and not on the basis of empirical findings. Since the ordinal utility concept is still reigning in consumer theory, a considerable gap exists between the theories mentioned on the one hand and consumer theory on the other hand, although they are related by their common subject-matter: the choice behaviour of human beings confronted with scarce means.

One of the main reasons of the difficulty inherent in utility estimation seems to me the implicit assumption that a utility concept has been defined *by nature* and that it only has to be discovered by the scientist. Actually most physical magnitudes like temperature, time, electricity, and sound can only be observed as the result of more or less sophisticated experiments and are only properly *defined* by a suitable measurement method devised by the experimenter, provided that the outcome of the measurement method does not depend on the specific experimenter. It is the measurement method that defines the concept. Obviously the terminology should be adapted as much as possible to the meaning that everyday language already assigns to the concept, albeit in a pre-scientific way. So it stands to reason that the concept defined and measured by a thermometer should be related to the pre-scientific notions of 'hot' and 'cold' and not to 'light' and 'dark'.

In the same way the concept of utility or, as we prefer to call it from now on, *individual welfare*, has to correspond to the notions 'unsatisfied', 'satisfied'. In order to get a quantifiable concept, we shall define individual welfare as the evaluation by an individual of his position. It is well known that an individual is able to evaluate many things even if objective measurement is impossible. We think of the sound quality of a gramophone, the taste of wine or the outcome of an oral examination on literature, the quality of an actor, etc. As a rule such an evaluation is performed on a more or less continuous finite scale. There is an evaluation 'very bad' and an evaluation 'excellent' and other evaluations in between. Frequently such evaluations, when performed by professionals, are on a numerical scale or indicated by letters, or by a set of ordered symbols, e.g., minus- and plus-signs. This suggests that the human mind is able to *evaluate* fairly complicated phenomena on a finite scale, and not only by words but also: by ordered symbols or numbers.

Now there is nothing which excludes the possibility for human beings of evaluating their own welfare position, characterized by any set of variables they assume to be relevant at the moment, in precisely such a way, viz., either in terms of verbal qualifications 'good', 'sufficient', 'bad' or after some experience on a numerical scale e.g. the (0, 10)- or (0, 1)-interval. The characteristics assumed to be relevant to describe the individual's welfare position may be the quantities $x_1, \ldots, x_k$ of specific commodities $X_1, \ldots, X_k$ held or consumed by the consumer. It is not necessary, and physically and philosophically impossible, that $x = (x_1, \ldots, x_k)$ refers to *all* existing commodities. As a rule the consumer will be aware at any given moment of only a small number of commodities he possesses or would like to possess. Other variables may be defined as aggregates representing a consumption level with respect to a whole subgroup of commodities, more or less corresponding to the needs they satisfy, like 'clothes', 'housing', 'food', etc. In the latter case x_1 is an index referring to a specific commodity group. A rather simple index is used when x_1 is the *money amount* spent on commodities in a specific commodity group X_1, where the price structure within that subgroup is assumed to be fixed and given. The simplest way in which an individual may characterize his welfare position is by the total money amount y he may spend during a certain reference period. In that case we shall call the welfare evaluation $U(y)$ the individual's *welfare function* (of income). It goes without saying that we do not pretend that the individual's welfare evaluation refers to all aspects of life, it is only an evaluation of the welfare characteristics assumed to be relevant at the moment. On the other hand it is evident that this welfare evaluation will be conditioned by other variables, e.g. the individual's environment.

In this paper we shall restrict ourselves to the case of this simplified space of characteristics, where income is the only relevant characteristic (cf. Van Praag [16]). Now we shall make the so-called *evaluation assumption*:

> An individual is able to evaluate his income on a finite numerical scale by comparison with the two extreme income levels, namely $y = 0$ and $y \to \infty$, by means of an evaluation function $U(y)$.

Introduction of a suitable normalization yields

$$U(0) = 0, \lim_{y \to \infty} U(y) = 1,$$

$$0 \leq U(y) \leq 1.$$

Assuming that $U(y)$ is a non-decreasing function U is isomorphic with a probability distribution function. In [16] it has been shown that, when some additional assumptions are made, Central Limit Theorem arguments can be transplanted from the probability context to this welfare evaluation model. This yields a.o. the following result:
Income is approximately evaluated by a lognormal distribution function i.e.

$$U(y) = \Lambda(y; \mu, \sigma) = \frac{1}{\sigma\sqrt{2\pi}} \int_{-\infty}^{\ln y} e^{-\frac{1}{2}\frac{(t-\mu)^2}{\sigma^2}} dt$$

The parameters μ and σ are individually determined.
The function Λ has been sketched in fig. 1a and 1b for various values of μ and σ. The income level $\exp(\mu)$ yields a welfare evaluation 0.5; it is called the individual's *natural unit* (of income). This magnitude which varies from individual to individual seems to be a representative measuring-rod to compare income levels. For further explanation we refer to [16].
The parameter σ determines the slope of the welfare function and it has been called the individual's welfare sensitivity. If σ is large, an individual is sensitive to income increases over a large income interval; if σ is small the individual experiences income differences only over a small interval. It should be noticed that these *S*-curves are intuitively plausible and well-known from portfolio theory and the theory of risk-bearing; they have been repeatedly found from Von Neumann-Morgenstern-type gambling experiments.

Measurements of the Individual Welfare Function

In [17] and [18] it has been attempted for the first time to measure the individual welfare function in practice. As observed before the individual is able to evaluate income levels in verbal terms like 'good', 'bad', and so on. This experimental fact was the basis for a written question in a survey, which runs as follows:

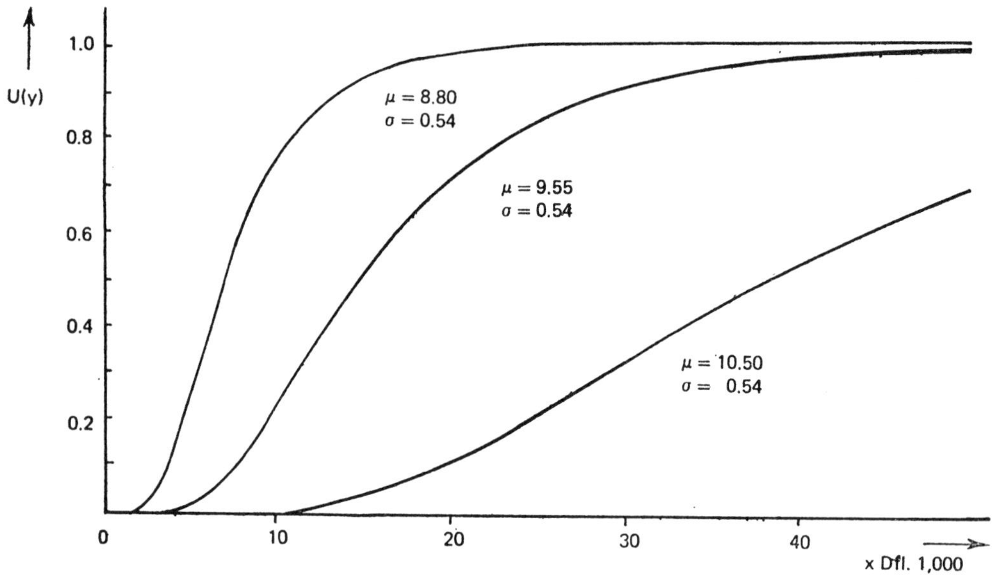

Figure 1a. The welfare function of income for different values of σ.

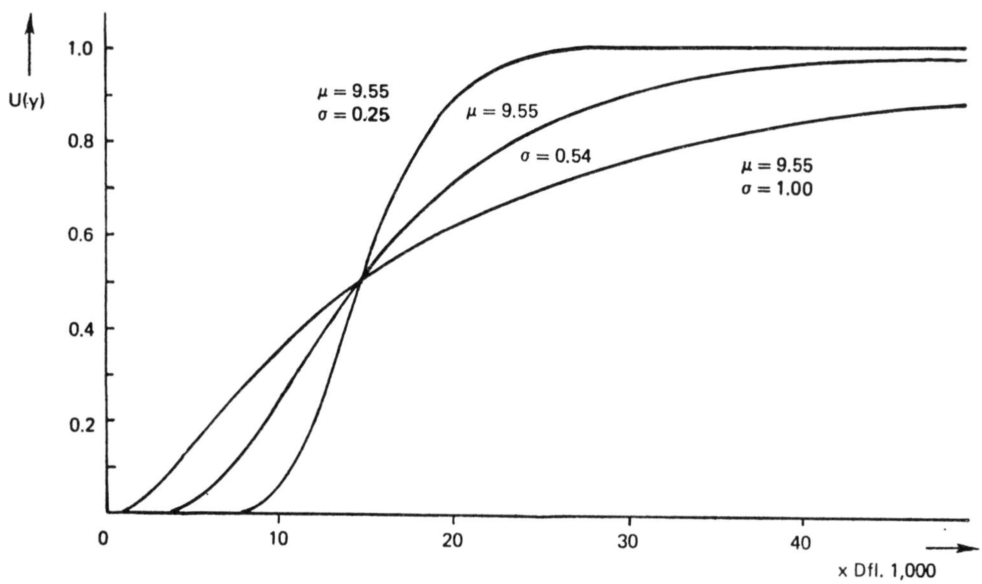

Figure 1b. The welfare function of income for different values of μ.

'Taking into account your own situation with respect to family and job you would call your *net-income* (including fringe benefits and with subtraction of social security premiums)

per $\begin{cases} \text{week} & \text{A} \\ \text{month} & \text{B} \\ \text{year} & \text{C} \end{cases}$ (encircle A, B or C)

excellent	if it were over *f* 45,000
good	if it were between *f* 35,000 and *f* 45,000
amply sufficient	if it were between *f* 30,000 and *f* 35,000
sufficient	if it were between *f* 25,000 and *f* 30,000
barely sufficient	if it were between *f* 22,000 and *f* 25,000
insufficient	if it were between *f* 20,000 and *f* 22,000
very insufficient	if it were between *f* 17,000 and *f* 20,000
bad	if it were between *f* 12,000 and *f* 17,000
very bad	if it were under *f* 12,000

We have added a typical answer as found in the questionnaires. Evidently the answer differs from individual to individual but the pattern is nearly always the same: the extreme brackets are wider than the brackets in the middle. It is not unreasonable to assume that the individual attempts to inform us as exactly as possible about the specification of his welfare function. Actually, he tries to describe a continuous function by supplying eight points, and it seems reasonable to assume that the points are chosen in such a way that the additions in income correspond to equal welfare increments.

This would imply that the points on the income axis define an equal partition of the welfare unit mass over the income axis. For the specific individual quoted above this would mean:

$$U_i(12{,}000) = 1/9,\ U_i(17{,}000) = 2/9, \ldots, U_i(45{,}000) = 8/9$$

This intuitive reasoning can be made more exact if we specify an inaccuracy-measure according to which the individual tries to select the points in his answer in an optimal way. A suitable criterion function is

$$\sum_{j=0}^{8} \int_{y_j}^{y_{j+1}} [U(y) - U(\bar{y}_j)]^2 \, dU_i(y)$$

where $y_1, \ldots, y_8$ are the individual's answers, $y_0 = 0$, $y_9 = \infty$, and where $\bar{y}_j$ is the representative income level in the jth bracket, defined by

$$U_i(\bar{y}_j) = \tfrac{1}{2}[U_i(y_j) + U_i(y_{j+1})]$$

The inaccuracy-measure is a sum of mean-square errors within the brackets selected. Minimization of this inaccuracy measure with respect to $y_1, \ldots, y_8$ yields

$$U_i(y_1) = 1/9, \ldots, U_i(y_8) = 8/9$$

Obviously the method applies to any number of answers. When the mean square expression is replaced by absolute errors or other reasonable loss function specifications we find the same solution. To what extent the solution depends on the specific wording of the question is not self-evident. We conjecture that replacing the verbal qualifications by school-marks familiar to the respondent would make no difference, provided that the labelling suggests a one-dimensional monotonous ordening.

It is clear that this method of measurement yields eight points of a function U, and we may attempt to fit a lognormal curve as predicted by the theory to the scatter of eight points. Applying the well-known transformation formulae of the lognormal-distribution (Aitchison and Brown [1]) there holds

$$\Lambda(y; \mu, \sigma) = N(lny; \mu, \sigma) = N\left(\frac{lny - \mu}{\sigma}; 0, 1\right)$$

where $N(.)$ is the normal distribution function. If $U_i(y_1) = 1/9$ this implies

$$U_i(y_1) = \Lambda(y_1; \mu_i, \sigma_i) = N\left(\frac{lny_1 - \mu_i}{\sigma_i}; 0, 1\right) = 1/9$$

from which follows

$$\frac{lny_1 - \mu_i}{\sigma_i} = u_1$$

where u_1 is the 1/9-quantile of the standard normal distribution.
For the eight answers we get

$$ln(y_j) = \sigma_i u_j + \mu_i \qquad (j = 1, \ldots, 8)$$

where u_j is the $(j/9)$-quantile.

Evidently this relation will suffer from error terms ε_j which we suppose to be mutually independent and of the N(0, σ^2)-type. Then the parameters σ_i, μ_i may be estimated from the eight individual observations $y_1, \ldots, y_8$ by linear regression. As a by-product we get standard-deviations for σ_i, μ_i, and a correlation coëfficient.

This procedure has been followed in several surveys with a total of about 12,000 observations. The standard deviations were nearly always very small, while the (corrected) correlation coefficient R^2 of such an individual regression was nearly always about 0.98 (in a minority of cases not all answers were given in which case we applied a modified regression procedure on less than eight observations). We reported in detail on these investigations in the articles quoted in the beginning of this section and in Van Herwaarden et al [6].
Our conclusion is that our theoretical hypothesis that individuals evaluate income (money) approximately according to a log-normal distribution function cannot be rejected.

It stands to reason that the individual welfare function of income differs a lot from individual to individual with respect to the parameter values μ_i, σ_i that have been found. We have therefore investigated whether the individual (μ_i, σ_i)-values could be explained by objective determinants or that the variables were purely individual variables. With respect to σ_i it was found that its value cannot be explained by objective factors except for a slight influence of education. Higher education is correlated with a higher σ. The observations of σ_i varied according to a more or less normal distribution about a mean value of 0.54. The value σ does not depend on the money unit used.

The explanation of μ_i was more successful. The principal determinants of μ_i were the *actual net income* y_a, being a proxy for the actual consumption level, and the *family size* fs. The estimated relationship was

$$\mu_i = \beta_1 \, ln(fs_i) + \beta_2 \, ln(y_{a,i}) + \beta_3 + \varepsilon_i \tag{1}$$

where β_1 and β_2 are dimensionless elasticities. For the total Dutch 1971-sample on which we reported in [18] we estimated this equation as

$$\begin{array}{llll} \mu = 0.13 \, ln(fs) & + \, 0.60 \, ln(y_a) & + \, 3.50 & (N = 2952) \\ \quad\;\; (0.01) & \quad\;\; (0.01) & \quad (0.11) & (R^2 = 0.60) \end{array}$$

Table 1

Estimates from six surveys

Source	Date and year	Sample drawn from	Type of survey	Number of observations	Average σ	Fs-elasticity β_1	Preference drift β_2	Corrected R^2
Van Praag [17]	December, 1969	Membership of Belgian Consumer Union	Anonymous, by mail, no reminder	2522	0.56	0.14	0.68	0.61
V. Herwaarden, Kapteyn, Van Praag [6]	December, 1970	Membership of Belgian Consumer Union	Anonymous, by mail, no reminder	2268	0.57	0.13	0.66	0.59
Van Herwaarden, Kapteyn, Van Praag [6]	December, 1973	Membership of Belgian Consumer Union	Anonymous, by mail, no reminder	2179	0.54	0.14	0.60	0.51
Van Praag, Kapteyn [18]	October, 1971	Membership of Dutch Consumer Union	Anonymous, by mail, no reminder	2592	0.51	0.14	0.60	0.63
Van Herwaarden, Kapteyn, Van Praag [6]	March, 1974	Membership of Dutch Consumer Union (60%) *and* non-members (40%) with similar socio-economic traits	written, after oral introduction	919	0.43	0.11	0.66	0.66
Van Herwaarden, Kapteyn, Van Praag [6]	January, 1975	Dutch population	written, after oral introduction, reminder	1748	0.40	0.13	0.53	0.57

The difference between the σ-values in the first four and the latter two samples is probably caused by a slight modification in the income-evaluation

The welfare evaluation of actual income y_a is

$$U(y_a) = N\left(\frac{lny_a - \mu}{\sigma};0,1\right) = N\left(\frac{lny_a - \beta_1 lnfs - \beta_2 lny_a - \beta_3}{\sigma}; 0, 1\right)$$

where we substituted (1).

Keeping in mind that σ varies randomly among individuals and notably does not depend on y_a or fs, we observe two interesting features.

a. Given a specific actual income, the welfare evaluation decreases with increasing family size. We call β_1 the family size elasticity.

b. For a given family size an increase of actual income by a factor $(1 + \alpha)$ yields an *ex ante* evaluation

$$N\left(\frac{lny_a + ln(1 + \alpha) - \beta_1 lnfs - \beta_2 lny_a - \beta_3}{\sigma}; 0, 1\right)$$

and an *ex post* evaluation of

$$N\left(\frac{lny_a + (1 - \beta_2)\, ln(1 + \alpha) - \beta_1 lnfs - \beta_2 ln(y_a) - \beta_3}{\sigma}; 0, 1\right)$$

If β_2 were zero, there would be no difference between the *ex ante* and *ex post* evaluations of the income increase; if β_2 were equal to one, the income rise would not yield any welfare increase. In the Dutch context we find a sizable coefficient value of about 0.64. This phenomenon, which is easily interpreted as the established psychological fact that people adapt their needs to their income, has been termed by us 'preference drift'.

Other surveys yielded the same result (Kapteyn, Van Praag, Van Herwaarden [10]). We present the main results in Table 1 without discussion. We refer to the original sources for an extensive discussion. Here we only observe how remarkably stable the results are.

Before we continue our report on the empirical findings a few words on the issue of interpersonal utility comparison. It is tempting to say that people who evaluate their income by the same number on a zero-one-scale experience the same degree of well-being. However, this statement should be qualified at least in two respects. First, the income evaluation question refers to *money income* and there are evidently other variables $x_1, \ldots, x_k$, which also contribute to someone's feeling of welfare. Hence, the individual welfare function of income measures a *partial* welfare concept, say U_m, while the evaluation of life in total may be a function

$$U(U_m(y; x_1, \ldots x_k), U_0(x_1, \ldots, x_k))$$

where U_0 is the evaluation of the other (non-monetary) aspects of the welfare situation. It may be that the other variables (e.g. environmental variables, family situation) influence the evaluation of income as well; in that case they appear as parameters in the individual welfare function of income U_m.

Secondly, even when keeping in mind the restriction outlined above, we may question whether two individuals who evaluate their income by the same number experience the same degree of well-being. This boils down to the *semantic* question whether the qualifications 'good' and 'bad' mean the same thing to the two individuals. This cannot be taken for granted when we take it in the strictest sense. Its truth cannot be proved nor disproved. Words are only an imperfect vehicle to communicate feelings between human beings, but even if we admit all other instruments of human communication like gestures, singing, etc, still we cannot expect communication to be perfect. There is always noise and loss of information. Nevertheless, we think that the connotation of qualifications like 'good' and 'bad' will not vary systematically between people with the same frame of reference. This implies that welfare comparison between people by means of their individual welfare functions seems admissible, if the individuals belong more or less to the same social reference group (including the emotional meaning assigned to words). Now we turn to the applications which we shall discuss briefly.

Welfare-Based Family Equivalence Scales

In the previous section we reported about the explanation of the individual welfare parameter μ by objectively measurable determinants. We found for the total Dutch 1971-sample

$$\underset{}{\mu} = \underset{(0.01)}{0.13\, ln(fs)} + \underset{(0.01)}{0.60\, ln(y)} + \underset{(0.11)}{3.50}$$

This influence of increasing family size is easily interpretable, as we have shown in [8].

An increase of $fs_1 = 2$ to $fs_2 = 4$ implies an increase of μ_1 by $0.13\, ln(fs_2/fs_1)$,

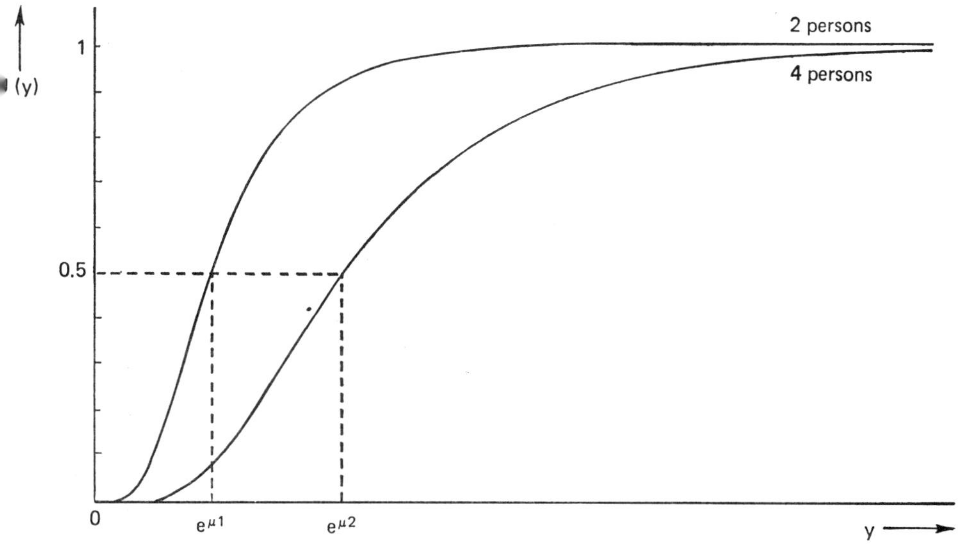

Figure 2. The influence of a family increase on the individual welfare function.

hence the median value shifts to the right as a consequence of the family size increase and so does the welfare function (see fig. 2). (It goes without saying that this is a result of comparative statics and that such a transition is not realized overnight). The same income is valued less than before due to the fact that it has to serve more family members. Consider the equation

$$\mu = \beta_1 \, lnfs + \beta_2 \, lny_a + \beta_3 \tag{2}$$

and the welfare level associated with actual income

$$\Lambda(y_a) = N\left(\frac{lny_a - \beta_1 \, lnfs - \beta_2 \, lny_a - \beta_3}{\sigma}; 0, 1\right) \tag{3}$$

If σ is constant, the welfare evaluation depends on the variable z defined as

$$z = (1 - \beta_2) lny_a - \beta_1 \, lnfs - \beta_3 \tag{4}$$

Hence, if fs increases we may keep z at the intial level by increasing y_a in such a way that z remains constant. Then equation (4) may be interpreted as describing an *iso-welfare-curve* in (fs, y_a)-space for any welfare level $N(z)$. For any income level

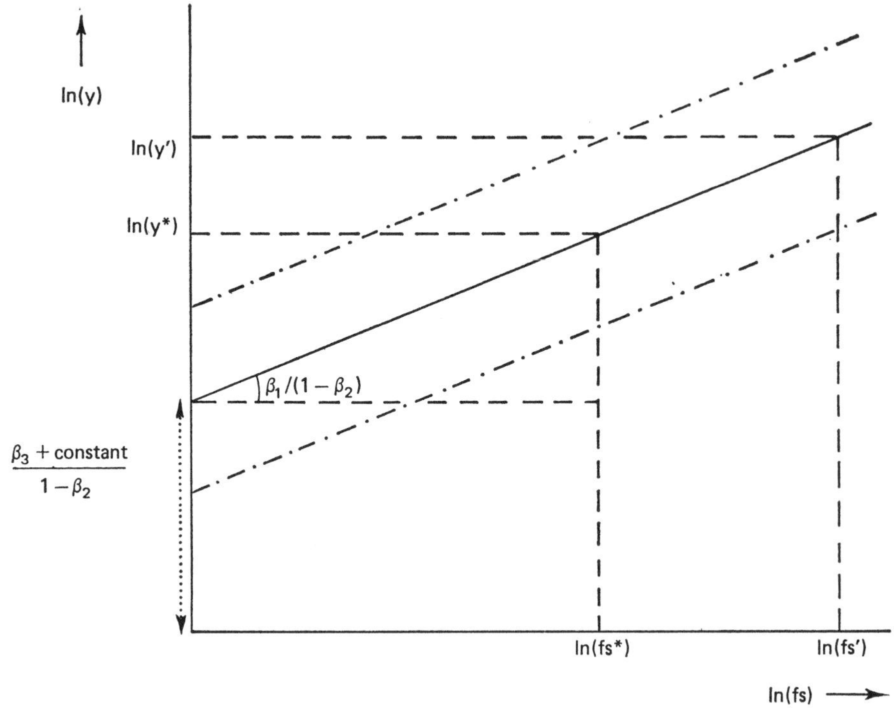

Figure 3. Iso-welfare curves in ln(fs), ln(y_a)-space.

y_a a family size increase by a factor $(1 + \alpha)$ should be compensated by an income increase by a factor $(1 + \alpha)^{\beta_1/(1-\beta_2)}$, in order to keep welfare constant.

We observe that this scale does not depend on income nor welfare level (there was only a slight intercorrelation between family size and actual income). It is this simple analysis which served as starting point for an advice on a revision of the family allowance system in the Netherlands, requested by the State Commission on Population Problems [9].

However, the definition of family size by the mere number of family members irrespective of their ages is clearly unsatisfactory. Anybody feels that adults should count for more than babies and that children should be in between. In order to do justice to this intuitive feeling we made *fs* a function of the age distribution of the family by the following specification

$$fs = \sum_{i=1}^{n} \alpha_i f(a_i)$$

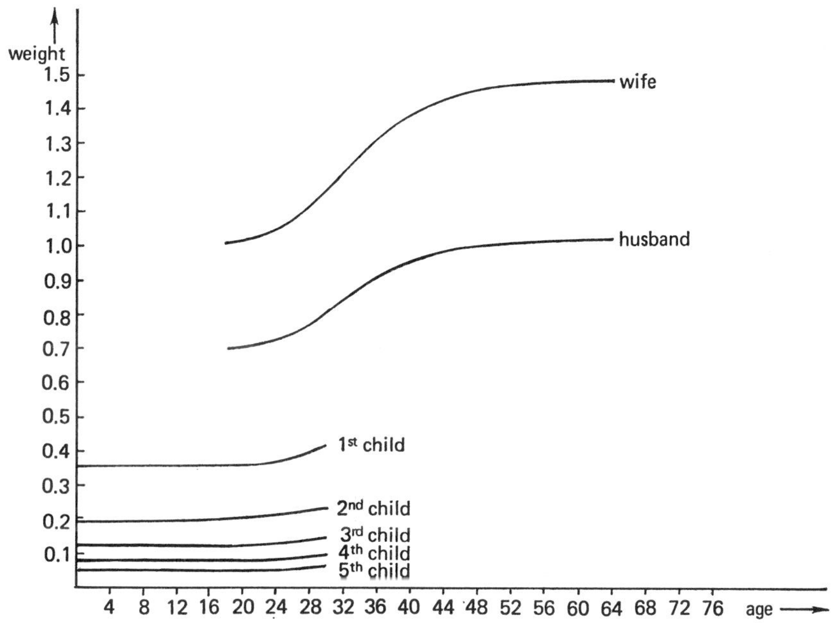

Figure 4. Nomograph for the construction of family equivalence scales.

where n is the unweighted family size, and where a_i is the age of the ith family member, the family being arranged in a definite order spouse, husband, oldest child, next-oldest child, . . . The contribution of each person to *fs* is transformed according to his age into an *age-equivalent* $f(a_i)$. The age-equivalents weighted by α_i according to their rank i in the family are added to each other. The positive weights α_i have been normalized so that $\sum_{i=1}^{\infty} \alpha_i = 1$. By the introduction of this weight-distribution a possible 'economies of scale'-effect ('children are cheaper by the dozen') will be discovered if it exists. We shall not dwell at this place on technical matters for which we refer to [8]. A considerable 'economies of scale'-phenomenon has been found. The estimated function $f(a_i)$ was typically of the shape as sketched in fig. 4 where the range of increase was between the ages 20–45. We call this range the 'career-span'.

From the analysis of homogeneous social subgroups it turned out that there was quite a difference between the functions. For all subgroups the career-span starts at 20, except for people with academic education of the breadwinner, where the age-equivalent function started to increase at an earlier age, viz., about 12 years of age. From the other results we mention here only the striking difference between families where both partners work in a full-time paid job and families where only one partner works in a paid job. The difference may be interpreted as the cost of day-care for the children, which had to be supplied by outsiders in the former case.

These results may be used as a basis for constructing family allowance schemes and family equivalence scales. This approach is diametrically opposed to the usual approach which is based on the cost of a 'food-basket', or of a 'basket of necessities', or on observed behavior as estimated by Engel-curves. We are inclined to believe that the above-sketched subjective procedure is superior to the traditional so-called objective methods in one respect. In most traditional methods there is a good deal of arbitrariness involved in selecting the normative basket of commodities and/or the choice of the normative consumer. Such a preliminary selection clearly is not needed here. For a more elaborate comparison we refer to [8].

The Poverty Line Concept

In the last decade poverty as a socio-economic concept has become an issue of primary importance in scientific research. One of the major problems is the definition of 'being poor'. Even more so than in the case of family equivalence scales a multitude of arbitrary elements slipped into the analysis. For poverty appeared not to be fit for an objective definition. The only way out seemed to be the *a priori* statement of characteristics (e.g. social indicators) of poor people contrasted with non-poor people. ('house' or 'no house', 'meat at least once a week' or 'not'). The definition of these test characteristics and their threshold values is mainly based on *value judgments* of the social scientist or, perhaps a bit more refined, on value judgments made explicit by politicians or by a political body. Consequently it is no miracle that there are so many widely differing estimates about the percentage of poor people in the U.S.-population. This is caused by the differences in the criterion applied. One of the simpler criteria employed is the one-dimensional *poverty line*. It states that one is considered 'poor' if one does not earn a certain minimum amount of income that makes ends meet. In some Western welfare states this approach is linked up with a statutory minimum wage (or income) policy. It involves the same arbitrariness, for the question when 'ends meet' cannot be answered in an objective way. Is it necessary to have meat once a week or should it be twice a week? Poverty is not an objectively observable condition but rather a feeling of the individual concerned.

The least subjective method seems to be to question the people *themselves* what income they consider to be the *absolute minimum* in order that *they* can make 'ends meet', given their circumstances. Such a survey should not be restricted to a specific bracket of the population, aprioristically stamped as poor people; this would introduce a circular reasoning, because we do not know beforehand whether one is 'poor' or not. We are out to define such a concept. In [4] we operationalized this idea by posing to a representative sample of the Dutch population the following question:

> 'We would like to know what net family income would, in *your* circumstances be the absolute minimum for *you*. That is to say, that you would not be able to make both ends meet if you earned less.'

The answer to this question will be referred to as the respondent's *minimum income* ($y_{\min}$). In January 1975 the survey was conducted and a sample of about 1750 individuals was analyzed. As was to be expected the answers varied from individual to individual, each individual stating his own 'poverty line'. There was a statistically very satisfactory explanation of the $y_{\min}$-level stated. We found the following regression

$$\begin{aligned} ln(y_{\min}) &= \underset{(0.15)}{3.60} + \underset{(0.01)}{0.12}\, lnfs + \underset{(0.02)}{0.60}\, lny_a \quad \begin{matrix}(R^2 = 0.57)\\(N = 1748)\end{matrix} \end{aligned} \tag{5}$$

where the numbers in parentheses are standard deviations and *fs* is family size, simply defined as the number of family members. Graphically the relationship can be sketched in (lny_a, $lny_{\min}$)-space for various values of *fs* as in fig. 5.

This variation in stated minimum income, corresponding to the individual circumstances like *net* actual income and the number of more or less dependent family members, clearly demonstrates that the poverty level defined merely as an income level does not have any objective basis.

Equation (5) resembles (2) and it appeared worthwhile to estimate the individual's welfare functions and the corresponding overall-relation (2) for this 1975-sample as well. We found

$$\mu = \underset{(0.12)}{4.39} + \underset{(0.01)}{0.13}\, lnfs + \underset{(0.01)}{0.53}\, lny_a \quad \begin{matrix}(R^2 = 0.60)\\(N = 1748)\end{matrix} \tag{6}$$

As in other samples, σ could not be explained, but it varied randomly about 0.40 instead of about the usual 0.50 (see footnote to table 1).

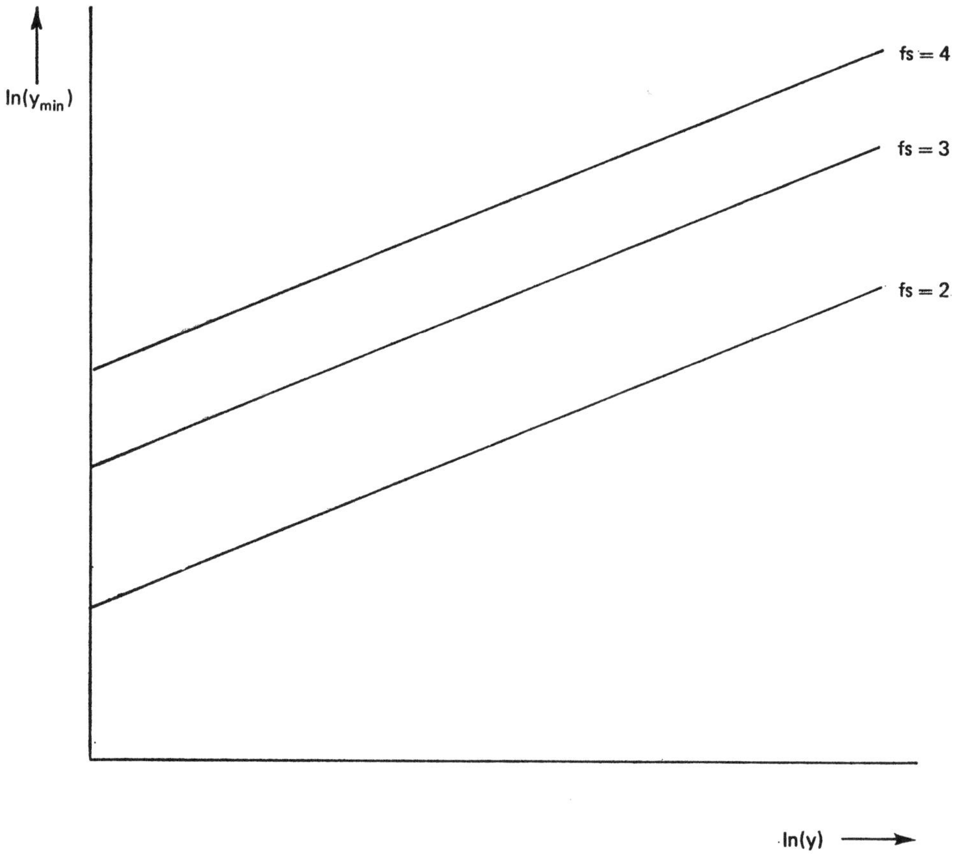

Figure 5. The relation between $ln(y_{min})$ and $ln(y_a)$ for various family sizes.

Combining (5) and (6) we may find the individual's welfare evaluation assigned to the stated 'poverty level' (or minimum income) to be

$$N\left(\frac{ln y_{\min} - \mu}{\sigma}; 0, 1\right) = N\left(\frac{-0.79 + 0.07 ln y_a}{\sigma}; 0, 1\right) \tag{7}$$

where we ignore the difference between the almost identical family size elasticities in (5) and (6). It appears that the evaluation assigned to the minimum income level varies a great deal less than $y_{\min}$ itself. The evaluation starts at

$$N\left(\frac{-\ 0.79\ +\ 0.07 ln(10{,}000)}{\sigma}\right),$$

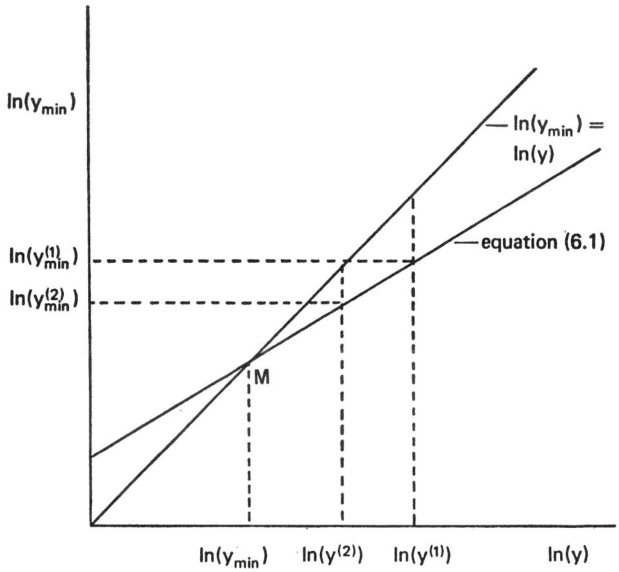

Figure 6. The search for the „general" poverty line.

where *f*. 10,000 is approximately the minimum net family income in the Netherlands (1975) and it increases slightly with increasing y_a. Actually, when regressing $(ln y_{\min} - \mu)$ directly on $ln y_a$ we get the result

$$ln(y_{\min}) - \mu = -0.77 + 0.07\, ln(y_a) \qquad (\bar{R}^2 = 0.02) \tag{8}$$
$$(0.12) \quad (0.01)$$

Our conclusion is that richer people are slightly more demanding with respect to their minimum welfare level than poorer people. The welfare level assigned to the poverty line $y_{\min}$ varies from 0.30 at an actual *net* income of *f*. 10,000 to about 0.45 at an actual *net* income level of *f*. 60,000.

The average evaluation is about 0.39. In view of the $\bar{R}^2$ for (8) which is almost equal to zero, we conclude that for practical purposes the minimum welfare-level is identified with an income evaluation of about 0.39 on a (0,1)-scale. In other words, although the minimum *income level* is not objectively defined, the *welfare level* assigned to the poverty line is quite well-defined and independent of the individual situation.

This provides a clue for the definition of a *general* statutory minimum *income* level. Consider the following exercise. Let an individual with actual income $y_a^{(1)}$ be put in the position of his 'poverty line' $y_{\min}^{(1)}$, i.e. $y_a^{(2)} = y_{\min}^{(1)}$. After a transition period he will have adapted his idea on a 'poverty line' to his new standards, and it will equal $y_{\min}^{(1)}$. Giving him a new setback to $y_a^{(3)} = y_{\min}^{(2)}$ the next step begins. In this way the process will converge to the point where $ln y_a = ln y_{\min}$. In fig. 6 it corresponds to the point of intersection of the $y_{\min}$-line and the 45°-line. If the poverty level would be prescribed by politicians at a welfare level which is higher than what the individuals themselves call 'poor', say of $x\%$, the analysis can be done in the same way. We would have

$$\frac{ln\tilde{y}_{\min} - \mu}{\sigma} = u_x$$

where $N(u_x) = x\%$

which yields $ln\tilde{y}_{\min} = 4.89 + 0.13\ lnfs + 0.53\ lny_a + \sigma u_x$,

where $\tilde{y}_{\min}$ stands for the income level which yields the politically prescribed welfare level of $x\%$. The equilibrium would then be given by $ln\tilde{y}_{\min} = lny_a$ yielding an $x\%$-poverty line.

The Concept of Social Influence

One of the oldest issues in economics is certainly the question whether welfare of society as a whole can be evaluated. A social welfare function is invariably assumed to be of the type

$$W = W(U_1, \ldots, U_n)$$

where U_i is the individual welfare of the ith individual. There is almost no discussion about the idea that

$$\frac{\partial W}{\partial U_i} > 0$$

If $\dfrac{\delta W}{\delta U_i} = 0$, the ith individual's welfare is of no importance to society. So it is tempting to interpret the first-order derivatives as representing the *social influence* individuals have.

One may even imagine that one reduces the ith individual's welfare by ΔU_i in order to increase U_j by ΔU_j. In order that social welfare remains constant there must hold

$$\frac{\partial W}{\partial U_i} \Delta U_i + \frac{\partial W}{\partial U_j} \Delta U_j = 0$$

Now it may be that $\Delta U_i = 0.1$ and $\Delta U_j = -0.01$. In that case we may infer that the increase of j's welfare counts ten times as heavy in the eyes of society as the decrease of i's welfare, leaving us with the impression that $\left(\frac{\partial W}{\partial U_1}, \ldots, \frac{\partial W}{\partial U_n}\right)$ (all elements being non-negative) might represent a *social weight distribution*.
Evidently, this simple utilitarian calculus is not new, but it is still horrifying to many authorities in the profession. Nevertheless this naive reasoning has some charm and reasonings like this are more or less explicitly applied by politicians. The construct may have some value in the light of our newly developed individual welfare function concept.
The primary difficulty in standard literature is that the arguments $U_1, \ldots, U_n$ are specified as *ordinal* utility functions. It stands to reason that the whole social influence interpretation then shatters. However, if U_i is specified as a cardinal welfare function, prospects become brighter. The reader will not be surprised when we propose our individual welfare function (of income) to be inserted as argument in the W-function. We observe that we define every U_i-function on the same (0, 1)-interval in order to avoid the still present ambiguity due to the restriction 'up to a positive linear transformation'.

Nevertheless, the specification of the W-function presents a real problem. As we already saw, someone's individual welfare is not unambiguously defined. For instance, individual i will evaluate a specific welfare position with a value 0.8 while individual j would evaluate that same position by 0.4. So we cannot exclude the possibility that social welfare itself is not uniquely defined but that there are a number of social welfare functions W_i, corresponding to the individuals who evaluate W. Accepting the idea that individual i will evaluate social welfare with a look to his fellow-citizen's welfare, the problem remains how i should evaluate j's welfare. Two possibilities lie at hand: he may employ his own individual welfare function, evaluating j's position by U_{ij}, or he may borrow j's evaluation scheme in which case he will evaluate j's position by U_{jj}. The latter case being contradictory to normal psychology, we stick to the idea that

$$W_i = W_i(U_{i1}, \ldots, U_{in})$$

where we admit the possibility that the functional specification of W_i depends on the individual observer as well. Time and again a social welfare function has been specified as a weighted sum of individual welfare (see e.g. Harsanyi [5]), and this is the specification which seems also to us most reasonable, i.e.,

$$W_i = \sum_{j=1}^{n} \alpha_{ij} U_{ij}$$

where we apply the harmless normalization

$$\sum_{j=1}^{n} a_{ij} = 1.$$

We call $\alpha_i = (\alpha_{i1}, \ldots, \alpha_{in})$ the *distribution of social influence as perceived by individual i.*

In [19] and [20] an attempt was made to estimate this distribution of social influence. (In the earlier paper we used the less fortunate term 'economic power'). We characterize individuals by their income y. Let the income distribution be given by the density element $dN(y)$ with $\int_0^\infty dN(y) = 1$, then the social welfare function of i assumes the form

$$W_i = \int_0^\infty \alpha_i(y)\, U_i(y)\, dN(y) \tag{9}$$

We have to look for the density function of social influence $\alpha_i(y)$. Now we have to make a rather sophisticated distinction. At first we may think of $\alpha_i(y)$ as the social influence distribution, most desired by the individual i. Frequently this will be a homogeneous distribution, assigning equal weight to everyone. However, the individual i is aware that this ethically most desirable situation does not obtain in reality. In reality social influence is unequally distributed. But how can the individual estimate this latter distribution, not corresponding to how it *ought* to be but how it *is*?

We propose the following method, derived by analogy from consumer behaviour theory. In consumer behaviour theory the individual utility function is frequently defined implicitly as follows. Let (p, M) be a price-income-constellation and let the vector-function $x(p, M)$ be the individual's preferred commodity bundle, then $U(x)$ is a utility function for this individual if and only if for all $(p, M) > 0$, $x(p, M)$ is a solution of the maximum problem

$$\max U(x)$$

$$\text{sub} \quad p'x \leqslant M, \quad x \geqslant 0$$

If (p, M) is varying, $x(p, M)$ varies as well and so we get an indirect (or dual) estimate of the class of ordinal utility functions which can be considered as describing the individual's behaviour (see Samuelson [13]). We notice in passing that the solution(s) U will change if the space of feasible solutions changes, e.g. by the addition of integer constraints on x, equality constraints if joint buying is the only possibility, and so on. On the other hand, the solution x will change if the objective function $U(x)$ changes.

Now we propose the same approach in order to estimate the social welfare function as it is perceived by the individual. Let the income distribution N be in a set $\bar{N}$ of feasible income distributions and let $\bar{N}$ be an element of the class of sets $\tilde{N}$. The individual i believes $W_i(N)$ to be a *social* welfare function for the perceived society if and only if for the set of all feasible income distributions $\bar{N} \varepsilon \tilde{N}$ the perceived income distribution N is a solution of the maximum problem

$$\max W(N)$$

$$\text{sub} \quad N \varepsilon \bar{N}$$

(Notice that $\bar{N}$ is the analogon of the feasible set $\{x \mid p'x \leq M\}$ and $\tilde{N}$ the analogon of the class of sets of the type $\{x \mid p'x \leq M\}$ when (p, M) is allowed to vary).

Considering the consumer problem it is evident that the estimation of $U(x)$ becomes easier as one is able to observe more and more different (p, M)-constellations. Inversely, if the set of (p, M)-observations is reduced, estimation becomes more difficult, unless one resorts to a second device, the *a priori* restriction of U to a more or less narrow class of admitted functions.

In the social welfare problem we face a specific instance of this general problem.

The class of functions from which a social welfare function is to be chosen is restricted to the type (9). The class of sets $\tilde{N}$ contains only *one* set $\bar{N}$ and this set is specified, as a first attempt, by the following equality constraint

$$\int_0^\infty y\,dN(y) = Y$$

or in words, the addition of individual incomes yields a constant national product Y. Even this restriction of the problem does not yield a unique estimate of the social influence density function $\alpha_i(y)$. So we have made some assumptions which are more or less plausible but which are open to discussion. First, we assume the income distribution to be of the lognormal type $\Lambda(\mu_2, \sigma_2)$, which is supported by empirical analysis, provided the sample has been purified from holiday workers and other irregulars. Secondly, we make three hypotheses with respect to the $\alpha_i(y)$-function, viz.

1. richer people have more influence, i.e., $\alpha_i(y)$ is an increasing function of y;
2. the proportion of social influence depends solely on income proportions. – This second assumption is quantified as

$$\frac{d \ln(\alpha(y))}{d \ln y} = \delta$$

3. the same absolute income proportions mean less difference in social influence, the skewer the actual income distribution is. More precisely we refine assumption 2 to

$$\frac{d \ln(\alpha(y))}{d \ln y} = \frac{\varepsilon}{\sigma_2}$$

where σ_2^2 is the log-variance of the income-distribution, and ε a parameter. By these assumptions $\alpha(y)$ is specified up to one parameter ε as

$$\alpha(y) = Cy^{\varepsilon/\sigma_2},$$

where C is a suitable normalization constant such that

$$\int_0^\infty \alpha(y)\,dN(y) = 1.$$

We call ε/σ_2 the *social influence elasticity* with respect to income. Subject to these restrictions the maximum problem is reduced to

$$\max_{\substack{\mu_2,\,\sigma_2 \\ \sigma_2 > 0}} \int_0^\infty C y^{\varepsilon/\sigma_2}\, U_i(y)\, dN(y)$$

$$\text{sub} \qquad \int_0^\infty y\, dN(y) = Y$$

where $U_i(y)$ is the observer's individual welfare function of income. This problem has a unique (μ_2, σ_2)-solution. If this solution is equated to the real (μ_2, σ_2)-values of the observed income distribution, it becomes possible after some calculation to estimate the ε which will yield the observed income distribution. We find for the social influence elasticity ε/σ_2

$$\frac{\varepsilon}{\sigma_2} = \tfrac{1}{2}\left(\frac{\sigma_2}{\sigma_1}\right)^2 + 1 - \frac{(\beta_1 \ln y_a + \beta_2' - \ln \bar{y})}{\sigma_1^2}$$

where σ_1 is the individual's welfare sensitivity, y_a the observer's actual income, β_2' a constant, β_1 the preference drift rate, $\bar{y}$ is average private net income, σ_2^2 the log-variance of the distribution of net incomes. The value ε/σ_2 has been estimated for the Netherlands in 1971. It is seen that the distribution of social influence is perceived as skewer, the smaller the income y_a of the observer is.

Moreover a definition of the political mean is given, being the median of the social influence distribution (see [19]).

We are aware of the subjectivity of the perceived social influence concept developed above. It can be refined in many ways, and the first extensions seem to be the introduction of a production function constraint and a collective good distribution next to the distribution of private incomes. The difficulty, however, is to find relevant data. Also the conceptual side of the problems invites a lot of discussion, which we shall avoid here. This branch of development described in this progress report is perhaps the most audacious but also the most debatable. In the next sections we have recourse to firmer ground.

The Estimation of Social Reference Groups

The scheme by which people evaluate money, i.e. their individual welfare function,

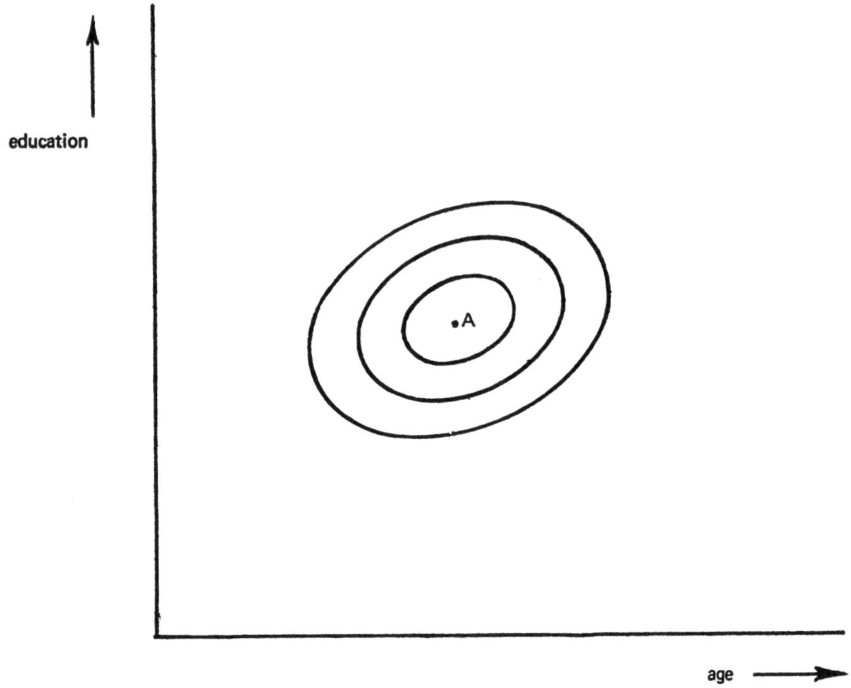

Figure 7. A two-dimensional social characteristics space.

is not formed by the individual in splendid isolation. If an individual considers a net income of *f* 60.000,– and he evaluates it as a large income, then this is partly due to the fact that he knows only a few other people who have at least such an income. Actually, the evaluation of income levels has a lot to do with the income distribution by which the individual is surrounded. Incomes which are low in that distribution are evaluated as low by the individual, and relatively high incomes are evaluated as high. The simplest proposition would be the following:

> the individual's welfare function (being approximately lognormal) equals the income distribution (being approximately lognormal) in the society of which he he is a member.

If this hypothesis is tested with reference to the income distribution of the entire Dutch population it evidently has to be rejected. However, when it is suitably modified by replacing the Dutch population by its *subjective* counterpart, the *social reference group* of the individual concerned, it deserves some second thoughts.

Every person may be characterized by a set of social characteristics like age, education, marital status, sex, income, etc. We may sketch a 2-dimensional social characteristics space as in fig. 7.
Consider an individual *A* described by point *A*. Over this space the population is distributed according to a specific objective distribution. However, individual *A* will not communicate with every population member at the same rate, secondly not every contact will have the same importance to *A* as reference point for his own behaviour, values, etc., and thirdly there may be asymmetry in the sense that the same contact between *B* and *A* is perceived by *B* and *A* in a different way and evaluated by them with different importance. An extreme example is a radio speech by the Queen to the population. The speech will influence the citizen, but the citizen is not even known to the Queen. Hence, we may conceive of the reference group of *A* as of a system of inner and outer spheres around *A* in the social characteristics space corresponding to spheres with more or less influence on *A*. More formally speaking we may define the social reference group of *A* as a mass distribution on the space of social characteristics which depends on:

a. the objective distribution of the population on the social characteristics space;
b. the position of individual *A* (probably the gravity point of the distribution);
c. the subjective reflection of the objective distribution as transformed by a 'social distance'-mechanism applied by individual A.

Returning to our starting point we put forward as a first conjecture that the individual's welfare parameters μ and σ equal μ_y and σ_y where

$$\mu_y = \int_C ln(y(c))dR(c|A)$$

$$\sigma_y^2 = \int_C (ln(y(c)) - \mu_y)^2 dR(c|A)$$

and where $dR(c|A)$ is the density on the social characteristics space C describing the reference group of A, and $y(c)$ the average income corresponding to a person of type c, where c is the vector of social characteristics. This proved to be a too naive conjecture. We tested then the relationships

$$\mu = \beta_0 + \beta_1 \, ln(fs) + \beta_2 \, ln(y_a) + \beta_3 \, \mu_y \tag{10}$$

$$\sigma^2 = \gamma_0 + \gamma_1 \, ln(fs) + \gamma_2 \, ln(y_a) + \gamma_3 \sigma_y^2 \tag{11}$$

which imply that the individual welfare parameters are partly determined by objective individual characteristics, viz. fs and y_a, and partly by the income distribution in the social reference group of the individual considered. Equations (10) and (11) were estimated by the method of *seemingly unrelated regressions*. The distribution $R(c|A)$ was functionally specified and its parameters were estimated simultaneously with the parameters β and γ in (10) and (11) by a non-linear estimation method. We refer to [10] for further details.

The main results are:

1. the estimates of (10) and (11) are

$$\underset{}{\mu(c)} = \underset{(0.44)}{1.92} + \underset{(0.02)}{0.13}\, ln[fs(c)] + \underset{(0.01)}{0.50}\, ln[y(c)] + \underset{(0.05)}{0.30}\, \mu_y(c) \quad (\bar{R}^2 = 0.649)$$

$$\sigma_2(c) = \underset{(0.02)}{0.13} + \underset{(0.15)}{0.82}\, \sigma_y^2(c) \qquad (\bar{R}^2 = 0.024) \quad N = 2774$$

2. the social characteristics space was differentiated according to the characteristics: 'education', 'job', 'working status', (being independent, wage earner, or not-working), 'urbanization' and 'region'.
   It turned out that 'education', 'age', 'job', and 'working status', are important characteristics while 'urbanization' and 'region' are less important in Dutch society as determinants of the social reference group.
3. with respect to the characteristics 'education', 'working status', and 'urbanization' there is a marked asymmetry in the sense that people in some classes look nearly always to their own classes, while other classes also look to different classes than their own.
4. Calling a society closed if the society is divided in isolated social layers having no intercommunication, measures of closedness have been defined and calculated for Dutch society and several subgroups on the basis of the 1971-sample. Use has been made of the information concepts introduced by Theil [14].

Municipal Welfare Functions

The previous sections dealt with individual welfare functions and their offspring. In this section we shall devote a little space to another interesting extension. The methodology outlined to measure individual welfare functions may be used as well outside its original context. Consider the municipal authorities who have to allocate municipal expenditures. They do the job on the basis of a more or less explicit evaluation scheme. This led Linthorst and the present author to the idea of posing the following questions to municipal authorities (Aldermen):

'Taking into account the specific circumstances and needs for your municipality (number of inhabitants, location, ect.) you would call the level of welfare as regards *public works*

Welfare level		*Expenditure level* ($\times f100$)
excellent	if the expenditure level were over	f 5.800
good	if the expenditure level were between	f 5.500 and f 5.800
amply sufficient	if the expenditure level were between	f 5.200 and f 5.500
sufficient	if the expenditure level were between	f 5.000 and f 5.200
barely sufficient	if the expenditure level were between	f 4.000 and f 5.000
insufficient	if the expenditure level were between	f 3.800 and f 4.000
very insufficient	if the expenditure level were between	f 3.600 and f 3.800
bad	if the expenditure level were between	f 3.500 and f 3.600
very bad	if the expenditure level were under	f 3.500'

where we have added answers given by the alderman of Public Works of a Dutch municipality of about 28,000 inhabitants.

This question has been asked with reference to the portfolios of 'public works', 'education', 'culture, sports and recreation', 'social affairs' as well as with respect to 'total expenditures' to all Dutch municipal authorities in 1974.

In this way we measured for about 530 out of the 842 municipalities 'partial' municipal welfare functions pertaining to the specific fields of municipal care and their welfare function of *total* expenditures. As in the individual case the lognormal distribution function yielded an excellent fit for municipalities. Then we tried to explain the welfare parameters by objective determinants like the number of inhabitants, the urbanization degree, the percentage of unemployed, the number of youth under 18 years of age, the distance to the nearest large city, the age distribution of buildings, etc. For the σ-parameter this appeared impossible, at least by the objective determinants, tried up to now. We think that the political composition of the municipality may explain a lot more. The results with respect to μ were strikingly good for the larger municipalities, while the small communites (up to 5,000 inhabitants) seem to be influenced by a number of incidental particularities, which cannot be taken into account in a nation-wide survey. As an instance we quote the explanation for 'public works' per inhabitant. For the class of municipalities of over 50,000 inhabitants we found

$$(\mu_{PW} - ln\ (\text{Inhabitants})) = \underset{(0.325)}{0.080} + \underset{(0.076)}{0.444}\ ln\ (\text{Inhabitants})$$

$$- \underset{(0.084)}{0.050}\ ln\ (\text{Area}) + \underset{(0.181)}{0.129}\ ln(\text{Houses built after 1965}) \quad (\bar{R}^2 = 0.879) \quad N = 27$$

The coefficient of Inhabitants is significantly positive, 0.444, which indicates a considerable 'diseconomies of scale'-effect, since it would be zero when there were no economies or diseconomies. The negative coefficient of Area (although non-significant) may reflect the fact that less public works facilities are needed if the area increases, meaning a reduction of the urban congestion.

Just as the individual results have been used to construct family equivalence scales, the municipal results may be used to construct *municipal equivalence scales.* This is not a theoretical question, because Dutch municipalities are almost completely dependent on the state budget for their revenues, which are administered to them by the state according to precisely such objective norms like 'inhabitants', 'area', etc., as we introduced as explanatory variables. The present norms seem to be intuitive approximations of the more 'exact' municipal equivalence scales derivable from our data on municipal welfare functions. This research will be deepened in the years to come where we shall bring into play the regional communication network, the political variables and other additional variables.

Conclusion

In this paper we attempted to sketch a new body of empirical research based on the individual welfare function concept. This author feels that this approach, which is definitely more psychologically oriented than is usual in economics, has yielded sufficient results to justify the idea that this is a new and valuable tool for economic analysis. Nevertheless, we recognize the fact that his method is not intended to replace the older methods of a more objective nature, but is only to be used side by side with them.

It goes without saying that those methods may be applied also in other countries than Belgium and The Netherlands. We are happy that this development is probable, since the European Community has expressed its willingness to promote this type of research in the member-countries of the EEC from the fall of 1976 onwards, notably in the 'struggle against poverty'.

References

[1] Aitchison, J., and J. A. C. Brown: *The Lognormal Distribution*, Cambridge 1960.

[2] Aumann, R. J.: Values of Markets with a Continuum of Traders, *Econometrica*, 1975.

[3] Frisch, R.: A Complete Scheme for Computing all Direct and Cross Demand Elasticities in a Model with Many Sectors, *Econometrica*, 1959.

[4] Goedhart, Th., V. Halberstadt, A. Kapteyn and B. M. S. van Praag: *The Poverty Line: Concept and Measurement*. Report of the Economic Institute, Leiden 1975.

[5] Harsanyi, J. C.: Cardinal Welfare, Individualistic Ethics and Interpersonal Comparisons of Utility. *Readings in Welfare Economics*, ed. by K. J. Arrow, T. Scitovsky and D. Irwin, Homewood 1969.

[6] van Herwaarden, F. G., A. Kapteyn and B. M. S. van Praag: *Twelve Thousand Individual Welfare Functions of Income: a Comparison of Six Samples in Belgium and the Netherlands*. Report of the Economic Institute, Leiden 1976.

[7] Houthakker, H. S.: The Present State of Consumption Theory, *Econometrica*, 1961.

[8] Kapteyn, A., and B. M. S. van Praag: A New Approach to the Construction of Family Equivalence Scales, *European Economic Review*, 1976.

[9] Kapteyn, A. and B. M. S. van Praag: Enige subjectieve en materiële gevolgen van verschillen in gezinsstructuur: een kwantitatieve beschouwing en een voorstel voor een nieuw KBA-stelsel. Report to the *Staatscommissie voor het Bevolkingsvraagstuk*, 1975.

[10] Kapteyn, A., B. M. S. van Praag and F. G. van Herwaarden: *Individual Welfare Functions and Social Reference Groups*. Report of the Economic Institute, Leiden 1976.

[11] Pareto, V.: *Manuel de l'Economie Politique*, Paris 1906.

[12] Robertson, D. V.: Utility and all that. *Manchester School of Economic and Social Studies*, 1951.

[13] Samuelson, P. A.: *Foundations of Economic Analysis*, Cambridge, Mass. 1947.

[14] Theil, H.: *Economics and Information Theory*, Amsterdam 1967.

[15] Tinbergen, J.: *Income Distribution-Analysis and Policies*, Amsterdam 1975.

[16] van Praag, B. M. S.: *Individual Welfare Functions and Consumer Behavior*, Amsterdam 1968.

[17] van Praag, B. M. S.: The Welfare Function of Income in Belgium: an Empirical Investigation, *European Economic Review*, 1971.

[18] van Praag, B. M. S. and A. Kapteyn: Further Evidence on the Individual Welfare Function of Income: an Empirical Investigation in the Netherlands, *European Economic Review*, 1973.

[19] van Praag, B. M. S. and A. Kouwenhoven: *The Concept and Measurement of Economic Power: Theory and Empirical Results for the Netherlands*. Report of the Economic Institute, Leiden 1974.

[20] van Praag, B. M. S.: De verdeling van inkomen en macht, *De Economist*, 1975.

[21] van Praag, B. M. S. and J. M. Linthorst: Municipal Welfare Functions, *Regional Science and Urban Economics*, 1976.

An Approach to Economics Education

Judith Yates

Over the past decade there have been significant developments in research in economics education, particularly in the areas of evaluation, programmed instruction, audio-visual techniques (including TV) and games and simulations. See Lumsden [41] and Villard [65] for brief reviews of these developments and Dawson [20] and Lewis and Orvis [40] for comprehensive surveys. The burgeoning literature in this fields has varied from the primarily descriptive case study with little concern for evaluation to carefully controlled experimental research devoted to a specific question. However, as Lewis and Orvis note, there has been a large imbalance in the type of research being done, with a heavy emphasis on alternative techniques of teaching and on the evaluation of the efficiency of these techniques. It is only rarely that 'there have been co-ordinated attempts to evaluate or research all three dimensions of a course or curriculum in economics – the goals, content and the techniques and resources' ([40], p. 8). In a footnote on the same page as the quote above Lewis and Orvis go on to say that much of the research which has been done to date on the effectiveness of alternative teaching methods may well have yielded the all too common and disheartening 'no significant difference' (if the author has bothered to calculate significant differences) in these comparative studies simply because the studies themselves were too small scale in design. Only studies which look to wholly new teaching-learning models are likely to be of any use. Commenting on the British situation, Scott ([59], p. 73) makes a related point by claiming that 'unless some serious work is carried out in sorting out the underlying conceptual problems, as well as those of an empirical nature, there is little likelihood of economists coming out with any useful results in this important field' (i.e., in the evaluation of teaching effectiveness).

This paper aims to provide some explanation as to why much of the current research in economics education does yield inconclusive results and, in so doing, to simultaneously provide some guidelines for the 'wholly new teaching-learning models' claimed earlier to be necessary before significant advances can be made in the area of economics education.

The central hypothesis consists of several parts, none of which are either difficult or new when taken individually; and it is one which the educational technologists have swung back to after an enthusiastic foray into specific technological advances. The first part is that the approach to education must be a systems approach, whereby aims, methods and evaluation are closely inter-related; the second part is that different methods of teaching will achieve different objectives and, finally, the third part is that alternative teaching techniques will have differential impacts on students. It is claimed that if this three part hypothesis is accepted then the search for a rationale to justify the incorporation of innovative teaching methods into existing courses has been carried out along the wrong lines and the conclusions reached by so many of the studies which have already been undertaken are a logical consequence of this and could have largely been predicted in advance. In part II of the paper, the current state of the art in relation to each of the three parts of the hypothesis will be discussed; in part III some relevant empirical evidence will be discussed and used to illustrate the points being made; and, finally, in part IV some recommendations concerning economics education will be made.

II

The claim that the education process must be regarded as a whole, rather than as the sum of its parts, has increasingly become the central theme of the recent literature on curriculum development and educational technology [3, 8, 27, 29, 31, 62, 68]. According to the U.S. Commission on Instructional Technology ([14], p. 5), instructional technology, to use the American rather than the British term, 'is more than the sum of the parts. It is a systematic way of designing, carrying out and evaluating the total process of learning and teaching in terms of specific objectives, based on research in human learning and communication, and employing a combination of human and non-human resources to bring about more effective instruction.' Despite an emerging consensus amongst the educational technologists as to the desirability of such a definition, the Commission goes on to claim that 'the widespread acceptance and application of this broad definition belongs to the future.' This broad perspective has grown out of an earlier and much more limited concern about the role of technology in general and programmed learning in particular in education and from an increasing realization that such a narrow perspective could lead to recent technological advances simply being 'tacked on' to existing courses and fulfilling only a peripheral role [31, 38] rather than providing the scope for a radical re-appraisal of the whole learning environment [51]. The global consensus concerning the definition of educational technology also extends to what actually constitutes a systematic design of the learning process [13, 29, 46]. It is described as the process of identifying goals in specific terms; determining the nature and quality of the students involved; examining the resources available; choosing appropriate teaching and learning strategies; and evaluating the effectiveness of the whole process in the light of the specified goals. The notion of a systems approach is, according to Mesarovic [49], introduced to denote the existence of relationships between the data and variables being observed, but it is in the area of curriculum development rather than in educational technology, that the possibility of a non-sequential process involving the previous five steps has been suggested. Hall [27] lists several reasons why a learning system which proceeds linearly in successive stages from aims and objectives to evaluation (such as, for example, that advocated by Davies [18] is inadequate: the first reason is the assumption that aims and objectives can be and are defined at the start of a course; the second is the assumption that all the outcomes of an educational process are amenable to evaluation (or assessment); and the third is the assumption that evaluation, rather than revision in the light of this, is the final step in the process).

The concentration of the educational technologists on specific objectives—such as the behavioural or instructional objectives advocated in economics education by the Joint Council on Economic Education [32] and Phillips [54]—is claimed to have certain limitations (Eisner [22], MacDonald-Ross [44]. It may be that specific objectives are not clear, even though the aims are; the objectives may not be observable (for example, the development of certain attitudes); evaluation could be limited to those objectives specified and hence ignore other learning (whether intended or unintended) which has taken place; alternatively, they may result in concentration on an end point rather than on the process of development up to that point; and, finally, though not necessarily least importantly, they can take a long time to specify. However, whether or not behavioural objectives can, or should, be specified, there is still widespread agreement on the desirability of being aware of the broader aims of a course so that students can be told where they are going and so that teaching and assessment programmes can be directed towards the achievement of those aims.

That the right choice of assessment method is important because of the effect this choice has on the achievement of the stated (and even non-stated) aims has been widely discussed. See, for example, Cox [16] for a survey of this, and also other articles in the June 1967 issue of the *Universities Quarterly.* It has been well documented, for example, that the traditional three hour written exam assesses knowledge and concentration (among other things) very well, but creative ability rather poorly, whereas projects, or theses, have exactly the reverse characteristics. See, for example, an Adelaide University report ([64], p. 11) for a tabular presentation of the characteristics of different methods of assessment commonly used in economics education and a rating of these from poor to excellent according to which objective is being assessed. A slightly different example of the interaction between assessment and objectives is that given by Bloom [12] who claims that the type of assessment used determines which qualities are prized (e.g., competitiveness vs co-operation; specific attitudes vs achievement) and these, in turn, affect the objectives of any educational process. Likewise, the choice of teaching method should also be dependent on the aims or objectives which have been set: for example, to efficiently convey information, use lectures or programmed instruction; to bring about attitude changes, use simulations or role playing; to apply skills, use projects or case studies and so on. See Bligh [11] or Hall [27] for a fuller listing. A particular technique which is very effective for one objective may not be appropriate for another. Gregory [26], for example, claims that evidence shows that 'lectures are efficient for passing on factual material but (are) much less suited to the development of high intellectual skills and attitudes'. Bligh [11] surveys a vast array of literature on the relative effectiveness of the various methods of teaching and arrives at the conclusion which is the second part of the central hypothesis of this paper; namely (see p. 185)

'1. different kinds of objectives are best achieved by different methods;
2. teachers usually have a number of objectives in any one lesson;
3. therefore, the objectives in any one lesson are usually best achieved by different methods.'

For the purposes of this paper, this multi-part conclusion, although made with respect to a single lecture, could be taken to apply equally well, and perhaps even more strongly, to a whole course. The conclusion taken in isolation is a little simplistic as it tends to imply that any learning which has been undertaken can be attributed to a specific technique and, secondly, that it is possible to make a fairly clear cut distinction between objectives, which is often unlikely to be the case [27, 58]. However, even if there is some blurring of the various distinctions between teaching methods and objectives achieved and between objectives themselves, there is no reason why the general principles of the conclusion should not still apply.

So far, the argument has been developed to the point where the necessity of considering the whole process should be obvious because of the dependence of one aspect of the learning process on other aspects (in particular, those considered have been the dependence of the choice of teaching method and the choice of assessment on the objectives or aims). If recognition of this alone was all that was required, then the 'no significant difference' results of so much of the so-called academically sound research on economics education could not be explained away on the basis of a non-consideration of the whole process since most research has recognised the dependence of the choice of methods of teaching on objectives chosen. Most research has, in fact, considered a predetermined objective and attempted to determine how successfully one or another method has been in attaining this objective. Many of these studies are based on carefully controlled experiments using nationally validated objective tests, such as the *American Economic Association's TUCE*—test of understanding college economics—commissioned in 1967 and consisting of three parts which are used to test ability in the areas of 1. recognition and understanding, 2. simple application and 3. complex application[1] or the *British TEC*—test of economic comprehension—prepared by the staff of the *Economics Education Project* in 1971, based primarily on testing ability to apply principles and designed to be effective in discriminating between students rather than in evaluating methods.[2] There are also similar validated tests which have been developed to test specialized skills such as critical thinking alibity (for example, the Watson-Glaser test [66] as used by Kourilsky [37]) or to evaluate attitudes (for example, the OAIS attitude sophistication test [24] as used by Mann and Fusfeld [47]).

There are, however, two problems arising out of these studies. Firstly, what they have done is to take a predetermined objective (or even several objectives in a few isolated cases) and evaluated the effectiveness of alternative methods of teaching in achieving these objectives. What they have not taken into consideration is that any particular choice of teaching method will simultaneously contribute towards the attainment of several objectives and the relative advantage of one method over another can not and should not be wholly measured by the consideration of just one or two of the whole range of objectives. For example, programmed learning, on the basis of nationally validated tests, has been shown to be as effective in imparting information as lectures (see Bligh [11] for broadly based evidence or Attiyeh, Bach and Lumsden [4] or Soper [60] for results in economics education). However, it does not contribute to any note-taking skills, to take an arbitrary secondary objective.[3] On the other hand, programmed learning has been shown to be more efficient in achieving the stated objectives by taking less time than the more conventional lecture method (again, choosing a possible secondary objective rather arbitrarily). See Attiyeh et al. Considering a second example, computer simulations have been shown to be no more effective in imparting information than lectures [17, 23] but they are far more effective in teaching students what economists do and how they do it [61] and are also more effective in developing a positive student attitude towards a course [30]. Regarding the different characteristics necessary for effective teaching, Mann and Fusfeld [47], on the basis of a controlled experiment on attitude sophistication, tentatively conclude that if the course grade or knowledge of subject matter are the only objectives of a course, then the general teaching characteristics such as knowledge of subject, organization and preparation of lectures, ability to put information across in an interesting way, and so on are generally the characteristics which will ensure effective teaching. However, if attitude sophistication is also a course objective, then effective teaching requires less emphasis on the former characteristics and a greater emphasis on value problems, a greater questioning of beliefs in economic matters, creation of an atmosphere of active discussion in the classroom and the like. In general, then, this first problem is that the studies have not fully considered what alternative or secondary objectives are or can be achieved by the alternative methods being evaluated and they have not discussed whether these were deemed relevant or important to the course's initial aims.

The second, and somewhat related problem, is that most of the comparative studies have proceeded on the assumption of a linear nature of the curriculum development process – that is, from aims to methods of evaluation, without taking into account the point made earlier; namely, that the process should be an interactive one, with objectives not only affecting the choice of methods, but the methods or resources available affecting the choice of objectives as well. This point raises the much more difficult philosophical question of what should be the aims or objectives of a particular economics course. It is not the intention of this paper to attempt to answer this obviously essential question but, instead, to use the question as an excuse for raising several important points. With the advent of rapid advances in educational technology, advances in learning theory and increases in student expectations, should objectives remain unchanged? Should economics education be content to achieve only those objectives which can be and largely have been achieved by conventional methods? The fact that the advent of new technological innovations means that new objectives can be achieved should lead to a continual re-evaluation of the objectives which ought to be achieved. Any amount of empirical evidence can be brought into consideration to determine the relative effectiveness of one method over another with regard to a specific objective but it remains in the area of value judgements to determine which objective is more important than another. Different (implicit or explicit) weighting applied to secondary objectives will lead to a greater importance being attached to one method or another regardless of the efficacy of this method in achieving a specific primary objective. This is particularly likely to be the case when the ease or validity of measuring the secondary objective is questionable. It could be argued that these conclusions are supported by the fact that, although the general results of most research on education methods is largely inconclusive, innovation continues to take place. This innovation is not only in the form of new, untried methods but also consists of the implementation of tried, tested and 'not proven' methods by researchers who are well aware of current developments and yet remain committed to the innovation and convinced that improvements do exist, even if they have not been able to prove it as yet. Davies [19] supports this view and argues that continuing innovation occurs despite the evidence primarily because most evaluation is based on an examination of some sort, which usually measures the lower order cognitive skills (such as knowledge, comprehension and application) and rarely measures attitudes, beliefs and values. It could also reflect a feeling that many present teaching methods do not extend students to their maximum capacity. In other words, those introducing the innovation or continually seeking for alternatives could be doing so because their objectives (again, whether stated explicitly or held implicitly) have not been effectively achieved. A further reason also, could be that continual innovation in a course leads to successful exploitation of the Hawthorne effect and generally increases interest and motivation of both students and teacher, regardless of the usefulness of the actual innovation being introduced.[4] Trow [63] claims that innovation usually arises because of the instructor's boredom with the current situation, from a sense of inadequacy or from a changing function of higher education which means that it is relating to students' needs and interests more than to the traditional academic achievements. He claims that because of these reasons, innovation is justified by its intrinsic qualities, without regard to outcomes and points out that, because it would usually be undertaken anyway, evaluation is more often than not aimed at the person or institution funding the project, rather than for the innovator's own information.

The last part of this section of the paper is that which attempts to explain why the no significant differences occur, rather than explaining why researchers do not accept them. The main argument is that different students will achieve the objectives set most effectively in different ways, regardless of what the objectives actually are. Individualized instruction has been a catch-cry for many years, and it is this principle of differences between students that it is ideally based upon. However, what it has often resulted in is, firstly, interpretation as independent instruction where each student follows the same activity in the same way, working at his own pace. Examples of this are the programmed learning approach (see Hartley [29] for a general survey and there are many examples of this in economics, but the seminal works are those prepared by Attiyeh, Bach and Lumsden [5, 7, 43]); audio-tutorial approaches (developed by Postlethwait [55] and extended to economics by, for example, Martin [48] and see also Noble [52]); personalized systems of instruction (such as that envisaged by the Keller plan [33] and applied in economics education by Allison [1]). With these methods, students are freed from rigid timetables and lack of feedback and are able to work at their own pace with constant indicators as to their progress. The second interpretation of individualized instruction is as individualized feedback on learning in large group teaching situations such as that available from the feedback classroom and effectively applied in economics education by Kelley [34, 35, 36].

Many of these approaches, however, only cater for differences in the rate of learning rather than for catering for all the possible different ways in which students may learn. The factors which are generally shown to be of importance in learning at the tertiary level are intelligence, aptitude, previous experience, motivation, personality, sex, age and socio-economic background [9]. Many studies on the relative effectiveness of alternative approaches in economics education support these general findings, as many of the variables show up as significant in regression analyses. For example, taking a selection of empirically verified studies reported in the *Journal of Economic Education*, Bellico [10], Cox [17], Emery and Enger [23], Mann and Fusfeld [47] and Weidenaar and Dodson [67] all find one or more of the above factors as having significant effects on the course grade, or *TUCE* score or some similar cognitive objective over a wide range of teaching methods, even though in almost all of these studies the authors found no significant difference in the effect of the actual method they were experimenting with compared with the conventional lecture method. Most of the studies which have been undertaken in economics education have been concerned with only one objective – namely performance in some test – and it is in relation to this objective that the various student characteristics have been shown to be relevant. However, Mann and Fusfeld did show that these characteristics were sometimes also important in determining attitude sophistication as well. When the same characteristic was significant in explaining the achievement of both objectives, it did not necessarily work in the same direction; for example, being a female contributed positively towards course grade but negatively towards attitude sophistication.

Although all of the studies mentioned can be used to reach the conclusion that the various characteristics being considered are significant in determining whether or not a specific objective is achieved, very few of them have attempted to determine whether the non-significant result of the particular method being tested was due to differential impacts on all students cancelling each other out so that a positive impact on some was cancelled out by a negative impact on others, or whether it was due to a zero impact on all students. Hansen, Kelley and Weisbrod [28] illustrate the point being made here (and it is a point, they claim, which was made much earlier by McKeachie [45]) with the aid of a simple diagram. Considering the effect of just one characteristic on one objective they claim that, on average, it is possible that two methods, overall, are equally effective but that, in fact, the second method is better for low achievers and the first method better for high achievers. See diagram 1.

Kelley [35], in studying the differential impact of his *TIPS* innovation, shows that in principle this possibility exists as he shows that lower achievers perform relatively better than higher achievers as a result of *TIPS*.[5] Cox, on the other hand, shows that both low and high achievers perform better than the average students as a result of his computer simulations and so derives an obviously non-linear relationship between a specific characteristic and the achievement of a specific objective. Emery and Enger claim that they could determine no differential impact on their test score on the basis of *SAT*-math and *SAT*-total scores[6] but they do not report on the possible differential impact on the basis of other student characteristics.

Athough what work has been done fairly strongly indicates that student characteristics are important in achieving various objectives, there has been very little work done on determining these effects, particularly in relation to economics education. The evidence which is available and which was mentioned earlier does indicate

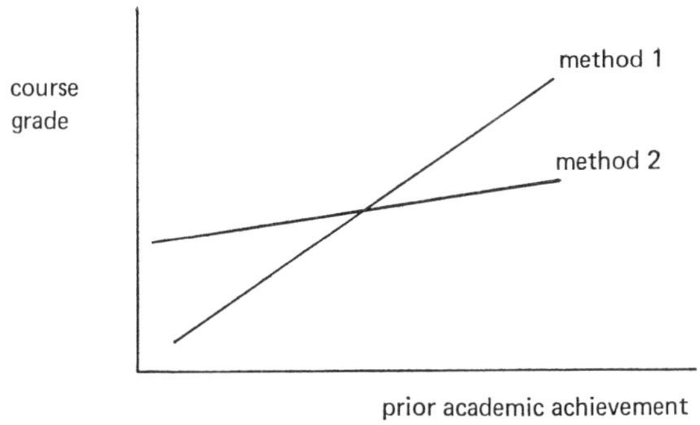

Diagram 1. Possible differential impact of alternative teaching methods.

that there is a differential impact of alternative methods of instruction on different students, but this is not conclusive or widespread enough to determine which technique can be best used to achieve a specific objective for a particular type of student.

Those characteristics of students which have been mentioned so far are the more readily available ones. However, there are other characteristics of students which could well affect the way in which they learn and which are not so readily available or even so readily measurable, although some attempts can usually be made. On the theoretical level, Messick [50], for example, claims that a student's 'cognitive style', which describes both his perceptual and intellectual characteristics, will more effectively characterize him then intellectual tests alone. In illustration he claims that the field dependence or independence of a particular student can be regarded as being the perceptual component of his cognitive style,[7] and he reports that measures of field independence were found to correlate with analytic intelligence, whereas field dependent subjects have been found to be better in situations requiring attention or concentration. From his observations regarding just a few of these characteristics he concludes (p. 197) that 'there is a possibility that, in the sciences at least, students with an articulated field approach,[8] and perhaps reflective students as well, might learn better with an inductive or 'discovery' method of teaching, since it would probably capitalize upon their propensities for analysis and careful consideration of alternatives. More global[9] and more impulsive students, on the other hand, might learn content information better with a direct method of teaching in which rules and principles are specified rather than induced.' One warning that Messick points out to those using these conclusions to adjust teaching methods to ensure maximum learning is that there is a danger of solidifying a global student's cognitive style so that he never learns to discover anything. In other words, if the manner of thinking is an objective in itself, the unintended effects of optimally achieving the specific objective of content information (for example) may work in the opposite direction to the intended effects.

This argument on the theoretical level has not been developed at all fully, but has been included to indicate that there are possibly many factors which have not been taken into account in the evaluation of education to date but which could well determine the way in which a student learns best. Because of these many factors, and the factors already considered earlier, different methods of teaching are likely to be differentially effective in achieving a particular objective.

III

Once it can be shown that different techniques of teaching have differential impacts on students and the direction of these impacts has been determined, the problem of choosing a specific technique will be complicated by the same problem as was raised with regard to the weight to be attached to the various desired objectives. In this case, the problem arises from the weights to be attached to the various characteristics of students; for example, should low achievers be helped relatively more to even out the level of achievement, or should high achievers be pushed to their maximum to provide an intellectual elite? Whether made explicitly or implicitly, these choices have to be made. The choice could be made more easily by the availability of more information on the differential impact of a wide range of teaching methods on an equally wide range of objectives and considered for as many of the student characteristics that are readily measurable and available. In this section a start is made in support of the case that there is a differential impact of teaching methods but this is not related to student characteristics because of lack of data.

Using the students' own evaluations of the usefulness of alternative teaching methods as a measure of their effectiveness, an indication of the differential impact of some alternative methods can be obtained by examination of the following data.[10] Table 1 gives the information obtained in response to the question:

'How helpful did you find each of the following:

	detracted				helpful
1. text books	1	2	3	4	5
2. lectures	1	2	3	4	5
3. class discussions	1	2	3	4	5
4. assignments	1	2	3	4	5
5. computer exercises	1	2	3	4	5
6. programmed instruction	1	2	3	4	5'

Table 1

Student Evaluation of Alternative Teaching Methods

Teaching method	Percentage in each category					Total	Mean	s.d.	t
1.	21.6	28.3	30.0	10.0	10.0	60	2.5	1.2	—2.6*
2.	8.3	10.0	28.3	40.0	13.3	60	3.4	1.0	2.7*
3.	8.3	18.3	35.0	26.6	11.6	60	3.1	1.1	1.0
4.	1.6	3.3	1.6	40.0	53.3	60	4.4	0.8	13.1*
5.	10.0	20.0	35.0	26.6	8.3	60	3.0	1.0	0.2
6.	2.2	4.4	24.4	35.5	33.3	45	3.9	0.9	6.3*

* Significantly different from 3 at 1% level of significance.

On the basis of a straightforward interpretation, it would be concluded that, on average, the students found that

1. texts detracted slightly (possibly because no single text was available and students were required to seek out the relevant information from one of four or five different texts);
2. lectures helped slightly (possibly because they defined the course in the absence of a single text);
3. assignments helped very much (the result is, in fact, significantly greater than an average rating of 4, and possibly occurs because the assignments closely integrated all sections of the course and were based on all methods of teaching);
4. programmed instruction, on average, was also regarded as helpful (again, possibly because it served to fairly rigidly define what was required of students).

Further naive analysis of results would also suggest that neither class discussions (in small groups of 12) nor computer exercises (including both simulations and

Table 2

Correlation Matrix for Alternative Teaching Methods

	1	2	3	4	5	6
1	1.0	.499*	.111	.044	—.219	—.075
2		1.0	.390*	.256**	.003	.124
3			1.0	.107	.214	—.095
4				1.0	.301**	.255
5					1.0	.131
6						1.0

For methods 1 to 5, $n = 60$, for method 6, $n = 45$
* significant at 1%
** significant at 5%

individualized exercises) were regarded either favourably or unfavourably. From this information alone, it would be tempting to conclude that both class discussion and the computer exercises could be dropped and that a drastic reappraisal of the no single textbook policy could be beneficial.

However, on closer analysis, it is obvious that the average rating of 3 in method 5 (computer exercises) results from approximately 30% of students who found it detracted from their understanding cancelling out the 30% of students who felt it was helpful. Approximately the same thing has occurred in method 3 (class discussions), so that the advantages as seen by some students were cancelled out by the disadvantages as seen by others.

Ideally, of course, the methods in question should be available to, or required of, those students who gain something from them. If this were the case then the overall effect must be beneficial. This is what a true individualized instruction system would do. However, it is possible that some students feel as though all methods are helpful and others feel as though no methods are. If this were the case it would not be possible to provide the latter students with suitable teaching methods geared to their particular needs. To determine whether this was the case for the data used above, the correlations between the various responses were looked at, and the information is given in table 2. From this table it is very obvious that students are not ranking each method in a similar way. If one group of students, possibly those who felt they gained most from the course over-all, all tended to rate each method high and a different group of students all tended to rate each method low, then there would be no case for arguing that alternative methods of teaching have

differential impacts on students. In this case, the elements of the correlation matrix would all be positive and significantly different from zero.
The highest positive correlation (significant at the 1% level) is between lectures and text books. This could be largely expected on a priori grounds since these teaching methods both have the potential for providing the student with a direct and ordered approach with rules and principles specified, allowing very little scope for enquiry beyond the predetermined framework or initiative for self-discovery. It is not suprising that students who found that lectures provided an adequate framework and rated them accordingly, also rated text books (despite the fact that no single one was available) as adequate, since they already had a base from which to study. Similarly, those students who rate lectures poorly could be expected to find the profusion of text books confusing and hence equally unhelpful.

The lower, but still significant at the 1% level, correlation between lectures and class discussions is somewhat harder to explain, unless it can be explained in terms of the common contact with the lecturer who conducted both lectures and tutorials. The correlation between assignments and computer exercises (significant at the 5% level) would presumably arise from students either liking (at the top end of the scale) or disliking (at the bottom end of the scale) the challenge of working out something for themselves. In other words, again there is a common characteristic between the two types of teaching methods which could certainly result in their obtaining a similar rating and again the significant (although still rather low) correlation could be expected on a priori grounds.

Finally, the last remaining correlation significant at the 5% or less level is that between lectures and assignments which, as with that between lectures and text books, could be due to those students who regarded both lectures and assignments as providing a framework for the course giving each a similar rating. On the whole, though, it can be seen from the data given in table 2 that the rating students give to the usefulness or otherwise of a particular method of teaching bears little relation to the rating they give to an alternative method (except in the few fairly readily explainable instances considered above). The general conclusion which can be thus derived from these largely insignificantly different from zero correlations is that different students do perceive the usefulness of different methods of teaching differently, thus reinforcing the points being made earlier in this paper.

A similar conclusion could also be reached by examining the regressions given in table 3. Although, on average, class discussions and computer exercises are not

Table 3

Effect of Teaching Methods on Course Evaluation

	(1)		(2)	
Independent variables	β	t	β	t
constant				
teaching methods[1]				
1. text books	—.07	—.49	—.09	— 6.4
2. lectures	.14	7.1	.12	6.4
3. class disc.	.17	10.9	.13	8.1
4. assignments	.32	14.4	.26	12.2
5. computer ex.	.24	16.0	.09	5.5
6. P.I.	.08	4.1	.02	1.1
relation to other areas[2]				
7. usefulness in relation to macroeconomics			—.23	— 8.7
8. increased understanding of application of mathematics to economics			—.30	— 10.2
R^2	.43		.52	

[1] Rated 1 for detracted to 5 for helpful

[2] Rated 1 for strongly agreeing with statement that course helped to 5 for strongly disagreeing.

Dependent variable: course was a worthwhile learning experience, rated 5 for strongly agreeing to 1 for strongly disagreeing.

regarded as being helpful or otherwise, both contribute significantly to the students' over-all rating of the course as a worthwhile learning experience.

In regression (1), based on a rather low 42 observations, textbooks still show up perversely, which is in agreement with the earlier interpretation of the data given in table 1. However, class discussions and computer exercises together contribute more than the highly rated assignments and all teaching methods, with the exception of textbooks, are both significant and of the right sign. Once the additional independent variables (based on students' perception of the usefulness of the course in relation to macroeconomics which is a course being concurrently undertaken by all students and on the usefulness of the course in increasing their understanding of the application of mathematical techniques to economics) were included in the regressions the significance of the contribution of the computer exercises decreased slightly (although it still remained positive and significant), due undoubtedly to the fact that the new variable 7 picked up some of the credit previously being granted to the computer exercises (which were largely based on macroeconomic simulations or macroeconometric models). The value of the coefficient of determination, although low by many standards, is quite reasonable for this type of work.

These results thus also support the contention that there will be at least one method of teaching which is relatively more efficient in enabling a particular student to achieve a specific objective. In the example above, all methods contribute significantly to the perception of the 'worthwhileness' of the course despite the lack of correlation between the evaluation of one method with another. However, if the rating of a particular method is based on an average over all students, then its desirability may not be as apparent and the researcher could be led falsely from his observations that no significant difference was apparent on average to the conclusion that the method in question served no useful purpose.

The measure being used in all of these results, of course, is only an indication of the student's perception of the usefulness of the various approaches rather than any measure based on test or exam results or related to the achievement of other specific objectives. Lumsden [42] shows that there is, in fact, very little association between students' evaluation and examination results, but points out that this could simply indicate that test scores do not give very good information about what students gain from a course. A further disadvantage of the data used in this analysis, and thus of the analysis itself, is that it does not provide any information as to why students rate alternative teaching methods in different ways. Their objectives and their weightings of these are not known, nor are their personal characteristics, and hence it cannot be determined which of these the differential impact results from. For the point being made in this paper, though, it should not matter; it is only necessary to know that there is a differential impact.

Thus, the point being made remains: different students can be shown to value alternative approaches to teaching in different ways and there is good reason to believe that, although their average over-all evaluation of a particular method may not differ significantly from a non-committal evaluation, their over-all evaluation of the course does. That is to say, the whole is greater than the sum of the parts.

To briefly summarize the general conclusions so far: firstly, researchers have found that any particular innovation in education has generally resulted in no significant change on previous methods because they have applied the innovation equally to all students and have not taken into account the differential impact it will have on students; secondly, they have tended to evaluate only a very narrow range of possible objectives and have generally not considered either the possibility that the introduction of new technology in the classroom often provides the potential for achieving objectives not earlier considered or the possibility that their methods of evaluation could affect their objectives; and, finally, they have not been prepared to accept their empirical results because they (either implicitly or explicitly) hold different objectives than those which they have tested for in evaluating the effectiveness of the innovation in question.

IV

The primary recommendations arising from the work done in this paper concerns both economics education and research into economics education. Regarding the first, it should be abundantly clear that the most appropriate approach to individualizing instruction is not that which depends on using the same method for all students, even if this is varied for each student by the use of suitably chosen additional reading or assignments etc. when shown necessary. It must depend, instead, on the suitable choice of teaching method for each student.[11] This recommendation is somewhat contrary to the current trends in educational innovation as it explicitly accepts that any particular innovation will not necessarily be an improvement for all students. It is also contrary to common current practice where all students work within the same framework and have the same teaching method(s) imposed upon them. It does not argue that the current approaches used (typically a lecture–seminar or tutorial–essay or assignment approach in most economics courses) are undesirable; in fact, quite the reverse. It is highly probable that for a certain group of students this method is the most effective. However, it is equally probable that for other groups of students it is far from effective. Because of the lack of information on the differential impact of alternative teaching methods there is some difficulty in determining in advance which method will be best in achieving a specific objective for any particular student. The logical consequence of this is that the educational process can be most effectively undertaken by a conscious use of a wide variety of teaching methods. Ideally, these would not all be compulsory for all students, but available as needed.

The second recommendation arising from the points made in this paper is that concerning further research into economics education; it is that any further research will have to begin by considering the whole process of objectives–resources – assessment – evaluation and will have to take into account the possible interaction of one on the other. It can no longer avoid the problem of explicitly stating (as far as possible) the values to be placed on the various objectives, because only once these are known can the whole education process be effectively evaluated. There is also a great need for specific research into the differential impact of alternative teaching methods on students according to which objectives are to be achieved.

Notes

1 Work done by Lewis and Dahl [39] indicates some doubt as to the construct validity of the *TUCE* with regard to this complex application aspect. Emery and Enger [23] suggest that it is possibly related to analytical ability.

2 For information on the *TUCE*, see [56] and on the *TUE* see [21].

3 To my knowledge, the relative efficiency of either method in producing this rather arbitrarily chosen objective has not been evaluated, although research reported in Beard [9] indicates that generally the time permitted in lectures does not permit satisfactory note-taking, with only something like one half of the important points made in a lecture being recorded. Intuitively, though, this only partially successful result contributes more than the stimulus-response type of approach used in the programmed learning evaluated to date.

4 The Hawthorne effect was named after an experiment on worker productivity at the *Hawthorne plant* of the *Western Electric Company* in the late 1920's. It was found that every change made improved productivity even though some of the changes meant reverting back to an earlier situation. In other words, it was the experimental situation itself which was providing the positive results.

5 In fact, Kelley's results are not amongst those that yield no significant differences; even controlling for prior academic achievement, Kelley's innovation shows a significant improvement over conventional techniques. Hence, in terms of diagram 1, his method 2 (*TIPS*) would lie wholly above the method 1 (conventional lecture) curve but, because of the differential impact, the relative slopes would remain as in the present diagram.

6 *S*cholastic *A*ptitude *T*ests, applied widely in the USA to determine a student's ability to perform well in college.

7 In describing these terms he claims that 'the perception of relatively field dependent subjects is dominated by the overall organization of the field, whereas relatively field independent subjects readily perceive elements as discrete from their backgrounds'. Females have been shown to be relatively more field dependent and males relatively more field independent, and perception also becomes more field independent with age.

8 Corresponds to field independence.

9 Corresponds to field dependence.

10 Data were obtained from student questionnaires, handed out and filled in during a lecture period. The response rate was approximately 85% with 60 questionnaires returned. The lower response rate on category 6 was due to the fact that this had been omitted from the original questionnaire and some students neglected to add it on when requested to do so.

11 In the *HERDSA newsletter* 2/75, Stanton claims that a particular method of individualized instruction that he tried out was a 'highly significant learning experience' for approximately one

third of his students but 'a considerable minority loafed . . . and did not use the learning opportunities provided'. This further reinforces the points being made; obviously in the case being cited some students benefitted from taking responsibility for their own learning, which is what the innovation entailed, but others did not.

References

[1] Allison, E.: *Self-paced Instruction in Introductory Economics* discussion paper no. 368, Harvard Institute of Economic Research, Harvard 1974.

[2] Armstrong, R. H. R. and J. L. Taylor: *Instructional Simulation System in Higher Education*, Cambridge 1970.

[3] Atkins, K. J. and J. C. Clift: Application of Educational Technology in the Development of a Learning Experience for a First Year Engineering Course, *Programmed Learning and Educational Technology*, 1975.

[4] Attiyeh, R. E., G. L. Bach and K. G. Lumsden: The Efficiency of Programmed Learning in Teaching Economics: the Results of a Nationwide Survey, *American Economic Review*, 1969.

[5] Attiyeh, R. E., G. L. Bach and K. G. Lumsden: *Basic Economics: Theory and Cases*, Englewood Cliffs, N.J., 1973.

[6] Attiyeh, R. E. and K. G. Lumsden: Some Modern Myths in Teaching Economics: the U.K. Experience, *American Economic Review*, 1972.

[7] Attiyeh, R. E., K. G. Lumsden and G. L. Bach: *Macroeconomics: a Programmed Book*, Englewood Cliffs, 1970.

[8] Beard, R. M.: Some Perspectives on Research in Higher Education. In: [2].

[9] Beard, R. M.: *Teaching and Learning in Higher Education*, Harmondsworth 1972.

[10] Bellico, R.: Prediction of Undergraduate Achievement in Economics, *Journal of Economic Education*, 1972.

[11] Bligh, D.: *What's the Use of Lectures?*, Harmondsworth 1972.

[12] Bloom, B.: Toward a Theory of Testing which includes Measurement—Evaluation—Assessment. In: [69].

[13] Chadwick, C.: Educational Technology: Progress, Prospects and Comparisons, *British Journal of Educational Technology*, 1973.

[14] Commission on Instructional Technology: *To Improve Learning*, reprinted in Tickton, S. (ed.), *To Improve Learning; an Evaluation of Educational Technology*, vols. 1 and 2, Bowker, N.Y., 1970.

[15] Costin, F.: Lecturing Versus Other Methods of Teaching: a Review of Research, *British Journal of Educational Technology*, 1972.

[16] Cox, R.: Examinations and Higher Education: A Survey of the Literature. *Universities Quarterly*, 1967.

[17] Cox, S. R.: Computer-Assisted Instruction and Student Performance in Macro-Economic Principles, *Journal of Economic Education*, 1974.

[18] Davies, I. K.: *The Management of Learning*, New York, 1971.

[19] Davies, I. K.: *Competency Based Learning: Technology, Management and Design*, New York 1973.

[20] Dawson, G.: *Research in Economic Education: a Bibliography*, Center for Economic Education, New York 1969.

[21] Economics Education Project: *Test of Economic Comprehension*, Secretary, EEP, dept. of economics, Heriot-Watt University, Edinburgh.

[22] Eisner, E. W.: Educational Objectives, Help or Hindrance?, *School Review*, 1967.
[23] Emery, E. D. and T. R. Enger: Computer Gaming and Learning in an Introductory Economic Course, *Journal of Economic Education*, 1972.
[24] Fricke, B. G.: *Opinion, Attitude and Interest Survey*, Ann Arbor 1962.
[25] Gage, N. L. (ed.): *Handbook of Research on Teaching*, Chicago 1963.
[26] Gregory I. D.: A New Look at the Lecture Method, *British Journal of Educational Technology*, 1975.
[27] Hall, W. C.: *University Teaching*, Advisory Centre for University Education, University of Adelaide, South Australia 1975.
[28] Hansen, W. L., A. C. Kelly, B. A. Weisbrod: Economic Efficiency and the Distribution of Benefits from College Instruction, *American Economic Review*, 1970.
[29] Hartley, J.: Programmed Instruction 1954—1974: a Review, *Programmed Learning and Educational Technology*, 1974.
[30] Holbrook, R. S.: The Use of Economic Policy Games as an Aid to Student Understanding, in *Proceedings of a Conference on Computers in the Undergraduate Curriculum*, 1970, University of Iowa.
[31] Hooper, R.: The National Development Programme in Computer-Assisted Learning—Origins and Starting Point, *Programmed Learning and Educational Technology*, 1974.
[32] Joint Council on Economic Education, Special Report on Behavioural Objectives and Student Learning Contracts in the Teaching of Economics, *Journal of Economic Education*, 1972.
[33] Keller, F. S.: Goodbye Teacher . . ., *Journal of Applied Behaviour Analysis*, 1968.
[34] Kelley, A. C.: An Experiment with TIPS: a Computer-Aided System for Undergraduate Education, *American Economic Review*, 1968.
[35] Kelley, A. C.: TIPS and Technical Change in Classroom Instruction, *American Economic Review*, 1972.
[36] Kelley, A. C.: Individualizing Instruction through the Use of Technology in Higher Education, *Journal of Economic Education*, 1973.
[37] Kourilsky, M.: Learning through Advocacy, *Journal of Economic Education*, 1972.
[38] Layard, R.: The Cost Effectiveness of the New Media in Higher Education, In: [42].
[39] Lewis, D. R. and T. Dahl: The Test of Understanding in College Economics and its Construct Validity, *Journal of Economic Education*, 1971.
[40] Lewis, D. R. and C. C. Orvis: *Research in Economic Education*, Joint Council of Economic Education, Washington 1971.
[41] Lumsden, K. G.: On Crossing the 'Pons Asinorum'. In: *Recent Research in Economics Education*, Englewood Cliffs, N.J. 1970.
[42] Lumsden, K. G.: *Efficiency in Universities: the La Paz Papers*, Elsevier, Amsterdam 1974.
[43] Lumsden, K. G., R. E. Attiyeh and G. L. Bach: *Microeconomics: a Programmed Book*, Englewood Cliffs, N.J. 1970.
[44] MacDonald-Ross, M.: Behavioural Objectives: a Critical Review, *Instructional Science*, 1973.
[45] McKeachie, W. J.: Research on Teaching at the College and University Level. In: [25].
[46] McLeish, J.: Systems, Models, Simulations and Games in Education: a Description and Bibliography. In: [2].
[47] Mann, W. R. and D. R. Fusfeld: Attitude Sophistication and Effective Teaching in Economics, *Journal of Economic Education*, 1970.
[48] Martin, D. A.: *Introductory Economic Theory: an Audio-Visual Tutorial Approach*, New York 1971.

[49] Mesarovic, M. D.: *General Systems and Economic Problems*, New York 1969.
[50] Messick, S.: The Criterion Problem in the Evaluation of Instruction. In: [69].
[51] Mitchell, P. D.: Educational Technology: Panacea or Piacebo?, *Aspects of Educational Technology*, 1970.
[52] Noble, P.: Learning Theory and the Audio-Visual Element in Economics. In: [68].
[53] Paden, D. W. and M. E. Moyer: The Relative Effectiveness of Three Methods of Teaching Principles of Economics, *Journal of Economic Education*, 1969.
[54] Phillips, J. A.: Instructional Objectives and Economic Understanding, *Journal of Economic Education*, 1972.
[55] Postlethwait, S. N., J. Novak and H. Murray: *The Audio-Tutorial Approach to Learning*, New York 1972.
[56] The Psychological Corporation, *The Test of Understanding College Economics: Manual*, 1968.
[57] Rao, P. and R. L. Miller: *Applied Econometrics*, Belmont 1971.
[58] Ryba, R. and K. Drake: Towards a Taxonomy of Educational Objectives for Economics? In: [68].
[59] Scott, A.: Research into Economic Efficiency in the Teaching of Economics: Some Fundamental Problems, In: [68].
[60] Soper, J. C.: Programmed Instruction in Large-Lecture Courses, *Journal of Economic Education*, 1973.
[61] Soper, J. C.: Computer-Assisted Instruction in Economics: a Survey, *Journal of Economic Education*, 1974.
[62] Squires, G.: Resources and Systems in Education, *British Journal of Educational Technology*, 1972.
[63] Trow, M.: Methodological Problems in the Evaluation of Innovation, In: [69].
[64] University of Adelaide, Faculty of Economics: *Report of the Sub-Committee Appointed to consider means of Assessing Undergraduate Performance*, 1971, mimeo.
[65] Villard, H. H.: Where we now Stand, *Journal of Economic Education*, 1969.
[66] Watson, G. and E. M. Glaser: *Watson-Glaser Critical Thinking Appraisal Test*, New York 1964.
[67] Weidenaar, D. J. and J. A. Dodson: The Effectiveness of Economics Instruction in two-year Colleges, *Journal of Economic Education*, 1972.
[68] Whitehead, D.: *Curriculum Development in Economics*, Londen 1974.
[69] Wittrock, M. C. and D. E. Wiley: *The Evaluation of Instruction*, New York 1970.

The authors

Jan Tinbergen (1903), emeritus professor of economics, University of Rotterdam.

Erik Lundberg (1907), emeritus professor of economics, Stockholm School of Economics.

P. Hennipman (1911), emeritus professor of economics, University of Amsterdam.

Lloyd Ulman (1920), professor of economics, University of California.

P. E. Venekamp (1922), professor of economic statistics, University of Amsterdam.

H. S. Houthakker (1924), professor of economics, Harvard University.

Henri Theil (1924), professor of economics, University of Chicago.

J. S. Cramer (1928), professor of econometrics, University of Amsterdam.

A. Pais (1930), professor of economics, University of Amsterdam.

D. van der Werf (1932), Deputy director of general economic affairs, Ministry of Social Affairs, The Hague.

A. Heertje (1934), professor of economics, University of Amsterdam.

C. R. Wichers (1935), associate-professor of economics, University of Pittsburgh.

B. M. S. van Praag (1939), professor of economics, University of Leyden.

Judith Yates (1943), lecturer, University of Sidney.

Printed in the Netherlands

Colophon

Letter: Times
Printing: VanderLoeff/Drukkers bv, Enschede
Binding: Binderij Callenbach bv, Nijkerk
Photo: Jesse Knopper, Heemstede